Indiana
Grade 6

interactive
SCIENCE

PEARSON

Boston, Massachusetts
Chandler, Arizona
Glenview, Illinois
Upper Saddle River, New Jersey

AUTHORS

You're an author!

As you write in this science book, your answers and personal discoveries will be recorded for you to keep, making this book unique to you. That is why you are one of the primary authors of this book.

✏️ **In the space below, print your name, school, town, and state. Then write a short autobiography that includes your interests and accomplishments.**

YOUR NAME _____

SCHOOL _____

TOWN, STATE _____

AUTOBIOGRAPHY _____

_____

_____

_____

_____

_____

_____

_____

Your Photo

Acknowledgments appear on pages 377–380, which constitute an extension of this copyright page.

Copyright © 2012 Pearson Education, Inc., or its affiliates. All Rights Reserved. Printed in the United States of America. This publication is protected by copyright, and permission should be obtained from the publisher prior to any prohibited reproduction, storage in a retrieval system, or transmission in any form or by any means, electronic, mechanical, photocopying, recording, or likewise. For information regarding permissions, write to Rights Management & Contracts, Pearson Education, Inc., One Lake Street, Upper Saddle River, New Jersey 07458.

Pearson, Prentice Hall, Pearson Prentice Hall, Lab zone, and Planet Diary are trademarks, in the U.S. and/or other countries, of Pearson Education, Inc., or its affiliates.

Bakelite® is a registered trademark of Momentive Chemical Investments, Inc. Use of the trademark or company name implies no relationship, sponsorship, endorsement, sale, or promotion on the part of Pearson Education, Inc., or its affiliates.

Certain materials herein are adapted from *Understanding by Design, 2nd Edition*, by Grant Wiggins & Jay McTighe © 2005 ASCD. Used with permission.

UNDERSTANDING BY DESIGN® and UbD™ are trademarks of ASCD, and are used under license.

ISBN-13: 978-0-13-253475-8
ISBN-10: 0-13-253475-4

7 8 9 10 V011 17 16

ON THE COVER
Northern Cardinal
The Northern Cardinal is the state bird of Indiana. The male is bright red and the female is brown with a dull red crest, wings, and tail. Cardinals do not migrate, so look for them year-round. Listen for their distinctive cheer-cheer-cheer or purty-purty-purty song.

Program Authors

DON BUCKLEY, M.Sc.
Information and Communications Technology Director,
The School at Columbia University, New York, New York
Mr. Buckley has been at the forefront of K–12 educational
technology for nearly two decades. A founder of New York City
Independent School Technologists (NYCIST) and long-time chair
of New York Association of Independent Schools' annual IT
conference, he has taught students on two continents and
created multimedia and Internet-based instructional systems
for schools worldwide.

ZIPPORAH MILLER, M.A.Ed.
Associate Executive Director for Professional Programs
and Conferences, National Science Teachers Association,
Arlington, Virginia
Associate executive director for professional programs and
conferences at NSTA, Ms. Zipporah Miller is a former K–12 science
supervisor and STEM coordinator for the Prince George's County
Public School District in Maryland. She is a science education
consultant who has overseen curriculum development and staff
training for more than 150 district science coordinators.

MICHAEL J. PADILLA, Ph.D.
Associate Dean and Director, Eugene P. Moore School of
Education, Clemson University, Clemson, South Carolina
A former middle school teacher and a leader in middle school
science education, Dr. Michael Padilla has served as president of
the National Science Teachers Association and as a writer of the
National Science Education Standards. He is professor of science
education at Clemson University. As lead author of the *Science
Explorer* series, Dr. Padilla has inspired the team in developing a
program that promotes student inquiry and meets the needs of
today's students.

KATHRYN THORNTON, Ph.D.
Professor and Associate Dean, School of Engineering
and Applied Science, University of Virginia,
Charlottesville, Virginia
Selected by NASA in May 1984, Dr. Kathryn Thornton is a veteran
of four space flights. She has logged over 975 hours in space,
including more than 21 hours of extravehicular activity. As an
author on the *Scott Foresman Science* series, Dr. Thornton's
enthusiasm for science has inspired teachers around the globe.

MICHAEL E. WYSESSION, Ph.D.
Associate Professor of Earth and Planetary Science,
Washington University, St. Louis, Missouri
An author on more than 50 scientific publications, Dr. Wysession
was awarded the prestigious Packard Foundation Fellowship and
Presidential Faculty Fellowship for his research in geophysics. Dr.
Wysession is an expert on Earth's inner structure and has mapped
various regions of Earth using seismic tomography. He is known
internationally for his work in geoscience education and outreach.

Instructional Design Author

GRANT WIGGINS, Ed.D.
President, Authentic Education,
Hopewell, New Jersey
Dr. Wiggins is a co-author with
Jay McTighe of *Understanding by Design,
2nd Edition* (ASCD 2005). His approach
to instructional design provides teachers
with a disciplined way of thinking about
curriculum design, assessment, and instruction that moves teaching from covering
content to ensuring understanding.

UNDERSTANDING BY DESIGN® and
UbD™ are trademarks of ASCD, and are
used under license.

Planet Diary Author

JACK HANKIN
Science/Mathematics Teacher,
The Hilldale School, Daly City, California
Founder, Planet Diary Web site
Mr. Hankin is the creator and writer of
Planet Diary, a science current events
Web site. He is passionate about bringing
science news and environmental awareness
into classrooms and offers numerous Planet
Diary workshops at NSTA and other events
to train middle and high school teachers.

ELL Consultant

JIM CUMMINS, Ph.D.
Professor and Canada Research Chair,
Curriculum, Teaching and Learning
department at the University of Toronto
Dr. Cummins focuses on literacy development in multilingual schools and the role of
technology in promoting student learning
across the curriculum. *Interactive Science*
incorporates essential research-based
principles for integrating language with the
teaching of academic content based on his
instructional framework.

Reading Consultant

HARVEY DANIELS, Ph.D.
Professor of Secondary Education,
University of New Mexico,
Albuquerque, New Mexico
Dr. Daniels is an international consultant
to schools, districts, and educational
agencies. He has authored or coauthored
13 books on language, literacy, and education. His most recent works are *Compre-
hension and Collaboration: Inquiry Circles
in Action* and *Subjects Matter: Every
Teacher's Guide to Content-Area Reading*.

REVIEWERS

Contributing Writers

Edward Aguado, Ph.D.
Professor, Department of
Geography
San Diego State University
San Diego, California

Elizabeth Coolidge-Stolz, M.D.
Medical Writer
North Reading, Massachusetts

Donald L. Cronkite, Ph.D.
Professor of Biology
Hope College
Holland, Michigan

Jan Jenner, Ph.D.
Science Writer
Talladega, Alabama

Linda Cronin Jones, Ph.D.
Associate Professor of Science and
Environmental Education
University of Florida
Gainesville, Florida

T. Griffith Jones, Ph.D.
Clinical Associate Professor
of Science Education
College of Education
University of Florida
Gainesville, Florida

Andrew C. Kemp, Ph.D.
Teacher
Jefferson County Public Schools
Louisville, Kentucky

Matthew Stoneking, Ph.D.
Associate Professor of Physics
Lawrence University
Appleton, Wisconsin

R. Bruce Ward, Ed.D.
Senior Research Associate
Science Education Department
Harvard-Smithsonian Center for
Astrophysics
Cambridge, Massachusetts

Content Reviewers

Paul D. Beale, Ph.D.
Department of Physics
University of Colorado at Boulder
Boulder, Colorado

Jeff R. Bodart, Ph.D.
Professor of Physical Sciences
Chipola College
Marianna, Florida

Joy Branlund, Ph.D.
Department of Earth Science
Southwestern Illinois College
Granite City, Illinois

Marguerite Brickman, Ph.D.
Division of Biological Sciences
University of Georgia
Athens, Georgia

Bonnie J. Brunkhorst, Ph.D.
Science Education and Geological
Sciences
California State University
San Bernardino, California

Michael Castellani, Ph.D.
Department of Chemistry
Marshall University
Huntington, West Virginia

Charles C. Curtis, Ph.D.
Research Associate Professor
of Physics
University of Arizona
Tucson, Arizona

Diane I. Doser, Ph.D.
Department of Geological
Sciences
University of Texas
El Paso, Texas

Rick Duhrkopf, Ph.D.
Department of Biology
Baylor University
Waco, Texas

Alice K. Hankla, Ph.D.
The Galloway School
Atlanta, Georgia

Mark Henriksen, Ph.D.
Physics Department
University of Maryland
Baltimore, Maryland

Chad Hershock, Ph.D.
Center for Research on Learning
and Teaching
University of Michigan
Ann Arbor, Michigan

Jeremiah N. Jarrett, Ph.D.
Department of Biology
Central Connecticut State
University
New Britain, Connecticut

Scott L. Kight, Ph.D.
Department of Biology
Montclair State University
Montclair, New Jersey

Jennifer O. Liang, Ph.D.
Department of Biology
University of Minnesota–Duluth
Duluth, Minnesota

Candace Lutzow-Felling, Ph.D.
Director of Education
The State Arboretum of Virginia
University of Virginia
Boyce, Virginia

Cortney V. Martin, Ph.D.
Virginia Polytechnic Institute
Blacksburg, Virginia

Joseph F. McCullough, Ph.D.
Physics Program Chair
Cabrillo College
Aptos, California

Heather Mernitz, Ph.D.
Department of Physical Science
Alverno College
Milwaukee, Wisconsin

Sadredin C. Moosavi, Ph.D.
Department of Earth and
Environmental Sciences
Tulane University
New Orleans, Louisiana

David L. Reid, Ph.D.
Department of Biology
Blackburn College
Carlinville, Illinois

Scott M. Rochette, Ph.D.
Department of the Earth Sciences
SUNY College at Brockport
Brockport, New York

Karyn L. Rogers, Ph.D.
Department of Geological
Sciences
University of Missouri
Columbia, Missouri

Laurence Rosenhein, Ph.D.
Department of Chemistry
Indiana State University
Terre Haute, Indiana

Sara Seager, Ph.D.
Department of Planetary Sciences
and Physics
Massachusetts Institute of
Technology
Cambridge, Massachusetts

Tom Shoberg, Ph.D.
Missouri University of Science
and Technology
Rolla, Missouri

Patricia Simmons, Ph.D.
North Carolina State University
Raleigh, North Carolina

William H. Steinecker, Ph.D.
Research Scholar
Miami University
Oxford, Ohio

Paul R. Stoddard, Ph.D.
Department of Geology and
Environmental Geosciences
Northern Illinois University
DeKalb, Illinois

John R. Villarreal, Ph.D.
Department of Chemistry
The University of Texas–Pan
American
Edinburg, Texas

John R. Wagner, Ph.D.
Department of Geology
Clemson University
Clemson, South Carolina

Jerry Waldvogel, Ph.D.
Department of Biological Sciences
Clemson University
Clemson, South Carolina

Donna L. Witter, Ph.D.
Department of Geology
Kent State University
Kent, Ohio

Edward J. Zalisko, Ph.D.
Department of Biology
Blackburn College
Carlinville, Illinois

Museum of Science.

Special thanks to the Museum of Science,
Boston, Massachusetts, and Ioannis Miaoulis,
the Museum's president and director, for
serving as content advisors for the technology
and design strand in this program.

Teacher Reviewers

Herb Bergamini
The Northwest School
Seattle, Washington

David R. Blakely
Arlington High School
Arlington, Massachusetts

Jane E. Callery
Capital Region Education Council
(CREC)
Hartford, Connecticut

Jeffrey C. Callister
Former Earth Science Instructor
Newburgh Free Academy
Newburgh, New York

Colleen Campos
Cherry Creek Schools
Aurora, Colorado

Scott Cordell
Amarillo Independent School
District
Amarillo, Texas

Dan Gabel
Consulting Teacher, Science
Montgomery County Public
Schools
Montgomery County, Maryland

Wayne Goates
Kansas Polymer Ambassador
Intersociety Polymer Education
Council (IPEC)
Wichita, Kansas

Katherine Bobay Graser
Mint Hill Middle School
Charlotte, North Carolina

Darcy Hampton
Science Department Chair
Deal Middle School
Washington, D.C.

Sean S. Houseknecht
Elizabethtown Area Middle School
Elizabethtown, Pennsylvania

Tanisha L. Johnson
Prince George's County Public
Schools
Lanham, Maryland

Karen E. Kelly
Pierce Middle School
Waterford, Michigan

Dave J. Kelso
Manchester Central High School
Manchester, New Hampshire

Beverly Crouch Lyons
Career Center High School
Winston-Salem, North Carolina

Angie L. Matamoros, Ed.D.
ALM Consulting
Weston, Florida

Corey Mayle
Durham Public Schools
Durham, North Carolina

Keith W. McCarthy
George Washington Middle
School
Wayne, New Jersey

Timothy McCollum
Charleston Middle School
Charleston, Illinois

Bruce A. Mellin
Cambridge College
Cambridge, Massachusetts

John Thomas Miller
Thornapple Kellogg High School
Middleville, Michigan

Randy Mousley
Dean Ray Stucky Middle School
Wichita, Kansas

Yolanda O. Peña
John F. Kennedy Junior High
School
West Valley, Utah

Kathleen M. Poe
Fletcher Middle School
Jacksonville Beach, Florida

Judy Pouncey
Thomasville Middle School
Thomasville, North Carolina

Vickki Lynne Reese
Mad River Middle School
Dayton, Ohio

Bronwyn W. Robinson
Director of Curriculum
Algiers Charter Schools
Association
New Orleans, Louisiana

Sandra G. Robinson
Matoaca Middle School
Chesterfield, Virginia

Shirley Rose
Lewis and Clark Middle School
Tulsa, Oklahoma

Linda Sandersen
Sally Ride Academy
Whitefish Bay, Wisconsin

Roxanne Scala
Schuyler-Colfax Middle School
Wayne, New Jersey

Patricia M. Shane, Ph.D.
Associate Director
Center for Mathematics & Science
Education
University of North Carolina
at Chapel Hill
Chapel Hill, North Carolina

Bradd A. Smithson
Science Curriculum Coordinator
John Glenn Middle School
Bedford, Massachusetts

Sharon Stroud
Consultant
Colorado Springs, Colorado

Master Teacher Board

Emily Compton
Park Forest Middle School
Baton Rouge, Louisiana

Georgi Delgadillo
East Valley School District
Spokane Valley, Washington

Treva Jeffries
Toledo Public Schools
Toledo, Ohio

James W. Kuhl
Central Square Middle School
Central Square, New York

Bonnie Mizell
Howard Middle School
Orlando, Florida

Joel Palmer, Ed.D.
Mesquite Independent School
District
Mesquite, Texas

Leslie Pohley
Largo Middle School
Largo, Florida

Susan M. Pritchard, Ph.D.
Washington Middle School
La Habra, California

Anne Rice
Woodland Middle School
Gurnee, Illinois

Richard Towle
Noblesville Middle School
Noblesville, Indiana

REVIEWERS

Indiana Content Reviewers

Sandra Davis, Ph.D.
Department of Biology
University of Indianapolis
Indianapolis, Indiana

Klaus Neumann, Ph.D.
Department of Geological Sciences
Ball State University
Muncie, Indiana

Laurence Rosenhein, Ph.D.
Department of Chemistry
Indiana State University
Terre Haute, Indiana

Janet Vaglia, Ph.D.
Department of Biology
DePauw University
Greencastle, Indiana

Built especially for
Indiana

Indiana Interactive Science covers 100% of Indiana's Academic Standards for Science without extraneous content. Built on feedback from Indiana educators, *Interactive Science* focuses on what is important to Indiana teachers and students, creating a personal, relevant, and engaging classroom experience.

Indiana K-8 Science Teacher Advisory Board

Jodi Allen
Glen Acres Elementary School
Lafayette, IN

Rick Dubbs
Monrovia Middle School
Monrovia, IN

Margaret Flack
Vincennes University-Jasper Campus
Jasper, IN

Michael Gibson
New Haven Middle School &
East Allen County School
New Haven, IN

Jill Hatcher
Spring Mill School
Indianapolis, IN

Jamie Hooten
Lincoln Elementary School, NLCS
Bedford, IN

Jamil Odom
Mary Bryan Elementary School
Indianapolis, IN

Mike Robards
Franklin Community Middle School
Franklin, IN

Richard Towle
Noblesville Middle School
Noblesville, IN

CONTENTS

 Enter the Lab zone
for hands-on inquiry.

Chapter Lab Investigation:
• Directed Inquiry: Changing Pitch
• Open Inquiry: Changing Pitch

Inquiry Warm-Ups: • Exploring Science
• How to Think Scientifically • Doing Science Is
Asking Questions

Quick Labs: • Practicing Science Skills
• Exploring Scientific Thinking • Using
Scientific Reasoning • Scientific Discovery
• Making a Hypothesis • Theory or Not?

my science online.com

**Go to MyScienceOnline.com to
interact with this chapter's content.
Keyword: What Is Science?**

> **UNTAMED SCIENCE**
• What Is Science, Anyway?

> **PLANET DIARY**
• What Is Science?

> **INTERACTIVE ART**
• Inquiry Diagram • Scientific Stumbling
Blocks • Building a Theory • Science in the
Real World

> **VIRTUAL LAB**
• What Is Scientific Inquiry?

The Tools of Science

CHAPTER 2

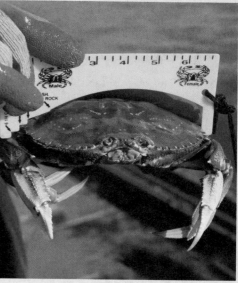

 Enter the Lab zone for hands-on inquiry.

Chapter Lab Investigation:
- Directed Inquiry: Super Models
- Open Inquiry: Super Models

Inquiry Warm-Ups: • Taking Measurements • Making Models • Picturing Information • Models and Science • Is Science Safe?

Quick Labs: • Measurement Systems • Measuring Volume in Metric • Understanding Significant Figures • Math Tools in Science • Making Graphs • Graphs and Predictions • Systems of Science • Models of Natural Systems • Be Prepared to Be Safe in the Lab. • In Case of an Emergency

my science online.com

Go to MyScienceOnline.com to interact with this chapter's content. Keyword: The Tools of Science

UNTAMED SCIENCE
- Measuring Up

PLANET DIARY
- The Tools of Science

INTERACTIVE ART
- Plotting a Line Graph • Modeling a System

VIRTUAL LAB
- How Are Units Useful?

CONTENTS

Enter the Lab zone for hands-on inquiry.

Chapter Lab Investigation:
• Directed Inquiry: Making Sense of Density
• Open Inquiry: Making Sense of Density

Inquiry Warm-Ups: • How Do You Describe Matter? • What Is a Mixture? • Which Has More Mass? • Is a New Substance Formed?

Quick Labs: • Observing Physical Properties • Modeling Atoms and Molecules • Separating Mixtures • Calculating Volume • What Is a Physical Change? • Demonstrating Tarnishing • Where Was the Energy?

my science online.com

Go to MyScienceOnline.com to interact with this chapter's content. Keyword: **Introduction to Matter**

> **UNTAMED SCIENCE**
• What's the Matter?

> **PLANET DIARY**
• Introduction to Matter

> **INTERACTIVE ART**
• Conservation of Matter • Properties of Matter

> **ART IN MOTION**
• What Makes Up Matter?

> **VIRTUAL LAB**
• How Do You Measure Weight and Volume?
• Will It Float? Density of Solids and Liquids

Solids, Liquids, and Gases

CHAPTER 4

Lab zone® **Enter the Lab zone for hands-on inquiry.**

Chapter Lab Investigation:
• Directed Inquiry: Melting Ice
• Open Inquiry: Melting Ice

Inquiry Warm-Ups: • What Are Solids, Liquids, and Gases? • What Happens When You Breathe on a Mirror? • How Can Air Keep Chalk From Breaking?

Quick Labs: • Modeling Particles • As Thick As Honey • How Do the Particles in a Gas Move? • Keeping Cool • Observing Sublimation • How are Pressure and Temperature Related? • Hot and Cold Balloons • It's a Gas

MY SCIENCE ONLINE.com

Go to MyScienceOnline.com to interact with this chapter's content. Keyword: Solids, Liquids, and Gases

> **UNTAMED SCIENCE**
• Building a House of Snow

> **PLANET DIARY**
• Solids, Liquids, and Gases

> **INTERACTIVE ART**
• Gas Laws • States of Matter

> **VIRTUAL LAB**
• Solid to Liquid to Gas: Changes of State

CONTENTS

Enter the Lab zone for hands-on inquiry.

Chapter Lab Investigation:
• Directed Inquiry: Can You Feel the Power?
• Open Inquiry: Can You Feel the Power?

Inquiry Warm-Ups: • How High Does a Ball Bounce? • What Makes a Flashlight Shine? • What Would Make a Card Jump?

Quick Labs: • Mass, Velocity, and Kinetic Energy • Determining Mechanical Energy • Sources of Energy • Soaring Straws • Law of Conservation of Energy

my science online.com

Go to MyScienceOnline.com to interact with this chapter's content.
Keyword: Energy

> UNTAMED SCIENCE
• The Potential for Fun

> PLANET DIARY
• Energy

> ART IN MOTION
• Kinetic and Potential Energy

> INTERACTIVE ART
• Types of Energy

> INTERACTIVE ART
• Energy Transformations

> VIRTUAL LAB
• Exploring Potential and Kinetic Energy

△ **Chapter Lab Investigation:**
  • Directed Inquiry: Reasons for the Seasons
  • Open Inquiry: Reasons for the Seasons

△ **Inquiry Warm-Ups:** • Earth's Sky • What Causes Day and Night? • What Factors Affect Gravity? • How Does the Moon Move? • When Is High Tide? • Why Do Craters Look Different From Each Other?

△ **Quick Labs:** • Observing the Night Sky • Watching the Sky • Sun Shadows • What's Doing the Pulling? • Around and Around We Go • Moon Phases • Eclipses • Modeling the Moon's Pull of Gravity • Moonwatching

my science online.com

Go to MyScienceOnline.com to interact with this chapter's content.
Keyword: Earth, Moon, and Sun

> **UNTAMED SCIENCE**
• Phased by the Moon!

> **PLANET DIARY**
• Earth, Moon, and Sun

> **INTERACTIVE ART**
•Constellations •Seasons and Earth's Revolution •Solar and Lunar Eclipses

> **ART IN MOTION**
• Cause of Tides

> **VIRTUAL LAB**
• What Affects Gravity?

CONTENTS

Lab zone® Enter the Lab zone for hands-on inquiry.

Chapter Lab Investigation:
• Directed Inquiry: Speeding Around the Sun
• Open Inquiry: Speeding Around the Sun

Inquiry Warm-Ups: • What Is at the Center? • How Big Is Earth? • How Can You Safely Observe the Sun? • Ring Around the Sun • How Big Are the Planets? • Collecting Micrometeorites

Quick Labs: • Going Around in Circles • A Loopy Ellipse • Clumping Planets • Layers of the Sun • Viewing Sunspots • Characteristics of the Inner Planets • Greenhouse Effect • Under Pressure • Make a Model of Saturn • Changing Orbits

my science online.com

Go to MyScienceOnline.com to interact with this chapter's content.
Keyword: The Solar System

> UNTAMED SCIENCE
• 100 Meters to Neptune

> PLANET DIARY
• The Solar System

> INTERACTIVE ART
• Objects of the Solar System • Anatomy of the Sun

> ART IN MOTION
• Formation of the Solar System

> VIRTUAL LAB
• Why Isn't Pluto a Planet?

CHAPTER 8
Populations and Communities

 The Big Question 270
How do living things affect one another?

Lab zone® Enter the Lab zone for hands-on inquiry.

Chapter Lab Investigation:
• Directed Inquiry: World in a Bottle
• Open Inquiry: World in a Bottle

Inquiry Warm-Ups: • What's in the Scene?
• Populations • Can You Hide a Butterfly?
• How Communities Change

Quick Labs: • Organisms and Their Habitats
• Organizing an Ecosystem • Growing and
Shrinking • Elbow Room • Adaptations for
Survival • Competition and Predation • Type
of Symbiosis • Primary or Secondary

my science online.com

Go to MyScienceOnline.com to interact with this chapter's content.
Keyword: Populations and Communities

> UNTAMED SCIENCE
• Clown(fish)ing Around

> PLANET DIARY
• Populations and Communities

> INTERACTIVE ART
• Changes in Population • Animal Defense Strategies

> ART IN MOTION
• Primary and Secondary Succession

> REAL-WORLD INQUIRY
• An Ecological Mystery

CONTENTS

Enter the Lab zone for hands-on inquiry.

Chapter Lab Investigation:
• Directed Inquiry: Ecosystem Food Chains
• Open Inquiry: Ecosystem Food Chains

Inquiry Warm-Ups: • Where Does the Energy Come From? • Where Did Your Dinner Come From? • Are You Part of a Cycle? • How Much Rain Is That?

Quick Labs: • Energy From the Sun • Looking at Pigments • Observing Decomposition • Following Water • Carbon and Oxygen Blues • Playing Nitrogen Cycle Roles • Inferring Forest Climates

my science online.com

Go to MyScienceOnline.com to interact with this chapter's content.
Keyword: **Ecosystems and Biomes**

▶ **UNTAMED SCIENCE**
• Give Me That Carbon!

▶ **PLANET DIARY**
• Ecosystems and Biomes

▶ **INTERACTIVE ART**
• Photosynthesis • Ocean Food Web
• Water Cycle • Cycles of Matter
• Earth's Biomes

▶ **VIRTUAL LAB**
• The Inner Workings of Photosynthesis
• Where's All the Food?

Untamed Science™

Video Series: Chapter Adventures

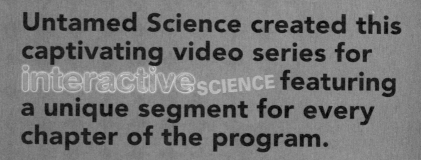

Untamed Science created this captivating video series for **interactive** SCIENCE featuring a unique segment for every chapter of the program.

Featuring videos such as

Chapter 1
What Is Science, Anyway?

Chapter 2
Measuring Up

Chapter 3
What's the Matter?

Chapter 4
Building a House of Snow

Chapter 5
The Potential for Fun

Chapter 6
Phased by the Moon!

Chapter 7
100 Meters to Neptune

Chapter 8
Clown(fish)ing Around

Chapter 9
Give Me That Carbon!

interactive SCIENCE

This is your book. You can write in it!

WHAT CAN SHARKS TEACH THESE CAGED SCIENTISTS?

 What does it mean to think like a scientist?

Would you ever go diving in a shark cage? If you were a marine biologist, this might be part of your job. To learn more about sharks, marine biologists study them in their natural environment. These Galápagos sharks were observed swimming off of the coast of Hawaii. Marine biologists have learned that a full-grown male Galápagos shark can grow to be 3.7 meters long and eat squid, octopus, and fish, including other sharks.

Infer **What information could scientists learn by watching these sharks?**

The scientists could estimate how old the sharks are and notice if they are males or females. They might also see how the sharks act around humans.

> **UNTAMED SCIENCE** Watch the **Untamed Science** video to learn more about science.

xxx What Is Science?

 THE BIG ?

Get Engaged!

At the start of each chapter, you will see two questions: an Engaging Question and the Big Question. Each chapter's Big Question will help you start thinking about the Big Ideas of Science. Look for the Big Q symbol throughout the chapter!

 **Untamed Science**

Follow the Untamed Science video crew as they travel the globe exploring the Big Ideas of Science.

Interact with your textbook.   **Interact with inquiry.**   **Interact online.**

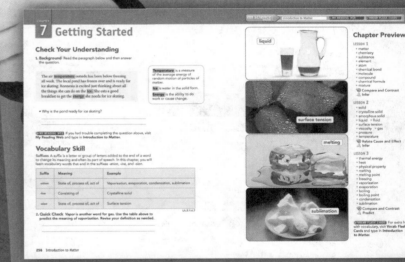

Build Reading, Inquiry, and Vocabulary Skills

In every lesson you will learn new ↻ Reading and ▲ Inquiry skills. These skills will help you read and think like a scientist. Vocabulary skills will help you communicate effectively and uncover the meaning of words.

Go Online!

Look for the MyScienceOnline.com technology options. At MyScienceOnline.com you can immerse yourself in amazing virtual environments, get extra practice, and even blog about current events in science.

Master Indiana Standards

Indiana Academic Standards for Science are indicated every step of the way throughout your book.

INTERACT... WITH YOUR TEXTBOOK...

Explore the Key Concepts.

Each lesson begins with a series of Key Concept questions. The interactivities in each lesson will help you understand these concepts and Unlock the Big Question.

my planet diary
for Indiana

At the start of each lesson, My Planet Diary will introduce you to amazing events, significant people, and important discoveries in Indiana or help you to overcome common misconceptions.

Desertification If the soil in a onc[...] of moisture and nutrients, the area c[...] advance of desertlike conditions int[...] fertile is called **desertification** (dih [...]

One cause of desertification is cli[...] is a period when less rain than norm[...] droughts, crops fail. Without plant c[...] blows away. Overgrazing of grasslan[...] cutting down trees for firewood can [...]

Desertification is a serious proble[...] and graze livestock where desertifica[...] people may face famine and starvati[...] central Africa. Millions of rural peo[...] cities because they can no longer sur[...]

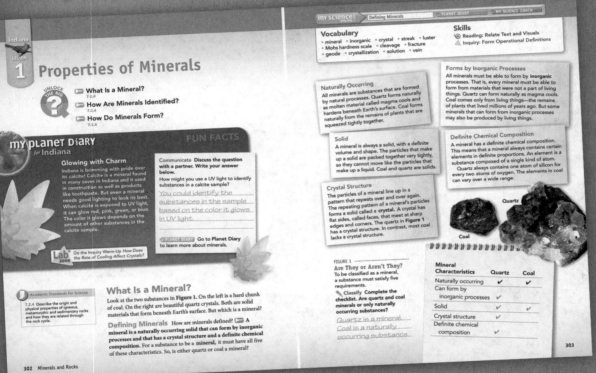

apply it!

Desertification affects many areas around the world.

1 Name Which continent has the most existing desert?

Africa

2 Interpret Maps Where in the United States is the greatest risk of desertification?

The western United Sta[...]

3 Infer Is desertification a threat [...] is existing desert? Explain. Circle an [...] your answer.

No; there are high-risk a[...] desert, such as along th[...]

4 CHALLENGE If an area is facing d[...] things people could do to possibly l[...]

Sample: People could limi[...] grow plants to provide s[...]

360   Land, Air, and Water Resource[...]

Explain what you know.

Look for the pencil. When you see it, it's time to interact with your book and demonstrate what you have learned.

apply it!

Elaborate further with the Apply It activities.

This is your opportunity to take what you've learned and apply it to new situations.

Lab Zone

Look for the Lab zone triangle. This means it's time to do a hands-on inquiry lab. In every lesson, you'll have the opportunity to do many hands-on inquiry activities that will help reinforce your understanding of the lesson topic.

Land Reclamation Fortunately, it is possible to replace land damaged by erosion or mining. The process of restoring an area of land to a more productive state is called **land reclamation**. In addition to restoring land for agriculture, land reclamation can restore habitats for wildlife. Many different types of land reclamation projects are currently underway all over the world. But it is generally more difficult and expensive to restore damaged land and soil than it is to protect those resources in the first place. In some cases, the land may not return to its original state.

FIGURE 4 ·······························

Land Reclamation
These pictures show land before and after it was mined.

✎ **Communicate** Below the pictures, write a story about what happened to the land.

Sample: Some trees were cut to make room for a mine. When the mining stopped, people replaced the soil and planted grass and trees. In time, the mine became a forest, but it is not the same as the original forest.

Do the Quick Lab
Modeling S...

📂 **Assess Your Understanding**

1a. Review Subsoil has (less/more) plant and animal matter than topsoil.   8.2.6

b. Explain What can happen to soil if plants are removed?
Soil particles can move, eroding the area.

c. Apply Concepts ...
that could prev...
land reclam...
Sample...
might ...
other ...
farmin...

got it?   8.2.6

O **I get it!** Now I know that soil management is important becau... ways, and poor management causes erosio... depletion, and desertification.

O **I need extra help with** See TE note.

Go to MY SCIENCE 🌐 COACH online for help with this subject.

Key
- Existing desert
- High-risk area
- Moderate-risk area

...tile area becomes depleted ...ecome a desert. The ...as that previously were ...uh fih KAY shun). ... For example, a **drought** ...lls in an area. During ... the exposed soil easily ... cattle and sheep and ... desertification, too. ...eople cannot grow crops ... has occurred. As a result, ...esertification is severe in ...ere are moving to the ... themselves on the land.

... areas where there
... on the map to support

...noderate-risk areas without existing
...st coast of South America.

...cation, what are some
... effects?

...estock overgrazing, limit tree cutting, and
...ver even during droughts.
                                          8.NS.8

Evaluate Your Progress.

After answering the Got It question, think about how you're doing. Did you get it or do you need a little help? Remember, MY SCIENCE 🅢 COACH is there for you if you need extra help.

Explore the Big Question.

At one point in the chapter, you'll have the opportunity to take all that you've learned to further explore the Big Question.

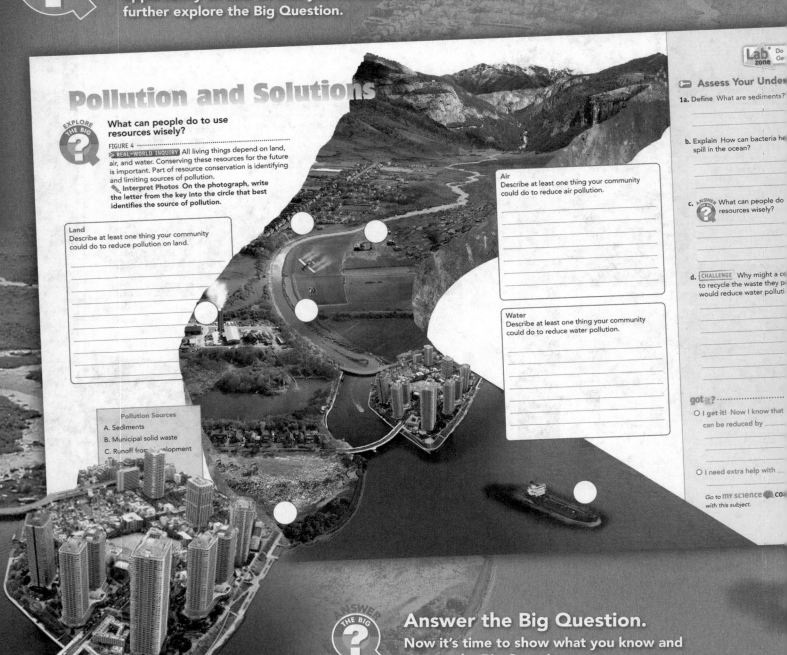

Pollution and Solutions

What can people do to use resources wisely?

FIGURE 4 ....

▶ REAL-WORLD INQUIRY All living things depend on land, air, and water. Conserving these resources for the future is important. Part of resource conservation is identifying and limiting sources of pollution.

✎ Interpret Photos On the photograph, write the letter from the key into the circle that best identifies the source of pollution.

Land
Describe at least one thing your community could do to reduce pollution on land.

Air
Describe at least one thing your community could do to reduce air pollution.

Water
Describe at least one thing your community could do to reduce water pollution.

Pollution Sources

A. Sediments

B. Municipal solid waste

C. Runoff from development

Lab zone

▷ Assess Your Under...

1a. Define What are sediments?

b. Explain How can bacteria he... spill in the ocean?

c. ANSWER What can people do resources wisely?

d. CHALLENGE Why might a co... to recycle the waste they p... would reduce water polluti...

got it? ....

○ I get it! Now I know that ... can be reduced by ...

○ I need extra help with ...

Go to MY SCIENCE COA... with this subject.

Answer the Big Question.

Now it's time to show what you know and answer the Big Question.

Review What You've Learned.

Use the Chapter Study Guide to review the Big Question and prepare for the quizzes and exams.

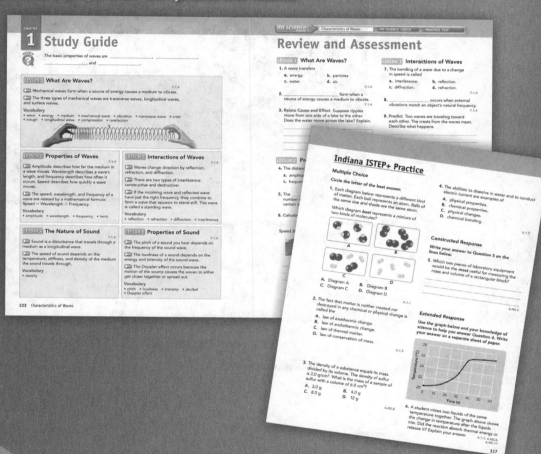

Practice Taking the ISTEP+.

Apply the Big Question and take a practice test in the ISTEP+ format.

Go to **MyScienceOnline.com** and immerse yourself in amazing virtual environments.

Go to **MyScienceOnline.com**

>> **THE BIG QUESTION**

Each online chapter starts with a Big Question. Your mission is to unlock the meaning of this Big Question as each science lesson unfolds.

Unit 4 > Chapter 1 > Lesson 1

The Big Question   Unlock the Big Question   Explore the Big Question

The Big Question   Check Your Understanding   Vocabulary Skill

Populations and Communities

Tools

The Big Question

Unit 2 > Chapter 4 > Lesson 1

Engage & Explore   Explain

Planet Diary

my planet diary

>> **VOCAB FLASH CARDS**

Practice chapter vocabulary with interactive flash cards. Each card has an image, definitions in English and Spanish, and space for your own notes.

Unit 4 > Chapter 1 > Lesson 1

The Big Question   Unlock the Big Question   Explore the Big Question   >>

The Big Question   Untamed Science   Check Your Understanding   Vocabulary Skill   Vocabulary Flashcards

Vocabulary Flashcards   Tools

Card List   Create-a-Card   10 Cards Left   Test Me

Lesson Cards   My Cards

Birth Rate   Science Vocabulary
Carrying Capacity
Commensalism   Term: **Community**
Community
Competition   Definition: All the different populations that live
Death Rate   together in a particular area.
Ecology
Ecosystem   View Spanish
Emigration
Habitat   Add Notes
Host
Immigration
Limiting Factor   Card 5 of

Unit 6 > Chapter 1 > Lesson

Engage & Explore   E

Apply It   Directed Virtual Lab

Color in Light

Exit

Reset Lab

Unit 6 > Chapter 1 > Lesson 1

Engage & Explore   Explain   Elaborate   Evaluate

Apply It   Do the Math   Art in Motion   Interactive Art   Real World Inquiry

The Nebraska Plains

▶ Bald Eagle

Information   Media

Haliaeetus leucocephalus
Bald Eagles are 80-95 cm tall with
a wingspan of 180-230 cm. These
birds are born with all brown
feathers but grow white feathers
on their head, neck, and tail.

Layers List   ▲ Show

Next

22
of
22

Back

>> **INTERACTIVE ART**

At MyScienceOnline.com, many of the beautiful visuals in your book become interactive so you can extend your learning.

interactive SCIENCE

GO ONLINE

my science online.com ⟩ Populations and Communities ⟩ PLANET DIARY ⟩ LAB ZONE ⟩ VIRTUAL LAB

⟲ ＋ 🌐 http://www.myscienceonline.com/

⟩ PLANET DIARY

My Planet Diary online is the place to find more information and activities related to lesson topics.

Elaborate | Evaluate

Everest

Tools
123

Still Growing! Mount Everest in the Himalayas is the highest mountain on Earth. Climbers who reach the peak stand 8,850 meters above sea level. You might think that mountains never change. But forces inside Earth push Mount Everest at least several millimeters higher each year. Over time, Earth's forces slowly but constantly lift, stretch, bend, and break Earth's crust in dramatic ways!

⟩ Planet Diary Go to Planet Diary to learn more about forces in the Earth's crust.

▶ Next

22 of 22

Back ◀

⟩ VIRTUAL LAB

Get more practice with realistic virtual labs. Manipulate the variables on-screen and test your hypothesis.

Find Your Chapter

1 Go to www.myscienceonline.com.

2 Log in with username and password.

3 Click on your program and select your chapter.

Keyword Search

1 Go to www.myscienceonline.com.

2 Log in with username and password.

3 Click on your program and select Search.

4 Enter the keyword (from your book) in the search box.

Other Content Available Online

⟩ **UNTAMED SCIENCE** Follow these young scientists through their amazing online video blogs as they travel the globe in search of answers to the Essential Questions of Science.

⟩ **MY SCIENCE COACH** Need extra help? My Science Coach is your personal online study partner. My Science Coach is a chance for you to get more practice on key science concepts. There you can choose from a variety of tools that will help guide you through each science lesson.

⟩ **MY READING WEB** Need extra reading help on a particular science topic? At My Reading Web you will find a choice of reading selections targeted to your specific reading level.

? BIG IDEAS OF SCIENCE

Have you ever worked on a jigsaw puzzle? Usually a puzzle has a theme that leads you to group the pieces by what they have in common. But until you put all the pieces together you can't solve the puzzle. Studying science is similar to solving a puzzle. The big ideas of science are like puzzle themes. To understand big ideas, scientists ask questions. The answers to those questions are like pieces of a puzzle. Each chapter in this book asks a big question to help you think about a big idea of science. By answering the big questions, you will get closer to understanding the big idea.

✎ **Before you read each chapter, write about what you know and what more you'd like to know.**

BIGIDEA

Scientists use scientific inquiry to explain the natural world.

Scientific inquiry requires a logical way of thinking based on gathering and evaluating evidence.

What do you already know about how scientists investigate the natural world?
✎ **What more would you like to know?**

_____
_____
_____

Big Question:

❓ What does it mean to think like a scientist? Chapter 1

✎ **After reading the chapter, write what you have learned about the Big Idea.**

_____
_____
_____

BIGIDEA

Scientists use mathematics in many ways.

Scientists rely on estimates as a quick way of determining how many insects are in this photo.

Which tools have you used to study science?
✎ **What more would you like to know?**

_____
_____
_____

Big Question:

❓ What tools do scientists use to understand the natural world? Chapter 2

✎ **After reading the chapter, write what you have learned about the Big Idea.**

_____
_____
_____

BIGIDEA
Atoms are the building blocks of matter.

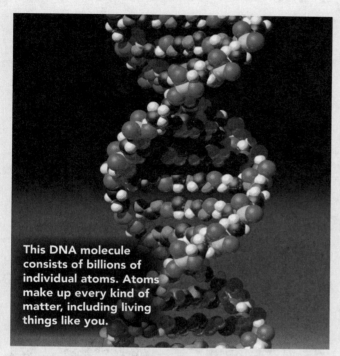

This DNA molecule consists of billions of individual atoms. Atoms make up every kind of matter, including living things like you.

If the building blocks of matter are the same, then what makes everything different?

✎ **What more would you like to know?**

_____

_____

_____

_____

Big Question:

❓ How is matter described? Chapter 3

✎ **After reading the chapter, write what you have learned about the Big Idea.**

_____

_____

_____

_____

_____

BIGIDEA
Mass and energy are conserved during physical and chemical changes.

Over the years, the Statue of Liberty has changed from a shiny copper to this bluish-green color because of its exposure to oxygen in the air. During these changes, the total mass and energy of the statue's atoms have been conserved.

If you burn a candle, gradually the candle becomes smaller. What happens to the part of the candle that burns away? Does it cease to exist?

✎ **What more would you like to know?**

_____

_____

_____

_____

Big Question:

❓ Why does a substance change states? Chapter 4

✎ **After reading the chapter, write what you have learned about the Big Idea.**

_____

_____

_____

_____

_____

Energy can take different forms but is always conserved.

As these snowboarders fall, they don't lose any energy—the energy just takes different forms.

What do you already know about what happens to the mass and energy of a candle as it burns? ✏️ **What more would you like to know?**

_____

_____

_____

_____

Big Question:

❓ How is energy conserved in a transformation? Chapter 5

✏️ **After reading the chapter, write what you have learned about the Big Idea.**

_____

_____

_____

_____

_____

Earth is part of a system of objects that orbit the sun.

Jupiter, its moons, and Earth are all parts of the solar system. Each of them is held in its orbit by gravity.

What do you already know about Earth and the other objects in the solar system? ✏️ **What more would you like to know?**

_____

_____

_____

_____

Big Questions:

❓ How do Earth, the moon, and the sun interact? Chapter 6

❓ Why are objects in the solar system different from each other? Chapter 7

✏️ **After reading the chapters, write what you have learned about the Big Idea.**

_____

_____

_____

_____

Living things interact with their environment.

What do you already know about how the animals and plants in your neighborhood live together?

✎ **What more would you like to know?**

_____

_____

_____

_____

Big Questions:

❓ How do living things affect one another?
Chapter 8

❓ How do energy and matter move through ecosystems? Chapter 9

✎ **After reading the chapters, write what you have learned about the Big Idea.**

_____

_____

_____

_____

_____

These prairie dogs live in grasslands and make their homes underground. To stay alive, prairie dogs search for food and water and hide from animals that eat them.

xxix

WHAT CAN SHARKS TEACH THESE CAGED SCIENTISTS?

What does it mean to think like a scientist?

Would you ever go diving in a shark cage? If you were a marine biologist, this might be part of your job. To learn more about sharks, marine biologists study them in their natural environment. These Galápagos sharks were observed swimming off of the coast of Hawaii. Marine biologists have learned that a full-grown male Galápagos shark can grow to be 3.7 meters long and eat squid, octopus, and fish, including other sharks.

Infer What information could scientists learn by watching these sharks?

_____

_____

_____

_____

> **UNTAMED SCIENCE** Watch the **Untamed Science** video to learn more about science.

What Is Science?

Academic Standards for Science

6.3.2, 6.3.3, 6.NS.1, 6.NS.2, 6.NS.3, 6.NS.4, 6.NS.5, 6.NS.6,
6.NS.7, 6.NS.8, 6.NS.9, 6.NS.10, 6.NS.11

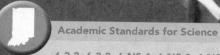

Check Your Understanding

1. **Background** Read the paragraph below and then answer the question.

Andy is watching a movie when the television suddenly turns off. He decides to **investigate**. Andy turns on a lamp but nothing happens. He tries the radio, but it doesn't work either. Then, he looks out the window and **observes** that all the houses on his street are dark. Andy **concludes** that the electricity has gone out in the neighborhood. He hopes the power returns soon.

To **investigate** is to observe or study closely.

To **observe** is to see or notice.

To **conclude** is to reach a decision.

• How did Andy investigate the problem?

_____

_____

> MY READING WEB) If you have trouble completing the question above, visit **My Reading Web** and type in *What Is Science?*

Vocabulary Skill

Identify Related Word Forms Learning related forms of words increases your vocabulary. The table lists forms of words related to vocabulary terms.

Verb	Noun	Adjective
predict, *v.* to state what will happen in the future	prediction, *n.* a statement about what will happen in the future	predictable, *adj.* able to state what will happen in the future
vary, *v.* to make a partial change in something	variation, *n.* the amount of change in something; the result of a change	variable, *adj.* able to change

2. **Quick Check** Complete the sentence with the correct form of the word.

• Can you _____ how long it will take to do your homework?

science

WHERE *I* COME FROM, WE DRINK A LOT OF *TEA,* SO I THINK IT'S OK IF WE DON'T HAVE *COFFEE* HERE.

cultural bias

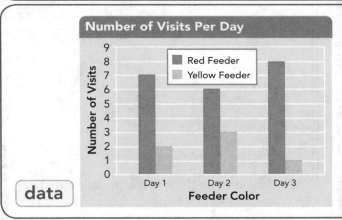

data

scientific law

Chapter Preview

LESSON 1
- science
- observing
- quantitative observation
- qualitative observation
- inferring
- predicting
- classifying
- making models
- evaluating
- scientific investigation

↻ **Sequence**

△ **Interpret Data**

LESSON 2
- skepticism
- personal bias
- cultural bias
- experimental bias
- ethics
- objective
- subjective
- deductive reasoning
- inductive reasoning

↻ **Ask Questions**

△ **Infer**

LESSON 3
- scientific inquiry
- hypothesis
- variables
- independent variable
- dependent variable
- controlled experiment
- data
- scientific theory
- scientific law

↻ **Relate Cause and Effect**

△ **Control Variables**

▷ **VOCAB FLASH CARDS** For extra help with vocabulary, visit **Vocab Flash Cards** and type in *What Is Science?*

The Skills of Science

UNLOCK
THE BIG
?

🔑 **What Are the Skills of Science?**
6.NS.1, 6.NS.3, 6.NS.8

my planet Diary

Underwater Science

Imagine being an explorer who has truly gone where no one has gone before. Imagine seeing pale crabs as large as cats and tall spirals of bamboo coral that glow blue when touched. Imagine walking in the ocean nearly 380 meters below the surface or swimming so close to a whale you can touch it. Well, none of this is imaginary for Dr. Sylvia Earle!

Dr. Earle is a marine biologist, a scientist who studies ocean life. She has spent more than 7,000 hours underwater, studying everything from algae to humpback whales. She is also an inventor who developed submersibles (a type of submarine) so she could study life in the ocean close-up.

Dr. Sylvia Earle shows algae to an engineer in an underwater habitat.

CAREERS

Answer the questions below. Then discuss your answers with a classmate.

1. What is one advantage and one disadvantage of actually being in the ocean to study ocean life?

_____
_____
_____
_____
_____
_____
_____

2. What do you think is the most interesting part of being a marine biologist?

_____
_____
_____

> PLANET DIARY Go to **Planet Diary** to learn more about science skills.

Lab zone® Do the Inquiry Warm-Up *Exploring Science.*

Vocabulary

- science
- observing
- quantitative observation
- qualitative observation
- inferring
- predicting
- classifying
- making models
- evaluating
- scientific investigation

Skills

↻ Reading: Sequence
△ Inquiry: Interpret Data

What Are the Skills of Science?

Dr. Earle is a scientist, or a person who practices science. Science is a way of learning about the natural world. Scientists gather information and explore the natural world using different science skills. ⚷ The skills of science include observing, inferring, predicting, classifying, evaluating, making models, and conducting scientific investigations.

Academic Standards for Science

6.NS.1 Make predictions and develop testable questions based on research and prior knowledge.
6.NS.3 Collect quantitative data.
6.NS.8 Analyze data.

Observing Scientists are always observing things. Observing means using one or more of your senses to gather information. It's the most important science skill. Dr. Earle, for example, has spent many hours observing ocean plants and animals, like those shown in Figure 1. By observing ocean life, she learned things such as which fish eat plants and which fish eat animals.

Observations can be either quantitative or qualitative. A quantitative observation deals with numbers, or amounts. For example, when you measure your height or your weight, or notice that there are 8 cars parked on your street, you are making a quantitative observation. A qualitative observation deals with descriptions that cannot be expressed in numbers. Noticing that a bird is blue or that a watermelon tastes sweet are qualitative observations.

Somryx Fish
These are Orange Fish
CORAL has Many colors

FIGURE 1 ·······················

Observing Ocean Life

 **Observe** Write at least one quantitative observation and one qualitative observation about these aquatic organisms. Discuss your observations with a classmate.

6.NS.3

⊙ **Sequence**
What did Dr. Earle do after she made her observations?

_____

_____

_____

_____

_____

Inferring Unlike many ocean scientists, Dr. Earle has actually lived under water. She spent two weeks in an underwater habitat near the Virgin Islands. There she studied fish and their behavior. One thing Dr. Earle noticed was that different fish eat different things. For example, parrotfish eat seaweed that grows on dead coral, while the damselfish eat a certain type of algae. Dr. Earle also noticed that none of the fish in the area she was studying ate the feathery green leaves of a plant called *Caulerpa*. She reasoned that although the plant looked good, it probably didn't taste good to the fish in the area.

Dr. Earle was not observing when she reasoned that *Caulerpa* doesn't taste good to fish. She was inferring. When you explain or interpret the things you observe, you are **inferring,** or making an inference. Inferring is not guessing. Inferences are based on reasoning from what you already know. Inferences could also be based on assumptions you make about your observations. See **Figure 2.**

FIGURE 2 ·······················
Inferring
Damselfish maintain and defend small "algal lawns" that they use for food, shelter, and nesting.
✎ **Complete these tasks.**

1. **Observe** Write one observation about the damselfish in the photo.
   the fish is orange
   _____
   _____
   _____
   _____

2. **Infer** Based on your observation, write one inference.
   The fish probably was spear colortul corals.
   _____
   _____

6.NS.8

3. [CHALLENGE] What sources might you use to research your inference?
   _____
   _____

Predicting Dr. Earle also followed humpback whales in the Hawaiian Islands. The more time she spent with the whales, the more she understood their behavior. Sometimes she could predict what a particular whale would do next. **Predicting** means making a statement or a claim about what will happen in the future based on past experience or evidence.

Inferences and predictions are closely related. While inferences are attempts to explain what is happening or *has* happened, predictions are statements or claims about what *will* happen. See what predictions you can make about the whales in **Figure 3.**

Classifying On one expedition, Dr. Earle was part of a team gathering information about plants found in the Gulf of Mexico. Team members collected samples from different underwater areas, and took detailed notes about the temperature, salt content, and amount of light present. They then classified the information they collected to make it easier to understand. **Classifying** is the grouping together of items that are alike in some ways. For example, the team grouped together in a data table the type of algae found in each area.

did you
know? N.O.

Scientists classify organisms into groups based on their common characteristics. For example, all animals belong to a group called the animal kingdom. Scientists use specific names to identify organisms. For example, the Indiana bat is classified as *Myotis sodalis.*

FIGURE 3 ·······················

Predicting Whale Behavior

Humpback whales eat krill, tiny shrimp-like animals. These panels show a sequence of humpback whale feeding behavior.

 Predict Draw a picture in the empty panel to show what you think will happen next. Write your prediction on the lines. 6.NS.1

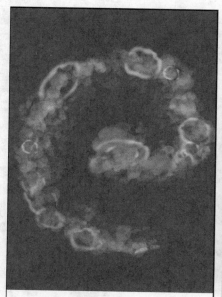

Humpback whales blow "bubble nets" when feeding.

The whales then move up through the center of the bubbles.

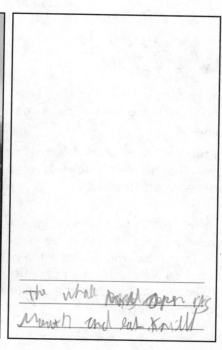

The whale will open its Mouth and eat krill

Making Models A data table is one way to present information. A model is another way. For example, Dr. Earle's team could have made a model showing the temperature and depth of the ocean at each algae collection point. **Making models** involves creating representations of complex objects or processes. Some models can be touched, such as a map. Others are in the form of mathematical equations or computer programs. Models help people study things that can't be observed directly. By using models, scientists can share information that would otherwise be difficult to explain.

Evaluating One of the reasons that Dr. Earle studied humpback whales was to see if she could determine if certain whale "songs"—a series of loud grunts and squeals repeated over and over—were associated with certain whale behaviors. Suppose she found that a whale sang a certain song each time it fed. What would this observation have told her about whale behavior? To reach a conclusion, Dr. Earle would first need to evaluate her observations and data. **Evaluating** involves comparing observations and data to reach a conclusion about them. For example, Dr. Earle would have needed to compare the whale's behaviors with those of the other whales in the group to reach a conclusion.

apply it!

This map shows ocean surface temperature along the Louisiana coast in January. **6.NS.8**

1 Interpret Maps Mark the areas on the map that have a surface temperature of about 12°C.

2 Interpret Data Phytoplankton are plantlike organisms that live in the ocean. Phytoplankton grow best in cold, nutrient-rich waters. Near which cities would you most likely find the greatest number of phytoplankton?

_____

_____

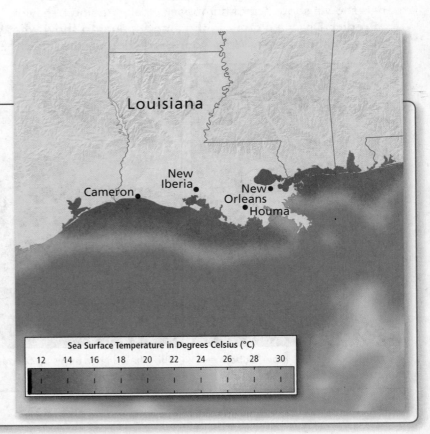

Louisiana

Cameron •   New Iberia •   New Orleans •   Houma •

Sea Surface Temperature in Degrees Celsius (°C)									
12	14	16	18	20	22	24	26	28	30

Conducting Scientific Investigations

Science is a continuous cycle of asking questions about the natural world, looking for answers, solving problems, and forming new ideas. A **scientific investigation** is the way in which scientists study the natural world. First, you ask a question. Then, you figure out a way to find the answer. Finally, you perform the actions necessary to find the answer. Recall that Dr. Earle first observed that bamboo coral glowed blue when touched, as shown in the first photo of **Figure 4**. Then, other scientists began investigating how and why the coral glows. Scientific investigations may occur in different ways, but they usually involve most or all of the other science skills.

FIGURE 4 ·······························

> **INTERACTIVE ART** **Scientific Investigation**
✎ **Pose Questions** For each image, write a question that could be answered by conducting a scientific investigation.   6.NS.1

2

1

why is the water red?

how does this coral glowing

> **Lab zone** ® Try the Quick Lab
Practicing Science Skills.

🔑 Assess Your Understanding

1a. Review Why do scientists make models?

_____

_____

_____

_____
    6.NS.1

b. Classify Identify each statement as an observation (*O*) or an inference (*I*).

The cat is fat. _____

The cat likes food. _____
    6.NS.1

got it?

◯ I get it! Now I know that the skills of

science include _____

_____

_____

_____

◯ I need extra help with _____

Go to **MY SCIENCE** 💬 **COACH** *online for help with this subject.*
    6.NS.1

LESSON

2 Scientific Thinking

UNLOCK
THE BIG
?

🔑 **What Are the Characteristics of Scientific Thinking?**
6.NS.1

🔑 **What Is Scientific Reasoning?**
6.NS.1

🔑 **How Does Scientific Knowledge Change?**
6.NS.2

MY PLANET DIARY for Indiana ⊗ ⊗ ⊗

Inventor Extraordinaire

What does it take to be an extraordinary inventor like Elwood Haynes? Born in 1857 in Portland, Indiana, Haynes was recognized at an early age for his determination and curiosity. As a student and as a scientist, he overcame obstacles and went on to distinguish himself with many technological "firsts". He constructed our nation's first long-distance, high-pressure natural gas pipeline. He created stainless steel and other metal combinations. Haynes designed the first successful gasoline-powered car in America, the Pioneer, pictured here.

BIOGRAPHY

Communicate Discuss the question with a partner. Then write your answer below.

1. How are curiosity and determination beneficial to a scientist or an inventor?

_____

_____

_____

_____

_____

_____

> PLANET DIARY Go to **Planet Diary** to learn more about thinking like a scientist.

Lab zone® Do the Inquiry Warm-Up
How to Think Scientifically.

Academic Standards of Science

6.NS.1 Make predictions and develop testable questions based on research and prior knowledge.

What Are the Characteristics of Scientific Thinking?

Have you ever taken apart a flashlight just to see how it works? Or thought about whether a magician really sawed a person in half? Or told a teacher the truth about why your homework was late? If so, you've demonstrated some of the key characteristics of scientific thinking. 🔑 **Scientific thinking involves characteristics such as curiosity, creativity, open-mindedness, skepticism, awareness of bias, honesty, and ethics.**

Vocabulary
- skepticism • personal bias • cultural bias
- experimental bias • ethics • objective
- subjective • deductive reasoning
- inductive reasoning

Skills
↪ Reading: Ask Questions
△ Inquiry: Infer

Curiosity and Creativity
Curiosity is one of the main characteristics that leads to new scientific knowledge. Scientists want to learn more about the topics they study. Curiosity helps them to make observations and ask questions.

In 1609, Galileo Galilei demonstrated his telescope, which would lead to many new astronomical observations. Although Galileo's curiosity inspired him to observe space, it was his creative thinking that allowed him to make improvements to the telescope. Creativity involves coming up with new sources and ways to help solve problems or produce new things.

Open-Mindedness and Skepticism
Scientists need to be open-minded, or capable of accepting new and different ideas. But open-mindedness should always be balanced by **skepticism,** which means having an attitude of doubt. Skepticism prevents scientists from accepting ideas that are presented without enough evidence or that may be untrue. Skeptics of scientific claims can help determine if something really exists. Practice using open-mindedness and skepticism in **Figure 1.**

✎ **Ask Questions** If you were a scientist studying the organism pictured below, what would you be curious to know about it?

_____
_____
_____

6.NS.1

FIGURE 1 ·········
Truth or Fiction?
This tabloid magazine is making a claim about the Florida Everglades.

✎ **Read the magazine's headline. Then answer the questions below.**

1. Make Judgments Would you respond to this headline with open-mindedness or skepticism?

_____
_____

2. Explain Why would you respond that way?

_____
_____
_____
_____
_____

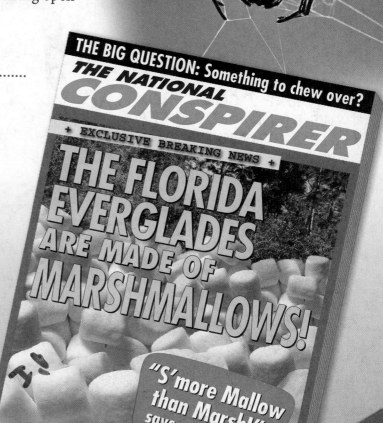

THE BIG QUESTION: Something to chew over?

THE NATIONAL CONSPIRER

+ EXCLUSIVE BREAKING NEWS +

THE FLORIDA EVERGLADES ARE MADE OF MARSHMALLOWS!

"S'more Mallow than Marsh!" says expert

Awareness of Bias

What scientists expect to find can influence, or bias, what they observe and how they interpret their observations. There are several different kinds of bias.

Personal Bias If a person's likes and dislikes influence how he or she thinks about something, that is called **personal bias.** For instance, if you like the taste of milk, you might think everyone else likes it, too.

Cultural Bias When the culture in which a person grows up affects the way that person thinks, this is called **cultural bias.** For example, a culture that regards milk as a food just for babies might overlook the nutritional benefits of drinking milk in later life.

Experimental Bias A mistake in the design of an experiment that makes a certain result more likely is called **experimental bias.** For example, suppose you want to compare the health effects of drinking low-fat milk and regular milk. Your experiment consists of two groups of people. One group drinks low-fat milk for a month, and the other drinks regular milk for a month. If either group had been less healthy than the other group before the experiment, your results would be biased.

I REALLY LIKE WATCHING MOVIES, SO I'LL BET THAT EVERYONE LIKES WATCHING MOVIES!

WHERE *I* COME FROM, WE DRINK A LOT OF *TEA,* SO I THINK IT'S OK IF WE DON'T HAVE *COFFEE* HERE.

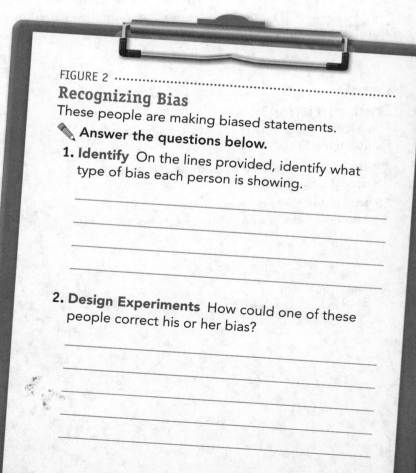

FIGURE 2 ....

Recognizing Bias

These people are making biased statements.

✎ **Answer the questions below.**

1. **Identify** On the lines provided, identify what type of bias each person is showing.

_____

_____

_____

_____

2. **Design Experiments** How could one of these people correct his or her bias?

_____

_____

_____

_____

_____

Honesty and Ethics Good scientists always report their observations and results truthfully. Honesty is very important when a scientist's results go against previous ideas or predictions. For example, in 1912, a group of scientists in Britain announced that they found a fossil that was the "missing link" between humans and apes. The fossil had the skull of a man and the jaw of an orangutan. They called the fossil "Piltdown Man," as shown in **Figure 3.** About 40 years later, careful testing determined that the fossil was a fake!

Scientists also need a strong sense of **ethics,** which refers to the rules that enable people to know right from wrong. Scientists must consider all the effects their research may have on people and the environment. They make decisions only after considering the risks and benefits to living things and the environment.

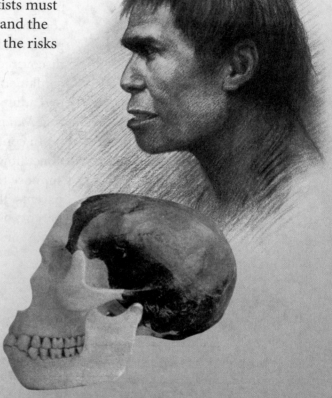

FIGURE 3 ··

The Piltdown Hoax
An artist has drawn what the Piltdown Man would have looked like, based on the fossilized skull parts.

✎ **Answer the questions below.**

1. **Name** What are two careers in which honesty and ethics are important?

_____

_____

2. CHALLENGE How might a fake fossil affect the work of other scientists?

_____

_____

_____

_____

Lab zone® Do the Quick Lab
Exploring Scientific Thinking.

🔑 **Assess Your Understanding**

1a. Describe What is bias?

_____
6.NS.1

b. Infer How might creativity help scientists come up with new scientific knowledge?

_____

_____
6.NS.1

got it?

○ **I get it!** Now I know that the characteristics of scientific thinking include _____

_____

_____

○ **I need extra help with** _____

Go to MY SCIENCE ⓢ COACH *online for help with this subject.*
6.NS.1

Academic Standards for Science

6.NS.1 Make predictions and develop testable questions based on research and prior knowledge.

What Is Scientific Reasoning?

You use reasoning, or a logical way of thinking, when you solve problems. For example, you notice that water on a stove boils when the stove is turned on. Because the water doesn't boil when the stove is off, you might logically conclude that heat causes water to boil. **Scientific reasoning requires a logical way of thinking based on gathering and evaluating evidence.**

Objective and Subjective Scientific reasoning involves being **objective,** which means that you make decisions and draw conclusions based on available evidence. For example, a paleontologist named Jack Horner and his partner, Robert Makela, discovered the nests of a dinosaur called *Maiasaura*. The nests contained fossilized eggs, newly hatched babies, young dinosaurs, and adults. Based on this evidence, Horner and Makela concluded that *Maiasaura* took care of their young.

In contrast, being **subjective** means that personal feelings affect how you make a decision or reach a conclusion. For example, suppose that a paleontologist thought that dinosaurs were bad parents. If she found a fossilized nest of eggs with no bones of parents nearby, she might ignore other evidence and conclude that dinosaurs did not care for their young.

PEDRO IS 1.7 M TALL.

NO ONE ELSE IN CLASS IS TALLER THAN 1.6 M.

Infer Read the comic above about measuring height. Write a conclusion and a title for the third picture. Is your conclusion based on subjective or objective reasoning? Explain.

_____

_____

Deductive and Inductive Reasoning

There are two main types of scientific reasoning: deductive reasoning and inductive reasoning. **Deductive reasoning** is a way to explain things by starting with a general idea and then applying the idea to a specific observation. You can think about deductive reasoning as being a process. First, you state the general idea. Then you relate the general idea to the specific case you are investigating. Finally, you reach a conclusion. For instance, you know that water freezes at 0 degrees Celsius. You see a frozen puddle of water. You know that the water has frozen because it was at or below 0 degrees Celsius.

Inductive reasoning can be considered the opposite of deductive reasoning. **Inductive reasoning** uses specific observations to make generalizations. Suppose you notice that every time a puddle freezes, the temperature outside is at or below 0 degrees Celsius. You might conclude that water freezes at 0 degrees Celsius.

FIGURE 4 ....

> INTERACTIVE ART **What Goes Up . . .**
Gene is playing with a basketball in his backyard.

✎ **Apply Concepts** Read the comic below. Is Gene's thinking an example of deductive or inductive reasoning? Explain your answer.

_____

_____

_____

_____

6.NS.1

FIGURE 5 ·····························

Chat Room Controversy
You are chatting online with three friends who live in other states.

✏️ **Communicate** In the space provided, explain to your friends why Jeff has shown faulty reasoning.

Faulty Reasoning If you make a conclusion without gathering enough data, your reasoning might lead you to the wrong general idea. Incorrect reasoning such as this is called faulty reasoning. For example, suppose you saw a number of people walking their dogs and observed that every person who was walking a yellow retriever that day was a young girl. You might use inductive reasoning to say that only young girls own yellow retrievers. However, this conclusion would be wrong. Scientists must be careful not to use faulty reasoning, because it can lead to faulty conclusions.

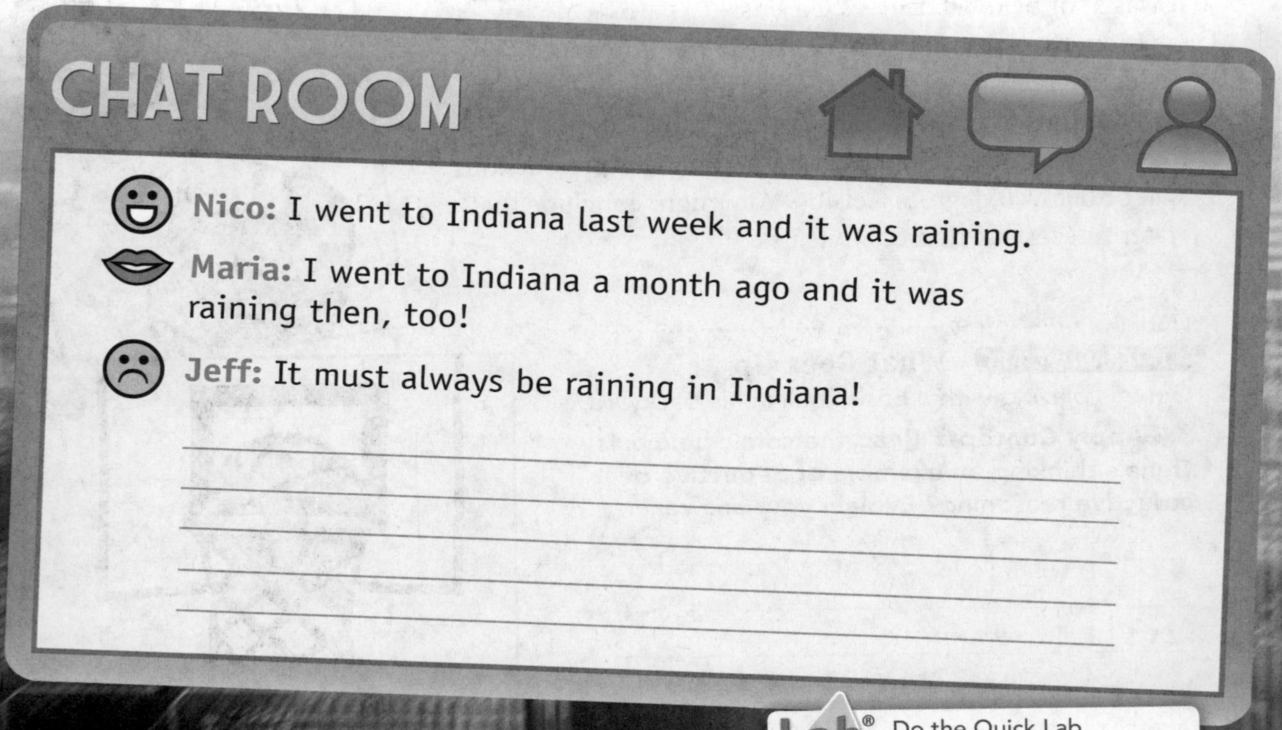

CHAT ROOM

😃 **Nico:** I went to Indiana last week and it was raining.

👄 **Maria:** I went to Indiana a month ago and it was raining then, too!

☹️ **Jeff:** It must always be raining in Indiana!

_____
_____
_____
_____
_____

Lab zone ® Do the Quick Lab
Using Scientific Reasoning.

🔑 Assess Your Understanding

2a. Summarize Why is subjective reasoning not an example of scientific thought?

_____
_____
_____

6.NS.1

b. Relate Cause and Effect What is a cause of faulty reasoning?

_____
_____
_____

6.NS.1

got it? ···

⭕ **I get it!** Now I know that scientific reasoning is _____
_____

⭕ **I need extra help with** _____

Go to **MY SCIENCE** 💬 **COACH** online for help with this subject.

6.NS.1

How Does Scientific Knowledge Change?

Academic Standards for Science

6.NS.2 Plan and carry out investigations as a class, in small groups or independently often over a period of several class lessons.

Our understanding of the natural world is always growing and changing. New technologies expand the ways scientists gather and interpret data. This increases and changes scientific knowledge. Today, scientists know about topics ranging from matter's smallest particles to the deepest regions of space. But this wasn't always the case. **Scientific knowledge is based on an ever-growing collection of facts about the natural world, but it changes with new evidence or new interpretations.** For example, 2,300 years ago, ancient astronomers thought that all the observable objects in the sky revolved around Earth. Later scientists proposed that Earth and other planets actually revolve around the sun. However, there was no evidence of this until Galileo used his improved telescope and witnessed moons moving around Jupiter. Today, scientists know that Earth and all other planets in the solar system revolve around the sun.

FIGURE 6 ·······················

Life in the Deep

Scientists used to think nothing lived at the bottom of oceans. But, in 1977, tube worms were found living at a depth of 2,000 meters!

✎ **Explain** How do you think scientists collected new evidence about deep oceans?

_____

_____

_____

_____

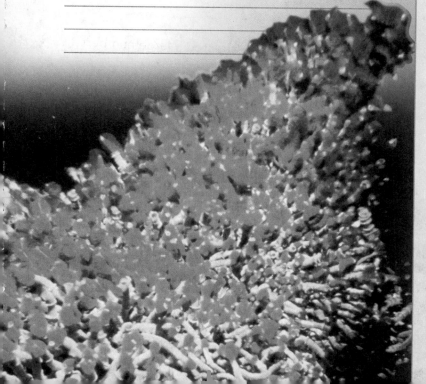

Lab zone® Do the Quick Lab *Scientific Discovery.*

🗝 Assess Your Understanding

3a. Identify A telescope expanded which of Galileo's senses?

_____
6.NS.2

b. Apply Concepts What kind of scientific knowledge has increased as a result of improvements to microscopes?

_____

_____
6.NS.2

got it? ·······································

○ I get it! Now I know scientific knowledge

changes _____

_____

○ I need extra help with _____

Go to **my science** ⬤ **coach** online for help with this subject.
6.NS.2

17

Answering Scientific Questions

UNLOCK THE BIG ?

🔑 **What Is Scientific Inquiry?**
6.NS.1

🔑 **How Do You Design and Conduct an Experiment?**
6.NS.1, 6.NS.2, 6.NS.3, 6.NS.4, 6.NS.6, 6.NS.7, 6.NS.8, 6.NS.9, 6.NS.10, 6.NS.11

🔑 **What Are Scientific Theories and Laws?**
6.NS.1, 6.NS.8, 6.NS.10, 6.NS.11

MY PLANET DIARY

MYSTERY

Bittersweet

In 2007, scientists found they had a mystery on their hands. In some countries, commercial honeybees began dying off in very large numbers. Honeybees pollinate crops such as apples, nuts, celery, and squash. If the mystery went unsolved, basic foods might become scarce!

Scientists began to investigate. In 2009, they compared the genes in healthy honeybees to the genes in sick honeybees. They found evidence that certain viruses attack proteins in honeybees. The afflicted bees seem unable to produce proteins that can fight the viruses. So the bees die.

This study was one of the first to identify a cause for the mystery. But scientists still need to investigate further to find a cure for the sick bees.

Write your answers to the questions below. Then discuss your answers with a partner.

1. Why did scientists have to keep investigating even after they thought they had found a reason why honeybees were dying?

_____

_____

2. How might your life be affected if large numbers of honeybees kept dying?

_____

_____

_____

> PLANET DIARY Go to **Planet Diary** to learn more about scientific investigations.

Lab zone® Do the Inquiry Warm-Up
Doing Science Is Asking Questions.

Vocabulary

- scientific inquiry • hypothesis • variables
- independent variables • dependent variables
- controlled experiment • data
- scientific theory • scientific law

Skills

- Reading: Relate Cause and Effect
- Inquiry: Control Variables

What Is Scientific Inquiry?

You hear a small whirring noise and look up. A ruby-throated hummingbird darts by, its wings a blur. It hovers over red salvia in the garden and then moves to an orange flower. It doesn't seem to go near any yellow flowers. What attracts a hummingbird to a flower? Do hummingbirds prefer some flower colors to others? Thinking and questioning in this way are the start of the **scientific inquiry** process. 🔑 **Scientific inquiry refers to the diverse ways in which scientists study the natural world and propose explanations based on the evidence they gather.**

Posing Questions Scientific inquiry often begins with a question about an observation. Your observation about the hummingbird's feeding habits may lead you to ask a question: Do hummingbirds prefer red flowers to other flower colors? Questions come from your experiences, observations, and inferences. Curiosity plays a role, too. Because others may have asked similar questions, you should do research to find what information is already known about the topic before you go on with your investigation. Look at **Figure 1** to pose a scientific question about an observation.

> **Academic Standards for Science**
>
> **6.NS.1** Make predictions and develop testable questions based on research and prior knowledge.

FIGURE 1 ··································

Posing Questions

The ruby-throated hummingbird is common in the eastern United States.

✎ **Complete these tasks.**   6.NS.1

1. **Pose Questions** Make an observation about this hummingbird. Then pose a question about this observation that you can study.

   _____

   _____

   _____

   _____

2. **Communicate** Share your questions with a group of classmates. Discuss which questions are the easiest and the most difficult to investigate.

Developing a Hypothesis How could you answer your question about hummingbirds and flower color? In trying to answer the question, you are developing a hypothesis. A **hypothesis** (plural: *hypotheses*) is a possible answer to a scientific question. In this case, you may suspect that hummingbirds can see red better than yellow. Your hypothesis would be that hummingbirds are more attracted to red flowers than yellow flowers. Use **Figure 2** to practice developing a hypothesis.

A hypothesis is *not* a fact. In science, a fact is an observation that has been confirmed repeatedly. For example, it is a fact that hummingbirds have tiny hairs on the tip of the tongue that help lap up nectar. A hypothesis, on the other hand, is one possible answer to a question. For example, perhaps the hummingbirds only seem to be feeding more at red flowers because the garden has fewer other colors of flowers. In science, a hypothesis must be testable. Researchers must be able to carry out investigations and gather evidence that will either support or disprove the hypothesis.

FIGURE 2 ·······························

Developing a Hypothesis
You may form a hypothesis about an everyday event.

✏️ **Develop Hypotheses** Why is the school bus always late? In the table, write two hypotheses for this question.   6.NS.1

Hypothesis A	Hypothesis B

Lab® zone Do the Quick Lab
Making a Hypothesis.

🔑 Assess Your Understanding

1a. Explain Can you test a hypothesis that hummingbirds spend most of their waking hours feeding? Explain.

_____

_____

_____

6.NS.1

b. Develop Hypotheses What is another hypothesis that might explain why hummingbirds seem to prefer red flowers?

_____

_____

_____

6.NS.1

got it? ··

○ **I get it!** Now I know that scientific inquiry is _____

_____

○ **I need extra help with** _____

Go to **MY SCIENCE** 🔊 **COACH** *online for help with this subject.*   6.NS.1

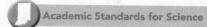
How Do You Design and Conduct an Experiment?

After developing your hypothesis, you are ready to test it by designing an experiment. **An experiment must follow sound scientific principles for its results to be valid.** The experiment needs to produce the kind of data that can answer your question. Also, the data collected need to be measurable. For example, to find out if the hummingbirds have a color preference, you could set up red and yellow feeders to test from which color, if any, the birds prefer to get food. Then you could collect data by counting how often hummingbirds feed from both the red and yellow feeders.

Controlling Variables
To test your hypothesis, you will observe hummingbirds feeding from different colored feeders. All other **variables,** or factors that can change in an experiment, must be the same. This includes variables such as the type of food, the shape and size of the feeder, and even the time of day when you observe the hummingbirds. By keeping these variables the same, you will know that any difference in how often a hummingbird feeds is due to feeder color alone.

The one variable that is purposely changed to test a hypothesis is the **independent variable.** The independent variable here is feeder color. The factor that may change in response to the independent variable is the **dependent variable.** The dependent variable here is the number of times the hummingbird visits a feeder.

Academic Standards for Science

6.NS.1 Make predictions and develop testable questions.
6.NS.2 Plan and carry out investigations.
6.NS.3 Collect quantitative data.
6.NS.4 Incorporate variables.
6.NS.6 Test predictions.
6.NS.7 Keep accurate records.
6.NS.8 Analyze data.
6.NS.9 Evaluate possible causes of different results.
6.NS.10 Compare results of an experiment with the prediction.
6.NS.11 Communicate findings.

Relate Cause and Effect
What is the effect of keeping all variables except the independent variable the same?

_____

_____

_____

_____

A student performs an experiment to determine if adding 1 milliliter of salt to bubble solution made from soap and water affects bubble making.

1 Control Variables Identify the independent variable and the dependent variable.

_____

_____

2 Identify What are two other variables in this experiment?

_____

_____

3 Draw Conclusions Write a hypothesis for this experiment.

_____

Setting Up a Controlled Experiment You can test your hypothesis in a controlled experiment. A **controlled experiment** is an experiment in which only one variable is changed at a time. You decide to test the hummingbirds at two different colored feeders: red and yellow. All other variables are kept the same. The feeders should be the same size, shape, and height above the ground. They should be in the same general area and contain the same amount and concentration of sugar water. The amount of time you observe the feeders should also be the same. Otherwise, your experiment would have more than one independent variable. Then you would have no way to tell which variable affected your results. Practice setting up a controlled experiment in **Figure 3.**

FIGURE 3 ···

A Controlled Experiment
The independent variable in this experiment is the color of the feeder. **6.NS.2, 6.NS.4, 6.NS.9**

✎ **Complete these tasks.**

1. **Design Experiments** On the lines below, write three variables for this experiment that must be kept the same. Then use the empty space to draw a picture of your experiment. Remember to include and label your variables.

   _____
   _____
   _____
   _____
   _____

2. **Compare and Contrast** With a group, discuss everyone's experiments and the different approaches that were used.

Collecting and Interpreting Data

Before you begin your experiment, decide what observations you will make and what data you will collect. **Data** are the facts, figures, and other evidence gathered through qualitative and quantitative observations. For the hummingbird experiment, you set up one feeder of each color. You decide to conduct three observations or trials because hummingbirds may behave differently from one trial to the next. You also decide to observe the feeders for 15 minutes at the same time for three days and count the number of visits to each feeder in that time period. You can use **Figure 4** to organize your hummingbird data.

After your data have been collected, they need to be interpreted. One tool that can help you interpret data is a graph. Graphs can reveal patterns or trends in data. You can use different graphs to present different types of information. Bar graphs are useful for comparing values across categories or treatments. Line graphs are used to show data points over time. Pie charts can be used to show the contribution of each item to the whole.

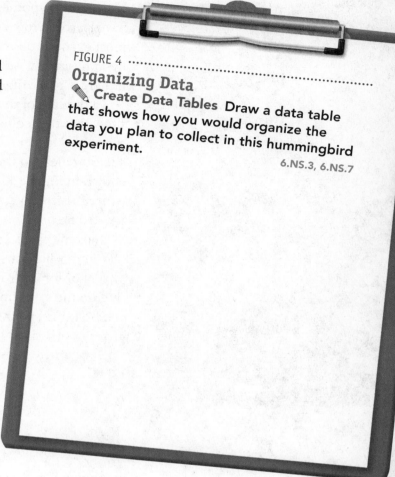

FIGURE 4 ....

Organizing Data

✎ **Create Data Tables** Draw a data table that shows how you would organize the data you plan to collect in this hummingbird experiment.

6.NS.3, 6.NS.7

do the math!

Graphing the data collected in an experiment may reveal whether there are patterns to the data.

❶ **Read Graphs** Identify the independent variable and the dependent variable.

_____

_____

_____

❷ **Interpret Data** Do the data support the hypothesis that hummingbirds prefer red flowers? Explain your answer.

_____

_____

_____

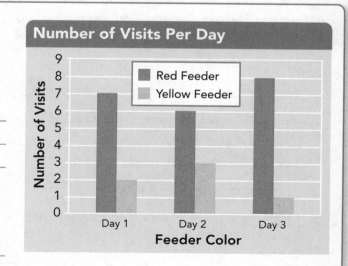

Number of Visits Per Day

Bar graph with y-axis "Number of Visits" (0–9) and x-axis "Feeder Color" showing Day 1, Day 2, Day 3. Legend: Red Feeder, Yellow Feeder.
Day 1: Red 7, Yellow 2. Day 2: Red 6, Yellow 3. Day 3: Red 8, Yellow 1.

6.NS.4, 6.NS.8

Drawing Conclusions Now you can draw conclusions about your hypothesis. A conclusion is a summary of what you have learned from an experiment. To draw your conclusion, you must examine your data objectively to see if they support your hypothesis. You must also consider if you collected enough data or if there is more than one interpretation for the set of data.

In the case of the hummingbirds' color preference, the data show that the red feeder had a greater average number of visits than the yellow feeder. Thus, the data support your hypothesis. Now, you should repeat your experiment to see if you get the same results, as shown in **Figure 5**. A conclusion is unreliable if it comes from an experiment with results that cannot be repeated. Many trials are needed before a hypothesis can be accepted as true.

In some cases, your data may not support your hypothesis. When this happens, check your experiment for things that went wrong or for improvements you can make. Then fix the problem and do the experiment again. If the experiment was done correctly the first time, your hypothesis was probably not correct. Propose a new hypothesis to test. Scientific inquiry usually doesn't end once an experiment is done. Often, one experiment leads to another.

FIGURE 5 ···

>**VIRTUAL LAB** **Drawing Conclusions**
Sometimes the same experiment can produce very different data.
✎ **Use the table to answer the questions.**   6.NS.6, 6.NS.8, 6.NS.9

1. **Interpret Tables** Suppose you retest your hypothesis. Do the new data in the table support your hypothesis? Explain.

_____

_____

2. **Analyze Sources of Error** If the data in this table were yours, what might you do next?

_____

_____

3. [CHALLENGE] Can you draw a conclusion from these data? Explain.

_____

_____

_____

Number of Visits Per Day		
	Red Feeder	**Yellow Feeder**
Day 1	4	5
Day 2	9	9
Day 3	5	4
Average	6	6

Communicating Communicating is the sharing of ideas and results with others through writing and speaking. Scientists give talks at scientific meetings, exchange information on the Internet, or publish articles in scientific journals to communicate.

When scientists share the results of their research, they describe their procedures so that others can repeat their experiments. Scientists wait until an experiment has been repeated many times before accepting a result. This way, scientists know that the result is accurate. Therefore, scientists must keep accurate records of their methods and results. Before the results are published, other scientists review the experiment for sources of error, such as bias, faulty data interpretation, and faulty conclusions. This review process helps prevent unreliable results from being published.

Sometimes, a scientific inquiry can be part of a huge project in which many scientists are working together around the world. On group projects, scientists share their ideas and results regularly. **Figure 6** asks you to come up with ideas for communicating the results of your hummingbird experiment.

FIGURE 6 ·······························
Communicating Results
Communicating results can lead to new questions, new hypotheses, and new investigations.

✎ **Communicate** With a group, write three ways to share the results of your hummingbird experiment.

_____

_____

_____

_____

6.NS.11

Lab zone® Do the Lab Investigation *Changing Pitch.*

🔑 Assess Your Understanding

2a. Name The _____ variable changes in response to the _____ variable in an experiment.　　6.NS.4

b. Summarize Why is it important for scientists to publish a description of their procedures with their results?

_____

_____

_____
　　　　　　　　　　　　　　　　6.NS.6

got it?

○ **I get it!** Now I know that an experiment must follow sound principles such as _____

_____

_____

○ **I need extra help with** _____

Go to MY SCIENCE Ⓢ COACH *online for help with this subject.*　　6.NS.2, 6.NS.3, 6.NS.4

Academic Standards for Science

6.NS.1 Make predictions and develop testable questions.

6.NS.8 Analyze data and use it to identify patterns and make inferences based on these patterns.

6.NS.10 Compare the results of an experiment with the prediction.

6.NS.11 Communicate findings using graphs, charts, maps and models.

What Are Scientific Theories and Laws?

Have you ever had a theory that your friends were planning a surprise party for you? Everyday theories you might have are different from scientific theories. **A scientific theory is a well-tested and widely accepted explanation of observations and experimental results.** Scientists are constantly testing scientific theories. If new observations or experiments do not support a theory, then the theory is changed or thrown out.

In a community, people make rules to help them live together. These rules are called laws. Science has laws, too. A **scientific law** is a statement that describes what scientists expect to happen every time under a particular set of conditions. **Scientific laws describe observed patterns in nature without trying to explain those patterns.** For example, according to the law of gravity, all objects in the universe attract each other. Learn about another scientific law in **Figure 7.**

FIGURE 7 ···

Scientific Laws

The law of superposition states that, in layers of rock, the oldest layer is at the bottom. The layers above it are younger.

✎ **Complete these tasks.**   6.NS.1, 6.NS.8

1. **Predict** Draw an arrow pointing to the rock layer that you think would contain the oldest fossils.

2. **Evaluate Scientific Claims** How could it be possible for a younger layer of rock to be below an older layer?

_____

_____

3. **Communicate** Explain to a classmate why the law of superposition is a scientific law.

EXPLORE THE BIG ?

In a Scientist's Shoes

What does it mean to think like a scientist?

FIGURE 8 ···
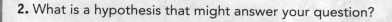

> INTERACTIVE ART When you think like a scientist, you conduct scientific investigations.

✎ **Apply Concepts** Think like a scientist to find out about whale songs. Answer these questions.

1. What question would you ask about whale songs?

_____

2. What is a hypothesis that might answer your question?

_____

_____

3. What three types of data could you collect to test your hypothesis?

_____

_____

_____

6.NS.1

Lab zone® Do the Quick Lab Theory or Not?

🗝 Assess Your Understanding

3a. Review Why are multiple experiments necessary before a theory is accepted?

_____

6.NS.6, 6.NS.8

b. Compare and Contrast How are scientific theories and scientific laws different?

_____

_____

6.NS.8

c. ANSWER THE BIG ? What does it mean to think like a scientist?

_____

_____

_____

_____

6.NS.1, 6.NS.8, 6.NS.11

got it? ···

○ **I get it!** Now I know that scientific theories and laws are _____

_____

○ **I need extra help with** _____

Go to MY SCIENCE ⓢ COACH *online for help with this subject.*   6.NS.1, 6.NS.8, 6.NS.10, 6.NS.11

27

Study Guide

To think like a scientist, you make _____ , develop _____ ,
design _____ , and collect data.

LESSON 1 The Skills of Science

6.NS.1, 6.NS.3, 6.NS.8

🔑 The skills of science include observing,
inferring, predicting, classifying, evaluating,
making models, and conducting scientific
investigations.

Vocabulary
- science • observing
- quantitative observation
- qualitative observation
- inferring • predicting
- classifying • making models
- evaluating • scientific investigation

LESSON 2 Scientific Thinking

6.NS.1, 6.NS.2

🔑 Scientific thinking involves characteristics such as curiosity, creativity,
open-mindedness, skepticism, awareness of bias, honesty, and ethics.

🔑 Scientific reasoning requires a logical way of thinking based on
gathering and evaluating evidence.

🔑 Scientific knowledge is based on an ever-growing collection of facts
about the natural world, but it changes with new evidence or new
interpretations.

Vocabulary
- skepticism • personal bias • cultural bias • experimental bias
- ethics • objective • subjective • deductive reasoning • inductive reasoning

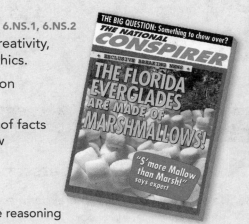

LESSON 3 Answering Scientific Questions

6.NS.1, 6.NS.2, 6.NS.3, 6.NS.4, 6.NS.6, 6.NS.7, 6.NS.8, 6.NS.9, 6.NS.10

🔑 Scientific inquiry refers to the ways in which scientists study
the natural world and propose explanations based on the
evidence they gather.

🔑 An experiment must follow sound scientific
principles for its results to be valid.

Vocabulary • scientific inquiry • hypothesis
- variables • independent variable
- dependent variable • controlled experiment
- data • scientific theory • scientific law

Review and Assessment

LESSON 1 The Skills of Science

1. An observation that deals with numbers is a(n)

  a. prediction.

  b. quantitative observation.

  c. inference.

  d. qualitative observation.

6.NS.1

2. Review When a scientist is evaluating, he or she is _____

_____

_____

6.NS.1

3. Apply Concepts A mother comes home to find her son holding a tennis racquet behind him, with a worried look on his face. A broken vase is on the floor next to him. What inference can you make about this situation?

_____

_____

_____

6.NS.1

4. A scientific investigation is _____

_____

_____

6.NS.1, 6.NS.2

5. Compare and Contrast How are the skills of inferring and predicting alike? How are they different?

_____

_____

_____

_____

6.NS.1

6. Explain Choose one scientific skill. Explain how it is useful in a scientific investigation.

_____

_____

_____

6.NS.1, 6.NS.11

LESSON 2 Scientific Thinking

7. A conclusion based on too little data is called

  a. cultural bias.   **b.** deductive reasoning.

  c. personal bias.   **d.** faulty reasoning.

6.NS.1

8. An attitude of doubt, or _____ can lead to new understanding.

6.NS.1

9. Review Experimental bias is _____

_____

_____

6.NS.2

10. Why do scientists need a strong sense of ethics?

_____

_____

_____

_____

6.NS.2

11. _____ reasoning uses specific observations to make generalizations.

6.NS.2

12. Draw Conclusions Why is it important that scientific reasoning be objective?

_____

_____

_____

_____

_____

_____

6.NS.8

13. Write About It Scientific knowledge changes with new evidence and new interpretations. Think of a scientific question you would like to answer, and then describe how you could collect evidence to answer it.

6.NS.1, 6.NS.2, 6.NS.3

LESSON 3 Answering Scientific Questions

14. Before you conduct an experiment, you must

   a. collect data.

   b. communicate your results.

   c. develop a hypothesis.

   d. draw conclusions.

6.NS.1

15. A variable is _____

_____

6.NS.4

16. Pose Questions Write a question about magnolia plants that you could test in a scientific investigation.

_____

_____

6.NS.1

17. Summarize What is a scientific theory and a scientific law?

_____

_____

_____

_____

_____

6.NS.6, 6.NS.8

18. Communicate Why do scientists review each other's work?

_____

_____

_____

_____

_____

6.NS.9, 6.NS.11

19. Write About It You're part of a research team that wants to determine the most popular type of cereal in your school. What type of scientific investigation would you conduct? How would you collect data and communicate the results?

6.NS.2, 6.NS.3, 6.NS.11

 What does it mean to think like a scientist?

20. People worldwide eat different kinds of tuna. One of the most popular types is the bluefin tuna. In fact, so many people eat bluefin tuna that the population has changed. Now only small bluefin are caught. You've been asked to investigate the cause of the decline in size of the bluefin tuna.

Think about the problem scientifically. What is a possible hypothesis? Could you test it? Mention how you would use at least one science skill in your investigation. Compare methods with a partner.

_____

_____

_____

_____

_____

_____

_____

_____

_____

_____

_____

_____

_____

6.NS.1, 6.NS.2

Indiana ISTEP+ Practice

Multiple Choice

Circle the letter of the best answer.

1. A scientist tested how long some modes of transportation took to travel between the two same cities. The data table shows the average amount of time each mode took.

Mode of Transportation	Average Time (minutes)
Airplane	80
Car	367
High-speed train	275
Maglev train	174

Which conclusion communicates the results of the investigation?

A. The car was the most efficient mode of transportation.

B. The airplane traveled faster than the car.

C. The maglev train is the world's fastest transportation.

D. The speed of the high-speed train was variable.

6.NS.8, 6.NS.11

2. Which of the following is a characteristic of a scientific theory?

A. It is an explanation of observations and results.

B. It is constantly being tested by scientists.

C. It is well supported and widely accepted.

D. All of the above

6.NS.1

3. Abbie took a trip to the beach. Which is a quantitative observation she may have made?

A. There were two lifeguards.

B. Everyone was wearing bathing suits.

C. It was a hot day.

D. The waves were big.

6.NS.1

4. Which describes an independent variable in a controlled experiment?

A. the factor that is purposely changed

B. the factor that changes in response

C. the factor that is kept the same

D. the factor that does not change

6.NS.4

Constructed Response

Write your answer to Question 5 on the lines below.

5. How does scientific knowledge change?

_____

_____

_____

_____

6.NS.1

Extended Response

Write your answer to Question 6 on another sheet of paper.

6. A scientist concludes that people prefer the smell of cinnamon more than any other scent. You find out that her data comes from the opinions of only three people. What is wrong with her conclusion? How might you improve her experiment?

6.NS.8, 6.NS.10

Indiana SCIENCE MATTERS

Sandy Habitats

The Indiana Dunes is now a national park that attracts more than 2 million visitors each year.

Do you enjoy taking field trips to natural places? Back in 1896, Dr. Henry Cowles, a botanist from the University of Chicago, visited the shores of Lake Michigan, now known as the Indiana Dunes.

Dr. Cowles set out to study plant species on the dunes. But he was fascinated by how many kinds of life he found. He noticed that the dunes supported greater varieties of life the farther away they were from the shore. He observed that interactions among organisms and between organisms and the environment changed over time.

Cowles looked at how factors such as rain, wind, and human development caused changes in the dunes. He also saw that these changes affected plant and animal life. Cowles noticed there was a connection between the diversity of species and environmental conditions.

Cowles's research contributed to the development of the science of ecology, the study of the relationships among organisms and between organisms and their environment. His study of the changes over time in organisms and the places they live became known as succession.

Communicate It Research the public efforts to protect the Indiana Dunes from human development. Write a persuasive letter to a public official giving your opinion as to whether public funds should be used to protect the dunes. Support your opinion with facts and details from your research.

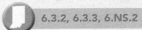

6.3.2, 6.3.3, 6.NS.2

Healing With MAGNETISM?

Magnetism is a powerful force with many uses. One claim is that it can relieve pain. The idea is that the magnetic field of a copper bracelet ionizes blood traveling through the wearer's wrist. This is supposed to change the electronic charge in the molecules of the blood. Supporters claim that the newly ionized blood improves circulation and oxygen flow. But what is really going on?

Doctors have done studies to test the claims made about these bracelets. A placebo is a control substance in experiments—something that looks like the material being tested, but doesn't do anything to the subject. In these studies, some patients wore ionic bracelets and others wore placebo bracelets, which looked the same but were not ionic. Doctors found no statistical difference in the pain relief from wearing an ionic bracelet versus a placebo bracelet. That means the bracelets don't work, but people experience pain relief because they believe the bracelets work. It's mind over matter!

Test It Find several sources presenting claims about magnetic bracelets. Write a letter to a friend who is considering buying one of these bracelets. Evaluate the claims made in the ads, and help your friend make an informed decision.

 6.NS.1, 6.NS.3, 6.NS.8

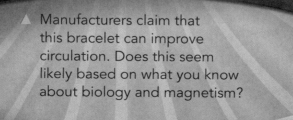

Manufacturers claim that this bracelet can improve circulation. Does this seem likely based on what you know about biology and magnetism?

WHAT MIGHT A CRAB'S SHELL SIZE TELL A SCIENTIST?

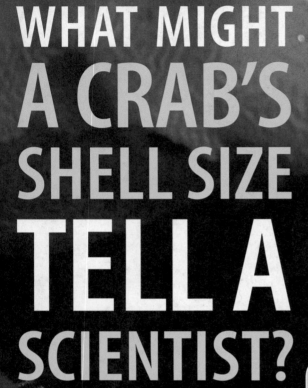

What tools do scientists use to understand the natural world?

This Dungeness crab's shell is being measured using a specialized tool. A crab ruler measures the shell at its widest point and is often used by fishermen to see if a crab is big enough to keep. For example, in Washington state, male crabs must be at least 15.9 cm (6 1/4 in) wide. Scientists studying this crab may record its shell size, weight, and the number of crabs that were found in the same area.

▲**Infer** **Why might a scientist measure a crab's size and record information about its surroundings?**

_____

_____

_____

_____

▶ UNTAMED SCIENCE Watch the **Untamed Science** video to learn more about how tools help scientists.

Female

Academic Standards for Science

6.NS.1, 6.NS.2, 6.NS.3, 6.NS.4, 6.NS.5, 6.NS.7,
6.NS.8, 6.NS.11, 6.DP.1, 6.DP.2, 6.DP.9, 6.DP.10

Check Your Understanding

1. **Background** Read the paragraph below and then answer the question.

Emi studied hard to prepare for her science lab investigation. Emi was concerned because her investigation was **complex.** She had been earning high marks all year and wanted to maintain this **trend.** Emi also wanted to use her lab report as a **sample** of her science work.

> To be **complex** is to have many parts.
>
> A **trend** is the general direction that something tends to move.
>
> A **sample** is a portion of something that is used to represent the whole thing.

- Why would preparing help Emi maintain her high marks?

_____

_____

> **MY READING WEB** If you had trouble completing the question above, visit **My Reading Web** and type in *The Tools of Science.*

Vocabulary Skill

Identify Multiple Meanings Some words have more than one meaning. The table below lists multiple meaning words used in science and in daily life.

Word	Everyday Meaning	Scientific Meaning
mean	*v.* to indicate; to intend **Example:** They didn't *mean* to hurt her.	*n.* the numerical average **Example:** The *mean* of 11, 7, 5, and 9 is 8.
volume	*n.* the loudness of a sound **Example:** Turn up the *volume* so we can hear the song.	*n.* the amount of space an object or substance takes up **Example:** Record the *volume* of water in the graduated cylinder.

2. **Quick Check** In the table above, circle the meaning of the word *volume* that is used in the following sentence.

- The *volume* of juice in the container is 1.89 liters.

density

estimate

model

safety symbol

Chapter Preview

LESSON 1
• metric system • International System of Units (SI) • mass • weight • volume • density

↺ Compare and Contrast
△ Predict

LESSON 2
• estimate • accuracy • precision • significant figures • percent error • mean • median • mode • range • anomalous data

↺ Ask Questions
△ Calculate

LESSON 3
• graph • linear graph • nonlinear graph

↺ Compare and Contrast
△ Graph

LESSON 4
• model • system • input • process • output • feedback

↺ Identify the Main Idea
△ Make Models

LESSON 5
• safety symbol • field

↺ Summarize
△ Infer

▶ VOCAB FLASH CARDS For extra help with vocabulary, visit **Vocab Flash Cards** and type in *The Tools of Science.*

37

Measurement in Science

🔑 **Why Is a Standard Measurement System Important?**
6.NS.3, 6.NS.4, 6.NS.5, 6.NS.7

🔑 **What Are Some SI Units of Measure?**
6.NS.1, 6.NS.3, 6.NS.5, 6.NS.7, 6.NS.8, 6.DP.1, 6.DP.2

MY PLANET DIARY

Measurements have helped people record and share information about some pretty amazing moments!

- In 2006 in Maui, Hawaii, a surfer rode the biggest wave on record: a 21-meter-tall wall of water!

- Growers compete every year for the heaviest pumpkin in the United States. The 2009 winner weighed more than 725 kilograms.

- In the winter of 1909 a severe cold front hit the East Coast, including Florida. Tallahassee holds the record for the coldest temperature in the state: -19°C.

 Do the Inquiry Warm-Up *Taking Measurements.*

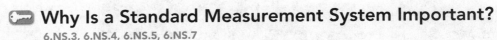

Read the following questions. Write your answers below.

1. What unit of measure is used to find both length and height?

_____

2. What problems could arise if scientists used different units to measure height?

_____

_____

> PLANET DIARY Go to **Planet Diary** to learn more about measurements.

Academic Standards for Science

6.NS.3 Collect quantitative data.
6.NS.4 Incorporate variables.
6.NS.5 Use principles of accuracy and precision when making measurement.
6.NS.7 Keep accurate records.

Why Is a Standard Measurement System Important?

Suppose you wanted to measure the width of a book. If you used your finger, the book might be 3 fingers wide. If you used paper clips, the book might be 5 paper clips wide. And if you used a ruler, the book might be 22 centimeters wide. These are three different ways of measuring the same thing.

Vocabulary

- metric system
- International System of Units (SI)
- mass
- weight
- volume
- density

Skills

- Reading: Compare and Contrast
- Inquiry: Predict

To avoid the problem of using different units of measurement, standard measurement systems were developed. **A standard measurement system is important because it allows scientists to compare data and communicate with each other about their results.**

In the 1790s, scientists developed the metric system of measurement. The **metric system** is a measurement system based on the number 10. Modern scientists use a version of the metric system called the **International System of Units,** or SI (from the French, *Système International d'Unités*). Prefixes are used to identify larger and smaller units. The prefixes used in the SI system are shown in **Figure 1.**

FIGURE 1 ···················

> VIRTUAL LAB **SI Prefixes**

The metric system is used to measure things like length, mass, and volume.

Identify Complete the tasks below.

1. Fill in the blanks to complete the chart of SI prefixes.

2. Identify something you would measure in each of the following:

Millimeters _____

Kilometers _____

_____

6.NS.3, 6.NS.5

Common SI Prefixes

Prefix	Meaning	Units
_____	1,000	kilometer
_____	100	hectometer
deka- (da)	10	dekameter
no prefix	1	meter
deci- (d)	_____ (one tenth)	decimeter
centi- (c)	_____ (one hundredth)	centimeter
milli- (m)	0.001 (one thousandth)	_____

Lab zone® Do the Quick Lab *Measurement Systems.*

Assess Your Understanding

got it? ···

O **I get it!** Now I know that a standard measurement system is important because _____

_____

_____

O **I need extra help with** _____

Go to **my science** s **COACH** online for help with this subject.

6.NS.3, 6.NS.4, 6.NS.5, 6.NS.7

Academic Standards for Science

6.NS.1 Make predictions.

6.NS.3 Collect quantitative data and use appropriate units to label numerical data.

6.NS.5 Use the principles of accuracy and precision.

6.NS.7 Keep accurate records during investigations.

6.NS.8 Analyze data.

6.DP.1 Identify a need or problem to be solved.

6.DP.2 Brainstorm potential solutions.

Conversions for Length

1 km	=	1,000 m
1 m	=	100 cm
1 m	=	1,000 mm
1 cm	=	10 mm

What Are Some SI Units of Measure?

Scientists regularly measure properties such as length, mass, volume, density, temperature, and time. Each property can be measured using an SI unit.

Length Length is the distance from one point to another. **A meter (m) is the basic SI unit used for measuring length.** One meter is about the distance from the floor to a doorknob. One tool used to measure length is a metric ruler.

Many distances can be measured in meters. For example, you can measure your height or a soccer kick in meters. For measuring lengths smaller than a meter, you use the centimeter (cm) and millimeter (mm). For example, the length of a piece of binder paper is about 29 centimeters. For measuring a long distance, such as the distance between cities, you use kilometers. The table at the left shows you how to convert between different metric length units. Try measuring the green anole in **Figure 2.**

FIGURE 2 ···

Measuring Length
The green anole is a small lizard native to southeastern parts of the United States.

✏ **Measure Do the activities at the right.**
6.NS.3, 6.NS.5

1. How long is the anole:

   In centimeters? _____

   In millimeters? _____

2. Choose three small items on or near your desk such as your pencil, finger, or eraser. Record their lengths below. How do your measurements compare with those of your classmates?

   _____

   _____

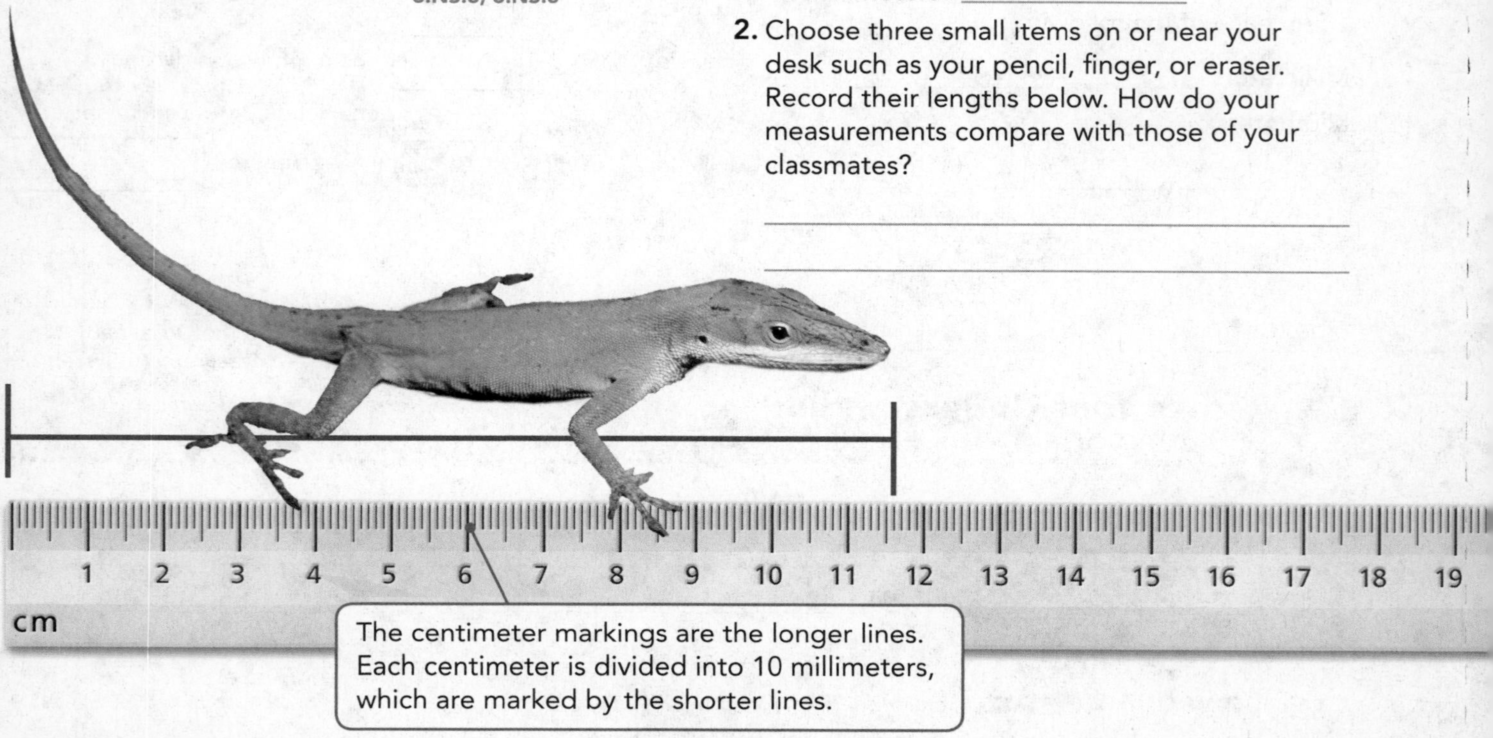

The centimeter markings are the longer lines. Each centimeter is divided into 10 millimeters, which are marked by the shorter lines.

Mass

Mass is a measure of the amount of matter in an object. 🔑 **In SI, the basic unit for measuring mass is the kilogram (kg).** The mass of cars, bicycles, and people is measured in kilograms. If you want to measure smaller masses, you would use grams (g) or milligrams (mg). The table at the right shows how to convert between kilograms, grams, and milligrams. The balance shown in **Figure 3** is used to measure mass. A balance compares the mass of an object to a known mass.

Weight is different than mass. **Weight** is a measure of the force of gravity acting on an object. A scale is used to measure weight. When you stand on a scale, gravity pulls you downward. This compresses springs inside the scale. The more you weigh, the more the springs compress.

Although mass and weight are related, they are not the same. The mass of an object is constant—it stays the same. The weight of the object is not constant. It can change because the force of gravity can change. For instance, on the moon, the force of gravity is weaker than it is on Earth. So you weigh less on the moon than you do on Earth. But your mass is the same no matter where you are.

✎ **Compare and Contrast**
In the space below, compare and contrast mass and weight. How are they similar? How are they different?

_____

_____

_____

_____

_____

_____

Conversions for Mass		
1 kg	=	1,000 g
1 g	=	1,000 mg

FIGURE 3 ·····
Measuring Mass

✎ **Use the triple-beam balance to complete this activity.**   6.NS.3

1. Review What does a triple-beam balance measure? _____

2. Identify What SI unit is used to measure mass?

_____

3. Measure What is the mass of the toy car?_____

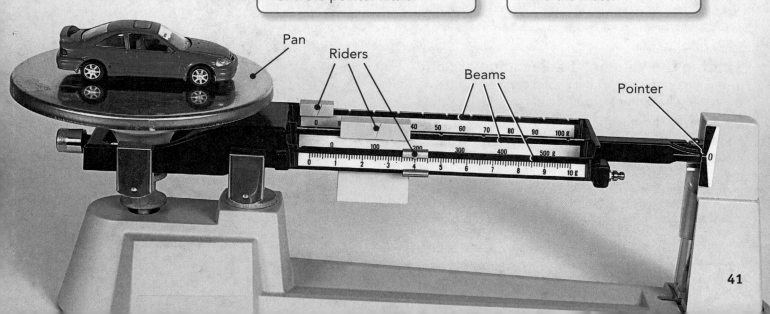

1 Place an object on the pan.

2 Shift the riders on the beams until they balance the object and the pointer hits 0.

3 Add up the grams shown on all three beams to find the mass.

Pan

Riders

Beams

Pointer

Conversions for Volume

1 m³	=	1,000,000 cm³
1 cm³	=	1 mL
1 L	=	1,000 mL
1 L	=	1,000 cm³

Volume

Have you ever looked at a box of your favorite food and seen the following line: "This package sold by weight, not by volume"? **Volume** is the amount of space an object or substance takes up. All objects with mass—whether they are solids, liquids, or gases—have volume. 🔑 **In SI, the basic unit for measuring volume is the cubic meter (m³).** Cubic meters and cubic centimeters (cm³) are used to measure the volume of solids. The unit for measuring the volume of liquids or gases is the liter (L). The table at the left shows how to convert between these units.

Calculating the Volume of Rectangular Solids

Suppose you want to know the volume of a rectangular solid, such as the gift box in **Figure 4.** To find this volume, you would first measure the length, width, and height of the box. Then you would multiply length times width times height. When you use this formula, you must use the same units for all the measurements.

length = 25 cm

height = 30 cm

width = 6 cm

FIGURE 4 ⋯⋯⋯⋯⋯⋯⋯⋯⋯⋯⋯⋯⋯⋯⋯⋯⋯⋯⋯⋯⋯⋯⋯⋯⋯⋯

Finding the Volume of a Rectangular Solid
The volume of a rectangular solid can be found by measuring its dimensions and multiplying the values.

✎ **Answer the questions below.**   6.NS.3, 6.NS.5

1. **Review** What unit should you use to measure the volume of a rectangular solid?

   _____

2. **Calculate** What is the volume of this gift box?

   _____

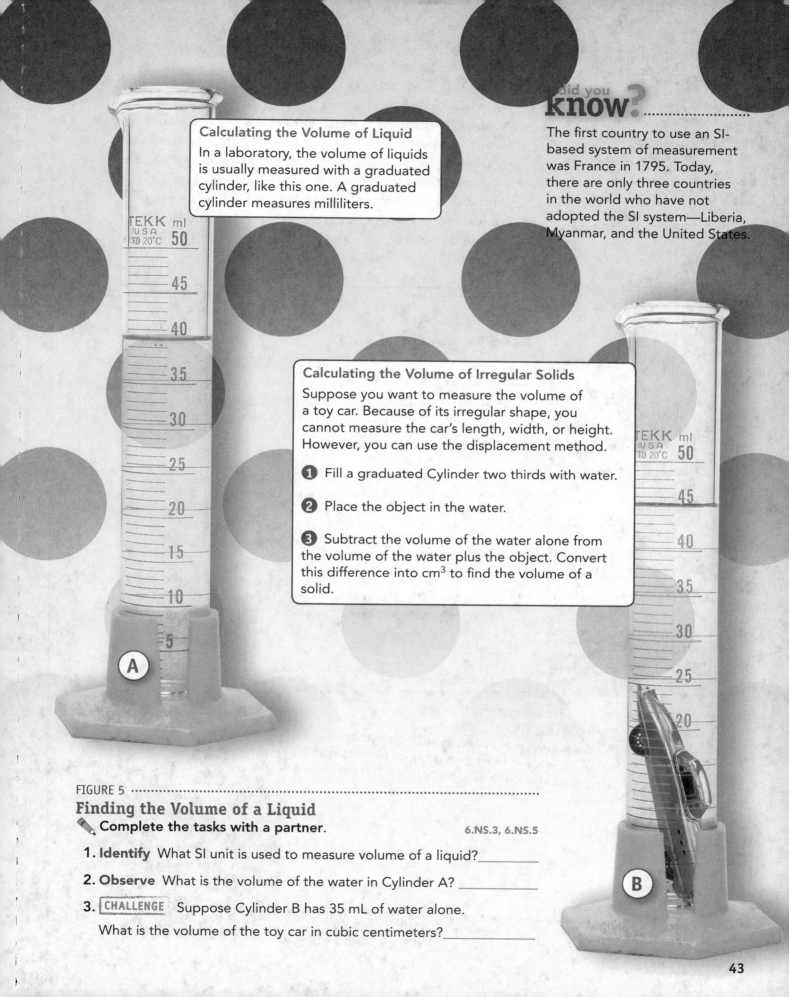

Calculating the Volume of Liquid
In a laboratory, the volume of liquids is usually measured with a graduated cylinder, like this one. A graduated cylinder measures milliliters.

did you know?
The first country to use an SI-based system of measurement was France in 1795. Today, there are only three countries in the world who have not adopted the SI system—Liberia, Myanmar, and the United States.

Calculating the Volume of Irregular Solids
Suppose you want to measure the volume of a toy car. Because of its irregular shape, you cannot measure the car's length, width, or height. However, you can use the displacement method.

❶ Fill a graduated Cylinder two thirds with water.

❷ Place the object in the water.

❸ Subtract the volume of the water alone from the volume of the water plus the object. Convert this difference into cm^3 to find the volume of a solid.

FIGURE 5
Finding the Volume of a Liquid
✎ **Complete the tasks with a partner.**

6.NS.3, 6.NS.5

1. **Identify** What SI unit is used to measure volume of a liquid?_____

2. **Observe** What is the volume of the water in Cylinder A? _____

3. **CHALLENGE** Suppose Cylinder B has 35 mL of water alone.

   What is the volume of the toy car in cubic centimeters?_____

43

Density Two objects of the same size, such as a block of wood and a brick, can have different masses. This is because different materials have different densities. **Density** is a measure of how much mass is contained in a given volume. Because density is made up of two measurements, mass and volume, the SI units for density come from the units for volume and mass. 🔑 **The standard SI unit for measuring density is kilograms per cubic meter (kg/m^3).** Other units of density include grams per cubic centimeter (g/cm^3) and grams per milliliter (g/mL). Look at **Figure 6.**

do the math!

Calculating Density

The density of an object is the object's mass divided by its volume. To find the density of an object, use the formula below.

$$\text{Density} = \frac{\text{mass}}{\text{volume}}$$

❶ Calculate Find the density of a piece of quartz that has a mass of 13 g and a volume of 5 cm^3.

_____

❷ Predict Suppose a mineral has the same mass as the quartz in Question 1 but a greater volume. How would its density compare to the quartz in Question 1?

_____

6.NS.3, 6.NS.5, 6.NS.8

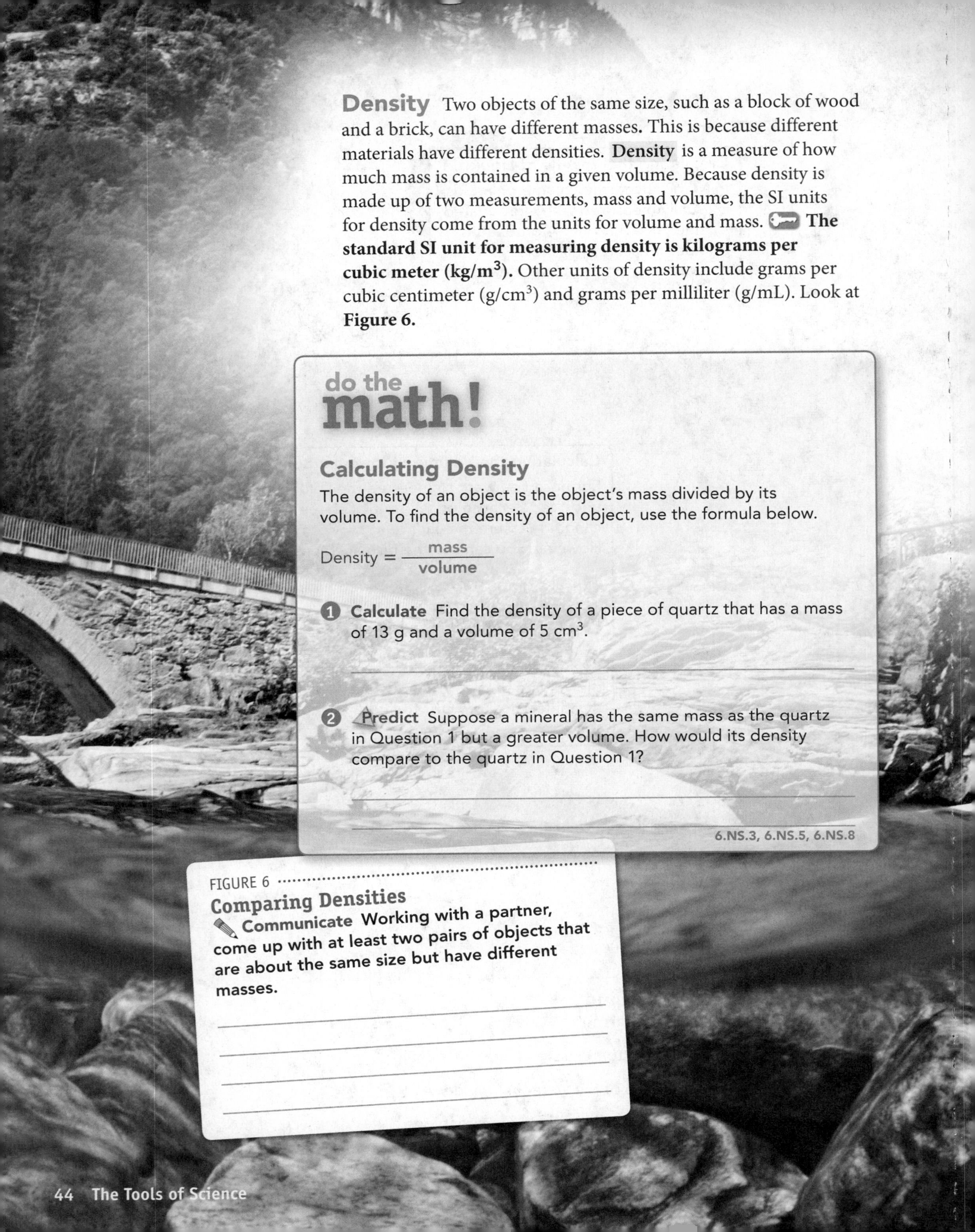

FIGURE 6 ••••••••••••••••••••••••••••••••

Comparing Densities

✏️ **Communicate** Working with a partner, come up with at least two pairs of objects that are about the same size but have different masses.

_____

_____

_____

_____

Density of Substances Different substances have different densities. Very dense materials contain a lot of matter in a given space or volume, while less dense materials contain smaller amounts of matter in the same space or volume. The density of a particular substance is the same for all samples of that substance, no matter how large or small. For example, a ring made of pure gold has the same density as a brick made of pure gold. The table in **Figure 7** lists the densities of some common substances.

Using Density If you know an object's density, you can determine whether the object will float in a given liquid. An object will float if it is less dense than the surrounding liquid. For example, the density of water is 1 g/cm^3. A piece of wood with a density of 0.8 g/cm^3 will float in water. However, a piece of copper, which has a density of 8.9 g/cm^3, will sink. Use the table to answer the question about using density in **Figure 7**.

Densities of Some Common Substances

Substance	Density (g/cm^3)
Air	0.001
Ice	0.9
Water	1.0
Aluminum	2.7
Lead	11.35

FIGURE 7 ·······························

Understanding Density
People who fish put small weights on their fishing line so the hook and bait sink below the surface of the water.

✎ **Complete the activities with a partner.**

1. **Identify** According to the chart, which substances will float in water?

_____

3. **Investigate** You need a lead weight for your fishing line, but your tackle box is unorganized. You have small weights of aluminum and lead but they look the same. How would you determine which weights are lead?

_____

_____

_____

6.NS.1, 6.NS.3, 6.DP.1, 6.DP.2

Lead fishing weight

Conversions for Temperature

0°C	=	273 K
100°C	=	373 K

Temperature Is it hot or cold outside today? You can answer this questions by measuring the temperature of the air.

Temperature is measured using a thermometer. A thermometer has numbers and units, or a temperature scale on it. When you place a liquid thermometer in a substance, the liquid inside will increase or decrease in volume. This makes the level rise or fall. To determine the temperature, you read the number next to the top of the liquid in the thermometer.

There are two temperature scales that are used in science—the Celsius scale and the Kelvin scale. On the Celsius scale, water freezes at 0°C and boils at 100°C. On the Kelvin scale, the lowest possible temperature is 0 K, or absolute zero. There are no negative numbers on this scale. 🗝 **The Kelvin scale is the basis for the SI temperature units, and the kelvin (K) is the SI unit for temperature. Figure 8** shows a comparison of the Celsius and Kelvin scales. The table shows how to convert between the two scales.

FIGURE 8 ·······································

Temperature Scales

✎ **Read the text and then complete the activity.** 6.NS.3, 6.NS.5

1. **Identify** Determine which thermometer is Kelvin and which is Celsius. Label them above the diagram.

2. **Interpret Diagrams** Find and shade in the freezing point on the Kelvin thermometer.

3. **Review** Identify one way the Kelvin and Celsius scales differ.

_____

_____

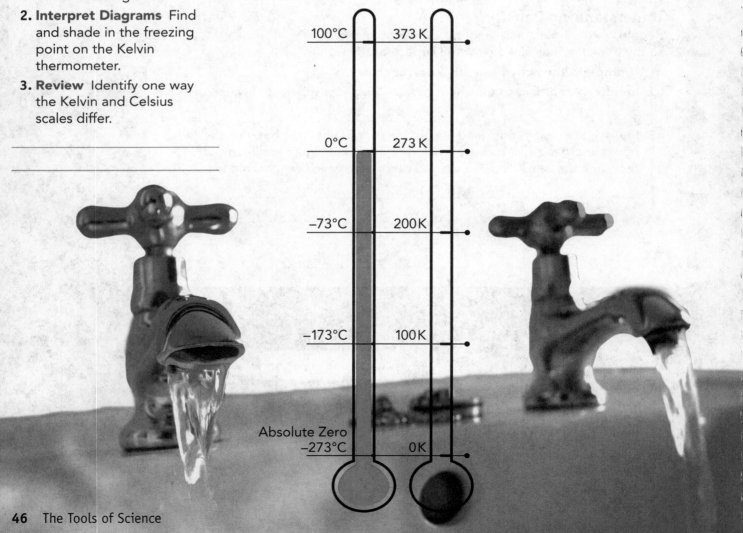

Time The race is on, and the finish line is in sight. But an opponent is catching up. Just one second can mean the difference between winning and losing. But what is a second?

Time is a measurement of the period between two events. 🔑 **The second (s) is the SI unit used to measure time.** In one second, light can travel about seven and a half times around Earth at the equator. Just like all SI units, the second can be divided into smaller units based on the number 10. For example, a millisecond (ms) is one thousandth of a second. However, for longer periods of time, minutes or hours are typically used. There are 60 seconds in a minute, and 60 minutes in an hour.

Clocks and watches are used to measure time. Some clocks are more accurate than others. Most digital stopwatches measure time accurately to one hundredth of a second, as shown in **Figure 9**. Devices used for timing Olympic events measure time to a thousandth of a second or less.

FIGURE 9 ······························
Measuring Time
✏️ **Review** Identify and record the minutes, seconds, and hundredths on the stopwatch.

_____

_____

Lab zone ® Do the Quick Lab *Measuring Volume in Metric.*

🔑 **Assess Your Understanding**

1a. Identify What tool would you use to measure the mass of an egg?

_____

6.NS.5

b. Sequence What steps would you take to determine the density of an egg?

_____

_____

_____

6.NS.3

got it?

⭕ **I get it!** Now I know that the basic SI units of

measurement are _____

_____

_____

_____

⭕ **I need extra help with** _____

Go to **MY SCIENCE** 🔵ˢ **COACH** *online for help with this subject.*   6.NS.3, 6.NS.5

Math in Science

🔑 **What Are Some Math Skills Used in Science?**
6.NS.3, 6.NS.5, 6.NS.8

🔑 **What Are Some Math Tools Used in Science?**
6.NS.3, 6.NS.4, 6.NS.5, 6.NS.8

MY PLANET DiARY *for* Indiana

BLOG

Posted by: Nikos

Location: Monrovia, Indiana

I was planning my birthday party when I realized that I needed to buy the tickets to the movie that my friends and I were going to see. Since it was my party, I thought I should pay for my friends' admission. I had three friends going, and each ticket was about 9 dollars. So I figured I should bring 40 dollars to be safe. This all happened within a minute, and I realized just how much we use math every day.

Write your answer to the question below.

How do you use math during a typical day?

_____

_____

_____

_____

▷ **PLANET DIARY** Go to **Planet Diary** to learn more about math in science.

Lab zone® Do the Inquiry Warm-Up *Making Models.*

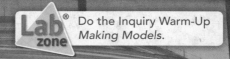

SCREEN 4: HAPPY BIRTHDAY!

$8.95

Vocabulary

- estimate • accuracy • precision • significant figures
- percent error • mean • median • mode • range
- anomalous data

Skills

↪ Reading: Ask Questions
△ Inquiry: Calculate

What Are Some Math Skills Used in Science?

Scientists in different fields use math to different degrees, but all use some math in their work. Scientists use math to collect, organize, analyze, and present data. ⟨━⟩ **Some math skills used in science when working with data include estimation, accuracy and precision, and significant figures.**

Estimation How could you measure the length of a book without using a measuring device? You might estimate the length by comparing it with a book you had already measured. An **estimate** is an approximation of a number based on reasonable assumptions. An estimate is not a guess. It is always based on known information.

Scientists often rely on estimates when they cannot obtain exact numbers. The estimates might be based on indirect measurements, calculations, models, or samples. For example, a scientist might estimate the number of insects living in an area based on a sample count in one part of the total area.

Academic Standards for Science

6.NS.3 Collect quantitative data and use appropriate units to label numerical data.

6.NS.5 Use the principles of accuracy and precision.

6.NS.8 Analyze data, using appropriate mathematical manipulation as required.

do the math!

Estimation

Estimating from a sample is a quick way to determine the large number of insects in this photo.

❶ **Interpret Photos** How many insects are in the yellow square? This number is your sample.

_____

❷ **Explain** By what number should you multiply the sample to find an estimate for the total number of insects in the area? Explain your answer.

_____

_____

❸ △ **Calculate** Calculate your estimate for the total number of insects. Show your work.

_____

6.NS.3, 6.NS.8

FIGURE 1 ·······················

Accuracy and Precision

In a dart game, accurate throws land close to the bull's-eye. Precise throws land close together. ✎ **Identify Are the darts thrown accurately or precisely? Explain.**   6.NS.5

_____

_____

_____

Accuracy and Precision

People often use the words *accuracy* and *precision* to describe the same idea. In science, these words have different meanings. **Accuracy** refers to how close a measurement is to the true or accepted value. **Precision** refers to how close a group of measurements are to each other.

How can you be sure that a measurement is both accurate and precise? First, use a high-quality measurement tool. Next, measure carefully. Finally, repeat the measurement a few times. If your measurement is the same each time, you can assume that it is reliable. A reliable measurement is both accurate and precise. Look at **Figure 1.**

Significant Figures

The precision of a measurement depends on the instrument you use to take the measurement. For example, if the smallest unit on a ruler is centimeters, then the most precise measurement you can make will be in centimeters. **Significant figures** communicate how precise measurements are. The significant figures in a measurement include all digits measured exactly, plus one estimated digit. If the measurement has only one digit, you must assume it is estimated. Use **Figure 2** to learn more about significant figures.

2

Adding and Subtracting Significant Figures

When measurements are added or subtracted, the answer can contain no more decimal places than the least accurate measurement.

Suppose you wanted to decorate a frame with shells. If a shell 2.3 centimeters long is added to a row of shells 10.23 centimeters long, what is the new length of the row? How many significant figures are in this measurement? Why?

_____

_____

_____

_____

FIGURE 2 ·······················

Significant Figures

When combining measurements with different degrees of accuracy and precision, the accuracy of the final answer can be no greater than the *least* accurate measurement. ✎ **Calculate Read about working with significant figures. Then complete the activities in the boxes.**

6.NS.5, 6.NS.8

1

Finding Significant Figures

What is length of the shell in centimeters? How many significant figures are in your measurement?

_____

3

Multiplying and Dividing Significant Figures

When measurements are multiplied or divided, the answer can contain no more significant figures than the least accurate measurement.

Suppose you have framed artwork that measures 1.25 meters by 2 meters. What is the area of the artwork? How many significant figures are in this measurement? Why?

_____

_____

_____

 Try the Quick Lab
Understanding Significant Figures.

🔑 Assess Your Understanding

1a. Compare and Contrast How does accuracy differ from precision?

_____

_____

_____

_____

_____

6.NS.5

b. Measuring A tortoise shell, measured with a meterstick divided into 0.01-m intervals, is 0.61 m long. How many significant figures are in this measurement?

_____

6.NS.8

got it?..

○ **I get it!** Now I know that some of the math skills used in science include _____

_____

○ **I need extra help with** _____

Go to **MY SCIENCE COACH** *online for help with this subject.*   6.NS.3, 6.NS.5, 6.NS.8

cm

1
2
3
4
5
6
7
8
9
10
11
12
13
14
15

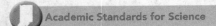
Academic Standards for Science

6.NS.3 Collect quantitative data and use appropriate units to label numerical data.

6.NS.4 Incorporate variables.

6.NS.5 Use the principles of accuracy and precision.

6.NS.8 Analyze data, using appropriate mathematical manipulation as required.

What Are Some Math Tools Used in Science?

Scientists also use certain math tools to analyze data. 🔑 **Some math tools used in science include calculating percent error; finding the mean, median, mode, and range; and checking the reasonableness of data.**

Percent Error Individual measurements can be accurate or inaccurate. For example, suppose you measure the temperature of boiling water and find the thermometer reads 100.6°C. You know that the accepted, or true, value for the boiling point of water is 100.0°C. Therefore, your measurement is not accurate. But how inaccurate is it? **Percent error** calculations are a way to determine how accurate an experimental value is. A low percent error means that the result you obtained was accurate. A high percent error means that your result was not accurate. It may not be accurate because you did not measure carefully or because something was wrong with your measurement tool.

Percent Error

The experimental value you obtained for the boiling point of water is 100.6°C. The true value is 100.0°C. Calculate percent error using the formula below. Substitute in the experimental and true values.

$$\text{Percent error} = \frac{\text{Difference between experimental value and true value}}{\text{True value}} \times 100\%$$

$$\text{Percent error} = \frac{100.6°C - 100.0°C}{100.0°C} \times 100\% = 0.6\%$$

The percent error in the calculation of the boiling point of water was 0.6%.

① **Calculate** Suppose you measure the density of copper to be 9.37 g/cm³, but you know the true value for the density of copper is 8.92 g/cm³. Find the percent error for the density you measured.

_____

_____

② **Explain** What is a possible source of the error in the density measurement?

_____

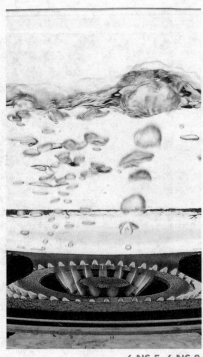

6.NS.5, 6.NS.8

Mean, Median, Mode, and Range

On a sight-seeing trip through the Florida Everglades, the sound of your boat startles a crocodile. The crocodile runs into the water, leaving behind its nest of eggs in the dirt. When you spot the nest, you get curious. How many eggs are there? Is this the typical number of eggs in a nest? What is the range of eggs in a group of nests? Scientists ask questions like these, too. Their answers come from analyzing data. Use **Figure 3** to analyze crocodile egg data yourself.

FIGURE 3 ···

American Crocodile Egg Data

You can use math to analyze the data in the table at the right about the number of American crocodile eggs in seven nests.

✎ **Calculate Fill in the boxes with the mean, median, mode, and range of the crocodile egg data.** 6.NS.8

Nest	Number of Eggs
A	40
B	32
C	24
D	40
E	37
F	40
G	39

Mean

The **mean** is the numerical average of a set of data. To find the mean, add up the numbers in the data set. Then divide the sum by the total number of items you added.
Find the mean for the egg data.

_____

Median

The **median** is the middle number in a set of data. To find the median, list all the numbers in order from least to greatest. The median is the middle entry. If a list has an even number of entries, add the two middle numbers together and divide by two to find the median.
Find the median for the egg data.

_____

_____

Mode

The **mode** is the number that appears most often in a list of numbers.
Find the mode for the egg data.

_____

Range

The **range** of a set of data is the difference between the greatest value and the least value in the set.
Find the range for the egg data.

_____

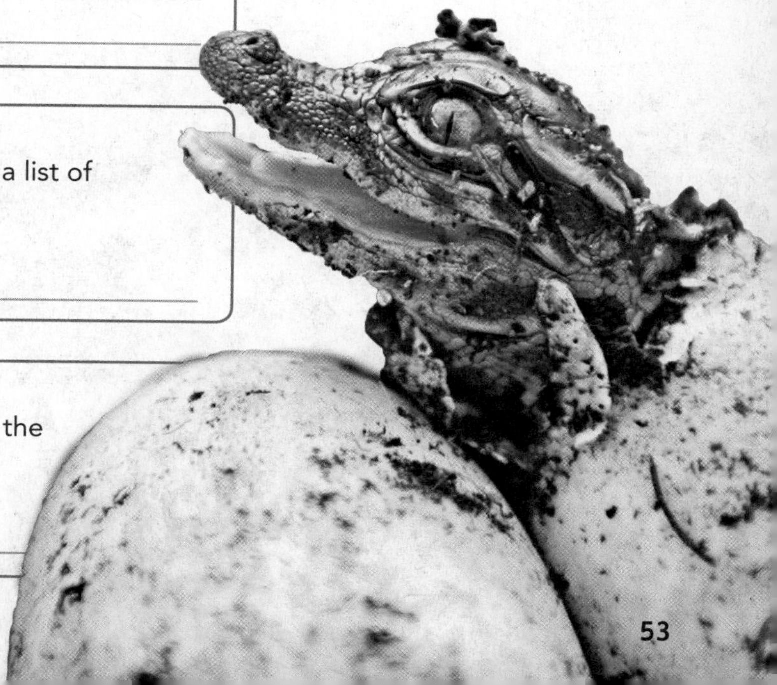

53

⤴ Ask Questions Before
you read this section, pose a
question about the topic. After
you read, try to answer it.

_____

_____

_____

_____

Reasonable and Anomalous Data   An important

part of analyzing any set of data is to ask, "Do they make sense?
Are these data reasonable?" Suppose a scientist studying American
crocodiles measures the air temperature near a nesting spot each
night for five nights. The data for the first four nights are 20°C,
19°C, 21°C, and 22°C. On the last night, a student is asked to make
the measurement. The student records 69°C in the data book.

Are the data reasonable? The reading on Day 5 is very different.
Some variation in air temperature makes sense within a small
range. But it doesn't make sense for the air temperature to rise 47°C
in one day, from 22°C to 69°C. The 69°C does not fit with the rest
of the data. Data that do not fit with the rest of a data set are
anomalous data. In this case, the anomalous datum is explainable.
The student measured temperature in °F instead of °C. Sometimes
asking whether data are reasonable can uncover sources of error.
Investigating the reason for anomalous data can lead to new
information and discoveries. See **Figure 4.**

FIGURE 4 ....

American Crocodile Nest Data
Researchers have been tracking the number of crocodile nests in
the Everglades for years. The table shows approximate nest data
from 1996 to 2000. During these years, the population of American
crocodiles in the region increased.

✏️ **Analyze Experimental Results** What variable
could have affected the number of nests?

_____

_____

_____

_____

6.NS.4

Year	Number of Nests
1996	10
1997	8
1998	11
1999	18
2000	22

apply it!

Until recently, the American crocodile was considered an endangered species. Even today, there are only about 2,000 in the United States. Most of these are in Florida. Studying crocodiles and their nesting habits have helped scientists better understand what affects the crocodile population.

1 Design Experiments How would you collect accurate and precise crocodile nest data?

_____

_____

_____

2 Explain How could you estimate the total number of nests in Florida?

_____

_____

_____

_____

_____

3 CHALLENGE How might a hurricane in Florida cause anomalous nest data?

_____

_____

6.NS.5, 6.NS.8

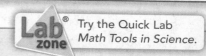
Try the Quick Lab
Math Tools in Science.

🗝 Assess Your Understanding

2a. Explain Why is it important for scientists to calculate percent error?

_____

_____

6.NS.5

b. Apply Concepts A scientists finds five crocodile egg nests, with the following egg counts: 26, 35, 35, 40, 34. What is the mean number of eggs?

_____

6.NS.8

got it? ....

○ **I get it!** Now I know that some math skills used in science include _____

_____

○ **I need extra help with** _____

Go to **MY SCIENCE COACH** *online for help with this subject.*

6.NS.3, 6.NS.5, 6.NS.8

Graphs

UNLOCK
THE BIG
?

🗝 **What Kinds of Data Do Graphs Display?**
6.NS.8

🗝 **How Are Different Graphs Used to Display Data?**
6.NS.1, 6.NS.3, 6.NS.8, 6.NS.11, 6.DP.9, 6.DP.10

my planet diary
for Indiana

SCIENCE STATS

Snow Day!

Brrr! Winters in Indiana can be cold. Snow emergencies can even cancel school! Average temperatures in January vary between –8°C and 2°C. The average annual snowfall for the entire state is about 56 centimeters. The bar graph shows the snowfall totals for each winter from 2003 to 2008 for Bloomington, Indiana.

Answer the question below.
What are the benefits of displaying this data in a graph rather than as a list of years and snowfall amounts?

_____

_____

_____

▷ **PLANET DIARY** Go to **Planet Diary** to learn more about graphs.

 Do the Inquiry Warm-Up *Picturing Information.*

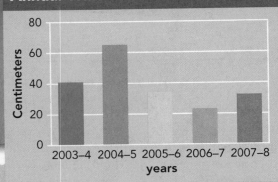

Annual Winter Snowfall Totals

Centimeters

80
60
40
20
0

2003–4 2004–5 2005–6 2006–7 2007–8
years

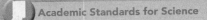

Academic Standards for Science

6.NS.8 Analyze data, using appropriate mathematical manipulation as required, and use it to identify patterns and make inferences based on these patterns.

What Kinds of Data Do Graphs Display?

Suppose you conduct an experiment about the number of calories burned in 30 minutes when bike riding, playing basketball, and watching television. You could simply list your results. This data would be difficult to analyze because it's only a summary of your results in word form.

Vocabulary
- graph
- nonlinear graph
- linear graph

Skills
- Reading: Compare and Contrast
- Inquiry: Graph

Instead, you could use a graph to organize your data. A **graph** is a picture of your data that allows you to visually analyze and compare information.

Kinds of Data Scientists frequently use graphs to display and analyze results of surveys and experiments. **Graphs can display categorical and numerical data.** Categorical data are information that can be grouped into categories. For example, you might take a survey of your classmates to find out their favorite sports. You would then group the results of your survey by type: basketball, football, baseball, tennis, soccer, and so on.

Numerical data, such as time, temperature, and weight, are continuous, ranging from small to large amounts. For example, you collect numerical data when you measure the temperature of a certain location for several days. Different kinds of graphs are used to display these different kinds of data.

The Martian atmosphere is very thin, which prevents liquid water from forming on the planet's surface.

FIGURE 1

Analyzing Data
The graph shows the amounts of different gases that make up the atmosphere of the planet Mars. By displaying this information visually, you can analyze and compare the data even in the absence of actual figures.

6.NS.8

✎ **Read Graphs** Use the graph to answer the questions below.

1. Estimate the percentage of carbon dioxide that makes up the Martian atmosphere.

_____

2. **Identify** Which two gases in the graph occur in almost equal amounts in the Martian atmosphere?

_____

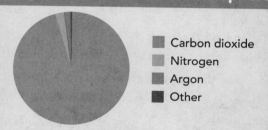

Composition of Martian Atmosphere

- Carbon dioxide
- Nitrogen
- Argon
- Other

Lab zone® Do the Quick Lab *Making Graphs.*

🔑 Assess Your Understanding

got it? ....

○ I get it! Now I know that graphs display both _____

_____

○ I need extra help with _____

Go to MY SCIENCE ⓢ COACH online for help with this subject.

6.NS.8

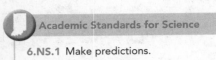

Academic Standards for Science

6.NS.1 Make predictions.

6.NS.3 Collect quantitative data with appropriate tools or technologies and use appropriate units to label numerical data.

6.NS.8 Analyze data.

6.NS.11 Communicate findings using graphs.

6.DP.9 Present evidence using mathematical representations.

6.DP.10 Communicate the solution including evidence using mathematical representations.

Compare and Contrast Read the text for Circle Graphs. How are bar graphs and circle graphs alike? How are they different?

_____

_____

_____

_____

_____

What Are the Different Types of Graphs and How Are They Used?

The most commonly used graphs in science include bar graphs, circle graphs, and line graphs. **Bar graphs and circle graphs are suitable for displaying categorical data, and line graphs and bar graphs are appropriate for displaying numerical data.**

Bar Graphs
A bar graph uses vertical or horizontal bars to display data for separate categories. Bar graphs are most often used when you want to show the amount of something in each category. Each bar in the graph represents the data for a single category and lets you compare data with the other categories.

Circle Graphs
Like a bar graph, a circle graph displays data in a number of separate categories. However, circle graphs can only be used when you have data for all the categories in your survey or experiment. A circle graph is sometimes called a pie chart. Each "slice" in the pie chart represents an individual category. The size of the slice indicates what percentage of the whole a particular category makes up.

FIGURE 2 ....

Types of Graphs
These three graphs show different kinds of data about amphibians.

✎ **Use the graphs to answer the questions below.**   6.NS.8

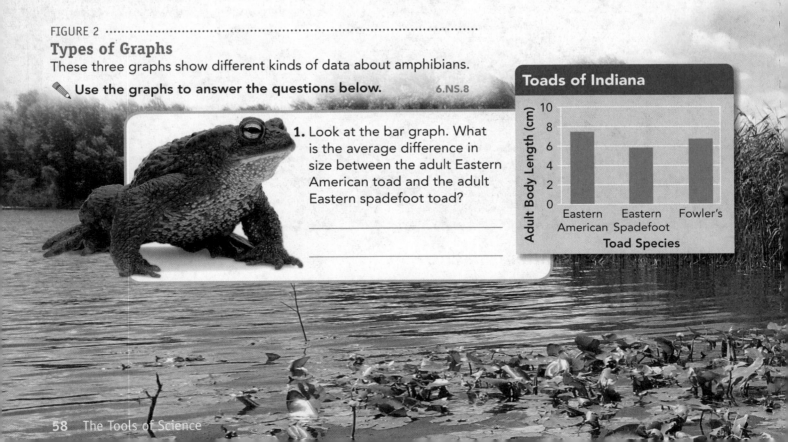

1. Look at the bar graph. What is the average difference in size between the adult Eastern American toad and the adult Eastern spadefoot toad?

_____

_____

Toads of Indiana

(Bar graph: Adult Body Length (cm) vs Toad Species — Eastern American, Eastern Spadefoot, Fowler's)

Line Graphs Line graphs are among the most common types of graphs used in science. Line graphs display data that show how one variable changes in response to another variable. Line graphs are useful for recording the results of many experiments.

Line Graphs in Experiments In experiments, scientists make changes to one variable, called the independent variable. The data they collect show how a second variable responds to these changes. This second variable is called the dependent variable. A line graph is used when an independent variable is continuous. A continuous variable has other points between the tested points. Temperature and time are examples of continuous variables.

For example, to see whether a relationship exists between a person's body mass and the number of calories burned when jogging, you could use a line graph. Body mass is a continuous variable because within the range of body masses you are studying, any value is possible.

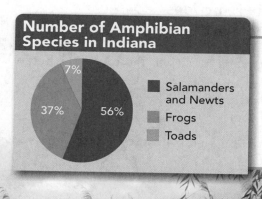

Number of Amphibian Species in Indiana

- 7%
- 37%
- 56%

■ Salamanders and Newts
■ Frogs
■ Toads

2. Look at the circle graph. About how many times more species of frogs are there in Indiana than species of toads?

_____

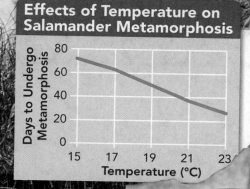

Effects of Temperature on Salamander Metamorphosis

Days to Undergo Metamorphosis

80
60
40
20
0

15 17 19 21 23

Temperature (°C)

3. Interpret Data What happens to the amount of time it takes for a salamander to undergo metamorphosis when the water temperature increases?

_____

_____

_____

Using Line Graphs
A line graph in which the data points form a straight line is a **linear graph.** A line graph in which the data points do not fall along a straight line, is called a **nonlinear graph.** If the data points form a jagged line, or no line at all, the variables may not have any clear relationship.

Line graphs are powerful tools in science because they allow you to identify trends and make predictions about those trends. Both linear and nonlinear graphs can show trends. A trend is the general direction in which a graph is changing. You can use lines on these graphs to predict the values of points that you have not measured. Use the graphs in **Figure 3** to explore trends and make predictions about the data that are shown.

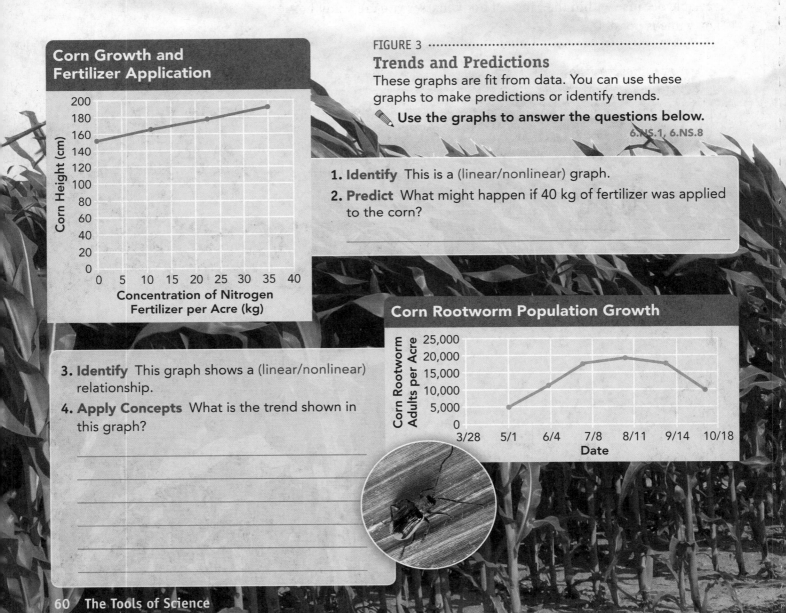

Corn Growth and Fertilizer Application

FIGURE 3 ·····························

Trends and Predictions
These graphs are fit from data. You can use these graphs to make predictions or identify trends.

✎ **Use the graphs to answer the questions below.**

6.NS.1, 6.NS.8

1. **Identify** This is a (linear/nonlinear) graph.
2. **Predict** What might happen if 40 kg of fertilizer was applied to the corn?

_____

3. **Identify** This graph shows a (linear/nonlinear) relationship.
4. **Apply Concepts** What is the trend shown in this graph?

_____

_____

_____

_____

_____

Corn Rootworm Population Growth

apply it!

Cell phones have changed the way we communicate.

1 ⟁ **Graph** Use the data to make a line graph.

2 **Describe** Does the graph show a linear or nonlinear relationship? Explain.

_____

_____

_____

_____

_____

_____

3 CHALLENGE Based on the data, predict the number of cell phone subscribers in 2009.

_____

_____

_____

_____

6.NS.3, 6.NS.8, 6.NS.11, 6.DP.9, 6.DP.10

Year	U.S. Subscribers
2002	140,000,000
2003	159,000,000
2004	182,000,000
2005	208,000,000
2006	233,000,000
2007	255,000,000
2008	263,000,000

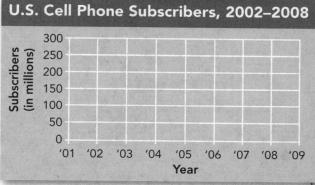

U.S. Cell Phone Subscribers, 2002–2008

 Do the Quick Lab
Graphs and Predictions.

🔑 Assess Your Understanding

1a. Review You are observing a _____ when you notice that the height of corn increases with increasing concentrations of fertilizer.

6.NS.8

b. Summarize Why is it often possible to make predictions from data in a line graph?

_____

_____

_____

_____

6.NS.8, 6.NS.11

got it?

○ **I get it!** Now I know that bar graphs and circle are used for _____ data and line graphs and bar graphs are used for _____ data.

○ **I need extra help with** _____

_____

Go to **MY SCIENCE** Ⓢ **COACH** *online for help with this subject.*

6.NS.8

Using Models

UNLOCK THE BIG ?

🔑 **Why Do Scientists Use Models?**
6.NS.8, 6.NS.11

🔑 **What Is a System?**
6.NS.1, 6.NS.8, 6.NS.11

🔑 **How Are Models of Systems Used?**
6.NS.8, 6.NS.11, 6.DP.9, 6.DP.10

my PLANET DiARY *for* Indiana

BLOG

Posted by: Maddie
Location: Monrovia, Indiana

One day in third grade my teacher said that the class was going to construct a model of the water cycle. At that time I had no idea what the water cycle was or how it worked. When I saw how the water cycle functioned in the model, it gave me a better perspective of how the water cycle worked than a book. Models can give a person a view of something that no book or website can give.

Write your answer to the question below.
Describe a time you used a model to help accomplish a task.

_____

_____

_____

_____

_____

> PLANET DIARY Go to **Planet Diary** to learn more about models.

Do the Inquiry Warm-Up
Models and Science.

Vocabulary
- model • system • input • process
- output • feedback

Skills
⟳ Reading: Sequence
△ Inquiry: Classify

Why Do Scientists Use Models?

So what exactly is a model? A **model** is a representation of a simple or complex object or process. Models can be pictures, diagrams, three-dimensional objects, mathematical equations, chemical equations, computer programs, or even written descriptions. **Scientists use models to understand things that they cannot observe directly.** Models help scientists to understand things that are very large, such as the universe, or things that are very small, such as an atom. Models can also help scientists to understand processes, such as weather systems. **Figure 1** shows how models can be used to predict earthquake damage.

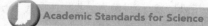

Academic Standards for Science

6.NS.8 Analyze data and use it to identify patterns and make inferences based on these patterns.

6.NS.11 Communicate findings using models.

FIGURE 1 ·····························

Shake, Rattle, and Roll

Look at how these two models of houses, built with different materials, react to an "earthquake" simulated by a shaking table.

✏ **Apply Concepts** How might scientists use the information from how the models reacted to the "earthquake"?

_____

_____

_____

_____

_____

6.NS.8, 6.NS.11

 Do the Lab Investigation
Super Models.

⊂⊃ Assess Your Understanding

got it? ···

○ I get it! Now I know scientists use models because _____

_____

○ I need extra help with _____

Go to MY SCIENCE ⑤ COACH online for help with this subject.

6.NS.8, 6.NS.11

Academic Standards for Science

6.NS.1 Make predictions.

6.NS.8 Analyze data and use it to identify patterns and make inferences based on these patterns.

6.NS.11 Communicate findings using models.

Sequence
Underline and number the steps that happen in your nervous system when you touch a hot stove.

What Is a System?

What happens when you touch a hot stove? Your nervous system sends a signal to your muscles to pull your hand away from the hot surface. Your response to the hot stove is an example of a system in action. 🔑 **A system is a group of parts that work together to perform a function or produce a result.**

Every system has an input, process, and output. **Input** is the material or energy that goes into the system. **Process** is what happens in the system. **Output** is the material or energy that comes out of the system. When you touch a hot stove, your skin sends a message to your nervous system. This is the input. Your nervous system understands that you are touching something hot. This is the process. The output is when your nervous system sends a signal to your muscles to pull your hand back. **Feedback** is output that changes the system in some way. For example, when you pull your hand back from the hot stove, your nervous system sends a message that your hand is no longer touching a hot object, so you can relax.

Classify You and your friends are sitting at the lunch table enjoying your food. You begin to eat an apple. In the chart below, fill in the input, process, and output of the digestive system. Circle and label the input and process on the diagram.

Mouth

Esophagus

Liver

Stomach

Large intestine

Small intestine

Rectum

Input	
Process	
Output	
Feedback	

6.NS.8, 6.NS.11

Mechanical Systems
People have designed many mechanical systems to keep them comfortable or to help them do work. Heating and air conditioning systems, elevators, and engines are examples of mechanical systems. **Figure 2** shows an example of a basic mechanical system.

FIGURE 2 ·······

A System on Wheels
This skateboarder may be having too much fun to realize it, but his skateboard is a mechanical system.

6.NS.8, 6.NS.11

✎ **Apply Concepts** Describe the input, process, and output of this system in the spaces provided. Then, in the empty space, draw an example of a mechanical system you use.

Vocabulary Prefixes The prefix *in-* can mean "into" or "within," such as in the word *input*. It can also mean "not." What do you think the word *inability* means?

_____

_____

_____

Input	
Process	
Output	

FIGURE 3 ·····················
Cloud Formation

Clouds form when warm, moist air rises and cools. Water vapor condenses onto tiny particles in the air. **6.NS.1, 6.NS.8**

✎ **On the lines provided, write the input, process, and output of this system.**

1. Identify What is the input of this system?

_____

_____

_____

2. Predict What would happen if there was no input?

_____

_____

_____

_____

_____

Environmental Systems There are many systems in nature. Environmental systems may involve biological, geological, and physical parts. The process that forms soil is one environmental system. Another is how a cloud forms, shown in **Figure 3.**

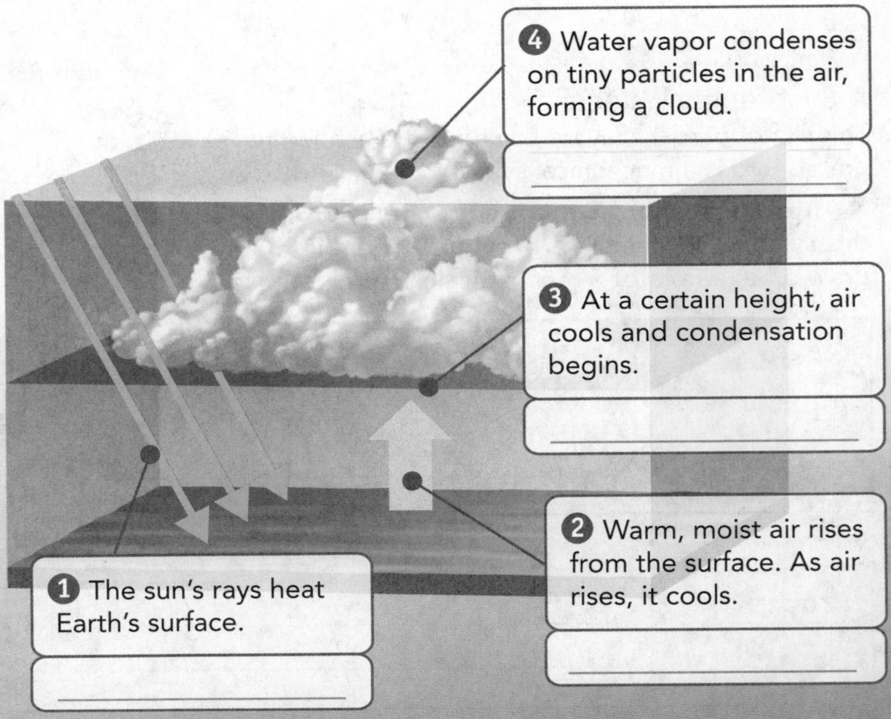

❹ Water vapor condenses on tiny particles in the air, forming a cloud.

_____

❸ At a certain height, air cools and condensation begins.

_____

❷ Warm, moist air rises from the surface. As air rises, it cools.

_____

❶ The sun's rays heat Earth's surface.

_____

Lab zone® Do the Quick Lab *Systems of Science.*

🔑 Assess Your Understanding

1a. Name _____ is the material or energy that comes out of a system. **6.NS.8**

b. Explain Why is a computer a system?

_____

_____

_____

6.NS.8

c. CHALLENGE What are the input, process, and output of an automatic paper towel dispenser?

_____

_____

_____

_____

6.NS.8, 6.NS.11

got it? ·····················

○ I get it! Now I know that a system is _____

_____

_____

○ I need extra help with _____

Go to MY SCIENCE ⒮ COACH online for help with this subject. **6.NS.8, 6.NS.11**

How Are Models of Systems Used?

Many systems are complex. Scientists cannot always observe all the inputs, processes, and outputs of a complex system. **Scientists often use models of systems to understand how systems work.** These models can help scientists to predict changes in a system as a result of a change in input or system feedback.

Using Basic Models Sometimes basic models of complex systems allow scientists, students, or the public to get a general knowledge of the system. These models do not show all the details of the system. However, they still show the major parts, processes, and relationships in the system. **Figure 4** shows a model of a basic system, the tick life cycle.

Academic Standards for Science

6.NS.8 Analyze data and use it to identify patterns and make inferences based on these patterns.

6.NS.11 Communicate findings using models.

6.DP.9 Present evidence using mathematical representations.

6.DP.10 Communicate the solution including evidence using mathematical representations.

FIGURE 4 ··

> INTERACTIVE ART **Life Cycle of the American Dog Tick**

American dog ticks are a common pest. They can spread diseases such as Rocky Mountain spotted fever to humans.

Interpret Diagrams Read the model of the life cycle of the American dog tick below. Then, fill in the sign with a title and information that could help you avoid ticks.
6.NS.8, 6.NS.11

WARNING!

Title: _____

Warning:

• _____
  _____

• _____
  _____

• _____
  _____

Female ticks lay eggs in moist, safe places on the ground.

Eggs

WINTER

SPRING

Nymphs develop into adults that climb onto low plants and attach to passing animals. They may feed on dogs or humans.

Adult

Larva

Eggs hatch into larvae. The larvae feed on the blood of small mammals such as mice, rats, and rabbits.

FALL

SUMMER

Larvae develop into nymphs. The nymphs feed on larger mammals such as dogs.

Nymph

67

Using Complex Models Some systems are complex, with many interactions. Scientists cannot understand these systems by using simple models. Scientists often use computer programs to represent all the interactions in a complex system.

The El Niño weather event is an example of a complex system because it involves both air and water. During some years, the difference in air pressure decreases across the tropical Pacific Ocean. You can think of this as the input of the system. It causes the trade winds to relax. Warm water spreads eastward toward the west coast of South America. The output of this system is thunderstorms, extra rainfall, and flooding in the southwestern United States. El Niño also causes warmer winters in the northeastern United States, and wetter winters in the southeastern United States. **Figure 5** shows a computer model of El Niño.

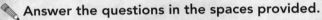

FIGURE 5

El Niño

Scientists used the computer models on these pages to study an El Niño event in 1997. The red color represents warm water spreading across the ocean between January and June.

✎ **Answer the questions in the spaces provided.**

1. **Draw Conclusions** How is this computer model limited in representing El Niño?

_____

_____

_____

did you know?

An El Niño year is usually followed by a La Niña year. La Niña happens when unusually cold water spreads across the Pacific Ocean. It causes warmer winters in the southeastern United States.

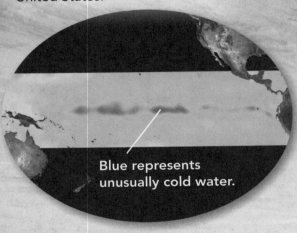

Blue represents unusually cold water.

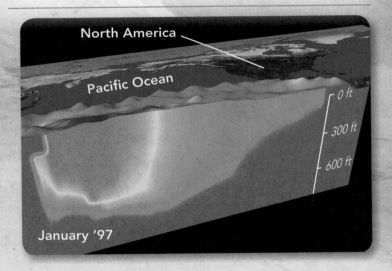

North America

Pacific Ocean

0 ft

300 ft

600 ft

January '97

do the math!

Although El Niño occurs in the Pacific Ocean, it also affects the weather patterns on the east coast of the United States.

Type of Year	Average Number of Hurricanes
Normal Year	5.8
El Niño Year	4

1 Interpret Tables Use the data table to make a bar graph in the space provided.

2 Graph Label the x- and y-axes. Write a title for the graph.

3 Interpret Data How did El Niño affect the average number of hurricanes?

_____

_____

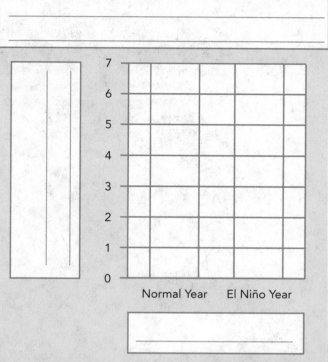

Normal Year   El Niño Year

6.NS.8, 6.NS.11, 6.DP.9, 6.DP.10

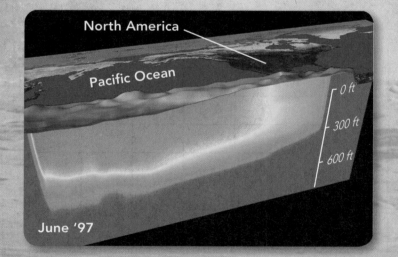

North America

Pacific Ocean

0 ft
300 ft
600 ft

June '97

2. Summarize How does the output of the El Niño system affect different areas of the United States?

_____

_____

_____

_____

6.NS.8

Out in Space

What tools do scientists use to understand the natural world?

FIGURE 6 ··

Scientists use models and math tools to study the solar system. The planets' distances are measured in units called astronomical units (AU). The time for one orbit of a planet is measured in Earth years. In this model, the planets' sizes and their distances from the sun are not shown to scale.

✎ **Complete the tasks in the boxes.**

6.NS.8, 6.NS.11, 6.DP.9, 6.DP.10

Sun

Mercury
0.4 AU
0.2 Earth year

Venus
0.7 AU
0.6 Earth year

Earth
1 AU
1 Earth year

Mars
1.5 AU
1.9 Earth years

1. **Graph** Complete the graph using the data points for Jupiter, Saturn, Uranus, and Neptune. The inner planets—Mercury, Venus, Earth, and Mars—have been done for you.

2. **Interpret Data** What does the trend of the graph show?

_____

_____

_____

_____

_____

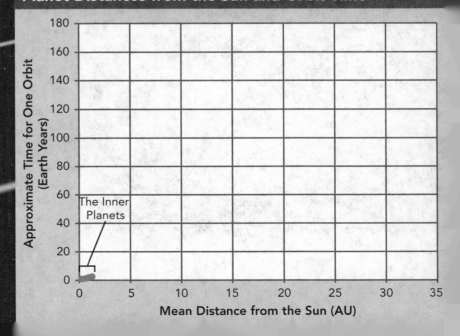

Planet Distances from the Sun and Orbit Time

The Inner Planets

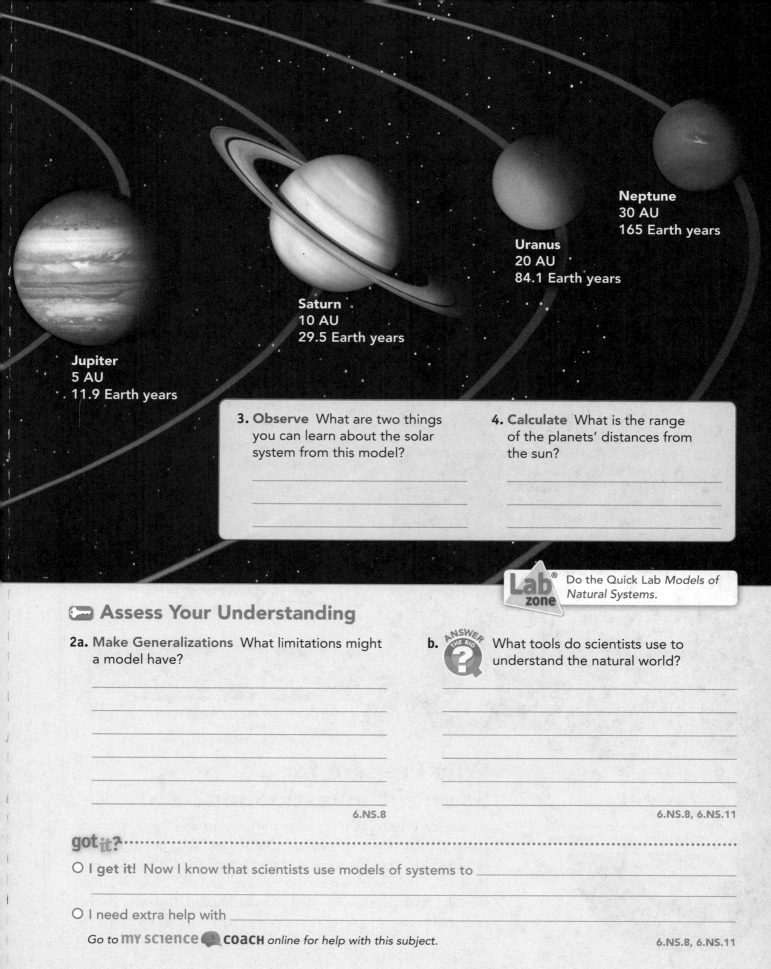

Neptune
30 AU
165 Earth years

Uranus
20 AU
84.1 Earth years

Saturn
10 AU
29.5 Earth years

Jupiter
5 AU
11.9 Earth years

3. Observe What are two things you can learn about the solar system from this model?

_____

_____

_____

4. Calculate What is the range of the planets' distances from the sun?

_____

_____

_____

Do the Quick Lab *Models of Natural Systems.*

🔑 Assess Your Understanding

2a. Make Generalizations What limitations might a model have?

_____

_____

_____

_____

_____

6.NS.8

b. ANSWER THE BIG **?** What tools do scientists use to understand the natural world?

_____

_____

_____

_____

_____

6.NS.8, 6.NS.11

got it? ....

○ **I get it!** Now I know that scientists use models of systems to _____

_____

○ **I need extra help with** _____

Go to MY SCIENCE ⬢ COACH *online for help with this subject.*

6.NS.8, 6.NS.11

Safety in the Science Laboratory

🔑 **Why Prepare for a Scientific Investigation?**
6.NS.2, 6.NS.3

🔑 **What Should You Do if an Accident Occurs?**
6.NS.2, 6.NS.3

MY PLANET DIARY

Staying Safe Among Snakes

What would you do if you saw a banded snake of black, red, and yellow slithering on the path in front of you? It could be the eastern coral snake, a venomous snake found in the southern United States. First, you should stop. Then walk away slowly. Often, a venomous snake will only bite if it feels threatened.

If you plan on hiking, take precautions to avoid snakebites. Always go with someone else. Once you are there, watch where you place your feet when you walk. If you see a snake, leave it alone!

FUN FACT

Communicate Discuss the question with a partner. Then write your answer below.

What are two other precautions you can take to avoid snakebite if you go hiking?

_____

_____

_____

_____

▶ PLANET DIARY Go to **Planet Diary** to learn more about safety in the laboratory.

Lab® zone Do the Inquiry Warm-Up *Is Science Safe?*

Academic Standards for Science

6.NS.2 Plan and carry out investigations.

6.NS.3 Collect quantitative data with appropriate tools and technologies.

Why Prepare for a Scientific Investigation?

As you start the test your teacher put on your desk, your stomach sinks. You knew you should have studied and then gone to bed early. But you couldn't resist going with your friends to a movie. Now you can barely keep your eyes open, and you have forgotten the calculator your teacher said you would need. If you had only prepared better, you would have done a lot better on the test.

Vocabulary
- safety symbol
- field

Skills
- Reading: Summarize
- Inquiry: Infer

Investigation Preparation Just like preparing for a test, you must prepare before you begin a science investigation. **Good preparation helps you stay safe when doing science investigations in a laboratory or in the field.** If you do not stay safe, you may not be able to finish the investigation or you may not obtain good results. To prepare for an investigation, first read through any procedures carefully and make sure you understand all the directions. Then, if anything is unclear, ask your teacher about it before you begin. Finally, use the safety equipment required, as indicated by an investigation's safety symbols. Also, observe the cautions of the other safety symbols. **Safety symbols** are signs that alert you to possible sources of accidents in a laboratory.

Safety Symbols

 Safety Goggles   Lab Apron   Breakage

 Heat-Resistant Gloves   Heating   Poison

 Physical Safety    Flames   Electric Shock

apply it!

You will perform different tasks in a science investigation.

1 Infer For each laboratory task below, list the safety symbols that best match the task. Each task has more than one safety symbol.

Task 1: adding food coloring to a liquid

_____

_____

Task 2: measuring the temperature of hot water

_____

_____

Task 3: dissolving a solid material in alcohol

_____

_____

Task 4: heating a liquid on a hot plate

_____

_____

_____

2 CHALLENGE Electrical appliances in the laboratory can cause shocks. What is another safety issue that all electrical appliances have?

_____

_____

_____

6.NS.2

73

Performing an Investigation

Whenever you are in a laboratory, your main concern must be the safety of you, your teacher, and your classmates. One safety rule is the most important. *Always follow your teacher's instructions and the investigation directions exactly.* Never try anything on your own without asking your teacher first.

When performing an investigation, you can do many things to make your laboratory experience safe and successful. In **Figure 1**, the students are not following many of the rules listed.

FIGURE 1 ·····························

Laboratory Safety

Recognizing and avoiding safety hazards are important lab skills.

✎ **Read the rules on the notebook below. Then complete these tasks.**

1. **Interpret Photos** Identify two safety hazards shown in each picture, and list them on the lines provided.

2. **Identify** Explain why it is important to wear plastic gloves when handling plants.

_____

_____

_____

6.NS.2

Rules

- Wear safety goggles to protect your eyes from chemical splashes, glass breakage, and sharp objects.
- Wear an apron to protect yourself and your clothes from chemicals.
- Use heat-resistant gloves when handling hot objects.
- Keep your work area clean and organized.
- Tie back long hair to keep it away from flames, chemicals, or equipment.
- Provide appropriate care for live animals.
- Handle live animals and plants with care.
- Wear plastic gloves to protect your skin when handling animals, plants, or chemicals.
- Make sure electric cords are untangled and out of the way.
- Wear closed-toe shoes when working in the laboratory.

End-of-Investigation Procedures Just because you have completed an investigation does not mean you are finished. You still need to clean up your work area. Also, turn off and unplug any electrical equipment and return it to its proper place. Dispose of any waste materials properly. Some wastes should not be thrown in the trash or poured down the drain. Follow your teacher's instructions about proper disposal. Finally, always be sure to wash your hands thoroughly after working in the laboratory.

Summarize You have just completed an investigation. Summarize what your next tasks should be.

_____

_____

_____

_____

_____

6.NS.2

Working Safely in the Field Some of your science investigations may be done in the **field,** which is any area outside a science laboratory. Just as in the laboratory, good preparation helps you stay safe because there can be many safety hazards outdoors. You could encounter severe weather, traffic, wild animals, or poisonous plants. Whenever you set out to work in the field, you should always tell an adult where you will be. Never carry out a field investigation alone. Wear appropriate clothing. Use common sense to avoid any potentially dangerous situations. You can see some scientists working in the field in **Figure 2.**

FIGURE 2 ·······························

Working in the Field

These scientists are collecting groundwater samples.

✎ **Apply Concepts** **Describe one way these scientists are working safely in the field.**

_____

_____

_____

_____

6.NS.2

 Do the Quick Lab *Be Prepared to Be Safe in the Lab.*

🔑 Assess Your Understanding

1a. Describe Suppose a student holds an insect by its wings during an investigation. How should the student observe the insect instead?

_____

_____

_____

6.NS.2, 6.NS.3

b. Relate Cause and Effect What might happen if you were to wear open-toed shoes on a field investigation?

_____

_____

_____

6.NS.2, 6.NS.3

got it? ··

○ **I get it!** Now I know that preparing for a science investigation is important because _____

_____

○ **I need extra help with** _____

Go to MY SCIENCE Ⓢ COACH *online for help with this subject.*

6.NS.2, 6.NS.3

What Should You Do if an Accident Occurs?

Although you may have prepared carefully, an accident may occur at some point. **When any accident occurs, no matter how minor, tell your teacher or another adult immediately. Then listen to their directions and carry them out quickly.** Make sure you know the location and the proper use of all the emergency equipment in your laboratory. **Figure 3** shows a lab that contains some emergency equipment.

Academic Standards for Science

6.NS.2 Plan and carry out investigations.
6.NS.3 Collect quantitative data with appropriate tools and technologies.

FIGURE 3 ···

Safety Equipment

In case of an emergency in the lab, you should recognize some basic safety equipment and know how to use it.

✏ **Observe** Circle all the lab safety equipment shown in the picture.

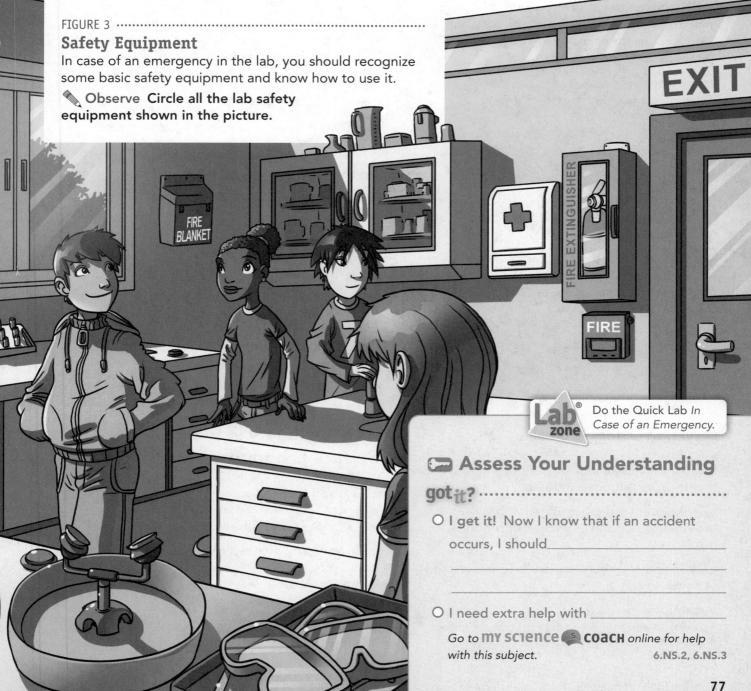

Lab zone ® Do the Quick Lab *In Case of an Emergency.*

Assess Your Understanding

got it? ···

○ **I get it!** Now I know that if an accident occurs, I should_____

_____

○ **I need extra help with** _____

Go to my science ⓢ coach *online for help with this subject.*   6.NS.2, 6.NS.3

CHAPTER 2 Study Guide

Scientists use _____ of systems and _____ tools, such as calculating percent error, to study the natural world.

LESSON 1 Measurement in Science
6.NS.1, 6.NS.3, 6.NS.4, 6.NS.5, 6.NS.7, 6.DP.1, 6.DP.2

🔑 A standard measurement allows scientists to compare data and communicate results.

🔑 SI measurement units include the meter (length), kilogram (mass), cubic meter (volume), kilograms per cubic meter (density), kelvin (temperature), and seconds (time).

Vocabulary
- metric system • SI • mass • weight
- volume • density

LESSON 2 Math in Science
6.NS.3, 6.NS.4 6.NS.5, 6.NS.8

🔑 Math skills used in science when working with data include estimation, accuracy and precision, and significant figures.

🔑 Math tools include calculating percent error; finding the mean, median, mode, and range; and checking the reasonableness of data.

Vocabulary
- estimate • accuracy • precision
- significant figures • percent error • mean
- median • mode • range • anomalous data

LESSON 3 Graphs
6.NS.1, 6.NS.3, 6.NS.8, 6.NS.11, 6.DP.9, 6.DP.10

🔑 Graphs can display categorical and numerical data.

🔑 Bar graphs and circle graphs are suitable for displaying categorical data and line graphs and bar graphs are appropriate for displaying numerical data.

Vocabulary
- graph • linear graph • nonlinear graph

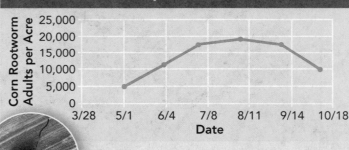

Corn Rootworm Population Growth

LESSON 4 Using Models
6.NS.1, 6.NS.8, 6.NS.11, 6.DP.9, 6.DP.10

🔑 Scientists use models to understand things that they cannot observe directly.

🔑 A system is a group of parts that work together to perform a function or produce a result.

🔑 Scientists often use models to understand systems.

Vocabulary
- model • system • input • process • output
- feedback

LESSON 5 Safety in the Science Laboratory
6.NS.2, 6.NS.3

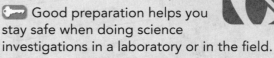

🔑 Good preparation helps you stay safe when doing science investigations in a laboratory or in the field.

🔑 When any accident occurs, no matter how minor, tell your teacher or another adult immediately. Then listen to their directions and carry them out quickly.

Vocabulary
- safety symbol • field

Review and Assessment

LESSON 1 Measurement in Science

1. The metric system is a measurement system based on the number
   a. 1.   **b.** 10.
   c. 100.   **d.** 1000.
   6.NS.3

2. Review The basic SI unit of time is _____
   6.NS.3

3. Calculate If your calculator is 5 centimeters wide, what is its width in millimeters?
   6.NS.3, 6.NS.5, 6.NS.8

4. Compare and Contrast How do you find the volume of a regular solid? An irregular solid?
   6.NS.3, 6.NS.5, 6.NS.8

LESSON 2 Math in Science

5. An estimate is a(n)
   a. guess.   **b.** observation.
   c. precise number.   **d.** approximation.
   6.NS.5

6. _____ do not fit with the rest of a data set.
   6.NS.8

7. Interpret Data Suppose you have a row of tiles that is 26.7 cm long. How many significant figures are in this measurement? Which digit is estimated?
   6.NS.3, 6.NS.8

8. math! Find the mean, median, mode, and range for this data: 24, 16, 11, 10, 16, 4, 17.
   6.NS.3, 6.NS.8

LESSON 3 Graphs

9. The factor that scientists change is called a
   a. manipulated variable.
   b. prediction.
   c. responding variable.
   d. trend.
   6.NS.4

10. _____ data are information that can be grouped into categories.
   6.NS.8

11. You want to include a graph showing the different species of animals on display at a local zoo. What is the most appropriate type of graph to use?
   6.NS.8

Use the graph to answer Questions 12 and 13.

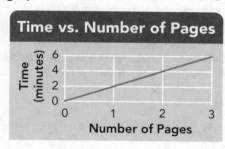

12. Interpret Graphs The graph shows how many pages Sarah read over time. Describe the relationship that the data have.
   6.NS.8

13. Predict How many pages do you expect Sarah to have read after 10 minutes? Explain.
   6.NS.8

79

LESSON 4 **Using Models**

LESSON 4 **Using Models**

14. A representation of a simple or complex object or process is a

   a. theory.   **b.** system.

   c. model.   **d.** output.

                             6.NS.11

15. A _____ is a group of parts that work together to perform a function or produce a result.

                             6.NS.11

16. Explain You are a scientist studying the energy given off by a distant star. Why might you use a computer model to study this star?

_____

_____

_____

_____

_____

                             6.NS.11

17. Make Generalizations Why would a complex model make more accurate predictions about a system than a basic model?

_____

_____

_____

_____

_____

_____

_____

_____

_____

_____

_____

                  6.NS.8, 6.NS.11

LESSON 5 **Safety in the Science Laboratory**

18. To protect your eyes from chemical spills, wear

   a. plastic gloves.   **b.** safety goggles.

   c. an apron.   **d.** closed-toe shoes.

                            6.NS.2

19. Signs that alert you to possible sources of accidents are _____

                           6.NS.2

20. Sequence You accidentally cut yourself during an investigation. What are the first two steps you should take?

_____

_____

                           6.NS.2

21. **Write About It** Suppose you observe animals in their habitats as part of a field investigation. Give at least three examples of how you would keep yourself and the animals safe.

                            6.NS.2

APPLY THE BIG ❓

What tools do scientists use to understand the natural world?

22. Suppose you are studying the energy use in your school. What math tools might you use to help collect data? How might you use a model?

_____

_____

_____

_____

_____

_____

_____

_____

          6.NS.2, 6.NS.3, 6.NS.11

Indiana ISTEP+ Practice

Multiple Choice

Circle the letter of the best answer.

1. What is this tool used to measure?

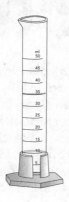

- **A.** weight
- **B.** length
- **C.** volume
- **D.** mass

6.NS.3

2. In the event that a glass beaker breaks in the laboratory, the first thing you should do is

- **A.** alert your teacher.
- **B.** clean up the broken glass.
- **C.** obtain another beaker.
- **D.** wash your hands.

6.NS.2

3. The data points on a linear graph form

- **A.** a straight line.
- **B.** a curve.
- **C.** a jagged line.
- **D.** no line.

6.NS.8

4. Find the range for this set of data: 22, 36, 7, 19, 56.

- **A.** 28
- **B.** 49
- **C.** 7
- **D.** 22

6.NS.8

Constructed Response

Write your answer to Question 5 on the lines below.

5. You have recorded data about the height of a seedling each day for a month. What is the best type of graph to use to display your data? Explain your choice.

_____

_____

_____

_____

6.NS.8

Extended Response

Write your answer to Question 6 on another sheet of paper.

6. You are finding the density of a substance. Write the steps you would follow. What metric units would you use? What is a possible source of error in your measurement?

6.NS.3, 6.NS.5, 6.NS.8

BAKELITE®:
Molding the Future

In 1907, Dr. Leo Baekeland created the first artificial plastic. Bakelite, as he called it, was an instant hit. It was strong and didn't easily melt. It could be molded into any shape in any color. At the time, more and more people were using electricity. Bakelite did not conduct electricity, so it was an excellent insulator. It was used to make electric plugs and cases for electronic devices like telephones.

Soon, Bakelite was everywhere. People found a lot of uses for such a valuable yet inexpensive material. It was used to make everything from engine parts to jewelry. And that was just the beginning.

Later, chemists created other, more useful types of plastic. Now over a century later, can you imagine life without plastic?

The benefits of plastic are obvious. But what are the downfalls? Plastics do not break down easily in landfills. They are not easily recycled, either. The production of plastic can release chemical pollutants into the environment. Companies are developing technologies to solve these problems, but doing so can be costly. The history of plastic shows that sometimes a new technology can create unforeseen challenges for society.

Analyze It Working with a partner, choose a new technology. Learn about the benefits and drawbacks of this technology. Then, do a cost-benefit analysis.

 6.NS.2, 6.NS.8

CAFFEINE CAUSES HALLUCINATIONS!

A new study reports that the equivalent of seven cups of coffee a day could cause people to see "ghosts."

Reading Between the Lines

Headlines grab your attention. That's their job—to get you to read more. Sometimes, though, when headlines promise interesting news, the report doesn't deliver accurate scientific data.

Recently, some newspapers reported that caffeine caused people to hallucinate. The report cited a study that showed that people who drank seven or more cups of coffee in a day saw things that weren't really there.

The newspapers reported the results of the study because a lot of people drink coffee and tea, which both have caffeine. So, a lot of people would find the study interesting. However, the study had some flaws.

It had a small sample of only 219 people. Also, the sample came from a specific group of people—university students. The study took the form of a survey, which means the researchers did not directly observe the subjects. Finally, the researchers did not have a control group. There was no way for them to determine if other factors, besides the caffeine, had affected the subjects. Many scientists later agreed that more tests still needed to be done.

Science doesn't always make for interesting news. Most scientific discoveries happen slowly. They are the result of many trials performed over long periods of time. So be critical of catchy headlines that promise an interesting story. You may not be reading accurate science.

Analyze It Compare articles about science in two or three news sources. Are the headlines more eye-catching in one source? Identify the science claims that the articles make. Identify the evidence that supports these claims. Which source provides the clearest evidence? Which source relies mostly on opinions and assumptions? Create a table to compare the reporting in your sources.

 6.NS.8, 6.NS.11

WHAT ARE ALL OF THESE THINGS MADE OF?

How is matter described?

Imagine a warm day at Waikiki Beach on the island of Oahu, Hawaii. You can feel the warm breeze, the hot sand, and the cool water. Palm trees, hotels, shops, and the volcanic crater called Diamond Head, are all a part of the scenery around you. People swimming, surfing, and sailing are enjoying the ocean.

Classify **Categorize the items found at Waikiki Beach by what they are made of.**

> UNTAMED SCIENCE Watch the **Untamed Science** video to learn more about matter.

Introduction to Matter

Academic Standards for Science

6.1, 6.1.1, 6.1.3, 6.1.7, 6.NS.1–6.NS.8,
6.NS.11, 6.DP.1–6.DP.8, 6.DP.11

3 Getting Started

Check Your Understanding

1. **Background** Read the paragraph below and then answer the question.

On a hot day, Jorge decides to make a pitcher of cold lemonade. He combines **pure** water with lemon juice in a **ratio** of six to one. He adds sugar and ice and stirs all the ingredients together. The **properties** of the lemonade are that it is cold, yellow, and sweet.

A **pure** material is not mixed with any other matter.

A **ratio** tells you the relationship between two or more things.

A **property** is a characteristic that belongs to a person or thing.

- How would the properties of the lemonade change if the ratio of pure water to lemon juice were three to one? Assume the amount of sugar is the same.

_____

_____

> **MY READING WEB** If you had trouble completing the question above, visit **My Reading Web** and type in *Introduction to Matter.*

Vocabulary Skill

Prefixes A prefix is a word part that is added at the beginning of a root word to change the word's meaning. The prefixes below will help you understand some of the vocabulary in this chapter.

Prefix	Meaning	Example
endo-	in, within	endogenous, *adj.* describes something that arises from inside an organism's tissues or cells
exo-	out	exoskeleton, *n.* an outer shell or outer skeleton that protects animals, such as crustaceans

2. **Quick Check** The Greek root *therm* means "heat." Predict the meaning of the term *endothermic change.*

_____

_____

substance

mixture

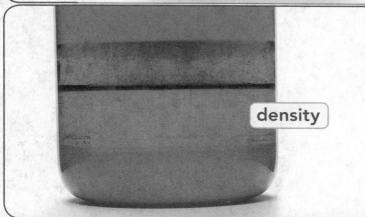

density

chemical energy

Chapter Preview

LESSON 1

- matter
- chemistry
- substance
- physical property
- chemical property
- Summarize
- Classify

LESSON 2

- element
- atom
- chemical bond
- molecule
- compound
- chemical formula
- mixture
- Compare and Contrast
- Infer

LESSON 3

- weight
- mass
- International System of Units
- volume
- density
- Identify the Main Idea
- Calculate

LESSON 4

- physical change
- chemical change
- law of conservation of mass
- temperature
- thermal energy
- endothermic change
- exothermic change
- chemical energy
- Relate Cause and Effect
- Draw Conclusions

> VOCAB FLASH CARDS For extra help with vocabulary, visit **Vocab Flash Cards** and type in *Introduction to Matter.*

Describing Matter

🔑 **What Properties Describe Matter?**
6.1, 6.1.1

my planeT DiaRY

CAREER

Art Conservation Scientist

Science and art may seem like two very different interests, but they are both part of the job for an art conservation scientist. Over time, art can fade, decay, or get dirty. Conservation scientists find ways to restore art by examining its properties. They look at texture, color and age of the paint, the condition of the canvas, and materials used to make the paint. Then, the scientists can determine chemical properties of the painting. For example, they can predict how the painting will react to light, changes in temperature, and the use of chemicals for cleaning. Thanks to art conservation scientists, masterpieces of art can be enjoyed for many years.

Before

After

Write your answers to the questions below.

1. Why is it important for an art conservation scientist to study the properties of a painting before it's repaired?

_____

_____

_____

_____

2. Name another career that combines science with another interest.

_____

_____

Medusa by Caravaggio, about 1598. Uffizi Gallery, Florence, Italy

▷ **PLANET DIARY** Go to **Planet Diary** to learn more about matter.

Lab zone® Do the Inquiry Warm-Up *How Do You Describe Matter?*

Vocabulary
- matter • chemistry
- substance • physical property
- chemical property

Skills
- Reading: Summarize
- Inquiry: Classify

What Properties Describe Matter?

You have probably heard the word *matter* used many times. "As a matter of fact…" or "Hey, what's the matter?" In science, **matter** is anything that has mass and takes up space. All the "stuff" around you is matter, and you are matter too. Air, plastic, metal, wood, glass, paper, and cloth are all matter.

Even though air and paper are both matter, you know they are different materials. Matter can have many different properties, or characteristics that can be used to identify and classify it. Materials can be hard or soft, hot or cold, liquid, solid, or gas. Some materials catch fire easily, but others do not burn. **Chemistry** is the study of matter and how matter changes.

Substances Some types of matter are substances and some are not. In chemistry, a **substance** is a single kind of matter that is pure, meaning it always has a specific makeup, or composition. For example, table salt has the same composition and properties whether it comes from seawater or a salt mine. **Figure 1** shows two examples of water that appear to be very different. Water is a substance. Pure water is always the same, whether it comes from a glacier or from a geyser.

FIGURE 1 ···

Properties of Matter

✎ **Compare and Contrast** Complete the Venn diagram with the properties of water from a glacier and from a geyser.

Glacier | Geyser

Academic Standards for Science

6.1 Core Standard Explain that all objects and substances in the natural world are composed of matter in different states with different properties.

6.1.1 Understand that the properties and behavior of matter can be explained by a model which depicts particles representing atoms or molecules in motion.

·················· ✏ ··················

Summarize How are matter and substances related?

_____

_____

_____

_____

_____

_____

Physical and Chemical Properties of Matter

Matter is described by its properties. ⬭ **Every form of matter has two kinds of properties—physical properties and chemical properties.** A **physical property** is a characteristic of a substance that can be observed without changing it into another substance.

Some properties of matter can't be seen just by observation or touch. A **chemical property** is a characteristic of a substance that describes its ability to change into different substances. To observe the chemical properties of a substance, you must try to change it into another substance. Physical and chemical properties are used to classify matter.

Basketball Hoop Two physical properties of metals are luster, or shine, and the ability to conduct electric current and heat. Another physical property is flexibility, which is the ability to be bent into shapes.

Mark all the objects that are flexible.

- ◯ Aluminum can
- ◯ Copper sheeting
- ◯ Brick house
- ◯ Glass window
- ◯ Silver spoon
- ◯ Wood drumstick

What do all of the flexible objects have in common?

_____

What physical property makes metal pots good for cooking?

_____

Water A physical property of water is that it freezes at 0°C. When liquid water freezes, it changes to ice, but it is still water. The temperatures at which substances boil and melt are also physical properties.

Rusty Metal Chain A chemical property of iron is that it combines slowly with oxygen in the air to form a different substance, rust. Silver reacts with sulfur in the air to form tarnish. In contrast, a chemical property of gold is that it does not react easily with oxygen or sulfur.

Frozen Fruit Bar Hardness, texture, temperature, and color are examples of physical properties. When you describe a material as a solid, a liquid, or a gas, you are describing its state of matter. State of matter is another physical property.

Describe three properties of a frozen fruit bar, including its state of matter.

_____

_____

Will any of these properties change after a couple of hours in the sun? Explain.

_____

_____

_____

Charcoal Briquettes Fuels, like charcoal, can catch fire and burn. When a fuel burns, it combines with oxygen in the air and changes into the substances water and carbon dioxide. The ability to burn, or flammability, is a chemical property.

How do you know that flammability is a chemical property?

_____

_____

_____

_____

apply it!

The wax in a burning candle can be described by both physical and chemical properties.

❶ **Describe** What are the physical properties of the wax in a burning candle?

_____

_____

_____

❷ **CHALLENGE** Why is melting a physical property of the wax, but flammability is a chemical property?

_____

_____

_____

_____

_____

_____

_____

Lab zone® Do the Quick Lab *Observing Physical Properties.*

🔑 Assess Your Understanding

1a. Classify The melting point of table salt is 801°C. Is this a physical or chemical property?

_____

6.1.1

b. Draw Conclusions Helium does not usually react with other substances. Does this mean that helium has no chemical properties? Explain.

_____

_____

6.1.1, 6.NS.8

got it?

○ **I get it!** Now I know that matter is described by its _____

_____

○ **I need extra help with** _____

_____

Go to **MY SCIENCE COACH** *online for help with this subject.* 6.1, 6.1.1

Classifying Matter

UNLOCK THE BIG ?

 **What Is Matter Made Of?**
6.1, 6.1.1, 6.NS.3

 **What Are Two Types of Mixtures?**
6.1

my planeT DiaRy

Smaller Than Small

What's the smallest thing you can think of? A grain of sand? A speck of dust? If you look at these items under a powerful microscope, you'll see that they're made up of smaller and smaller pieces. All matter is made up of very tiny particles called atoms. Atoms are so small, there is a special unit of measure used to describe them called a nanometer (nm). A nanometer is equal to 1/1,000,000,000 or one-billionth of a meter!

At least 50,000 of these tiny compounds called nanobouquets could fit on the head of a pin.

 Lab zone Do the Inquiry Warm-Up *What Is a Mixture?*

SCIENCE STATS

Write your answers to the questions below.

1. A nickel is about 2 millimeters thick, or 2/1,000 of a meter. How many nanometers is this?

_____

_____

2. Imagine being the size of an atom. Describe how something like a red blood cell might look to you.

_____

_____

_____

> PLANET DIARY Go to **Planet Diary** to learn more about atoms.

Common Objects in Nanometers (nm)

Object	Approximate Size
Compact disc diameter	120,000,000 nm
Grain of sand	3,000,000 nm
Grain of pollen	500,000 nm
Human hair diameter	100,000 nm
Red blood cell	7000 nm
Length of 3–10 atoms lined up	1 nm

Vocabulary

- element • atom • chemical bond
- molecule • compound • chemical formula
- mixture

Skills

↺ Reading: Compare and Contrast
△ Inquiry: Infer

What Is Matter Made Of?

What is matter? Why is one kind of matter different from another kind of matter? Around 450 B.C., a Greek philosopher named Empedocles attempted to answer these questions. He proposed that all matter was made of four "elements"—air, earth, fire, and water. Empedocles thought that all other matter was a combination of these elements. The idea of four elements was so convincing that people believed it for more than 2,000 years.

Elements In the late 1600s, experiments by early chemists began to show that matter was made up of many more than four elements. 🗝 Scientists know that all matter in the universe is made of more than 100 different substances, called elements. An **element** is a substance that cannot be broken down into any other substances by chemical or physical means. Elements are the simplest substances. Each element can be identified by its specific physical and chemical properties. You may already be familiar with some elements such as aluminum or tin. Elements are represented by one- or two-letter symbols, such as C for carbon, O for oxygen, and Ca for calcium.

Academic Standards for Science

6.1 Core Standard Explain that all objects and substances in the natural world are composed of matter in different states with different properties.

6.1.1 Understand that the properties and behavior of matter can be explained by a model which depicts particles representing atoms or molecules in motion.

6.NS.3 Collect quantitative data.

apply it!

The elements make up all the matter in the universe.

1 **Explain** How can you tell one element from another?

_____
_____
_____

2 △ **Infer** Match the pictures on this page of items containing common elements to the element's name.

A) helium   B) gold   C) copper
D) iron   E) neon

3 CHALLENGE Choose another element that you are familiar with and describe its properties.

_____
_____
_____

6.1

Atoms Imagine tearing a piece of aluminum foil in half over and over again. Would you reach a point where you had the smallest possible piece of aluminum? The answer is yes. The particle theory of matter explains that all matter is made of atoms. An **atom** is the basic particle from which all elements are made. An atom has a positively charged center, or nucleus, containing smaller particles. The nucleus is surrounded by a "cloud" of negative charge. The elements have different properties because their atoms are different.

Molecules Atoms of most elements are able to combine with other atoms. When atoms combine, they form a **chemical bond,** which is a force of attraction between two atoms. In many cases, atoms combine to form larger particles called molecules. A **molecule** (MAHL uh kyool) is a group of two or more atoms held together by chemical bonds. A molecule of water, for example, is made up of an oxygen atom chemically bonded to two hydrogen atoms. Two atoms of the same element can also combine to form a molecule. Oxygen molecules are made up of two oxygen atoms. **Figure 1** shows models of some common molecules.

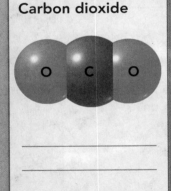

⟲ **Compare and Contrast** How are atoms and molecules the same? How are they different?

_____
_____
_____
_____
_____
_____

FIGURE 1 ⋯⋯⋯⋯⋯⋯⋯⋯⋯⋯⋯

6.NS.3

Atoms and Molecules
Molecules are made up of groups of atoms.

✎ **Use the molecule models to complete the activities.**

1. **Interpret Diagrams** Count the number of atoms of each element in the molecules and write it on the lines below.

2. [CHALLENGE] On the bottom line, write a representation for each molecule using letters and numbers.

Key
C = Carbon
H = Hydrogen
O = Oxygen
N = Nitrogen

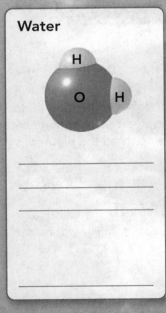

Carbon dioxide

_____
_____
_____
_____

[CHALLENGE]
_____

Water

_____
_____
_____

Oxygen

_____
_____
_____

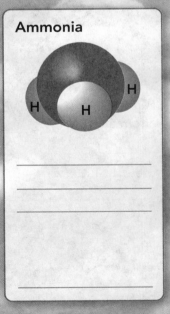

Ammonia

_____
_____
_____
_____

Compounds Water, ammonia, and carbon dioxide are all compounds. A **compound** is a substance made of two or more elements that are chemically combined in a set ratio. A compound is represented by a **chemical formula,** which shows the elements in the compound and the ratio of atoms. For example, the chemical formula for carbon dioxide is CO_2. The 2 below the O for oxygen tells you that the ratio of carbon atoms to oxygen atoms is 1 to 2. If there is no number after an element's symbol, it is understood that the number is 1. A different number of atoms in a formula represents a different compound. For example, the formula for carbon monoxide is CO. Here, the ratio of carbon atoms to oxygen atoms is 1 to 1.

When elements chemically combine, they form compounds with properties different from those of the elements. **Figure 2** shows that the element sulfur is a yellow solid and the element copper is a shiny metal. When copper and sulfur combine, they form a compound called copper sulfide. The new compound has different properties from both copper and sulfur.

FIGURE 2 ·······························

> **ART IN MOTION** **Compounds From Elements**
When elements combine, the compound that forms has different properties than the original elements.

✎ **Describe** **List the properties of copper, sulfur, and copper sulfide.** 6.1

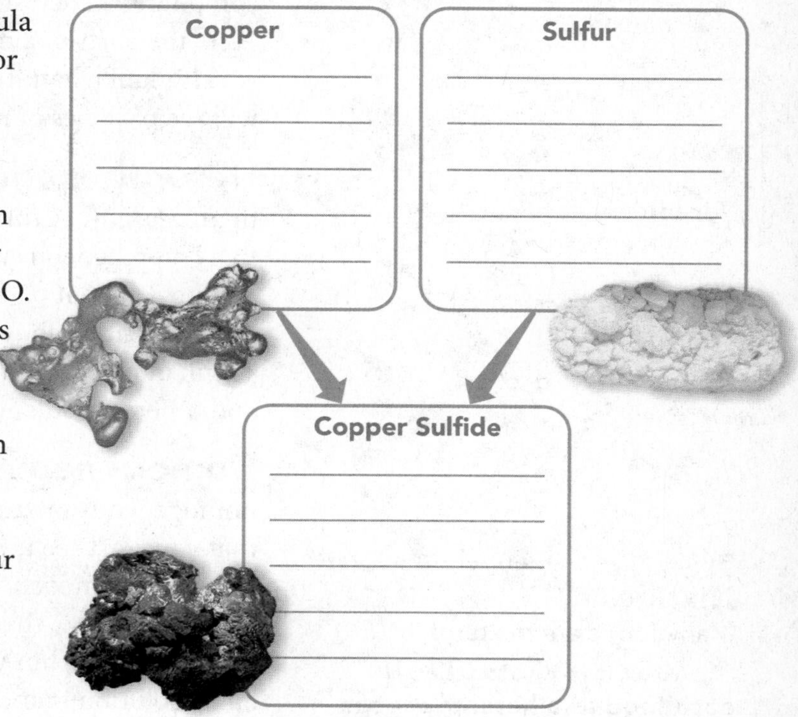

Copper

Sulfur

Copper Sulfide

Lab zone ® Do the Quick Lab *Modeling Atoms and Molecules.*

🗝 Assess Your Understanding

1a. Review What holds the hydrogen and oxygen atoms together in a water molecule?

_____
6.1.1

b. Identify Table sugar has the chemical formula $C_{12}H_{22}O_{11}$. What is the ratio of carbon atoms to oxygen atoms in this compound?

_____
_____
6.1.1

c. Draw Conclusions Two formulas for compounds containing hydrogen and oxygen are H_2O and H_2O_2. Do these formulas represent the same compound? Explain.

_____
_____
_____
_____
6.1.1

got it? ···

○ **I get it!** Now I know that all matter is made up of _____

_____

○ **I need extra help with** _____

Go to MY SCIENCE COACH *online for help with this subject.*

6.1.1

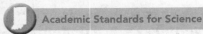
Academic Standards for Science

6.1 Core Standard Explain that all objects and substances in the natural world are composed of matter in different states with different properties.

What Are Two Types of Mixtures?

Elements and compounds are substances, but most materials are mixtures. **Figure 3** shows some common mixtures. A **mixture** is made of two or more substances that are together in the same place, but their atoms are not chemically bonded. Mixtures differ from compounds. Each substance in a mixture keeps its own properties. Also, the parts of a mixture are not combined in a set ratio.

Think of a handful of sand. If you look closely at the sand, you will see particles of rock, bits of shells, maybe even crystals of salt.

Heterogeneous Mixtures There are two types of mixtures. ⚷ **A mixture can be heterogeneous or homogeneous.** In a heterogeneous mixture (het ur oh JEE nee us), you can usually see the different parts and they can easily be separated out. The sand described above is a heterogeneous mixture. So is a salad. Think of how easy it is to see the pieces of lettuce, tomatoes, onions, and other ingredients that can be mixed in countless ways.

Homogeneous Mixtures The substances involved in a homogeneous mixture (hoh moh JEE nee us), are so evenly mixed that you can't see the different parts. It is difficult to separate the parts of a homogeneous mixture. Air is a homogeneous mixture of gases. You know that oxygen is present in the air because you are able to breathe, but you cannot identify where the oxygen is in the air. A solution is another example of a homogeneous mixture. Solutions can be liquids, gases, or even solids.

Vocabulary Prefixes The prefix *homo-* comes from a Greek word that means "the same or alike." Predict the meaning of the prefix *hetero-*.

○ more than one

○ different

○ equal

FIGURE 3 ·········

Mixtures

Many foods are mixtures.

✎ **Interpret Photos** Label each food as a heterogeneous or homogeneous mixture.

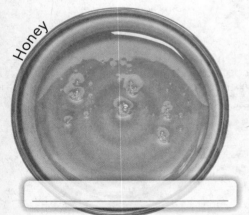

Honey

Guacamole

Soy sauce

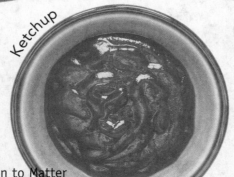

Ketchup

CHALLENGE Is ketchup a heterogeneous or homogeneous mixture? Explain your reasoning.

Separating Mixtures

Separating Mixtures Since the substances in a mixture keep their properties, you can use those properties to separate a mixture into its parts. Methods used to separate the parts of a mixture, including distillation, evaporation, filtration, and magnetic attraction, are shown in **Figure 4.**

FIGURE 4 ···

Separating a Mixture

Different methods can be used to separate mixtures.

✏ **Identify** Name the type of separation method being used in each photo.

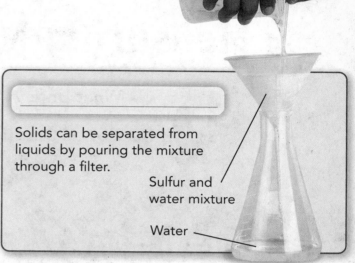

Solids can be separated from liquids by pouring the mixture through a filter.

Sulfur and water mixture

Water

Iron objects can be separated from a mixture using a magnet.

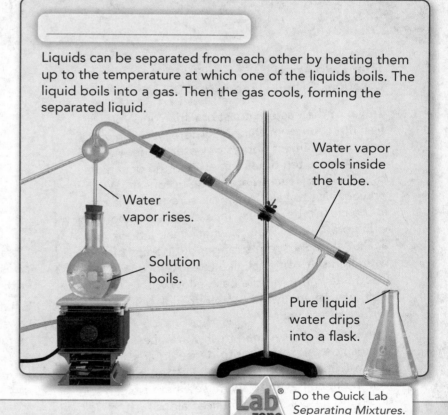

Liquids can be separated from each other by heating them up to the temperature at which one of the liquids boils. The liquid boils into a gas. Then the gas cools, forming the separated liquid.

Water vapor rises.

Solution boils.

Water vapor cools inside the tube.

Pure liquid water drips into a flask.

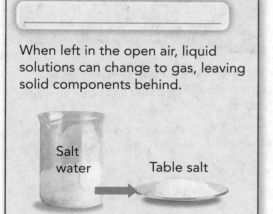

When left in the open air, liquid solutions can change to gas, leaving solid components behind.

Salt water

Table salt

Lab zone ®   Do the Quick Lab *Separating Mixtures.*

⚷ Assess Your Understanding

got it? ···

○ **I get it!** Now I know that the two types of mixtures are _____

_____

○ **I need extra help with** _____

Go to MY SCIENCE ⊕ COACH *online for help with this subject.*

6.1

Measuring Matter

 UNLOCK THE BIG ?

🔑 **What Units Are Used to Express Mass and Volume?**
6.NS.3, 6.NS.8

🔑 **How Is Density Determined?**
6.NS.1, 6.NS.3, 6.NS.8

MY PLANET DIARY

FIELD TRIP

Site: Lake Assal
Location: Djibouti, Republic of Djibouti

Travel to the eastern coast of Africa and you will find the country of Djibouti. There, you can visit one of the saltiest bodies of water in the world. Lake Assal is ten times saltier than the ocean. Its crystal white beaches are made up of salt. While on your visit to Lake Assal, be sure to take a dip in the clear blue waters. Take a book or magazine with you to read. Wait ... what? Take a book into a lake? It might seem strange, but bodies of water with high salt contents, like Lake Assal or the Dead Sea in the Middle East, allow you to float so well that it's nearly impossible to sink below the surface of the water.

Salt water is denser than fresh water. Less-dense liquids float on top of more-dense liquids. You, too, will float on top of the salty water. In fact, it will be difficult even to swim, so what else can you do? Read a book while you float along!

Floating in the Dead Sea

Communicate Write your answers to the questions below. Then discuss your answers with a partner.

What water activities might be easier to do in Lake Assal's salty water? What activities could be more difficult?

_____

_____

_____

▷ PLANET DIARY Go to **Planet Diary** to learn more about density.

 Lab zone® Do the Inquiry Warm-Up *Which Has More Mass?*

Vocabulary

- weight
- mass
- International System of Units
- volume
- density

Skills

- ↺ Reading: Identify the Main Idea
- △ Inquiry: Calculate

What Units Are Used to Express Mass and Volume?

Here's a riddle for you: Which weighs more, a pound of feathers or a pound of sand? If you answered "a pound of sand," think again. Both weigh exactly the same—one pound.

There are all sorts of ways to measure matter, and you use these measurements every day. Scientists rely on measurements as well. In fact, scientists work hard to make sure their measurements are as accurate as possible.

Weight Your **weight** is a measure of the force of gravity on you. On another planet, the force of gravity will be more if the planet is more massive than Earth and less if the planet is less massive than Earth. On the moon, you would weigh only about one sixth of your weight on Earth. On Jupiter, you would weigh more than twice your weight on Earth.

To find the weight of an object, you could place it on a scale like the ones shown in **Figure 1.** The object's weight pulls down on the mechanisms inside the scale. These mechanisms cause beams or springs inside the scale to move. The amount of movement depends on the weight of the object. From the movement of the beams, the scale displays the weight to you.

> **Academic Standards for Science**
>
> **6.NS.3** Collect quantitative data with appropriate tools or technologies and use appropriate units to label numerical data.
>
> **6.NS.8** Analyze data, using appropriate mathematical manipulation as required, and use it to identify patterns and make inferences based on these patterns.

↺ **Identify the Main Idea**
Underline the sentence(s) that describe how weight can be affected by location.

FIGURE 1 ················
Measuring Weight

✎ **Complete the tasks below.**

1. **Estimate** Use the weight of the first scale to estimate the weight of the fish on the other scales. Draw in the pointers.

2. **Describe** How would their weight change on a planet with less mass like Mercury? Or a planet with more mass like Neptune?

_____

_____

_____

_____

6.NS.3

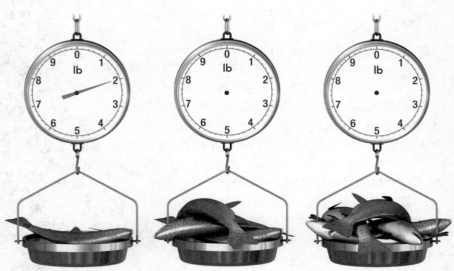

Lake Michigan, which borders Indiana, is the second largest of the Great Lakes in terms of volume, but third largest in terms of surface area. Its borders enclose a smaller surface area than that of Lake Huron (the Great Lake with the second largest surface area). But Lake Michigan has a greater average depth, giving it a greater volume than that of Lake Huron.

Mass How can you weigh less on the moon than on Earth when nothing about you has changed? Your weight is dependent on the gravity of the planet you are visiting. The amount of matter in an object is its **mass,** which does not change with location even if the force of gravity changes. If you travel to the moon, the amount of matter in your body—your mass—does not change. You are the same size. For this reason, scientists prefer to describe matter in terms of mass rather than weight. The mass of an object is a physical property.

To measure the properties of matter, scientists use a system called the **International System of Units** (abbreviated SI for the French name, *Système International d'Unités*). **The SI unit of mass is the kilogram (kg).** If you weigh 90 pounds on Earth, your mass is about 40 kilograms. Often, a smaller unit is used to measure mass, the gram (g). There are 1,000 grams in a kilogram, or 0.001 kilograms in a gram. The table in **Figure 2** lists the masses of some common items.

Mass of Common Objects		
Object	**Mass (g)**	**Mass (kg)**
Nickel	5	0.005
Baseball	150	_____
Pineapple	1,600	_____
Full can of soda	390	_____
Inflated balloon	3	_____

FIGURE 2 ···

Measuring Mass
The SI system uses grams and kilograms to measure mass.

✎ **Complete the following tasks about mass.**

1. **Calculate** In the table, convert the mass of each object from grams to kilograms.

2. **CHALLENGE** Suppose you are taking a flight to Europe. You are only allowed a 23-kg suitcase. How much is that in pounds? (*Hint:* 1 kg = 2.2 lbs.)

○ 50.6 lbs   ○ 46.2 lbs   ○ 10.5 lbs

6.NS.8

Volume All matter has mass and takes up space. The amount of space that matter occupies is called its **volume.** It's easy to see that solids and liquids take up space, but gases have volume, too.

🔑 **The SI unit of volume is the cubic meter (m³).** Other common SI units of volume include the cubic centimeter (cm³), the liter (L), and the milliliter (mL). Common plastic soda bottles hold 2 liters of liquid. A milliliter is 1/1,000 of a liter and is exactly the same volume as 1 cubic centimeter. A teaspoonful of water has a volume of about 5 milliliters. In a lab, volumes of liquid are often measured with a graduated cylinder.

Calculating Volume

Suppose you want to know the volume of a rectangular object, like one of the suitcases shown in **Figure 3**. First, measure the length, width, and height (or thickness) of the suitcase. Then, multiply the measurements together.

Volume = Length × Width × Height

When you multiply the three measurements, you must also multiply the units.

Units = cm × cm × cm = cm³

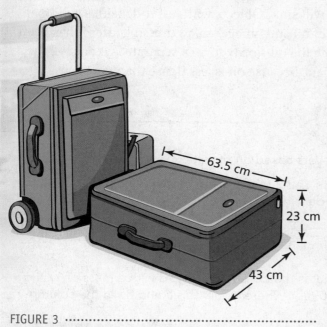

FIGURE 3 ···

⟩VIRTUAL LAB Calculating Volume
Calculate Find the volume of the suitcase.

_____

_____

6.NS.3, 6.NS.8

Measuring Irregular Objects

How do you measure the volume of an irregular object, such as a key or a raspberry? One way is to submerge the object in a liquid in a graduated cylinder. The liquid level will rise by an amount that is equal to the volume of the object in milliliters.

Lab® Do the Quick Lab
zone *Calculating Volume.*

🔑 **Assess Your Understanding**

1. **Explain** Why is mass more useful than weight for measuring matter?

_____

_____

_____

_____

_____

6.NS.3

got it? ···

○ **I get it!** Now I know that the SI unit for

mass is _____

and the SI unit for volume is _____

_____

○ **I need extra help with** _____

_____

Go to **MY SCIENCE ⓢ COACH** *online for help with this subject.* 6.NS.3

101

Academic Standards for Science

6.NS.1 Make predictions based on research and prior knowledge.

6.NS.3 Collect quantitative data with appropriate tools or technologies and use appropriate units to label numerical data.

6.NS.8 Analyze data using appropriate mathematical manipulation as required, and use it to identify patterns and make inferences based on those patterns.

How Is Density Determined?

Remember the riddle about the sand and the feathers? Although they weigh the same, a kilogram of sand takes up much less space than a kilogram of feathers. The volumes differ because sand and feathers have different densities—an important property of matter.

Calculating Density
Density is a measure of the mass of a material in a given volume. Density can be expressed as the number of grams in one cubic centimeter (g/cm^3). For example, the density of water at room temperature is stated as "one gram per cubic centimeter" ($1\ g/cm^3$). Recall that volume can also be measured in milliliters. So the density of water can also be expressed as 1 g/mL. 🔑 **You can determine the density of a sample of matter by dividing its mass by its volume.**

$$\text{Density} = \frac{\text{Mass}}{\text{Volume}}$$

Sinking or Floating?
Suppose you have a block of wood and a block of iron of equal mass. When you drop both blocks into a tub of water, you see that the wood floats and the iron sinks. You know the density of water is $1\ g/cm^3$. Objects with densities greater than that of water will sink. Objects with lesser densities will float.

Watch a bottle of oil and vinegar salad dressing after it has been shaken. You will see the oil slowly form a separate layer above the vinegar. This happens because oil is less dense than vinegar.

apply it!

Liquids can form layers based on density.

1 Apply Concepts Label the layers of colored liquid in the column according to their densities.

Water: 1.00 g/mL   Honey: 1.36 g/mL   Dish soap: 1.03 g/mL
Corn syrup: 1.33 g/mL   Vegetable oil: 0.91 g/mL

2 Calculate What is the density of a liquid with a mass of 17.4 g and a volume of 20 mL? Where would this liquid be in the column?

_____

_____

3 CHALLENGE In which layer(s) would a solid cube with 6-cm sides and a mass of 270 g float? Explain.

_____

6.NS.3, 6.NS.8

Using Density

Using Density Suppose you are a gold miner in the 1800s, like the men in **Figure 4**. One day, while panning through the sediment in a stream, you come across a shiny golden rock. How do you know if the rock is real gold? Since density is a physical property of a substance, it can be used to identify an unknown substance. You can measure the mass and volume of the rock and find its density. If it matches 19.3 g/cm³, the density of gold, then you have struck it rich!

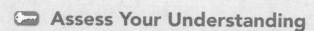

FIGURE 4 ···

> VIRTUAL LAB **Using Density**

Density can be used to identify substances.

✎ **Estimate** Hypothesize which rock sample is gold. Then, calculate the density of each sample. Circle the rock that is real gold.

My hypothesis is that the gold rock is:

○ A   ○ B   ○ C

A

Mass = 108 g
Volume = 12 cm³

Density = _____

B

Mass = 126 g
Volume = 15 cm³

Density = _____

C

Mass = 386 g
Volume = 20 cm³

Density = _____

6.NS.1, 6.NS.8

 Lab zone® Do the Lab Investigation *Making Sense of Density.*

🔑 Assess Your Understanding

2a. Identify Maple syrup will (float/sink) in water because its density is greater than 1 g/cm³. **6.NS.8**

b. ◢ **Calculate** What is the mass of a sample of a substance with a volume of 120 mL and a density of 0.75 g/mL?

_____

6.NS.3, 6.NS.8

c. |CHALLENGE| Liquid water and ice are the same substance, H_2O. How would you explain why ice floats in water?

_____

_____

6.NS.8

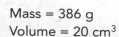

got it? ···

○ **I get it!** Now I know density is calculated by _____

_____

○ **I need extra help with** _____

Go to **MY SCIENCE** 💬 **COACH** *online for help with this subject.*

6.NS.3

Changes in Matter

UNLOCK THE BIG ?

🔑 **What Happens to a Substance in a Physical Change?**
6.1.3, 6.NS.1, 6.NS.11

🔑 **What Happens to a Substance in a Chemical Change?**
6.1.3, 6.NS.2, 6.NS.8, 6.DP.1, 6.DP.2

🔑 **How Are Changes in Energy and Matter Related?**
6.1.3, 6.1.7, 6.NS.3, 6.NS.7, 6.NS.8

MY PLANET DIARY

BLOG

Posted by: Dylan
Location: Fountain Valley, California

Whenever I go to the beach, I spend a majority of my time building a sand castle. I try to build it after a high tide comes. That way I have a lot of time to build up the walls and they will not be destroyed as quickly by the water.

Even though the waves will eventually destroy the castle and take the sand with them back to the ocean, the sand could be easily separated from the ocean. At the end of the day when I leave and kick and stomp on my sand castle, it is still sand. Only its appearance changes.

Write your answers to the questions below.

1. Describe the differences in the ways the sand castle is changed by an ocean wave and by Dylan stomping on it.

_____

_____

_____

2. Dylan changed a formless pile of sand into a sand castle. What other natural materials can be changed into art?

_____

_____

▶ PLANET DIARY Go to **Planet Diary** to learn more about changes in matter.

Lab zone ® Do the Inquiry Warm-Up
Is a New Substance Formed?

Vocabulary

- physical change • chemical change
- law of conservation of mass • temperature
- thermal energy • endothermic change
- exothermic change • chemical energy

Skills

↻ Reading: Relate Cause and Effect

△ Inquiry: Draw Conclusions

What Happens to a Substance in a Physical Change?

How can matter change? A **physical change** alters the form or appearance of matter but does not turn any substance in the matter into a different substance. In **Figure 1,** a butter artist has changed a formless block of butter into artwork. Although it looks different, the sculpture is still butter. ⟳ **A substance that undergoes a physical change is still the same substance after the change.** Many physical changes, such as snow melting into water, occur in nature.

Changes of State As you may know, matter occurs in three familiar states—solid, liquid, and gas. Suppose you leave a small puddle of liquid water on the kitchen counter. When you come back two hours later, the puddle is gone. Has the liquid water disappeared? No, a physical change happened. The liquid water changed into water vapor (a gas) and mixed with the air. A change in state, such as from a solid to a liquid or from a liquid to a gas, is an example of a physical change.

Academic Standards for Science

6.1.3 Using a model in which matter is composed of particles in motion, investigate that when substances undergo a change in state, mass is conserved.

6.NS.1 Make predictions based on prior knowledge.

6.NS.11 Communicated findings using models.

FIGURE 1 ·····················

Change of State

Changes between solids, liquids, and gases are physical changes.

✏ **Predict** Describe the changes the butter sculpture will undergo in a few hours if it is left out in the sun.

_____

_____

_____

_____

6.NS.1

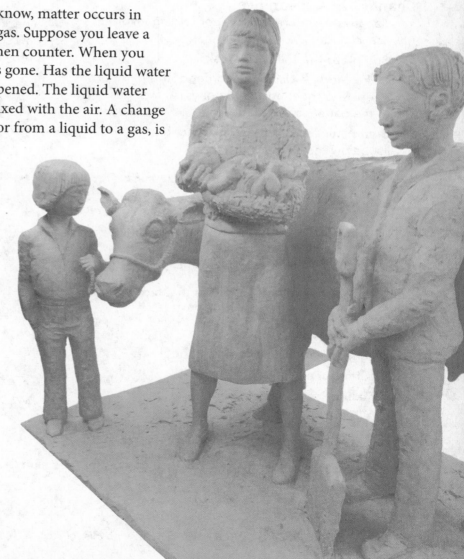

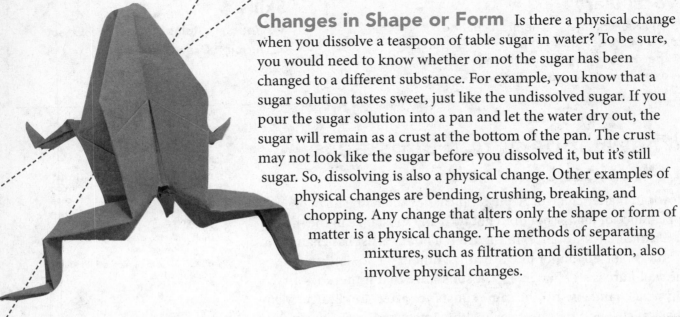

Changes in Shape or Form Is there a physical change when you dissolve a teaspoon of table sugar in water? To be sure, you would need to know whether or not the sugar has been changed to a different substance. For example, you know that a sugar solution tastes sweet, just like the undissolved sugar. If you pour the sugar solution into a pan and let the water dry out, the sugar will remain as a crust at the bottom of the pan. The crust may not look like the sugar before you dissolved it, but it's still sugar. So, dissolving is also a physical change. Other examples of physical changes are bending, crushing, breaking, and chopping. Any change that alters only the shape or form of matter is a physical change. The methods of separating mixtures, such as filtration and distillation, also involve physical changes.

FIGURE 2 ·······························

Changes in Appearance

The Japanese art of origami paper folding involves physical changes.

✏️ **Complete the following tasks.**

1. **Make Models** Using the corner of this page or a separate sheet, make two physical changes to the paper. **6.NS.11**

2. **Communicate** Ask a classmate to identify and list below the changes you made.

_____

_____

3. [CHALLENGE] Is it correct to say that dissolving a packet of juice powder in water makes a new substance, fruit punch, so it must not be a physical change?

_____

_____

_____

_____

_____

Lab zone Do the Quick Lab *What Is a Physical Change?*

🔑 Assess Your Understanding

1a. Classify Mark all the processes that are physical changes.

○ drying wet clothes
○ lighting a match from a matchbook
○ cutting snowflakes out of paper
○ melting butter for popcorn

6.1.3

b. Apply Concepts Describe three physical changes that occur in nature.

_____

_____

_____

_____

6.1.3

got it? ·······························

○ I get it! Now I know that a substance that undergoes a physical change is _____

○ I need extra help with _____

Go to **MY SCIENCE COACH** online for help with this subject. 6.1.3

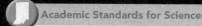

What Happens to a Substance in a Chemical Change?

Another kind of change occurs when a substance transforms into another substance. A change in matter that produces one or more new substances is a chemical change, or chemical reaction. In some chemical changes, a single substance breaks down into two or more other substances. For example, hydrogen peroxide breaks down into water and oxygen gas when it's poured on a cut on your skin. In other chemical changes, two or more substances combine to form different substances. Photosynthesis is a natural chemical change. Several compounds combine with energy from the sun to produce new substances.

Figure 3 shows chemical changes that are used in forensics to collect evidence. To make fingerprints more visible, a chemical found in super-strong glues is heated. Vapors from the glue react with sweat or other body chemicals in a fingerprint to form a white powder making the print visible. Luminol is a chemical that reacts with blood. It combines with traces of blood that are too small to see with the naked eye to form a new substance that glows in the dark. The footprint in Figure 3 has been treated with luminol. ⚡ Unlike a physical change, a chemical change produces new substances with new and different properties.

Academic Standards for Science

6.1.3 Using a model in which matter is composed of particles in motion, investigate that when substances undergo a change in state, mass is conserved.

6.NS.2 Plan and carry out investigations independently.

6.NS.8 Analyze data, and use it to identify patterns and make inferences based on these patterns.

FIGURE 3 ·······························
Chemical Changes
The prints are visible because of chemical change.

apply it!

You are a detective investigating a robbery. When you arrive at the scene, there are not many clues that you can see to help solve the crime. You're able to write down a few observations.

Solve Problems
Determine how you would use chemical changes to gather evidence at the crime scene.

An empty jewelry box is knocked over on a table.

Chemical treatment: _____
_____
_____

An open box of bandages is on the floor. Bandage wrappers are found nearby.

Chemical treatment: _____
_____
_____

Shattered glass from a window is scattered across the floor.

Chemical treatment: _____
_____
_____

6.NS.2, 6.DP.1, 6.DP.2

Copper: before

Copper: after

Examples of Chemical Change

One common chemical change is the burning of natural gas on a gas stove. Natural gas is mostly made up of the compound methane (CH_4). When it burns, methane combines with oxygen in the air and forms new substances. These new substances include carbon dioxide gas (CO_2) and water vapor (H_2O). Both of these substances can be identified by their properties, which are different from those of methane. The chemical change that occurs when fuels, such as natural gas, candle wax, or wood, burn in air is called combustion. Other processes resulting in chemical change include electrolysis, oxidation, and tarnishing. The table in **Figure 4** describes each of these types of chemical change.

FIGURE 4 ···················

Types of Chemical Change

The copper in the Statue of Liberty is exposed to oxygen in the air.

✎ **Observe** What chemical change did the Statue of Liberty likely undergo? Describe the properties before and after the chemical change.

_____

_____

_____

_____

_____

_____

Examples of Chemical Change		
Chemical Change	**Description**	**Example**
Combustion	Rapid combination of a fuel with oxygen; produces heat, light, and new substances	Gas, oil, or coal burning in a furnace
Electrolysis	Use of electricity to break a compound into elements or simpler compounds	Breaking down water into hydrogen and oxygen
Oxidation	Combination of a substance with oxygen	Rusting of an iron fence
Tarnishing	Slow combination of a bright metal with sulfur or another substance, producing a dark coating on the metal	Tarnishing of brass

Conservation of Mass Water may seem to "disappear" when it evaporates, but scientists long ago proved otherwise. In the 1770s, a French chemist, Antoine Lavoisier, measured mass both before and after a chemical change. His data showed that no mass was lost or gained during the change. The fact that matter is not created or destroyed in any chemical or physical change is called the **law of conservation of mass**. This law is also called the law of conservation of matter since mass is a measurement of matter.

Suppose you could measure all of the carbon dioxide and water produced when methane burns. You would find that it equals the mass of the original methane plus the mass of the oxygen from the air that was used in the burning. **Figure 5** demonstrates that during a chemical change, atoms are not lost or gained, only rearranged.

FIGURE 5 ·······························

> INTERACTIVE ART

Conservation of Mass

✏ **Interpret Diagrams** Count the atoms of each element before and after the chemical change. Is mass conserved in this reaction? Explain.

_____

_____

_____

_____

6.NS.8

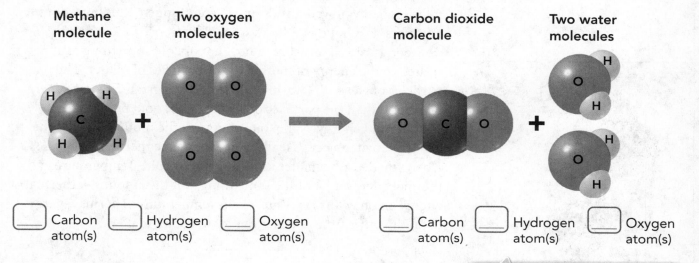

Methane molecule

Two oxygen molecules

Carbon dioxide molecule

Two water molecules

☐ Carbon atom(s) ☐ Hydrogen atom(s) ☐ Oxygen atom(s)   ☐ Carbon atom(s) ☐ Hydrogen atom(s) ☐ Oxygen atom(s)

Lab zone   Do the Quick Lab *Demonstrating Tarnishing.*

🔑 Assess Your Understanding

2a. Name A chemical reaction is another name for a chemical (combustion/change).   6.1.3

b. Predict What kind of chemical change do you think occurs when a banana peel turns brown in the open air? Explain.

_____

_____

6.1.3, 6.NS.1

c. CHALLENGE Assuming no mass escapes, explain why the mass of a rusted nail is greater than the mass of a nail before it rusted.

_____

_____

_____

6.1.3

got it? ···

○ **I get it!** Now I know that when a substance undergoes a chemical change, _____

_____

○ **I need extra help with** _____

   Go to MY SCIENCE Ⓢ COACH *online for help with this subject.*   6.1.3

109

Academic Standards for Science

6.1.3 Using a model in which matter is composed of particles in motion, investigate that when substances undergo a change in state, mass is conserved.

6.1.7 Explain that energy may be manifested as heat, light, electricity, mechanical motion, sound and is often associated with chemical reactions.

6.NS.3 Collect quantitative data and use appropriate units to label numerical data.

6.NS.7 Keep accurate records in a notebook.

6.NS.8 Analyze data, identify patterns and make inferences based on these patterns.

How Are Changes in Energy and Matter Related?

Do you feel as if you are full of energy today? Energy is the ability to do work or cause change. **Every chemical and physical change in matter includes a change in energy.** A change as simple as bending a paper clip takes energy. When ice changes to liquid water, it absorbs energy from the surrounding matter. When candle wax burns, it gives off energy as light and heat.

Like matter, energy is conserved in a chemical change. Energy is never created or destroyed. It can only be transformed from one form to another.

Temperature and Thermal Energy Think of how it feels when you walk inside an air-conditioned building from the outdoors on a hot day. Whew, what a difference in temperature! **Temperature** is a measure of how hot or cold something is. It is related to the energy of motion of the particles of matter. The particles of gas in the warm outside air have greater average energy of motion than the particles of air inside the cool building.

Thermal energy is the total energy of the motion of all of the particles in an object. Usually, you experience thermal energy when you describe matter as feeling hot or cold. Temperature and thermal energy are not the same thing, but the amount of thermal energy an object has is related to its temperature. Thermal energy naturally flows from warmer matter to cooler matter.

FIGURE 6 ·······

Thermal Energy

✎ **Apply Concepts** Shade in the arrow that indicates which direction energy will flow between the people and the icy water or warm mud pit.

Energy

Energy

Energy

Energy

Thermal Energy and Changes in Matter

Thermal energy is a form of energy that is often released or absorbed when matter changes. For example, ice absorbs thermal energy from its surroundings when it melts, leaving the surroundings feeling cold. That's why you can pack food and drinks in an ice-filled picnic cooler. The melting of ice is an **endothermic change,** a change in which energy is absorbed. Changes in matter can also occur when energy is given off. An **exothermic change** releases energy. Combustion is a chemical change that releases thermal energy and light.

Transforming Chemical Energy The energy stored in the chemical bonds between atoms is a form of energy called **chemical energy.** Chemical energy is stored in foods, fuels, and even the cells of your body. Animals, like the bear in **Figure 7,** gain chemical energy from food.

Burning fuels transforms chemical energy and releases some of it as thermal energy. When you ride a bike up a hill, chemical energy from foods you ate changes into energy of motion. Chemical energy can change into other forms of energy, and other forms of energy can change into chemical energy.

FIGURE 7 ....

Transforming Chemical Energy
Chemical energy from food can be transformed into other types of energy needed for activity.

> ✏️
> **⤺ Relate Cause and Effect**
> Underline the sentence that describes how your hand would be affected if you made a snowball or held a frozen treat.

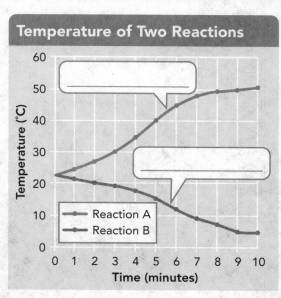

do the math! Analyzing Data

A student records the temperature of two reactions once per minute. Her data are plotted on the graph.

❶ Calculate What was the change in temperature for each reaction after 10 minutes?

_____

_____

❷ ◢ Draw Conclusions On the graph, label each reaction as exothermic or endothermic. How can you tell?

_____

_____

_____

_____

6.NS.3, 6.NS.8

Temperature of Two Reactions

Reaction A
Reaction B

(y-axis: Temperature (°C), 0 to 60; x-axis: Time (minutes), 0 to 10)

INDIANA JANE AND THE INVESTIGATION OF MATTER

How is matter described?

FIGURE 8 ....

> **INTERACTIVE ART** Indiana Jane is hunting for lost treasures of matter. Join her in following clues to describe different types of matter.

✎ **Review** Answer questions about Indiana's findings along the way. Then, complete the logbook with information you've gathered about the properties of matter.

Arrowhead This arrowhead, most likely carved by an ancient hunter, was discovered in a pile of rocks. **Describe the type of mixture the arrowhead was found in.**

_____

_____

_____

_____

Yellowed, torn map
Field notes: The paper of this ancient map has suffered from changes over the years making it nearly impossible to read.—IJ

Tarnished coins I found these coins near the opening of a foul-smelling cave. I believe they were a shiny metal at one point, perhaps silver, platinum, or aluminum. I've determined the mass of each coin to be 315 g and the volume to be 30 cm³.
What element are the coins made of?

○ Aluminum (density = 2.7 g/cm³)
○ Silver (density = 10.5 g/cm³)
○ Platinum (density = 21.5 g/cm³)

6.NS.3, 6.NS.8

Mummy The mummy we found today is badly decayed, probably because its sarcophagus is not sealed airtight. I translated a scroll found nearby that says the mummy and case originally had a mass of 200 kg. The mass is now 170 kg. **Explain how the mummy and its sarcophagus decreased in mass if the law of conservation of mass must be obeyed.**

_____

_____

_____

_____

_____

_____

_____

_____

Indiana Jane has to bring all the artifacts back to the museum. Describe each object's properties and the physical or chemical changes it underwent.

Object	Properties	Changes Undergone
1. Clay pot		
2. Coins		
3. Map		

6.NS.7

Broken clay pot Field notes: I've come across some clay pots. Many have been broken or cracked over time.—IJ

Wax statue I believe we have found the remains of the famous Carved Dove wax statue. It would have been a valuable artifact, but all that's left is a puddle of liquid.
Describe at least two changes the wax has undergone over time.

_____

_____

_____

Do the Quick Lab
Where Was the Energy?

🔑 Assess Your Understanding

3a. Identify What energy transformation takes place when you exercise?

_____

_____

6.1.7

b. ANSWER THE BIG ? How is matter described?

_____

_____

_____

_____

_____

_____

_____

_____

6.1.3, 6.1.7

got it? ....

○ **I get it!** Now I know that every chemical and physical change includes _____

_____

○ **I need extra help with** _____

_____

Go to **MY SCIENCE** 🅢 **COACH** *online for help with this subject.*   6.1.7

113

REVIEW THE BIG ?

Water is a _____ . A _____ property of water is that it boils at
100°C. The _____ of water is 1 g/cm^3.

LESSON 1 **Describing Matter**

6.1.1

🔑 Every form of matter has two kinds
of properties—physical properties and
chemical properties.

Vocabulary
• matter
• chemistry
• substance
• physical property
• chemical property

LESSON 2 **Classifying Matter**

6.1, 6.1.1, 6.NS.3

🔑 Scientists know that all matter in the universe
is made of more than 100 different substances,
called elements.

🔑 A mixture can be
heterogeneous or
homogeneous.

Vocabulary
• element • atom
• chemical bond • molecule • compound
• chemical formula • mixture

LESSON 3 **Measuring Matter**

6.NS.1, 6.NS.3, 6.NS.8

🔑 The SI unit of mass is
the kilogram (kg).

🔑 The SI unit of volume is the cubic
meter (m^3).

🔑 You can determine the density
of a sample of matter by dividing its
mass by its volume.

Vocabulary
• weight • mass • International System of Units
• volume • density

LESSON 4 **Changes in Matter**

6.1.3, 6.1.7, 6.NS.1, 6.NS.2, 6.NS.3, 6.NS.7, 6.NS.8, 6.NS.11, 6.DP.1, 6.DP.2

🔑 A substance that undergoes a physical change is still
the same substance after the change.

🔑 Unlike a physical change, a chemical change produces
new substances with new and different properties.

🔑 Every chemical and physical change in matter includes
a change in energy.

Vocabulary
• physical change • chemical change • law of conservation of mass
• temperature • thermal energy • endothermic change
• exothermic change • chemical energy

Review and Assessment

LESSON 1 Describing Matter

1. Which of the following is an example of a chemical property?

a. density
b. flammability
c. hardness
d. luster

6.1.1

2. A substance can be classified by its physical properties, which are properties that

_____

_____

_____

_____

6.1.1

3. Classify Which of the following is a substance: table salt, seawater, or sand? Explain how you know.

_____

_____

_____

_____

_____

6.1.1

4. Interpret Tables Write a title that describes the table below.

Helium	Colorless; less dense than air
Iron	Attracted to magnets; melting point of 1,535°C
Oxygen	Odorless; gas at room temperature

6.1.1

5. Write About It Write an e-mail to a friend explaining why the melting point of a substance is a physical property but flammability is a chemical property. Use examples to explain.

6.1.1, 6.NS.11

LESSON 2 Classifying Matter

6. Which of the following is an element?

a. water
b. carbon dioxide
c. oxygen
d. ammonia

6.1

7. Four methods that can be used to separate mixtures are _____

_____

6.1

Use the diagrams to answer Questions 8–10. Each diagram represents a different kind of matter. Each ball represents an atom. Balls of the same color are the same kind of atom.

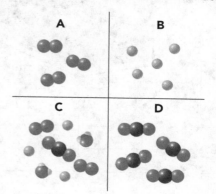

8. Interpret Diagrams Which diagram or diagrams represent a single element? Explain.

_____

_____

6.1, 6.1.1, 6.NS.8

9. Compare and Contrast How do the atoms in Diagram A differ from those in Diagram D?

_____

_____

_____

6.1, 6.1.1, 6.NS.8

10. Apply Concepts Which diagram or diagrams represent a mixture? Explain.

_____

_____

_____

6.1, 6.1.1, 6.NS.8

115

Measuring Matter

11. What is the SI unit of mass?

a. milliliter   b. kilogram

c. pound   d. cubic centimeter

6.NS.3

12. The density of a substance is calculated by

_____

_____

6.NS.8

13. Make Judgments Which measurement shown in the diagram is not needed to find the volume of the box? Explain.

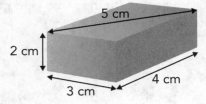

_____

_____

_____

_____

6.NS.3, 6.NS.8

14. math! A piece of metal has a volume of 38 cm³ and a mass of 277 g. Calculate the density of the metal and identify it based on the information in the table below.

Density of Common Metals	
Iron	7.9 g/cm³
Lead	11.3 g/cm³
Tin	7.3 g/cm³
Zinc	7.1 g/cm³

6.NS.8

Changes in Matter

15. Which of the following is a physical change?

a. burning   b. rusting

c. freezing   d. oxidation

6.1.7

16. The law of conservation of mass states that

_____

_____

_____

6.1.3

17. Solve Problems How could you prove that dissolving table salt in water is a physical change, not a chemical change?

_____

_____

_____

_____

_____

6.1.7

How is matter described?

18. Choose a substance you're familiar with. What are its physical and chemical properties? How would you measure its density? What are some physical and chemical changes it can undergo?

_____

_____

_____

_____

_____

_____

_____

_____

_____

6.1.3, 6.1.7

Indiana ISTEP+ Practice

Multiple Choice

Circle the letter of the best answer.

1. Each diagram below represents a different kind of matter. Each ball represents an atom. Balls of the same size and shade are the same atom.

   Which diagram *best* represents a mixture of two kinds of molecules?

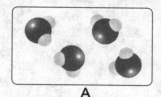
A

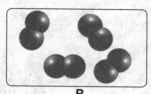
B

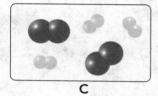
C

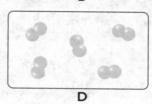
D

   A. Diagram A   **B.** Diagram B
   C. Diagram C   **D.** Diagram D

   6.1.1

2. The fact that matter is neither created nor destroyed in any chemical or physical change is called the

   A. law of exothermic change.
   B. law of endothermic change.
   C. law of thermal matter.
   D. law of conservation of mass.

   6.1.3

3. The density of a substance equals its mass divided by its volume. The density of sulfur is 2.0 g/cm³. What is the mass of a sample of sulfur with a volume of 6.0 cm³?

   A. 3.0 g   **B.** 4.0 g
   C. 8.0 g   **D.** 12 g

   6.NS.8

4. The abilities to dissolve in water and to conduct electric current are examples of

   A. physical properties.
   B. chemical properties.
   C. physical changes.
   D. chemical bonding.

   6.1.7

Constructed Response

Write your answer to Question 5 on the lines below.

5. Which two pieces of laboratory equipment would be the *most* useful for measuring the mass and volume of a rectangular block?

   _____

   _____

   _____

   6.NS.3

Extended Response

Use the graph below and your knowledge of science to help you answer Question 6. Write your answer on a separate sheet of paper.

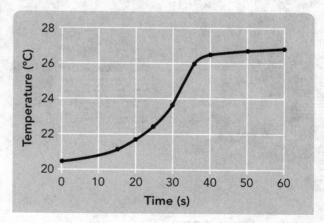

6. A student mixes two liquids of the same temperature together. The graph above shows the change in temperature after the liquids mix. Did the reaction absorb thermal energy or release it? Explain your answer.   6.1.7, 6.NS.8, 6.NS.11

TECH & DESIGN

Museum of Science

TENSION IN ALL THE
RIGHT
PLACES

Design It Use straws, rubber bands, and paper clips to build a tensegrity structure that can support weights. Working with a partner: brainstorm designs; document ideas with labeled sketches; select your best idea; and build a prototype. Test your prototype and identify any problems. Then redesign your prototype to improve your results. See Appendix A on page 350 for more information about the design process.

6.NS.1–6.NS.8, 6.NS.11, 6.DP.1–6.DP.8, 6.DP.11

Rock stars and football players play to huge crowds at the world-famous Georgia Dome. But what really makes the Georgia Dome legendary is that it's the largest cable-supported domed stadium in the world! A cool engineering idea called tensegrity gave engineers the inspiration for its famous domed roof.

A tensegrity structure spreads out tension and compression along all of its parts. In the Georgia Dome, three oval hoops sit high above the ground, held in place by vertical steel posts and a horizontal system of steel cable triangles. The steel posts push down on the corners of the cable triangles while the triangles pull on the posts. This constant compression and tension keeps the strong, lightweight fiberglass roof up. You can compare it to a giant, very stable umbrella!

Tensegrity structures use little material to cover a lot of space, so they can be very cost-effective. They are also incredibly strong and flexible. Rain or shine, the Georgia Dome's roof will be around for a long time, thanks to its inventive structure.

Museum of Science

An Antiuniverse?

What if the entire universe had a mirror or negative image? Would everything happen backward? Or, would there be an opposite you? Scientists working in the field of particle physics think there just might be a mirror universe, but they don't really expect it to be the stuff of science fiction movies.

A little over a hundred years ago, scientists thought that the smallest part of matter—a part not made up of anything else—was the atom. That wasn't true. An atom is made up of a nucleus that contains protons and neutrons, surrounded by electrons. A physicist named Paul Dirac added an interesting twist to this knowledge. He correctly predicted that the electron might have a reverse twin, which he called a positron. (He won the Nobel Prize for this leap of genius back in 1933.) The positron has the same mass as an electron but the opposite charge—it's the antielectron.

Electrons, neutrons, and protons all have these antiparticles, or at least they did when the particles formed. Scientists have been able to study them in the laboratory. Inside particle accelerators, scientists can even use positrons and electrons to form entirely new atoms. But outside of the controlled laboratory environment, where are these antiparticles? Are they now part of an antiuniverse somewhere? Physicists are hoping to find the answers in the twenty-first century— your century!

Research It Write down three questions you have about particle physics and antimatter. Research to find out the answers. Articles about the CERN laboratory in Switzerland would be a good place to start. Answer your questions in one or two paragraphs.

Paul Dirac predicted that positrons might exist as the opposites of electrons. ▼

◄ Inside a special chamber, two invisible photons enter and produce a pair of electrons (colored green) and antielectrons (colored red).

Hot Science

An Antiuniverse?

6.1.3, 6.NS.1, 6.NS.2

HOW DID THIS BUILDING TURN TO ICE?

Why does a substance change states?

Firefighters sprayed water on a blaze in this historic building in Maine. The air temperature was −14°F, which was uncomfortably cold. This made it difficult for firefighters to battle the flames. The building was in danger of falling down because it was covered in ice 6 to 10 inches thick. **Infer How did this building get covered in ice?**

_____

_____

_____

_____

_____

> UNTAMED SCIENCE Watch the **Untamed Science** video to learn more about changing states.

Solids, Liquids, and Gases

Academic Standards for Science

6.1.2, 6.1.3, 6.NS.1, 6.NS.3, 6.NS.8, 6.NS.11, 6.DP.9, 6.DP.10

4 | Getting Started

Check Your Understanding

1. **Background** Read the paragraph below and then answer the question.

The air **temperature** outside has been below freezing all week. The local pond has frozen over and is ready for ice skating. Ronnesia is excited just thinking about all the things she can do on the **ice.** She eats a good breakfast to get the **energy** she needs for ice skating.

Temperature is a measure of the average energy of random motion of particles of matter.

Ice is water in the solid form.

Energy is the ability to do work or cause change.

• Why is the pond ready for ice skating?

_____

_____

> MY READING WEB If you had trouble completing the question above, visit **My Reading Web** and type in **Solids, Liquids, and Gases.**

Vocabulary Skill

Suffixes A suffix is a letter or group of letters added to the end of a word to change its meaning and often its part of speech. In this chapter, you will learn vocabulary words that end in the suffixes *-ation, -ine,* and *-sion.*

Suffix	Meaning	Example
-ation	State of, process of, act of	Vaporization, evaporation, condensation, sublimation
-ine	Consisting of	Crystalline solid
-sion	State of, process of, act of	Surface tension

2. **Quick Check** *Vapor* is another word for gas. Use the table above to predict the meaning of *vaporization.* Revise your definition as needed.

_____

_____

liquid

surface tension

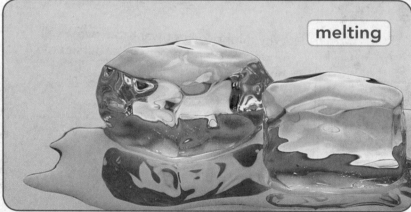

melting

sublimation

Chapter Preview

LESSON 1
- solid
- crystalline solid
- amorphous solid
- liquid
- fluid
- surface tension
- viscosity
- gas
- pressure

 Relate Cause and Effect

▲ Infer

LESSON 2
- melting
- melting point
- freezing
- vaporization
- evaporation
- boiling
- boiling point
- condensation
- sublimation

Compare and Contrast

▲ Predict

LESSON 3
- Charles's Law
- directly proportional
- Boyle's Law
- inversely proportional

Identify the Main Idea

▲ Graph

▷ VOCAB FLASH CARDS For extra help with vocabulary, visit **Vocab Flash Cards** and type in *Solids, Liquids, and Gases.*

Indiana

LESSON

1 States of Matter

UNLOCK THE BIG ?

🔑 **How Do You Describe a Solid?**
6.1.2, 6.NS.11

🔑 **How Do You Describe a Liquid?**
6.1.2

🔑 **How Do You Describe a Gas?**
6.1.2, 6.NS.3, 6.NS.8

MY PLANET DiaRY

Liquid Crystals

Have you ever wondered why some television sets are referred to as LCD TVs? *LCD* stands for "liquid crystal display." An LCD is a thin, flat screen. LCDs have replaced the picture tubes in many computer monitors and television sets because they are lighter and use less power. LCDs are also found in cell phones and clock radio faces.

Liquid crystals are neither solid nor liquid—instead they fall somewhere in between. But it takes just a small amount of thermal energy to change a liquid crystal to a liquid. As a result, LCDs tend to be very sensitive to heat.

FUN FACTS

Communicate Discuss these questions with a classmate. Write your answers below.

1. List some things that contain LCDs.

_____

_____

2. Why might you not want to leave a cell phone or a laptop computer outside on a hot day?

_____

_____

_____

_____

▶ PLANET DIARY Go to **Planet Diary** to learn more about solids, liquids, and gases.

 Lab zone® Do the Inquiry Warm-Up *What Are Solids, Liquids, and Gases?*

LCD display with crystals cooling (background)

Vocabulary

- solid • crystalline solid • amorphous solid • liquid
- fluid • surface tension • viscosity • gas • pressure

Skills

- Reading: Relate Cause and Effect
- Inquiry: Infer

How Do You Describe a Solid?

Look at the bowl in **Figure 1.** It contains the metal bismuth.
Notice that the shape and size of the piece of bismuth are different
from the bowl's shape and size. What would happen if you took the
bismuth out of the bowl and placed it on a tabletop? Would
it become flatter? What would happen if you put it in a larger
bowl? Would it become larger? Of course not, because it's a solid.
A **solid** has a definite shape and a definite volume. Your pencil is
another example of a solid. If your pencil has a cylindrical shape
and a volume of 6 cubic centimeters, it will keep this shape and
volume in any position in any container.

Particles in a Solid The particles that make
up a solid are packed very closely together. Also, each
particle is tightly fixed in one position. 🗝 **This
fixed, closely packed arrangement of particles in a
solid causes it to have a definite shape and volume.**
Do the particles that make up a solid move at all?
Yes, but not much. The particles in a solid are closely
locked in position and can only vibrate in place. This
means that the particles move back and forth slightly,
like a group of people running in place.

Place a check in each category that describes a solid.	Definite	Indefinite
Shape	_____	_____
Volume	_____	_____

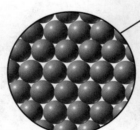

Particles in
a solid

> **Academic Standards for Science**
>
> **6.1.2** Explain the properties of solids,
> liquids and gases using drawings and
> models that represent matter as par-
> ticles in motion whose state can be
> represented by the relative positions
> and movement of the particles.
> **6.NS.11** Communicate findings using
> graphs, charts, and models.

FIGURE 1 ···

Solid

A solid does not take the shape or volume of its container.
✎ **Interpret Diagrams** Describe the arrangement of
particles in a solid.

_____

_____

_____

FIGURE 2 ·····························
Types of Solids

Solids are either crystalline or amorphous. Butter is an amorphous solid. The mineral fluorite is a crystalline solid.

✏️ **Compare and Contrast** Use the Venn diagram to compare the characteristics of amorphous and crystalline solids.

6.NS.11

Types of Solids In many solids, the particles form a regular, repeating pattern. These patterns create crystals. Solids that are made up of crystals are called **crystalline solids** (KRIS tuh lin). Salt, sugar, and snow are examples of crystalline solids. The fluorite crystal shown in **Figure 2** is an example of a colorful crystalline solid. When a crystalline solid is heated, it melts at a distinct temperature.

In **amorphous solids** (uh MAWR fus), the particles are not arranged in a regular pattern. Unlike a crystalline solid, an amorphous solid does not melt at a distinct temperature. Instead, it may become softer and softer or change into other substances. Glass is an example of an amorphous solid. A glass blower can bend and shape glass that has been heated. Plastics and rubber are other examples of amorphous solids.

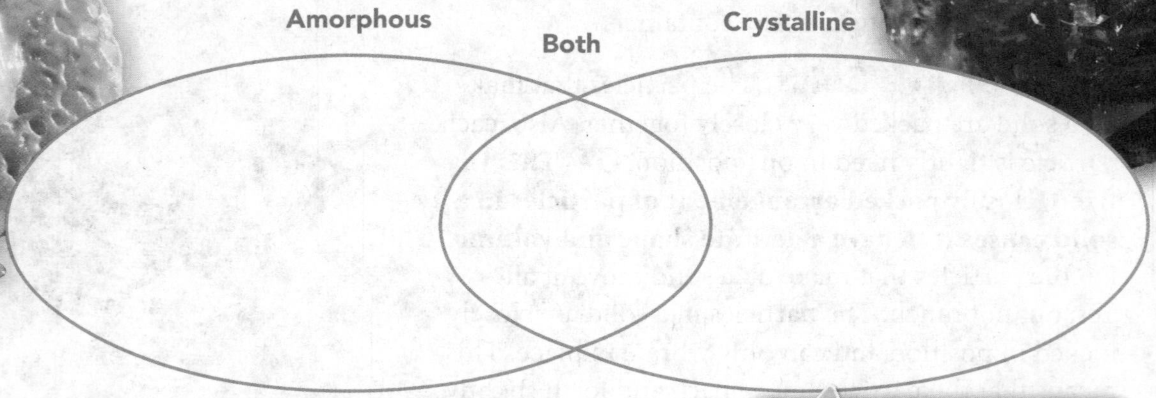

Amorphous   Both   Crystalline

Lab zone® Do the Quick Lab *Modeling Particles.*

🔑 Assess Your Understanding

1a. Identify The two types of solids are

_____ and _____.

6.1.2

b. Explain Are the particles in a solid motionless? Explain your answer.

_____

_____

6.1.2

c. Draw Conclusions Candle wax gradually loses its shape as it is heated. What type of solid is candle wax? Explain.

_____

_____

_____

_____

_____

6.1.2

got it? ···

○ I get it! Now I know that a solid has a definite shape and volume because _____

_____

○ I need extra help with _____

Go to MY SCIENCE 🗨️ COACH *online for help with this subject.*   6.1.2

How Do You Describe a Liquid?

Without a container, a liquid spreads into a wide, shallow puddle. Like a solid, however, a liquid does have a constant volume. A **liquid** has a definite volume but no shape of its own. **Figure 3** shows equal volumes of iced tea in two different containers. The shape of a liquid may change with its container, but its volume remains the same.

Particles in a Liquid In general, the particles in a liquid are packed almost as closely together as those in a solid. However, the particles in a liquid move around one another freely. You can compare this movement to the way you might move a group of marbles around in your hand. Like the particles of a liquid, the marbles slide around one another but still touch. **Because its particles are free to move, a liquid has no definite shape. However, it does have a definite volume.** These freely moving particles allow a liquid to flow from place to place. For this reason, a liquid is also called a **fluid,** meaning a "substance that flows."

 Academic Standards for Science

6.1.2 Explain the properties of solids, liquids and gases using drawings and models that represent matter as particles in motion whose state can be represented by the relative positions and movement of the particles.

🔄 **Relate Cause and Effect**
Underline the cause and circle the effect in the boldface sentences.

Place a check in each category that describes a liquid.

	Definite	Indefinite
Shape	____	____
Volume	____	____

FIGURE 3 ·······
Liquid
Each container contains 300 cm³ of iced tea. The iced tea takes the shape of its container, but its volume does not change.
✏️ **Interpret Diagrams** Describe the arrangement of particles in a liquid.

_____
_____
_____
_____

Particles in a liquid

Properties of Liquids

One characteristic property of liquids is surface tension. **Surface tension** is an inward force, or pull, among the molecules in a liquid that brings the molecules on the surface closer together. You may have noticed that water forms droplets and can bead up on many surfaces, such as the leaves shown in **Figure 4.** That's because water molecules attract one another strongly. These attractions cause molecules at the water's surface to be pulled slightly toward the water molecules beneath its surface. Due to surface tension, the surface of water can act like a sort of skin. For example, a sewing needle floats when you place it gently on the surface of water, but it quickly sinks if you push it below the surface. Surface tension lets an insect called a water strider walk on the calm surface of a pond.

Another characteristic property of liquids is **viscosity** (vis KAHS uh tee), or a liquid's resistance to flowing. A liquid's viscosity depends on the size and shape of its particles and the attractions between the particles. Some liquids flow more easily than others. Liquids with high viscosity flow slowly. Honey is an example of a liquid with a very high viscosity. Liquids with low viscosity flow quickly. Water and vinegar have relatively low viscosities.

FIGURE 4 ·······················

Surface Tension

Infer Circle the correct answer.
Water beads up on the surface of the leaves because water molecules (attract/repel) each other strongly.

Lab® zone   Do the Quick Lab *As Thick as Honey.*

🔑 Assess Your Understanding

2a. Name A substance that flows is called a

_____
6.1.2

b. Describe Why is a liquid able to flow?

_____
_____
6.1.2

c. Compare and Contrast How do liquids with a high viscosity differ from liquids with a low viscosity?

_____
_____
_____
6.1.2

got it? ···

○ **I get it!** Now I know that a liquid has a definite volume but not a definite shape because _____
_____

○ I need extra help with _____

Go to MY SCIENCE 🔵ˢ COACH *online for help with this subject.*   6.1.2

How Do You Describe a Gas?

Like a liquid, a gas is a fluid. Unlike a liquid, however, a **gas** has neither a definite shape nor a definite volume. If a gas is in a closed container such as the flask in **Figure 5,** the gas particles will move and spread apart as they fill the container.

If you could see the particles that make up a gas, you would see them moving in all directions. 🔑 **As gas particles move, they spread apart, filling all the space available. Thus, a gas has neither definite shape nor definite volume.** When working with a gas, it is important to know its volume, temperature, and pressure. So what exactly do these measurements mean?

Volume Remember that volume is the amount of space that matter fills. Volume is measured in cubic centimeters (cm^3), cubic meters (m^3), milliliters (mL), liters (L), and other units. Because gas particles move and fill all of the space available, the volume of a gas is the same as the volume of its container. For example, a large amount of helium gas can be compressed—or pressed together tightly—to fit into a metal tank. When you use the helium to fill balloons, it expands to fill many balloons that have a total volume much greater than the volume of the tank.

Academic Standards for Science

6.1.2 Explain the properties of solids, liquids and gases using drawings and models that represent matter as particles in motion whose state can be represented by the relative positions and movement of the particles.

6.NS.3 Collect quantitative data with appropriate tools or technologies and use appropriate units to label numerical data.

6.NS.8 Analyze data.

Place a check in each category that describes a gas.		
	Definite	**Indefinite**
Shape	_____	_____
Volume	_____	_____

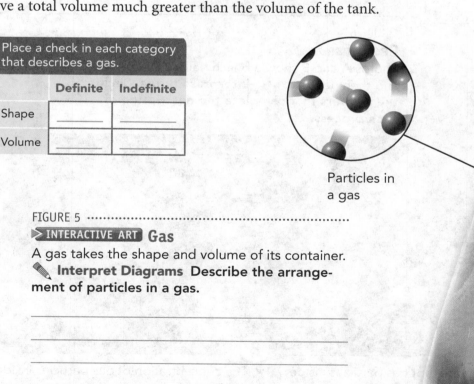

Particles in a gas

FIGURE 5 ···

▶ INTERACTIVE ART **Gas**

A gas takes the shape and volume of its container.
✎ **Interpret Diagrams** Describe the arrangement of particles in a gas.

_____

_____

_____

_____

_____

do the math!

Calculating Pressure

When calculating pressure, force is measured in newtons (N). If the area is measured in square meters (m²), pressure is expressed in pascals (Pa), where 1 Pa = 1 N/m². Suppose a gas exerts a force of 252 N on a piston having an area of 0.430 m². What is the pressure on the piston in Pascals?

$$\text{Pressure} = \frac{\text{Force}}{\text{Area}}$$

$$= \frac{252 \text{ N}}{0.430 \text{ m}^2}$$

$$= 586 \text{ Pa}$$

Practice Problem A gas exerts a force of 5,610 N over an area of 0.342 m². What pressure does the gas exert in Pa?

_____

_____

6.NS.3, 6.NS.8

Pressure Gas particles constantly collide with one another and with the walls of their container. As a result, the gas pushes on the walls of the container. The **pressure** of the gas is the force of its outward push divided by the area of the walls of the container. Pressure is measured in units of pascals (Pa) or kilopascals (kPa) (1 kPa = 1,000 Pa).

$$\text{Pressure} = \frac{\text{Force}}{\text{Area}}$$

The firmness of a gas-filled object comes from the pressure of the gas. For example, the air inside an inflated ball has a higher pressure than the air outside. This higher pressure is due to the greater concentration of gas particles inside the ball than in the surrounding air. Concentration is the number of gas particles in a given unit of volume.

Why does a ball leak even when it has only a tiny hole? The higher pressure inside the ball results in gas particles hitting the inner surface of the ball more often. Therefore, gas particles inside the ball reach the hole and escape more often than gas particles outside the ball reach the hole and enter. Thus, many more particles go out than in. The pressure inside drops until it is equal to the pressure outside.

FIGURE 6 ···

Gas Pressure

Photos A and B show a beach ball being inflated and then deflated. ✎ **Interpret Photos** Circle the answers that complete the description of each process.

A

The concentration of gas particles inside the beach ball (increases/decreases). The gas pressure inside the beach ball (increases/decreases).

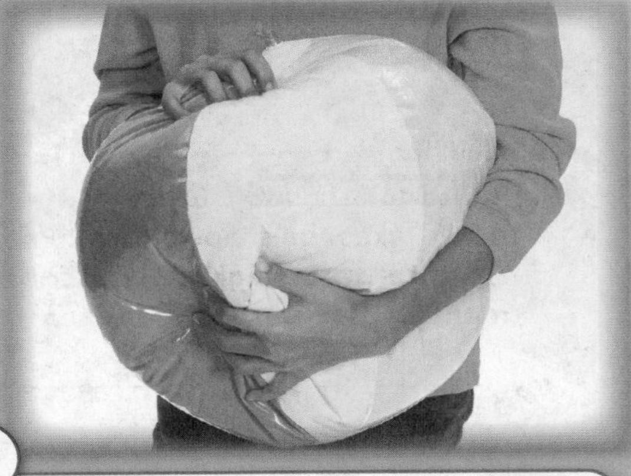

B

The concentration of gas particles inside the beach ball (increases/decreases). The gas pressure inside the beach ball (increases/decreases).

Faster-moving, hot gas particles

Slower-moving, cool gas particles

Temperature

The balloonists in **Figure 7** are preparing the balloon for flight. To do this, they use a propane burner to heat the air inside the balloon. Once the temperature of the air is hot enough, the balloon will start to rise. But what does the temperature tell you? Recall that all particles of matter are constantly moving. Temperature is a measure of the average energy of random motion of the particles of matter. The faster the particles are moving, the greater their energy and the higher the temperature. You might think of a thermometer as a speedometer for particles.

Even at room temperature, the average speed of particles in a gas is very fast. At about 20°C, the particles in a typical gas travel about 500 meters per second—more than twice the cruising speed of a jet plane!

FIGURE 7 ·····································

Temperature of a Gas

✎ **Explain** Why are the hot gas particles moving faster than the cool gas particles?

_____

_____

_____

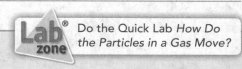 Do the Quick Lab *How Do the Particles in a Gas Move?*

🔑 Assess Your Understanding

3a. Describe Describe how the motions of gas particles are related to the pressure exerted by the gas.

_____

_____

_____

_____

_____

6.1.2

b. Relate Cause and Effect Why does pumping more air into a basketball increase the pressure inside the ball?

_____

_____

_____

_____

_____

6.1.2

got it? ···································

○ **I get it!** Now I know that a gas has neither a definite shape nor definite volume because_____

_____

○ **I need extra help with** _____

Go to MY SCIENCE ⓢ COACH *online for help with this subject*

6.1.2

Changes of State

🔑 **What Happens to the Particles of a Solid as It Melts?**
6.1.3, 6.NS.8

🔑 **What Happens to the Particles of a Liquid as It Vaporizes?**
6.1.3, 6.NS.1

🔑 **What Happens to the Particles of a Solid as It Sublimes?**
6.1.3

MY PLANET DIARY

On the Boil

You might have noticed that as an uncovered pot of water boils, the water level slowly decreases. The water level changes because the liquid is changing to a gas. As you heat the water, the thermal energy of its molecules increases. The longer you leave the pot on the hot stove, the more energy is absorbed by the water molecules. When the water molecules gain enough energy, they change state from a liquid to a gas.

The graph shows the temperature of a small pot of water on a stove set to high heat. The starting temperature of the water is 20°C.

SCIENCE STATS

Liquid to a Gas

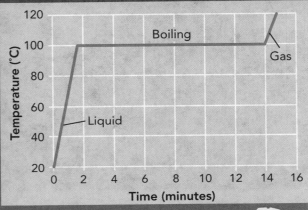

Answer the following questions.

1. How long does it take for the water to start boiling? At what temperature does the water boil?

_____

_____

_____

2. Does it take more energy to heat the water to 100°C or to boil it?

_____

_____

_____

▶ **PLANET DIARY** Go to **Planet Diary** to learn more about changes of state.

Do the Inquiry Warm-Up
What Happens When You Breathe on a Mirror?

Vocabulary

- melting • melting point • freezing • vaporization
- evaporation • boiling • boiling point • condensation
- sublimation

Skills

⟳ Reading: Compare and Contrast

△ Inquiry: Predict

What Happens to the Particles of a Solid as It Melts?

Particles of a liquid have more thermal energy than particles of the same substance in solid form. As a gas, the particles have even more thermal energy. A change from a solid to a liquid involves an increase in thermal energy. As you might guess, a change from a liquid to a solid is just the opposite: It involves a decrease in thermal energy.

Melting The change in state from a solid to a liquid is called **melting.** In pure, crystalline solids, melting occurs at a specific temperature, called the **melting point.** Because the melting point is a characteristic property of a substance, chemists often compare melting points when trying to identify an unknown material. The melting point of pure water, for example, is 0°C at sea level.

What happens to the particles of a solid as it melts? Think of an ice cube taken from the freezer. The energy needed to melt the ice comes mostly from the air in the room. At first, the added thermal energy makes the water molecules vibrate faster, raising their temperature. ⟳ **At a solid's melting point, its particles vibrate so fast that they break free from their fixed positions.** At 0°C, the temperature of the ice stops increasing. Any added energy continues to change the arrangement of the water molecules from ice crystals into liquid water. The ice melts.

> **Academic Standards for Science**
>
> **6.1.3** Using a model in which matter is composed of particles in motion, investigate that when substances undergo a change in state, mass is conserved.
>
> **6.NS.8** Analyze data, using appropriate mathematical manipulation as required, and use it to identify patterns and make inferences based on these patterns.

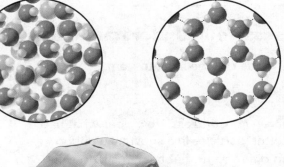

FIGURE 1 ······································

Melting

✏ **Relate Diagrams and Photos** Draw a line matching each illustration of water molecules to either ice or liquid water. Then describe how ice and liquid water differ in the arrangement of their molecules.

_____

_____

_____

_____

Freezing The change of state from a liquid to a solid is called **freezing.** It is just the reverse of melting.  **At a liquid's freezing point, its particles are moving so slowly that they begin to take on fixed positions.**

When you put liquid water into a freezer, for example, the water loses energy to the cold air in the freezer. The water molecules move more and more slowly as they lose energy. Over time, the water becomes solid ice. When water begins to freeze, its temperature stays at 0°C until freezing is complete. The freezing point of water, 0°C, is the same as its melting point.

apply it!

In metal casting, a liquid metal is poured into a container called a mold. The mold gives a shape to the metal when it cools and hardens.

1 Explain How does metal casting make use of the different characteristics of liquids and solids?

_____

_____

_____

_____

_____

_____

2 CHALLENGE The melting point of copper is 1084°C. How does the energy of the particles in a certain amount of liquid copper compare to the energy of the molecules in the same amount of liquid water? Why?

_____

_____

_____

_____

_____

_____

Lab zone Do the Lab Investigation
Melting Ice.

Assess Your Understanding

1a. Identify The change in state from a solid to a liquid is called _____
6.1.3

b. Compare and Contrast How does what happens to the particles in a substance during melting differ from what happens in freezing?

_____

_____

_____

_____

6.1.3

got it? ·····································

○ **I get it!** Now I know that melting occurs when the particles in a solid_____

_____

_____

_____

○ **I need extra help with** _____

Go to MY SCIENCE COACH *online for help with this subject.*
6.1.3

What Happens to the Particles of a Liquid as It Vaporizes?

Have you ever wondered how clouds form or why puddles dry up? To answer these questions, you need to look at what happens when changes occur between the liquid and gas states.

Evaporation and Boiling The change in state from a liquid to a gas is called **vaporization** (vay puhr ih ZAY shun). 🔑 **Vaporization occurs when the particles in a liquid gain enough energy to move independently.** There are two main types of vaporization—evaporation and boiling.

Vaporization that takes place only on the surface of a liquid is called **evaporation** (ee vap uh RAY shun). A shrinking puddle is an example. Water in the puddle gains energy from the ground, the air, or the sun. The added energy enables some of the water molecules on the surface of the puddle to escape into the air, or evaporate.

Vaporization that takes place both below and at the surface of a liquid is called **boiling.** When water boils, vaporized water molecules form bubbles below the surface. The bubbles rise and eventually break the surface of the liquid. The temperature at which a liquid boils is called its **boiling point.** As with melting points, chemists use boiling points to help identify unknown substances.

Academic Standards for Science

6.1.3 Using a model in which matter is composed of particles in motion, investigate that when substances undergo a change in state, mass is conserved.

6.NS.1 Make predictions based on prior knowledge.

🔄 **Compare and Contrast**
Compare and contrast the two types of vaporization.

_____

_____

_____

_____

_____

_____

_____

FIGURE 2

Types of Vaporization
Liquid water changes to water vapor by either evaporation or boiling.

✏️ **Interpret Diagrams** Label the type of vaporization occurring in each flask. Then draw arrows to indicate the paths of water molecules leaving each flask.

Suppose there is the same amount of water in both of the flasks. ▲ **Predict** Which flask does water vaporize from first? Why?

_____

_____

_____

_____

6.NS.1

135

Condensation Condensation is the reverse of vaporization. The change in state from a gas to a liquid is called **condensation.** You can observe condensation by breathing onto a mirror. When warm water vapor in your breath reaches the cooler surface of the mirror, the water vapor condenses into liquid droplets. 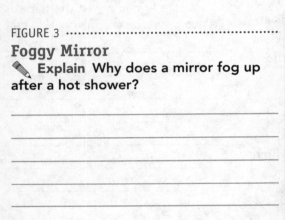 **Condensation occurs when particles in a gas lose enough thermal energy to form a liquid.**

Clouds typically form when water vapor in the atmosphere condenses into tiny liquid droplets. When the droplets get heavy enough, they fall to the ground as rain. Water vapor is a colorless gas that you cannot see. The steam you see above a kettle of boiling water is not water vapor, and neither are clouds or fog. What you see in those cases are tiny droplets of liquid water suspended in air.

Vocabulary Suffixes Complete the sentences using the correct forms of the word *condense.*

_____ is the change in state from a gas to a liquid. Clouds form because water vapor _____

FIGURE 3 ··························

Foggy Mirror
✎ **Explain** Why does a mirror fog up after a hot shower?

_____
_____
_____
_____
_____
_____

Lab® zone
Do the Quick Lab
Keeping Cool.

🔑 Assess Your Understanding

2a. Identify The change in state from a liquid to a gas is called _____
6.1.3

b. Apply Concepts How does the thermal energy of water vapor change as the vapor condenses?

_____
6.1.3

c. Relate Cause and Effect Why do clouds form before it rains?

_____
_____
_____
_____
_____
6.1.3

got it? ···············

○ **I get it!** Now I know that vaporization occurs when the particles in a liquid _____
_____

○ **I need extra help with** _____

Go to **MY SCIENCE COACH** *online for help with this subject.*
6.1.3

What Happens to the Particles of a Solid as It Sublimes?

In places where the winters are cold, the snow may disappear even when the temperature stays well below freezing. This change is the result of sublimation. **Sublimation** occurs when the surface particles of a solid gain enough energy that they form a gas. **During sublimation, particles of a solid do not pass through the liquid state as they form a gas.**

One example of sublimation occurs with dry ice. Dry ice is the common name for solid carbon dioxide. At ordinary atmospheric pressures, carbon dioxide cannot exist as a liquid. So instead of melting, solid carbon dioxide changes directly into a gas. As it sublimes, the carbon dioxide absorbs thermal energy. This property helps keep materials near dry ice cold and dry. For this reason, using dry ice is a way to keep the temperature low when a refrigerator is not available. Some fog machines use dry ice to create fog in movies or at concerts, as shown in **Figure 4.** When dry ice becomes a gas, it cools water vapor in the nearby air. The water vapor then condenses into a liquid, forming fog near the dry ice.

> **Academic Standards for Science**
>
> **6.1.3** Using a model in which matter is composed of particles in motion, investigate that when substances undergo a change in state, mass is conserved.

did you know? ....

Mosquitos are attracted to the carbon dioxide gas you exhale during breathing. A mosquito trap baited with dry ice can attract up to four or five times as many mosquitos as traps baited with a light source alone.

FIGURE 4 ....

Dry Ice

A fog machine uses dry ice to create fog at this rock concert. ✎ **Explain** Why does fog form near dry ice?

_____

_____

_____

_____

_____

Dry ice subliming

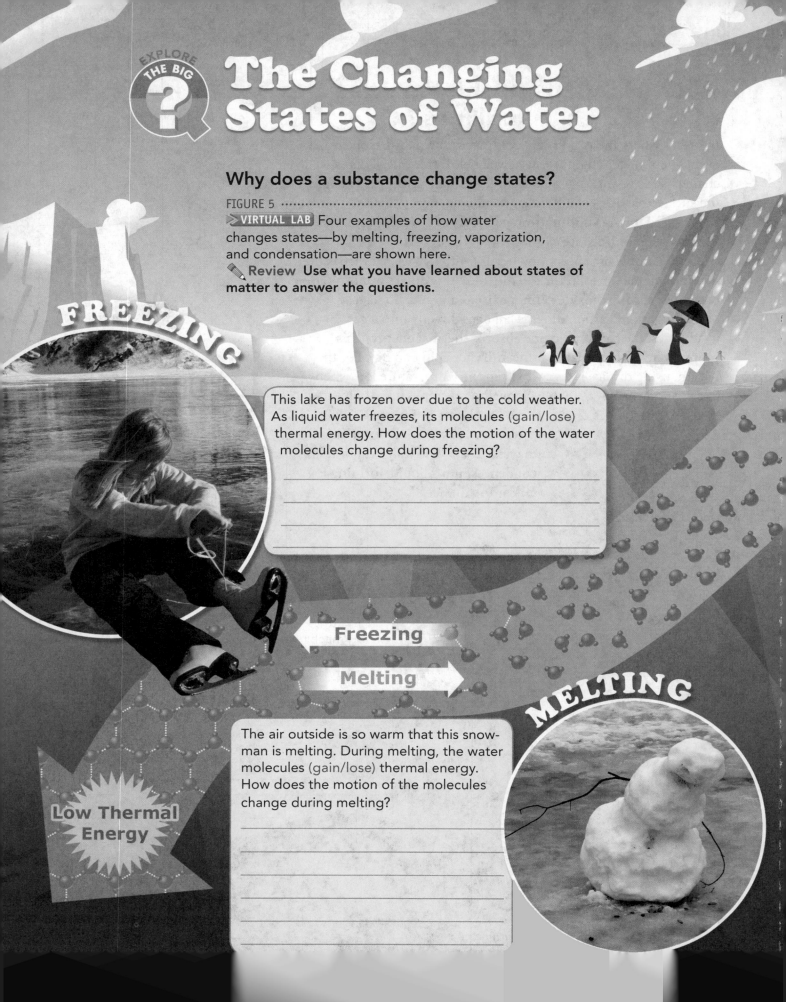

The Changing States of Water

Why does a substance change states?

FIGURE 5 ···

> VIRTUAL LAB Four examples of how water changes states—by melting, freezing, vaporization, and condensation—are shown here.

✏ Review Use what you have learned about states of matter to answer the questions.

FREEZING

This lake has frozen over due to the cold weather. As liquid water freezes, its molecules (gain/lose) thermal energy. How does the motion of the water molecules change during freezing?

_____
_____
_____

Freezing

Melting

MELTING

Low Thermal Energy

The air outside is so warm that this snowman is melting. During melting, the water molecules (gain/lose) thermal energy. How does the motion of the molecules change during melting?

_____
_____
_____
_____
_____

These wet footprints are disappearing due to evaporation. As water evaporates, its molecules (gain/lose) thermal energy. How does the motion of the molecules change during evaporation?

_____

_____

_____

_____

_____

VAPORIZATION

High Thermal Energy

← **Condensation**

Vaporization →

CONDENSATION

During the night, water vapor in the air condensed on this spider web. As water vapor condenses, its molecules (gain/lose) thermal energy. How does the motion of the molecules change during condensation?

_____

_____

_____

_____

Lab zone® Do the Quick Lab *Observing Sublimation.*

🔑 Assess Your Understanding

3a. Identify What is dry ice?

_____

_____

6.1.3

b. **Predict** If you allowed dry ice to stand in a bowl at room temperature for several hours, what would be left?

_____

_____

6.1.3, 6.NS.1

c. **ANSWER THE BIG ❓** Why does a substance change states?

_____

_____

_____

_____

_____

6.1.3

got **it**? •••••••••••••••••••••••••••••••••••••

○ **I get it!** Now I know that sublimation

occurs when the particles in a solid_____

_____

_____

○ **I need extra help with** _____

Go to MY SCIENCE ⓢ COACH *online for help with this subject.* 6.1.3

Gas Behavior

MY PLANET DIARY

BIOGRAPHY

Jacques Charles (1746–1823)

French scientist Jacques Charles is best known for his work on gases. But he also made contributions to the sport of ballooning. On August 27, 1783, Charles released the first hydrogen-filled balloon, which was about 4 meters in diameter. This balloon, which did not carry any people, rose to a height of 3,000 feet. Charles also improved the design of hot-air balloons. He added a valve line that allowed the pilot to release gas from the balloon. He also added a wicker basket that attached to the balloon with ropes. Charles was elected to the French Academy of Sciences in 1785.

Communicate Discuss this question with a classmate. Write your answer below.

What sport or hobby inspires you to want to know more about science? Why?

_____

_____

_____

_____

▶ PLANET DIARY Go to **Planet Diary** to learn more about gases.

Lab zone® Do the Inquiry Warm-Up *How Can Air Keep Chalk From Breaking?*

🏛 **Academic Standards for Science**

6.1.2 Explain the properties of solids, liquids and gases using drawings and models that represent matter as particles in motion whose state can be represented by the relative positions and movement of the particles.

How Are Pressure and Temperature of a Gas Related?

If you dropped a few grains of sand onto your hand, you would hardly feel them. But what if you were caught in a sandstorm? Ouch! The sand grains fly around very fast, and they would sting if they hit you. Although gas particles are much smaller than sand grains, a sandstorm is a good model for gas behavior. Like grains of sand in a sandstorm, gas particles travel at high speeds. The faster the gas particles move, the greater the force with which they collide with the walls of their container.

Vocabulary
- Charles's law
- directly proportional
- Boyle's law
- inversely proportional

Skills
- ↻ Reading: Identify the Main Idea
- △ Inquiry: Graph

Consider a gas in a closed, rigid container. If you heat the gas, its particles will move faster on average. They will collide with the walls of their container with greater force. The greater force over the same area results in greater pressure. ⚷ **When the temperature of a gas at constant volume is increased, the pressure of the gas increases. When the temperature is decreased, the pressure of the gas decreases.**

On long trips, especially in the summer, a truck's tires can become very hot. As the temperature increases, so does the pressure of the air inside the tire. If the pressure becomes greater than the tire can hold, the tire will burst. For this reason, truck drivers need to monitor and adjust tire pressure on long trips.

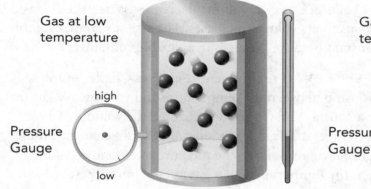
Gas at low temperature
Pressure Gauge
high
low
No heat

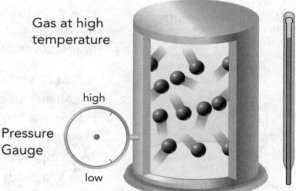
Gas at high temperature
Pressure Gauge
high
low
Heat added

FIGURE 1 ·······················
Temperature and Gas Pressure
When a gas is heated in a closed, rigid container, the particles move faster and collide more often.

✎ **Infer** Draw an arrow in each pressure gauge to show the change in pressure of the gas.

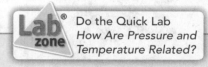
Lab zone® Do the Quick Lab
How Are Pressure and Temperature Related?

⚷ Assess Your Understanding

got it? ···

○ **I get it!** Now I know that when the temperature of a gas at a constant volume increases, _____

_____

○ **I need extra help with** _____

Go to **MY SCIENCE** ⬤ **COACH** online for help with this subject.

6.1.2

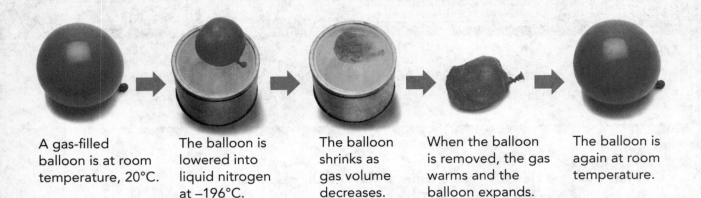

A gas-filled balloon is at room temperature, 20°C.

The balloon is lowered into liquid nitrogen at −196°C.

The balloon shrinks as gas volume decreases.

When the balloon is removed, the gas warms and the balloon expands.

The balloon is again at room temperature.

FIGURE 2 ···

Cooling a Balloon
The volume of a gas-filled balloon decreases as temperature decreases and then increases as temperature increases.

Academic Standards for Science

6.1.2 Explain the properties of solids, liquids and gases using drawings and models that represent matter as particles in motion whose state can be represented by the relative positions and movement of the particles.

6.NS.1 Make predictions based on research and prior knowledge.

6.NS.8 Analyze data, and use it to identify patterns and make inferences from these patterns.

FIGURE 3 ·····················

Charles's Law
A gas in a cylinder with a movable piston is slowly heated.

✎ **Predict** Draw the piston and gas particles when the temperature reaches 200°C and 400°C.   6.NS.1

How Are Volume and Temperature of a Gas Related?

Figure 2 shows what happens when a balloon is slowly lowered into liquid nitrogen at nearly −200°C and then removed. As the air inside the balloon cools, its volume decreases. When the air inside warms up again, its volume increases. The pressure remains more or less constant because the air is in a flexible container.

Charles's Law French scientist Jacques Charles examined the relationship between the temperature and volume of a gas that is kept at a constant pressure. He measured the volume of a gas at various temperatures in a container that could change volume. (A changeable volume allows the pressure to remain constant.) 🔑 **When the temperature of a gas at constant pressure is increased, its volume increases. When the temperature of a gas at constant pressure is decreased, its volume decreases.** This principle is called **Charles's law.**

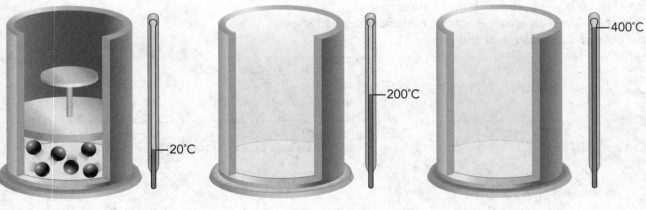

No heat   Some heat added   More heat added

Graphing Charles's Law

Graphing Charles's Law Suppose you do an experiment to test Charles's law. The experiment begins with 50 mL of gas in a cylinder with a movable piston similar to the one in **Figure 3**. The gas is slowly heated. Each time the temperature increases by 10°C, the gas volume is recorded. The data are recorded in the data table in **Figure 4.** Note that the temperatures in the data table have been converted to kelvins, the SI unit of temperature. To convert from Celsius degrees to kelvins (K), add 273.

As you can see in the graph of the data, the data points form a straight line. The dotted line represents how the graph would look if the gas could be cooled to 0 K. Notice that the line passes through the point (0, 0), called the origin. When a graph of two variables is a straight line passing through the origin, the variables are said to be **directly proportional** to each other. The graph of Charles's law shows that the volume of a gas is directly proportional to its kelvin temperature at constant pressure.

Temperature		Volume
(°C)	(K)	(mL)
0	273	50
20	293	54
40	313	58
60	333	62
80	353	66
100	373	70
120	393	74

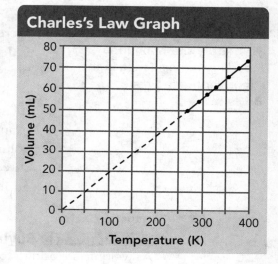

Charles's Law Graph

FIGURE 4 ···

Temperature and Gas Volume

🖊 In an experiment, a gas is heated at a constant pressure. The data shown in the table are plotted on the graph.

1. Draw Conclusions What happens to the volume of a gas when the temperature is increased at constant pressure?

_____

2. CHALLENGE Suppose the data formed a line with a steeper slope. For the same change in temperature, how would the change in volume compare?

_____

_____

6.NS.8

Lab zone® Do the Quick Lab
Hot and Cold Balloons.

🔑 Assess Your Understanding

1a. Identify The graph of Charles's law shows that the volume of a gas is

_____ to its

kelvin temperature at constant pressure.
6.1.2

b. Predict Suppose the gas in **Figure 4** could be cooled to 100 K (−173°C). Predict the volume of the gas at this temperature.

_____

6.1.2, 6.NS.1, 6.NS.8

got it? ···

○ **I get it!** Now I know that when the temperature of a gas is decreased at constant pressure _____

_____

○ **I need extra help with** _____

Go to MY SCIENCE ⓢ COACH *online for help with this subject.*

6.1.2

Academic Standards for Science

6.1.2 Explain the properties of solids, liquids and gases using drawings and models that represent matter as particles in motion whose state can be represented by the relative positions and movement of the particles.

6.NS.8 Analyze data, using appropriate mathematical manipulation as required, and use it to identify patterns and make inferences based on these patterns.

6.DP.9 Present evidence using mathematical representations.

6.DP.10 Communicate the solution including evidence using mathematical representations.

✏️

Identify the Main Idea

Underline the main idea in the text under the red heading "Boyle's Law."

How Are Pressure and Volume of a Gas Related?

Suppose you use a bicycle pump to inflate a tire. By pressing down on the plunger, you force the gas inside the pump through the rubber tube and out of the nozzle into the tire. What happens to the volume of air inside the pump cylinder as you push down on the plunger? What happens to the pressure?

Boyle's Law In the 1600s, the scientist Robert Boyle carried out experiments to try to improve air pumps. He measured the volumes of gases at different pressures. Boyle's experiments showed that gas volume and pressure were related. 🔑 **When the pressure of a gas at constant temperature is increased, the volume of the gas decreases. When the pressure is decreased, the volume increases.** This relationship between the pressure and the volume of a gas is called **Boyle's law.**

Boyle's law describes situations in which the volume of a gas is changed. The pressure then changes in the opposite way. For example, as you push down on the plunger of a bicycle pump, the volume of air inside the pump cylinder gets smaller, and the pressure inside the cylinder increases. The increase in pressure forces air into the tire.

FIGURE 5 ···

▶ **INTERACTIVE ART** **Boyle's Law**

As weights are added to the top of each piston, the piston moves farther down in the cylinder. ✎ **Interpret Diagrams** First, rank the pressure in each of the cylinders. Then rank the volume. A ranking of 1 is the greatest. A ranking of 3 is the lowest.

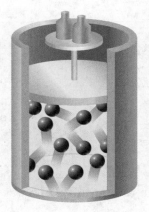

1a. _____ pressure   1b. _____ pressure   1c. _____ pressure

2a. _____ volume   2b. _____ volume   2c. _____ volume

do the math! Analyzing Data

In an experiment, the volume of a gas was varied at a constant temperature. The pressure of the gas was recorded after each 50-mL change in volume. The data are in the table below.

1 **Graph** Use the data to make a line graph. Plot volume on the horizontal axis. Plot pressure on the vertical axis. Write a title for the graph at the top.

2 **Control Variables** The manipulated variable in this experiment is _____. The responding variable is _____.

3 **Make Generalizations** What happens to the pressure of a gas when the volume is decreased at a constant temperature?
_____
_____

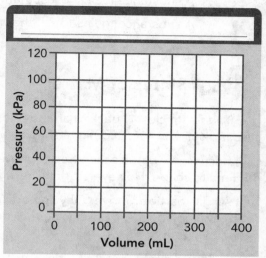

6.NS.8, 6.DP.9, 6.DP.10

Volume (mL)	Pressure (kPa)
300	20
250	24
200	30
150	40
100	60
50	120

Graphing Boyle's Law Look at the graph that you made above. Notice that the points lie on a curve and not a straight line. The curve is steep at lower volumes, but it becomes less steep as volume increases. If you multiply the two variables at any point on the curve, you will find that the product does not change.

$$300 \text{ mL} \times 20 \text{ kPa} = 6{,}000 \text{ mL·kPa}$$
$$250 \text{ mL} \times 24 \text{ kPa} = 6{,}000 \text{ mL·kPa}$$

When the product of two variables is constant, the variables are **inversely proportional** to each other. The graph for Boyle's law shows that gas pressure is inversely proportional to volume at constant temperature.

Lab zone Do the Quick Lab *It's a Gas.*

🔑 Assess Your Understanding

2a. Identify The graph of Boyle's law shows that the gas pressure is

_____ to volume at constant temperature.

6.1.2

b. Read Graphs Use the graph that you made in Analyzing Data above to find the pressure of the gas when its volume is 125 mL.

_____

6.1.2, 6.NS.8

got it? ....

○ **I get it!** Now I know that when the pressure of a gas at a constant temperature is increased, _____
_____

○ **I need extra help with** _____

Go to **MY SCIENCE** ⑤ **COACH** online for help with this subject.

6.1.2

REVIEW THE BIG ?

A substance (gains/loses) thermal energy when it melts or vaporizes.

A substance (gains/loses) thermal energy when it freezes or condenses.

LESSON 1 States of Matter

6.1.2, 6.NS.3, 6.NS.8, 6.NS.11

🔑 The fixed, closely packed arrangement of particles causes a solid to have a definite shape and volume.

🔑 Because its particles are free to move, a liquid has no definite shape. However, it does have a definite volume.

🔑 As gas particles move, they spread apart, filling all the space available. Thus, a gas has neither definite shape nor definite volume.

Vocabulary
• solid • crystalline solid • amorphous solid • liquid
• fluid • surface tension • viscosity • gas • pressure

LESSON 2 Changes of State

6.1.3, 6.NS.1, 6.NS.8

🔑 At a solid's melting point, its particles vibrate so fast that they break free from their fixed positions.

🔑 Vaporization occurs when the particles in a liquid gain enough thermal energy to move independently.

🔑 During sublimation, particles of a solid do not pass through the liquid state as they form a gas.

Vocabulary
• melting • melting point • freezing • vaporization • evaporation
• boiling • boiling point • condensation • sublimation

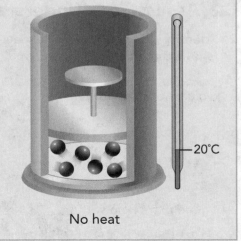

LESSON 3 The Behavior of Gases

6.1.2, 6.NS.1, 6.NS.8, 6.DP.9, 6.DP.10

🔑 When the temperature of a gas at constant volume is increased, the pressure of the gas increases.

🔑 When the temperature of a gas at constant pressure is increased, its volume increases.

🔑 When the pressure of a gas at constant temperature is increased, the volume of the gas decreases.

Vocabulary
• Charles's law • directly proportional • Boyle's law
• inversely proportional

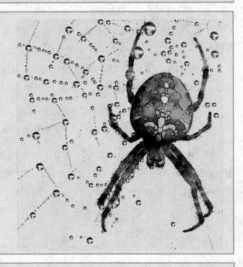

20°C

No heat

Review and Assessment

States of Matter

1. A substance with a definite shape and definite volume is a

   a. solid   **b.** liquid

   c. gas   **d.** fluid

                              6.1.2

2. Rubber is considered a(n) _____ solid because it does not melt at a distinct temperature.

                              6.1.2

3. Compare and Contrast Why do liquids and gases take the shape of their containers while solids do not?

_____

_____

_____

_____

                              6.1.2

4. Predict What happens to the gas particles in an inflated ball when it gets a hole? Why?

_____

_____

_____

_____

_____

                        6.1.2, 6.NS.1

5. math! Earth's atmosphere exerts a force of 124,500 N on a kitchen table with an area of 1.5 m². What is the pressure in pascals?

_____

_____

_____

                        6.1.2, 6.NS.8

6. **Write About It** Write a short essay in which you create an analogy to describe particle motion. Compare the movements and positions of people dancing with the motions of water molecules in liquid water and in water vapor.

                        6.1.2

Changes of State

7. A puddle dries up by the process of

   a. melting   **b.** freezing

   c. condensation   **d.** evaporation

                              6.1.3

8. When you see fog or clouds, you are seeing water in the _____ state.

                              6.1.3

9. Classify Label the correct change of state on top of the arrows in the diagram below.

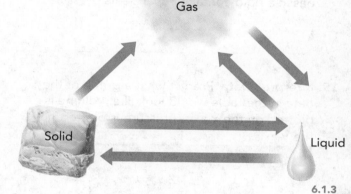

                              6.1.3

10. Draw Conclusions At room temperature, table salt is a solid and mercury is a liquid. What conclusion can you draw about the melting points of these substances?

_____

_____

_____

                              6.1.3

11. Apply Concepts When you open a solid room air freshener, the solid slowly loses mass and volume. How do you think this happens?

_____

_____

_____

_____

_____

                              6.1.3

LESSON 3 **The Behavior of Gases**

12. According to Boyle's law, the volume of a gas increases when its

    a. pressure increases. **b.** pressure decreases.

    c. temperature falls. **d.** temperature rises.

                            6.1.2

13. According to Charles's law, when the temperature of a gas is increased at a constant pressure, its volume _____

                            6.1.2

14. Relate Cause and Effect How does heating a gas in a rigid container change its pressure?

_____

_____

                            6.1.2

15. Interpret Data Predict what a graph of the data in the table would look like. Volume is plotted on the *x*-axis. Pressure is plotted on the *y*-axis.

Volume (cm³)	Pressure (kPa)
15	222
21	159
31	108
50	67

_____

_____

_____

_____

             6.1.2, 6.NS.1, 6.NS.8

16. Relate Cause and Effect Explain why placing a dented table-tennis ball in boiling water is one way to remove the dent in the ball. (Assume the ball has no holes.)

_____

_____

_____

_____

                            6.1.2

Why does a substance change states?

17. A fog forms over a lake. What two changes of state must occur to produce the fog? Do the water molecules absorb or release energy during these changes of state? What happens to the motion of the water molecules as a result?

_____

_____

_____

_____

_____

_____

_____

_____

_____

_____

_____

_____

_____

                            6.1.2

Indiana ISTEP+ Practice

Multiple Choice

Circle the letter of the best answer.

1. The graph below shows changes in 1 g of a solid as energy is added.

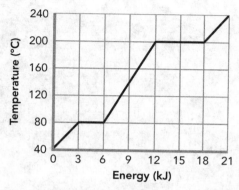

   What is the total amount of energy absorbed by the substance as it completely changes from a solid at 40°C to a gas at 200°C?

   A. 3 kJ   **B.** 6 kJ

   C. 12 kJ   **D.** 18 kJ

   6.1.2, 6.NS.8

2. Which of the following correctly describes a solid?

   A. The particles do not move at all.

   B. The particles are closely locked in position and can only vibrate in place.

   C. The particles are free to move about independently, colliding frequently.

   D. The particles are closely packed but have enough energy to slide past one another.

   6.1.2

3. A gas exerts a force of 1,000 N on a surface with an area of 5.0 m². What is the pressure on the area?

   A. 200 Pa

   B. 500 Pa

   C. 2,000 Pa

   D. 5,000 Pa

   6.1.2

4. A wet towel is hanging on a clothesline in the sun. The towel dries by the process of

   A. boiling.

   B. condensation.

   C. evaporation.

   D. sublimation.

   6.1.3

Constructed Response

Write your answer to Question 5 on the lines below.

5. A gas at constant temperature is in a cylinder with a movable piston. The piston is pushed into the cylinder, decreasing the volume of the gas. The pressure increases. What are the variables in this experiment?

   _____

   _____

   _____

   6.1.2

Extended Response

Use the diagrams to help you answer Question 6. Write your answer on a separate sheet of paper.

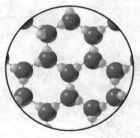 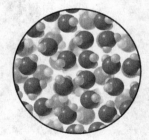

Before   After

6. The diagrams represent the molecules of water before and after a change of state. What change of state has occurred? Explain.

   6.1.3

SCUBA DIVING

When you swim to the bottom of a pool, you can feel the pressure of the water around you. That pressure increases rapidly during a deeper dive.

To make really deep dives, people use SCUBA (self-contained underwater breathing apparatus) gear. The SCUBA tank is filled with air at very high pressure. Boyle's law states that as pressure increases under conditions of constant temperature, the volume of the gas decreases. In other words, more air will fit into the tank when the pressure is high.

Breathing air straight from the tank could damage the diver's lungs. The pressure of the air entering the diver's lungs needs to match the pressure of the gases already inside the diver's body. Valves on the tank adjust the pressure of the air as it is released to match the pressure of the water around the diver, so that when it enters the diver's body, it matches the pressure of the gases in the body.

Write About It Make an instruction card for new divers explaining that it is dangerous for divers to hold their breath during a deep dive or ascent. Use Boyle's law to explain why this is true.

 6.1.2, 6.NS.11

◄ The regulator adjusts the pressure to match the surrounding water pressure.

A Shocking State

You touch a plasma globe, and lightning crackles. *Zap!* A plasma globe is a glass globe filled with partially ionized gas (that's the plasma!) and pumped full of high voltage power.

What's the Matter?

Plasma is different! In plasma, the electrons have been separated from the neutral atoms, so that they're no longer bound to an atom or molecule. Because positive and negative charges move independently, plasma can conduct electricity—causing the shocking light displays in a plasma globe. Plasma is its own state of matter. Like a gas, it has no shape or volume until it is captured in a container. Unlike a gas, it can form structures and layers, like the bolts in a plasma globe, or a bolt of lightning. It's shocking!

Find It Research and make a list of plasma objects. Compare your list with a partner, and discuss how plasma changes state to become a gas.

 6.1.3, 6.NS.2

Growing Snow

You may have heard that no two snowflakes look the same. Writers use the unique structures of snowflakes as a metaphor for things that are one-of-a-kind, and impossible to reproduce. And it's probably true! A snowflake forms when water begins to freeze around small particles of dust inside a cloud. The exact shape of the crystal depends on humidity and temperature, and because there are tiny variations in both of these factors, each snowflake will differ slightly from every other snowflake.

All snowflakes share a common shape, though. The hexagonal shape of a snow crystal forms as molecules come together during the phase change from liquid to solid. The oxygen atom has a partial negative charge and the hydrogen atoms a partial positive charge, so the atoms are attracted to one another.

Graphing Research to find out how the exact shape of snow crystals change as temperature and humidity change. Draw a line graph that illustrates your findings.

 6.1.2, 6.NS.8, 6.NS.11

The most stable arrangement of water molecules occurs when six molecules form a ring.

WHAT MAKES THESE SNOWBOARDERS "FLY" DOWNHILL?

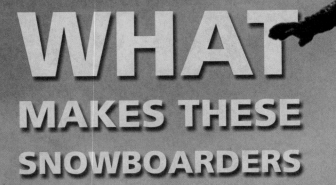

 How is energy conserved in a transformation?

These women are competing in the sport of snowboard cross. They "fly" down a narrow course, filled with jumps, steep sections, and ramps. Disaster looms at every turn. If they don't crash into each other or fall, then the first one across the finish line wins.

△Develop Hypotheses **What do you think makes these snowboarders go so fast?**

_____

_____

_____

_____

_____

_____

▷ UNTAMED SCIENCE Watch the **Untamed Science** video to learn more about energy.

Energy

Academic Standards for Science

6.1.4, 6.1.5, 6.1.6, 6.1.7, 6.4.1, 6.4.3, 6.NS.2, 6.NS.3, 6.NS.8, 6.NS.11

Check Your Understanding

1. **Background** Read the paragraph below and then answer the question.

While Chung works, his computer shuts down. Both the street and his house are dark, so he knows there is no **electricity.** A fallen tree has snapped an electric wire. The wire was the **conductor** that brought him power. Chung reaches for the light switch, but then remembers that no **electric current** will flow when he turns it on.

Electricity is a form of energy sometimes created by the movement of charged particles.

A material through which charges can easily flow is a **conductor.**

Electric current is the continuous flow of electric charges through a material.

• How can electricity be restored to Chung's house?

_____

_____

> MY READING WEB If you had trouble completing the question above, visit **My Reading Web** and type in **Energy.**

Vocabulary Skill

Identify Multiple Meanings Some familiar words may have different meanings in science. Look at the different meanings of the words below.

Word	Everyday Meaning	Scientific Meaning
energy	*n.* the ability to be active or take part in a vigorous activity **Example:** She had enough *energy* to run for miles.	*n.* the ability to do work or cause change **Example:** The wind can move objects because it has *energy.*
power	*n.* the ability to influence others **Example:** The coach has a lot of *power* over his young athletes.	*n.* the rate at which work is done **Example:** A truck's engine has more *power* than a car's engine.

2. **Quick Check** Review the sentences below. Then circle the sentence that uses the scientific meaning of the word *energy.*

• A puppy has too much *energy* to be inside the house all day.

• A wrecking ball has enough *energy* to knock down a building.

kinetic energy

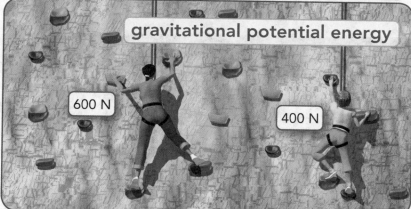

gravitational potential energy

600 N

400 N

mechanical energy

energy transformation

Chapter Preview

LESSON 1
- work
- energy
- power
- kinetic energy
- potential energy
- gravitational potential energy
- elastic potential energy

⟳ Relate Cause and Effect
△ Calculate

LESSON 2
- mechanical energy
- sound energy
- nuclear energy
- thermal energy
- electrical energy
- electromagnetic energy
- chemical energy

⟳ Identify the Main Idea
△ Classify

LESSON 3
- energy transformation
- law of conservation of energy

⟳ Identify Supporting Evidence
△ Infer

> VOCAB FLASH CARDS For extra help with vocabulary, visit **Vocab Flash Cards** and type in *Energy.*

What Is Energy?

UNLOCK
THE BIG

🔑 **How Are Energy, Work, and Power Related?**
6.1.7

🔑 **What Are Two Types of Energy?**
6.1.4, 6.1.5, 6.1.6, 6.4.1, 6.NS.3, 6.NS.8

my PLANeT DiaRY

FUN FACT

Wind Farms

Did you know that wind can be used to produce electricity? A wind farm is a group of very large wind-mills, or turbines, placed in a location that gets a lot of wind. The energy of the wind causes the propellers of the turbines to spin. The turbines are connected to generators. When the turbines are spinning, the generators produce electricity. The amount of electricity produced depends on the size of the propellers, the number of turbines, and the strength of the wind.

Write your answer to the question below.

Analyze Costs and Benefits What are some advantages and disadvantages of using wind energy to create electricity?

_____

_____

_____

_____

_____

▶ PLANET DIARY Go to **Planet Diary** to learn more about energy.

Lab zone® Do the Inquiry Warm-Up
How High Does a Ball Bounce?

Academic Standards for Science

6.1.7 Explain that energy may be manifested as heat, light, electricity, mechanical motion, and sound and is often associated with chemical reactions.

How Are Energy, Work, and Power Related?

Did you open a door when you left for school this morning? If so, you did work on the door. In scientific terms, you do **work** any time you exert a force on an object that causes the object to move.

Work and Energy The ability to do work or cause change is called **energy**. When you do work on an object, you transfer energy to it. Thus, you can think of work as the transfer of energy. Energy is measured in joules—the same units as work.

Vocabulary
- work • energy • power • kinetic energy
- potential energy • gravitational potential energy
- elastic potential energy

Skills
⏵ **Reading:** Relate Cause and Effect
△ **Inquiry:** Calculate

Power and Energy
If you carry a package up a flight a stairs, the work you do is the same whether you walk or run. The amount of work you do on an object is not affected by the time it takes to do the work. But scientists keep track of how fast work is done with a variable called power. **Power** is the rate at which work is done. 🔑 **Since the transfer of energy is work, then power is the rate at which energy is transferred, that is the amount of energy transferred in a unit of time.**

$$Power = \frac{Energy\ Transferred}{Time}$$

An object has more power when it can transfer more energy in the same amount of time as another object, or if it can transfer the same amount of energy in less time.

Different objects have different amounts of power. For example, you could use either a snowblower or a hand shovel, like the one in **Figure 1,** to remove snow from your driveway. Each transfers the same amount of energy when it moves the snow the same distance. However, you could move the snow faster using a snowblower than a hand shovel. The snowblower has more power because it removes the same amount of snow in less time than the person using a shovel.

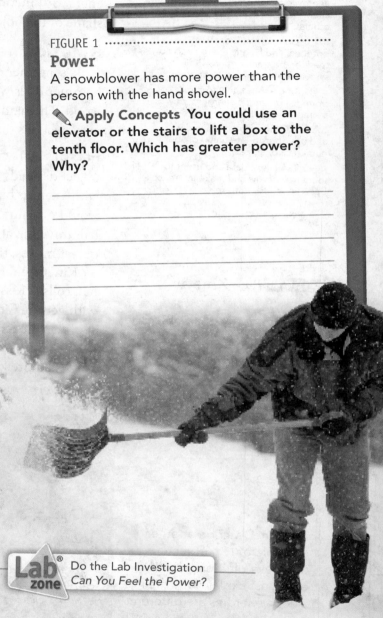

FIGURE 1 ....
Power
A snowblower has more power than the person with the hand shovel.

✎ **Apply Concepts** You could use an elevator or the stairs to lift a box to the tenth floor. Which has greater power? Why?

_____

_____

_____

_____

_____

Lab zone Do the Lab Investigation
Can You Feel the Power?

🔑 Assess Your Understanding

got it? ....

○ **I get it!** Now I know that energy is _____
and power is _____
_____

○ **I need extra help with** _____

Go to **my science** ⬤ **COACH** *online for help with this subject.*

Academic Standards for Science

6.1.4 Recognize that objects in motion have kinetic energy and objects at rest have potential energy.

6.1.5 Describe with examples that potential energy exists in several different forms (gravitational potential energy, elastic potential energy, and chemical potential energy, among others).

6.1.6 Compare and contrast potential and kinetic energy and how they can be transformed within a system from one form to another.

6.4.1 Understand how to apply potential or kinetic energy to power a simple device.

6.NS.3 Collect quantitative data and use appropriate units to label numerical data.

6.NS.8 Analyze data and use it to identify patterns and make inferences based on these patterns.

FIGURE 2 ·······················

> ART IN MOTION **Kinetic Energy**
The kinetic energy of an object depends on its speed and mass.

✎ **Use the diagram to answer the questions.**   6.NS.8

1. **Interpret Diagrams** List the vehicles in order of increasing kinetic energy.

   _____
   _____
   _____

2. **Explain** Describe another example of two objects that have different kinetic energies. Explain why their kinetic energies are different.

   _____
   _____
   _____
   _____
   _____
   _____

What Are Two Types of Energy?

Moving objects, such as the vehicles shown in **Figure 2,** have one type of energy. A rock perched on the edge of a cliff or a stretched rubber band has another type of energy. 🔑 **The two basic types of energy are kinetic energy and potential energy.** Whether energy is kinetic or potential depends on the motion, position, and shape of the object.

Kinetic Energy A moving object can do work when it strikes another object and moves it. For example, a swinging hammer does work on a nail as it drives the nail into a piece of wood. The hammer has energy because it can do work. The energy an object has due to its motion is called **kinetic energy.**

Factors Affecting Kinetic Energy The kinetic energy of an object depends on both its speed and its mass. Suppose you are hit with a tennis ball that has been lightly tossed at you. It probably would not hurt much. What if you were hit with the same tennis ball traveling at a much greater speed? It would hurt! The faster an object moves, the more kinetic energy it has.

Kinetic energy also increases as mass increases. Suppose a tennis ball rolls across the ground and hits you in the foot. Compare this with getting hit in the foot with a bowling ball moving at the same speed as the tennis ball. The bowling ball is much more noticeable because it has more kinetic energy than a tennis ball. The bowling ball has more kinetic energy because it has a greater mass.

30 m/s

20 m/s

20 m/s

Calculating Kinetic Energy You can use the following equation to solve for the kinetic energy of an object.

$$\text{Kinetic energy} = \tfrac{1}{2} \times \text{Mass} \times \text{Speed}^2$$

For example, suppose a boy is pulling a 10-kg wagon at a speed of 1 m/s.

$$\text{Kinetic energy of wagon} = \tfrac{1}{2} \times 10 \text{ kg} \times (1 \text{ m/s})^2$$

$$= 5 \text{ kg·m}^2/\text{s}^2 = 5 \text{ joules}$$

$$\text{Note that } 1 \text{ kg·m}^2/\text{s}^2 = 1 \text{ joule}$$

Do changes in speed and mass have the same effect on the kinetic energy of the wagon? No—changing the speed of the wagon will have a greater effect on its kinetic energy than changing its mass by the same factor. This is because speed is squared in the kinetic energy equation. For example, doubling the mass of the wagon will double its kinetic energy. Doubling the speed of the wagon will quadruple its kinetic energy.

Relate Cause and Effect
What has a greater effect on an object's kinetic energy—doubling its mass or doubling its speed? Explain.

_____
_____
_____
_____
_____

do the math!

A girl and her dog are running. The dog has a mass of 20 kg. The girl has a mass of 60 kg.

1 Calculate Suppose both the dog and the girl run at a speed of 2 m/s. Calculate both of their kinetic energies.

Kinetic energy of dog =

Kinetic energy of girl =

2 Calculate Suppose the dog speeds up and is now running at a speed of 4 m/s. Calculate the dog's kinetic energy.

Kinetic energy of dog =

3 Draw Conclusions Are your answers to Questions 1 and 2 reasonable? Explain.

_____
_____
_____
_____

6.NS.3, 6.NS.8

159

Review Write the SI unit for each quantity in the table.

Quantity	SI Unit
Force	_____
Height	_____
Work	_____
Mass	_____
Energy	_____

Potential Energy

An object does not have to be moving to have energy. Some objects have energy as a result of their shapes or positions. When you lift a book up to your desk from the floor or compress a spring by winding a toy, you transfer energy to it. The energy you transfer is stored, or held in readiness. It might be used later if the book falls or the spring unwinds. Energy that results from the position or shape of an object is called **potential energy.** This type of energy has the potential to do work.

Gravitational Potential Energy Potential energy related to an object's height is called **gravitational potential energy.** The gravitational potential energy of an object is equal to the work done to lift it to that height. Remember that work is equal to force multiplied by distance. The force you use to lift the object is equal to its weight. The distance you move the object is its height above the ground. You can calculate an object's gravitational potential energy using this equation.

$$\text{Gravitational potential energy} = \text{Weight} \times \text{Height}$$

For example, suppose a book has a weight of 10 newtons (N). If the book is lifted 2 meters off the ground, the book has 10 newtons times 2 meters, or 20 joules, of gravitational potential energy.

FIGURE 3 ·····································

Gravitational Potential Energy

The rock climbers have gravitational potential energy.

✎ **Use the diagram to answer the questions.**

1. **Identify** Circle the rock climber with the greatest potential energy. Calculate this potential energy. The height to be used is at the rock climber's lowest foot.

_____

_____

_____

_____

_____

2. [CHALLENGE] Where would the rock climbers at the top have to be to have half as much potential energy?

_____

_____

_____

6.NS.3, 6.NS.8

Elastic Potential Energy An object has a different type of potential energy due to its shape. **Elastic potential energy** is the energy associated with objects that can be compressed or stretched. For example, when the girl in **Figure 4** presses down on the trampoline, the trampoline changes shape. The trampoline now has potential energy. When the girl pushes off of the trampoline, the stored energy sends the girl upward.

FIGURE 4 ....

Elastic Potential Energy
The energy stored in a stretched object, such as the trampoline, is elastic potential energy.

✏️ **Interpret Diagrams Rank the amount of elastic potential energy of the trampoline from greatest to least. A ranking of one is the greatest. Write your answers in the circles. Then explain your answers in the space to the right.**

6.4.1, 6.NS.8

_____
_____
_____
_____
_____
_____

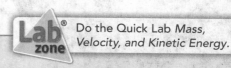
Do the Quick Lab *Mass, Velocity, and Kinetic Energy.*

🔑 Assess Your Understanding

1a. Identify The energy an object has due to its motion is called (kinetic/potential) energy. Stored energy that results from the position or shape of an object is called (kinetic/potential) energy.

6.1.4, 6.1.5, 6.1.6

b. Summarize What are the two factors that affect an object's kinetic energy?

_____

6.1.4

c. Apply Concepts What type of energy does a cup sitting on a table have? Why?

_____
_____
_____
_____
_____

6.1.6

got it? ....

○ **I get it!** Now I know that the two basic types of energy are _____

_____

○ **I need extra help with** _____

Go to MY SCIENCE COACH *online for help with this subject.*

6.1.4, 6.1.5, 6.1.6, 6.4.1

Indiana

LESSON

2 Forms of Energy

UNLOCK THE BIG ?

🔑 **How Can You Find an Object's Mechanical Energy?**
6.1.4, 6.1.5, 6.1.6, 6.4.1, 6.NS.8

🔑 **What Are Other Forms of Energy?**
6.1.7

MY PLANET DIARY for Indiana

Full of Energy

Today, people cannot do without their flat-screen TVs, cell phones, and digital music players. But where does the energy come from to power these devices? Most of the electricity in Indiana comes from fossil fuels, such as coal and natural gas. These fuels are burned at power plants. The energy released is used to power steam turbines that creates electricity for everyone to use. The graph below shows the fuel sources used to generate electricity in the state.

Fuel Sources for Electric Power Generation in Indiana in 2005

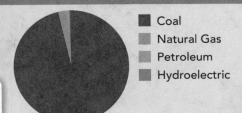

- Coal
- Natural Gas
- Petroleum
- Hydroelectric

® Do the Inquiry Warm-Up *What Makes a Flashlight Shine?*

FIELD TRIP

Interpret Data Analyze the graph to answer the questions.

1. Estimate the percentage of electricity generated in Indiana from coal.

_____

2. How do you think this graph might change in 10 years?

_____
_____
_____
_____

▷ PLANET DIARY Go to **Planet Diary** to learn more about populations.

🏛 **Academic Standards for Science**

6.1.4 Describe with examples that particles and objects in motion have kinetic energy.

6.1.5 Describe that potential energy exists in several different forms.

6.1.6 Compare and contrast potential and kinetic energy.

6.4.1 Understand how to apply potential or kinetic energy to power a simple device.

6.NS.8 Analyze data.

How Can You Find an Object's Mechanical Energy?

What do a falling basketball, a moving car, and a trophy on a shelf all have in common? They all have mechanical energy. The form of energy associated with the motion, position, or shape of an object is called **mechanical energy.**

Vocabulary
- mechanical energy
- sound energy
- nuclear energy
- thermal energy
- electrical energy
- electromagnetic energy
- chemical energy

Skills
- Reading: Identify the Main Idea
- Inquiry: Classify

Calculating Mechanical Energy An object's mechanical energy is a combination of its potential energy and its kinetic energy. For example, the basketball in **Figure 1** has both potential energy and kinetic energy. The higher the basketball moves, the greater its potential energy. The faster the basketball moves, the greater its kinetic energy. 🔑 **You can find an object's mechanical energy by adding together the object's kinetic energy and potential energy.**

Mechanical energy = Potential energy + Kinetic energy

Sometimes an object's mechanical energy is its kinetic energy or potential energy only. A car moving along a flat road has kinetic energy only. A trophy resting on a shelf has gravitational potential energy only. But both have mechanical energy.

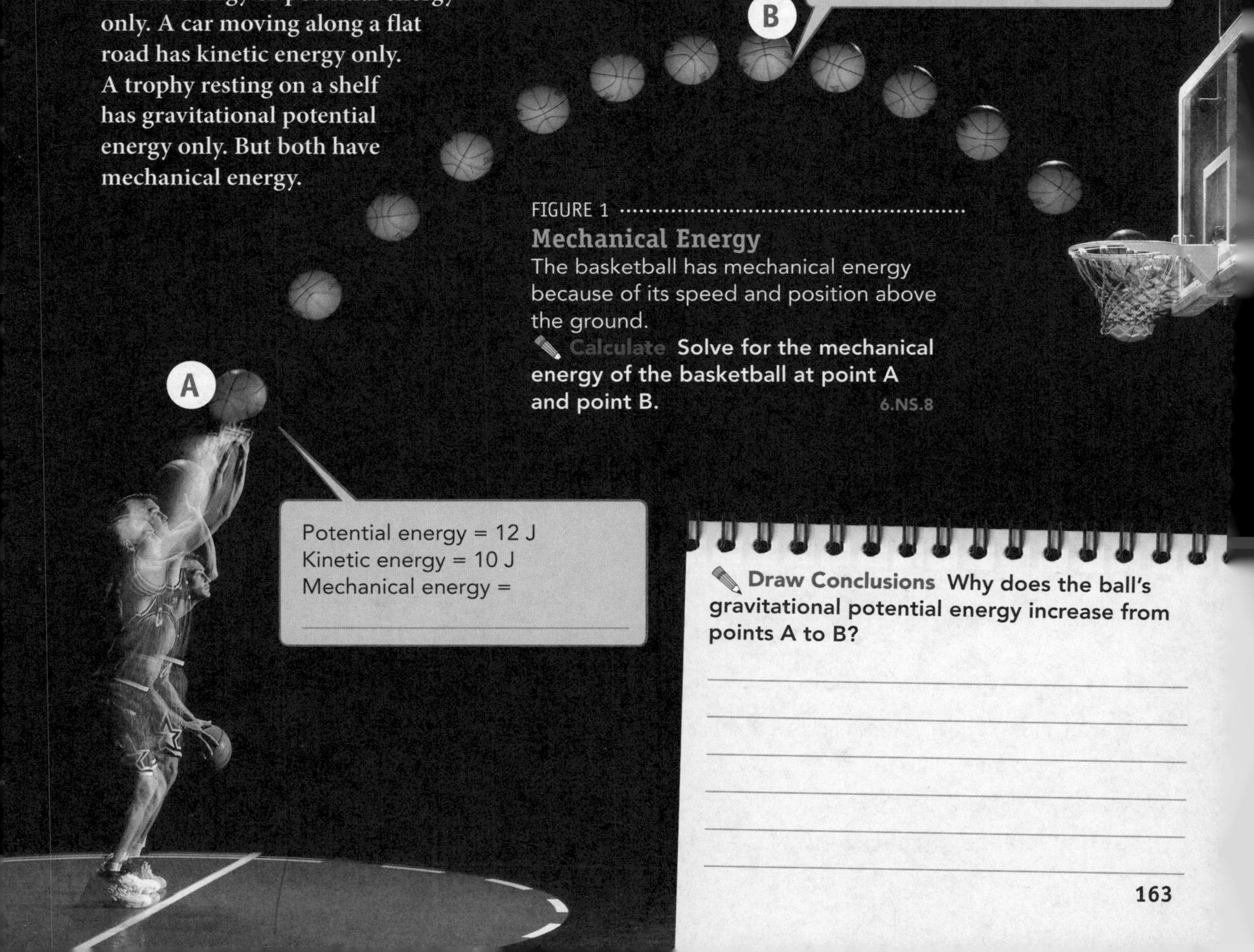

Potential energy = 20 J
Kinetic energy = 2 J
Mechanical energy =

B

FIGURE 1 ....

Mechanical Energy

The basketball has mechanical energy because of its speed and position above the ground.

✏️ **Calculate** Solve for the mechanical energy of the basketball at point A and point B.

6.NS.8

A

Potential energy = 12 J
Kinetic energy = 10 J
Mechanical energy =

✏️ **Draw Conclusions** Why does the ball's gravitational potential energy increase from points A to B?

_____

_____

_____

_____

_____

Mechanical Energy and Work An object with mechanical energy can do work on another object. In fact, you can think of mechanical energy, like all forms of energy, as the ability to do work. For example, a basketball does work on the net as it falls through the hoop. The net moves as a result. The more mechanical energy an object has, the more work it can do.

apply it!

The bowling ball does work on the pins when it hits them.

1 Why is the bowling ball able to do work?

_____

_____

_____

_____

2 How should you throw the ball to maximize the amount of work it does on the pins?

_____

_____

_____

_____

_____

3 CHALLENGE In the type of bowling shown in the photo, the ball has a mass of 7.0 kg. In candlepin bowling, the ball has a mass of about 1.0 kg. Does the ball with the greater mass always have the greater mechanical energy? Explain.

_____

_____

_____

_____

6.4.1, 6.NS.8

Lab zone® Do the Quick Lab *Determining Mechanical Energy.*

🔑 Assess Your Understanding

1a. Define Mechanical energy is the form of energy associated with the_____ ,

_____ , or _____ of an object.

6.1.4, 6.1.5, 6.1.6

b. Calculate At a certain point the kinetic energy of a falling apple is 5.2 J and its potential energy is 3.5 J. What is its mechanical energy?

_____

6.1.4, 6.1.5, 6.1.6, 6.NS.8

c. Infer If an object's mechanical energy is equal to its potential energy, how much kinetic energy does the object have? Explain.

_____

_____

_____

_____

_____

6.1.4, 6.1.5, 6.1.6, 6.NS.8

got it? ....

○ I get it! Now I know you can find an object's mechanical energy by _____

_____

○ I need extra help with _____

Go to MY SCIENCE ⓢ COACH online for help with this subject.

6.1.4, 6.1.5, 6.1.6, 6.4.1

What Are Other Forms of Energy?

So far, you have read about energy that involves the motion, position, or shape of an object. But an object can have other forms of kinetic and potential energy. These other forms are associated with particles. These particles are far too small to see with the naked eye. **Forms of energy associated with particles include sound energy, nuclear energy, thermal energy, electrical energy, electromagnetic energy, and chemical energy.**

Sound Energy You may not realize it, but the sounds you make and hear are forms of energy. **Sound energy** is a disturbance that travels through a medium as a wave. When you knock on a door, for example, the energy from your hand striking the door causes a disturbance. Particles in the door and the air begin to vibrate, or move back and forth. This energy travels as a wave through two mediums—the air and the door. Sound waves carry energy through a medium without moving the particles of the medium along. Each particle of the medium vibrates as the disturbance passes. When the disturbance reaches your ears, you hear the sound.

Nuclear Energy All objects are made up of particles called atoms. The region in the center of an atom is called the nucleus. A type of potential energy called **nuclear energy** is stored in the nucleus of an atom. Nuclear energy is released during a nuclear reaction. One kind of nuclear reaction, known as nuclear fission, occurs when a nucleus splits. A nuclear power plant, like the one shown in **Figure 2,** uses fission reactions to produce electricity. Another kind of reaction, known as nuclear fusion, occurs when the nuclei of atoms fuse, or join together. Nuclear fusion reactions occur constantly in the sun, releasing huge amounts of energy. Only a tiny portion of this energy reaches Earth as heat and light.

 Academic Standards for Science

6.1.7 Explain that energy may be manifested as heat, light, electricity, mechanical motion, and sound is often associated with chemical reactions.

Identify the Main Idea
Underline the main idea under the red heading Nuclear Energy.

FIGURE 2 ·······

Nuclear Energy
Controlled nuclear fission reactions occur at some power plants. Nuclear fusion reactions occur in the sun.

✎ **Compare and Contrast**
Use the Venn diagram to compare and contrast nuclear fission and nuclear fusion.

Nuclear Fission   Both   Nuclear Fusion

Thermal Energy The particles that make up objects are constantly in motion. This means that they have kinetic energy. These particles are arranged in specific ways in different objects, so they also have potential energy. The total kinetic and potential energy of the particles in an object is called **thermal energy.**

The higher the temperature of an object, the more thermal energy the object has. For example, suppose you heat a pot of water. As heat is applied to the water, the particles in the water move faster on average. The faster the particles move, the greater their kinetic energy and the higher the temperature. Therefore, a pot of water at 75°C, for example, has more thermal energy than the same amount of water at 30°C.

Electrical Energy When you receive a shock from a metal doorknob, you experience electrical energy. The energy of electric charges is **electrical energy.** Depending on whether the charges are moving or stored, electrical energy can be a form of kinetic or potential energy. Lightning is a form of electrical energy. You rely on electrical energy from batteries or electrical lines to run devices such as computers, handheld games, and digital audio players.

FIGURE 3 ·······························
▶ INTERACTIVE ART **Forms of Energy**
Many objects in this restaurant have more than one form of energy.

✎ **Classify** Circle three objects. Describe two forms of energy each object has.

Electromagnetic Energy The light you see is one type of electromagnetic energy. **Electromagnetic energy** is a form of energy that travels through space in waves. The source of these waves is vibrating electric charges. These waves do not require a medium, so they can travel through a vacuum, or empty space. This is why you can see the sun and stars.

The microwaves you use to cook your food and the X-rays doctors use to examine patients are also types of electromagnetic energy. Other forms of electromagnetic energy include ultraviolet rays, infrared (or heat) waves, and radio waves. Cell phones send and receive messages using microwaves.

Chemical Energy Chemical energy is in the foods you eat, in the matches you use to light a candle, and even in the cells of your body. **Chemical energy** is potential energy stored in chemical bonds. Chemical bonds are what hold atoms together. Often when these bonds are broken, this stored energy is released. For example, bonds are broken in your cells and release energy for your body to use.

Vocabulary Identify Multiple Meanings Review the multiple meaning words in the Getting Started section and complete the sentence. During a lightning storm, electric charges move between the clouds and the ground, releasing stored

_____

 Do the Quick Lab
Sources of Energy.

🔑 **Assess Your Understanding**

2a. Explain Why do the particles of objects have both kinetic and potential energy?

_____

_____

_____

_____

_____

_____

6.1.4, 6.1.5, 6.1.6

b. Classify The energy you get from eating a peanut butter and jelly sandwich is in the form of _____ energy.

6.1.7

got it? ....

○ **I get it!** Now I know the forms of energy associated with particles include _____

_____

_____

_____

○ **I need extra help with** _____

Go to MY SCIENCE Ⓢ COACH *online for help with this subject.*

6.1.7

Energy Transformations and Conservation

🔑 **How Are Different Forms of Energy Related?**
6.1.6, 6.4.3, 6.NS.8

🔑 **What Is the Law of Conservation of Energy?**
6.1.6, 6.NS.8

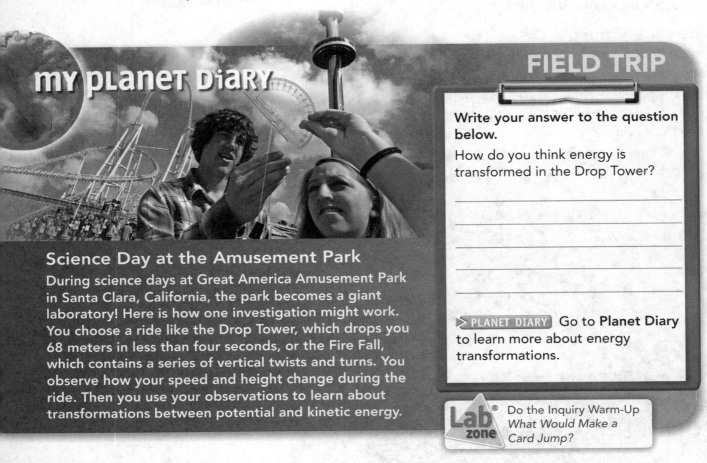

MY PLANET DIARY

Science Day at the Amusement Park

During science days at Great America Amusement Park in Santa Clara, California, the park becomes a giant laboratory! Here is how one investigation might work. You choose a ride like the Drop Tower, which drops you 68 meters in less than four seconds, or the Fire Fall, which contains a series of vertical twists and turns. You observe how your speed and height change during the ride. Then you use your observations to learn about transformations between potential and kinetic energy.

FIELD TRIP

Write your answer to the question below.

How do you think energy is transformed in the Drop Tower?

_____

_____

_____

_____

_____

▷ PLANET DIARY Go to **Planet Diary** to learn more about energy transformations.

 Lab zone® Do the Inquiry Warm-Up *What Would Make a Card Jump?*

Academic Standards for Science

6.1.6 Compare and contrast potential and kinetic energy and how they can be transformed within a system from one form to another.

6.4.3 Describe the transfer of energy amongst energy interactions.

6.NS.8 Analyze data and use it to identify patterns and make inferences based on these patterns.

How Are Different Forms of Energy Related?

What does flowing water have to do with electricity? In a hydro-electric power plant, the mechanical energy of moving water is transformed into electrical energy. 🔑 **All forms of energy can be transformed into other forms of energy.** A change from one form of energy to another is called an **energy transformation.** Some energy changes involve single transformations, while others involve many transformations.

Vocabulary

- energy transformation
- law of conservation of energy

Skills

- Reading: Identify Supporting Evidence
- Inquiry: Infer

Single Transformations Sometimes, one form of energy needs to be transformed into another to get work done. For example, a toaster transforms electrical energy to thermal energy to toast your bread. A cell phone transforms electrical energy to electromagnetic energy that travels to other phones.

Your body transforms the chemical energy in food to the mechanical energy you need to move your muscles. Chemical energy in food is also transformed to the thermal energy your body uses to maintain its temperature.

Multiple Transformations Often, a series of energy transformations is needed to do work. For example, the mechanical energy used to strike a match is transformed first to thermal energy. The thermal energy causes the particles in the match to release stored chemical energy, which is transformed to more thermal energy and to the electromagnetic energy you see as light.

In a car engine, another series of energy conversions occurs. Electrical energy produces a spark. The thermal energy of the spark releases chemical energy in the fuel. The fuel expands as it is broken down into smaller particles. The expansion of the fuel produces pressure on parts of the car. The increased pressure eventually causes the wheels to turn, transforming chemical energy into mechanical energy.

✏️ Identify Supporting Evidence

Underline the energy transformation that must occur for you to talk on your cell phone.

apply it!

A series of energy transformations must occur for you to ride your bike. Write the forms of energy involved in each transformation. 6.4.3

Reactions occur within the sun to transform _____ energy into _____ energy.

Plants transform _____ energy into _____ energy.

Your body transforms _____ energy into _____ energy to maintain your body temperature.

Your body also transforms _____ energy into _____ energy when you ride your bike.

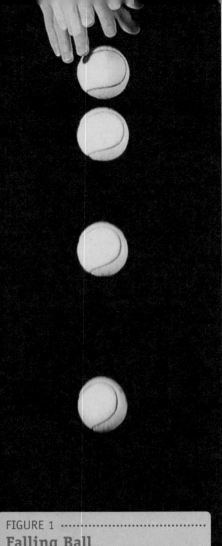

Kinetic and Potential Energy The transformation between potential and kinetic energy is one of the most common energy transformations. For example, when you stretch a rubber band, you give it elastic potential energy. If you let it go, the rubber band flies across the room. When the rubber band is moving, it has kinetic energy. The potential energy of the stretched rubber has transformed to the kinetic energy of the moving rubber band. Transformations between kinetic and potential energy can also occur in any object that rises or falls. A falling object, a pendulum, and a pole vault are all examples of these transformations.

Falling Object A transformation between potential and kinetic energy occurs in the ball in **Figure 1.** As the height of the ball decreases, it loses potential energy. At the same time, its kinetic energy increases because its speed increases. Its potential energy is transformed into kinetic energy.

Pendulum A pendulum like the one in **Figure 2** swings back and forth. At the highest point in its swing, the pendulum has no movement. As it swings downward, it speeds up. The pendulum is at its greatest speed at the bottom of its swing. As the pendulum swings to the other side, its height increases and its speed decreases. At the top of its swing, it comes to a stop again.

FIGURE 1 ·······························

Falling Ball
The ball was photographed at equal time intervals as it fell.

✏ **Interpret Photos** How can you tell that the ball's kinetic energy is increasing?

_____

_____

_____

_____

_____

_____

6.NS.8

FIGURE 2 ··

▷ **INTERACTIVE ART** **Pendulum**
A continuous transformation between potential and kinetic energy occurs in a pendulum. ✏ **Interpret Diagrams** Label the type of energy the pendulum has at positions A, B, and C.   6.4.3, 6.NS.8

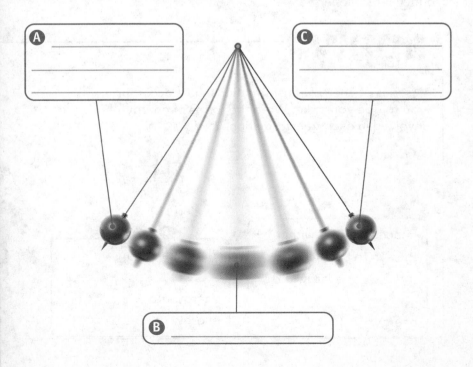

Ⓐ _____

Ⓒ _____

Ⓑ _____

Pole Vault The pole-vaulter in Figure 3 starts out by running forward. When the pole-vaulter plants the pole to jump, his speed decreases and the pole bends. As the pole straightens out, the pole-vaulter is lifted high into the air. Once he is over the bar, the pole-vaulter's speed increases as he falls toward the safety cushion.

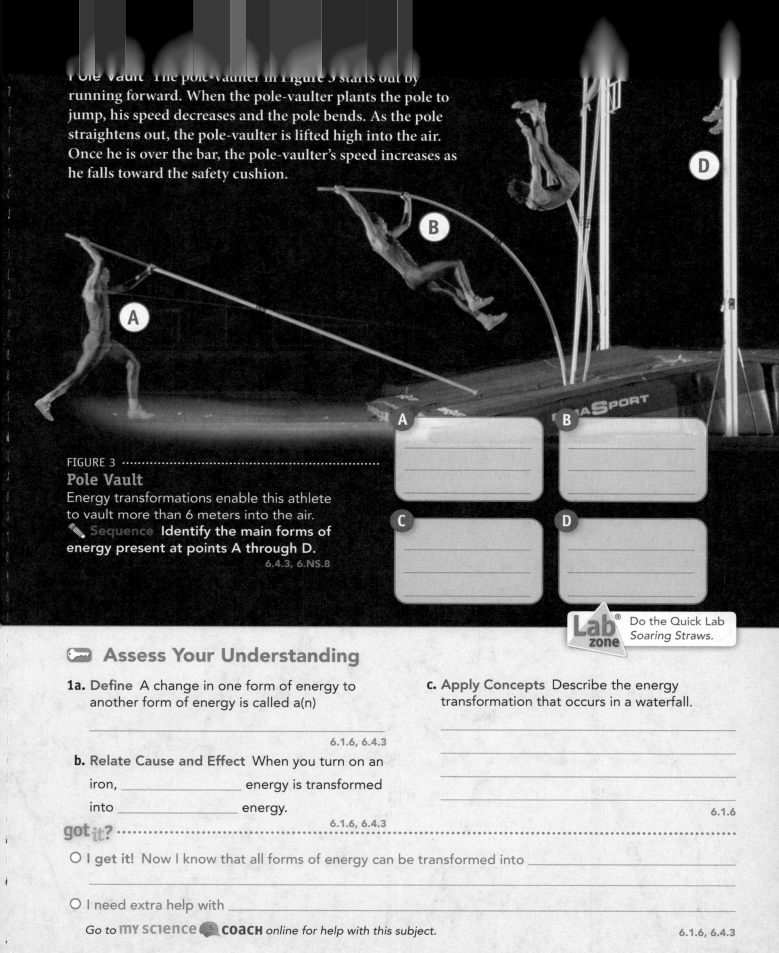

FIGURE 3 ···

Pole Vault
Energy transformations enable this athlete to vault more than 6 meters into the air.

✏️ Sequence **Identify the main forms of energy present at points A through D.**

6.4.3, 6.NS.8

Do the Quick Lab
Soaring Straws.

🔑 Assess Your Understanding

1a. Define A change in one form of energy to another form of energy is called a(n)

_____
6.1.6, 6.4.3

b. Relate Cause and Effect When you turn on an

iron, _____ energy is transformed

into _____ energy.
6.1.6, 6.4.3

c. Apply Concepts Describe the energy transformation that occurs in a waterfall.

_____
_____
_____
_____
6.1.6

got it? ··

○ **I get it!** Now I know that all forms of energy can be transformed into _____
_____

○ **I need extra help with** _____

Go to **MY SCIENCE** ⓢ **COACH** *online for help with this subject.*
6.1.6, 6.4.3

171

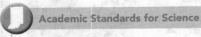

Academic Standards for Science

6.1.6 Compare and contrast potential and kinetic energy and how they can be transformed within a system from one form to another.
6.4.3 Describe the transfer of energy amongst energy interactions.
6.NS.8 Analyze data and use it to identify patterns and make inferences based on these patterns.

What Is the Law of Conservation of Energy?

Once you set a pendulum in motion, does it swing forever? No, it does not. Then what happens to its energy? Is the energy destroyed? Again, the answer is no. The **law of conservation of energy** states that when one form of energy is transformed to another, no energy is lost in the process. ⚷ **According to the law of conservation of energy, energy cannot be created or destroyed.** The total amount of energy is the same before and after any transformation. If you add up all of the new forms of energy after a transformation, all of the original energy will be accounted for. So what happens to the energy of the pendulum once it stops moving?

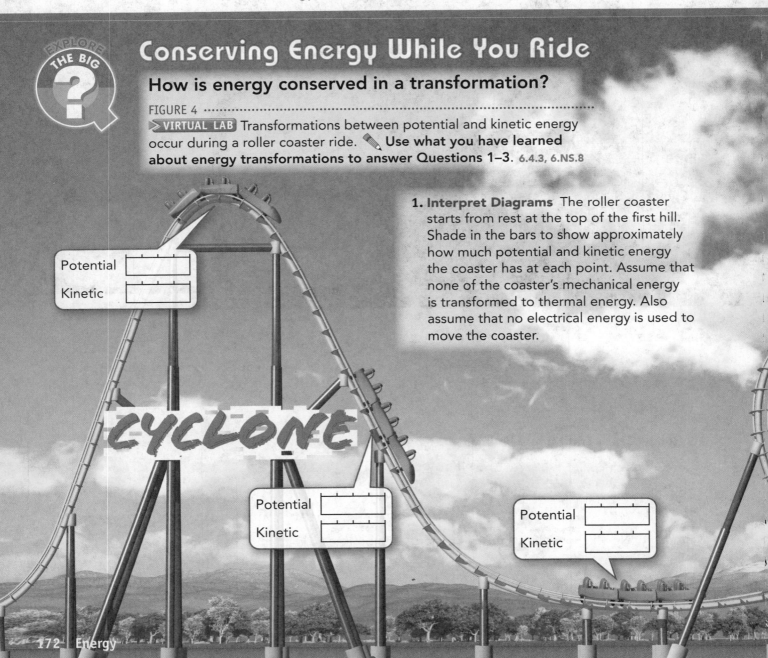

Conserving Energy While You Ride

How is energy conserved in a transformation?

FIGURE 4 ··································
▷ **VIRTUAL LAB** Transformations between potential and kinetic energy occur during a roller coaster ride. ✏ **Use what you have learned about energy transformations to answer Questions 1–3.** 6.4.3, 6.NS.8

1. **Interpret Diagrams** The roller coaster starts from rest at the top of the first hill. Shade in the bars to show approximately how much potential and kinetic energy the coaster has at each point. Assume that none of the coaster's mechanical energy is transformed to thermal energy. Also assume that no electrical energy is used to move the coaster.

Potential
Kinetic

CYCLONE

Potential
Kinetic

Potential
Kinetic

As the pendulum swings, it encounters friction at the pivot of the string and from the air through which it moves. Whenever a moving object experiences friction, some of its kinetic energy is transformed into thermal energy. So the mechanical energy of the pendulum is not destroyed. It is transformed to thermal energy.

The fact that friction transforms mechanical energy to thermal energy should not surprise you. After all, you take advantage of such thermal energy when you rub your cold hands together to warm them up. Friction is also the reason why no machine is 100 percent efficient. You may recall that the output work of any real machine is always less than the input work. This reduced efficiency occurs because some mechanical energy is always transformed into thermal energy due to friction.

did you
know?

When ancient animals and plants died, the chemical energy they had stored was trapped within their remains. This trapped energy is the chemical energy found in coal.

2. **Infer** Suppose you had taken thermal energy into account in Step 1. Would the total length of the shaded portion of the bars increase, decrease, or stay the same as as result?

◯ Increase ◯ Decrease ◯ Stay the same

3. **CHALLENGE** Why is the first hill of a roller coaster always the tallest?

_____

_____

_____

_____

Potential [ ]
Kinetic [ ]

Potential [ ]
Kinetic [ ]

Lab zone® Do the Quick Lab *Law of Conservation of Energy.*

🔑 Assess Your Understanding

2. **ANSWER THE BIG ?** How is energy conserved in a transformation?

_____

_____

_____

_____

6.1.6

got it? ··

◯ **I get it!** Now I know that according to the law of conservation of energy, energy _____

_____

_____

◯ **I need extra help with** _____

Go to **my science ⑤ coach** *online for help with this subject.* 6.1.6

5 Study Guide

REVIEW
THE BIG
?

The total amount of _____ is the same before and after any transformation.

LESSON 1 What Is Energy?

6.1.4, 6.1.5, 6.1.6, 6.1.7, 6.4.1, 6.NS.3, 6.NS.8

🔑 Since the transfer of energy is work, then power is the rate at which energy is transferred, that is the amount of energy transferred in a unit of time.

🔑 The two basic types of energy are kinetic energy and potential energy.

Vocabulary
• work • energy • power
• kinetic energy
• potential energy
• gravitational potential energy
• elastic potential energy

LESSON 2 Forms of Energy

6.1.4, 6.1.5, 6.1.6, 6.1.7, 6.4.1, 6.NS.8

🔑 You can find an object's mechanical energy by adding together the object's kinetic energy and potential energy.

🔑 Forms of energy associated with particles include sound energy, nuclear energy, thermal energy, electrical energy, electromagnetic energy, and chemical energy.

Vocabulary
• mechanical energy   • sound energy   • nuclear energy
• thermal energy   • electrical energy   • electromagnetic energy
• chemical energy

LESSON 3 Energy Transformations and Conservation

6.1.6, 6.4.3, 6.NS.8

🔑 All forms of energy can be transformed into other forms of energy.

🔑 According to the law of conservation of energy, energy cannot be created or destroyed.

Vocabulary
• energy transformation
• law of conservation of energy

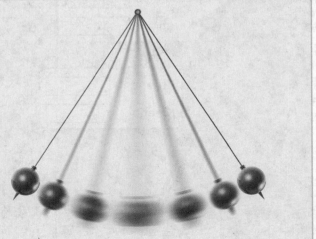

Review and Assessment

LESSON 1 **What Is Energy?**

1. When you stretch a rubber band, you give it

    a. kinetic energy.   **b.** electrical energy.

    c. potential energy.   **d.** chemical energy.

    6.1.5

2. To calculate power, divide the amount of energy transferred by _____

    6.1.7

3. Compare and Contrast In the illustration below, which vehicle has the greatest kinetic energy? Explain your answer.

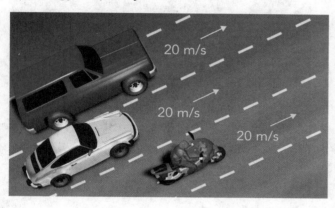

20 m/s

20 m/s

20 m/s

_____

_____

_____

    6.1.4

4. Apply Concepts If a handsaw does the same amount of work on a log as a chainsaw does, which has more power? Why?

_____

_____

_____

_____

    6.1.7

5. math! A 1,350-kg car travels at 12 m/s. What is its kinetic energy?

_____

_____

    6.1.4, 6.NS.3, 6.NS.8

LESSON 2 **Forms of Energy**

6. What is the energy stored in the nucleus of an atom called?

    a. electrical energy   **b.** chemical energy

    c. thermal energy   **d.** nuclear energy

    6.1.7

7. An object's mechanical energy is the sum of its

_____

    6.1.6

8. Classify When you heat a pot of water over a flame, what form of energy is added to the water?

_____

    6.1.7

The graph shows the kinetic energy of a 500-N diver during a dive from a 10-m platform. Use the graph to answer Questions 9 and 10.

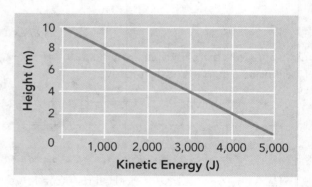

9. Read Graphs How does the diver's kinetic energy change as the diver falls? Why?

_____

_____

_____

    6.1.6, 6.NS.8

10. Calculate What is the diver's gravitational potential energy just before the dive?

_____

_____

_____

    6.1.5, 6.NS.8

LESSON 3 Energy Transformations and Conservation

11. As a car skids to a stop, friction transforms kinetic energy to

   a. thermal energy.   **b.** potential energy.

   c. chemical energy.   **d.** electrical energy.

6.1.6, 6.4.3

12. The law of conservation of energy states that

_____

_____

_____

_____

6.1.6

13. Classify Describe the energy transformation that occurs in a digital clock.

_____

_____

_____

6.1.6, 6.4.3

14. Apply Concepts Explain why a spinning top will not remain in motion forever.

_____

_____

_____

6.1.6, 6.4.3

15. Infer Why does a bouncing ball rise to a lower height with each bounce?

_____

_____

_____

_____

_____

6.1.6, 6.4.3

16. [Write About It] An eagle flies from its perch in a tree to the ground to capture and eat its prey. Describe its energy transformations.

6.1.6, 6.4.3, 6.NS.11

APPLY THE BIG ? How is energy conserved in a transformation?

17. The golfer in the photo is taking a swing. The golf club starts at point A and ends at point E. (1) Describe the energy transformations of the club from points A to E. (2) The kinetic energy of the club at point C is more than the potential energy of the club at point B. Does this mean that the law of conservation of energy is violated? Why or why not?

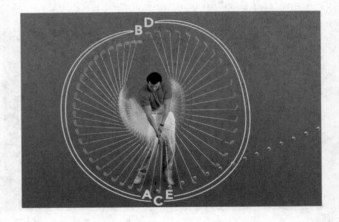

_____

_____

_____

_____

_____

_____

_____

_____

_____

_____

_____

6.1.6, 6.4.3, 6.NS.11

Indiana ISTEP+ Practice

Multiple Choice

Circle the letter of the best answer.

1. The table gives the kinetic and potential energy of a 6-kg cat doing various activities.

Activity	Kinetic Energy (J)	Potential Energy (J)
Running	200	0
Leaping	150	100
Climbing a tree	3	300
Sleeping on a chair	0	30

During which activity does the cat have the greatest mechanical energy?

A. climbing a tree   B. leaping

C. running   D. sleeping on a chair

6.1.6

2. Why does wind have energy?

A. It can change direction.

B. It can do work.

C. It moves through space as waves.

D. It is electrically charged.

6.1.7

3. What is the SI unit used to express gravitational potential energy?

A. newton

B. kilowatt

C. horsepower

D. joule

6.1.5

4. What causes a pendulum to eventually slow down and stop swinging?

A. friction

B. kinetic energy

C. weight

D. potential energy

6.1.6

Constructed Response

Write your answer to Question 5 on the lines below.

5. Which energy transformations take place when wood is burned?

_____

_____

_____

6.1.6, 6.4.3

Extended Response

Use the table below to answer Question 6. Write your answer on a separate sheet of paper.

Time	Speed at Bottom of Swing (m/s)
8:00 a.m.	2.2
10:00 a.m.	1.9
12:00 p.m.	1.7
2:00 p.m.	1.6

6. A large pendulum at a science museum is set in motion at the beginning of the day. The table shows how its speed at the bottom of the swing changes during the day. Use this data to determine how the height of the pendulum's swing changes. Explain your answer.

6.1.6, 6.4.3, 6.NS.8

Focus on **I**ndiana

Home-Grown Solution

Could biofuels be helpful in meeting Indiana's energy needs? Indiana has plenty of coal deposits, fertile farmland, and steady winds. Yet it gets more than 90% of its energy from other states.

If state and local officials could find ways to tap Indiana's energy sources, there might be several benefits. Costs to families in heating homes and fueling cars might be less. New jobs for workers would be created.

In August of 2007, one of the world's largest soybean-to-biofuel facilities was opened in Claypool, Indiana. The facility is located near vast stretches of Indiana's soy growing farmland. It uses advanced technology to crush soybeans and extract oils from them. These oils are then turned into biodiesel—a fuel alternative to petrolum.

Once the facility is fully functional, it will produce about 300–340 million liters of biodiesel each year. As a by-product, the process will also produce about 900 million kilograms of high-quality meal for local livestock.

▲ Use of biofuels is quickly increasing across the United States. Specially marked pumps like this one supply several types of biofuels.

Research It The amount of land available to grow crops is limited. Research biofuel production in Indiana, and describe a possible positive effect and a possible negative effect.

 6.1.5, 6.1.7, 6.NS.2

Grown for Biofuel

Going GREEN

Every time you turn on a light, you are using energy. We know this, but we don't always think about where the energy comes from. In most cases, that energy has come from fossil fuels, extracted from the ground, refined, and burned for their energy, in a process that causes a lot of pollution. Some scientists and government policymakers are exploring green (environmentally friendly) sources of energy.

According to the U.S. Environmental Protection Agency (EPA), green energy comes from technologies that don't produce waste products that will harm the environment. This includes resources like solar power and wind power, as well as geothermal energy from hot springs under the Earth's crust.

Reduced air pollution is just one of many benefits of green energy. Green energy also lowers greenhouse gas emissions and can cost less for consumers—like your family! Going green also creates jobs. Having many different sources makes the energy grid more stable. If one source stops working, we will still be able to get energy from other sources. What's not to love? Unfortunately, green energy technologies are expensive to develop.

▲ The flow of water is a renewable resource. But hydroelectric dams can damage habitats by changing the course of rivers.

Debate It Research the benefits and costs of developing green energy technologies. Organize a classroom debate about the costs and benefits of green energy. Be prepared to argue both sides of the issue.

 6.1.6, 6.NS.2

WHAT'S HAPPENING TO THE MOON?

THE BIG ?

How do Earth, the moon, and the sun interact?

This photograph shows a series of images of the moon taken over the course of an evening. Why do you think the moon looks different in each image? **Develop Hypotheses Explain what you think happened during the period of time shown in the photograph.**

> **UNTAMED SCIENCE** Watch the **Untamed Science** video to learn more about the moon.

_____
_____
_____
_____
_____
_____
_____

Earth, Moon, and Sun 6

Academic Standards for Science

6.2.1, 6.2.2, 6.2.4, 6.2.5, 6.NS.1, 6.NS.2,
6.NS.8, 6.NS.11, 6.DP.10

6 Getting Started

Check Your Understanding

1. **Background** Read the paragraph below and then answer the question.

Santiago is studying a globe. He sees that Earth has North and South poles. The globe **rotates** around a line through its center between the two poles. Another line called the **equator** divides Earth into two halves, the **Northern Hemisphere** and the **Southern Hemisphere.**

To **rotate** is to spin in place around a central line, or axis.

The **equator** is the imaginary line that divides Earth into two halves, the **Northern Hemisphere** and the **Southern Hemisphere.**

• Where is the equator found?

_____

_____

> **MY READING WEB** If you had trouble answering the question above, visit **My Reading Web** and type in *Earth, Moon, and Sun.*

Vocabulary Skill

Identify Multiple Meanings Words you use every day may have different meanings in science. Look at the different meanings of the words below.

Word	Everyday Meaning	Scientific Meaning
weight	*n.* a heavy object used for exercise **Example:** The athlete lifted *weights* to build strength.	*n.* a measure of the force of gravity on an object **Example:** The object's *weight* was 10 newtons.
force	*v.* to use power to make someone do something **Example:** She had to *force* herself to get up early.	*n.* a push or pull exerted on an object **Example:** You exert *force* when you open and close a door.

2. **Quick Check** Circle the sentence below that uses the scientific meaning of *force*.

• The *force* of gravity holds objects in their orbits.

• Her parents are trying to *force* her to get a job.

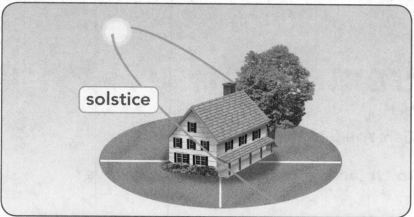

solstice

inertia

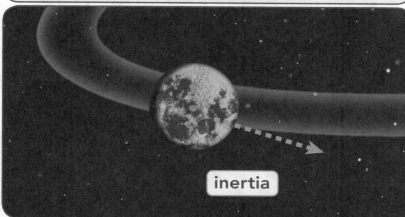

phase

solar eclipse

Chapter Preview

LESSON 1
- satellite • planet • meteor
- comet • star • constellation
↻ Identify the Main Idea
▲ Predict

LESSON 2
- axis • rotation • revolution
- orbit • calendar • solstice
- equinox
↻ Sequence
▲ Infer

LESSON 3
- force • gravity
- law of universal gravitation
- mass • weight • inertia
- Newton's first law of motion
↻ Ask Questions
▲ Draw Conclusions

LESSON 4
- phase • eclipse • solar eclipse
- umbra • penumbra
- lunar eclipse
↻ Relate Text and Visuals
▲ Make Models

LESSON 5
- tide • spring tide • neap tide
↻ Relate Cause and Effect
▲ Observe

LESSON 6
- maria • crater • meteoroid
↻ Compare and Contrast
▲ Develop Hypotheses

> VOCAB FLASH CARDS For extra help with vocabulary, visit **Vocab Flash Cards** and type in *Earth, Moon, and Sun.*

The Sky From Earth

UNLOCK
THE BIG

🔑 **What Can You See in the Night Sky?**
6.2.1, 6.2.4, 6.NS.2

🔑 **How Do Objects in the Sky Appear to Move?**
6.2.1, 6.2.5, 6.NS.1

MY PLANET DiARY

BIOGRAPHY

Communicate Discuss Aryabhata's discoveries with a partner. Then answer the questions below.

1. What did Aryabhata infer about the motion of Earth?

_____

_____

_____

2. What questions do you think about when you look at stars, the moon, or the planets?

_____

_____

_____

> PLANET DIARY Go to **Planet Diary** to learn more about the night sky.

Watching the Stars

When you look up at the night sky, what questions do you ask yourself? Do you wonder why the stars seem to move, or why the moon shines? Aryabhata (ar yah BAH tah) was an early Indian astronomer who thought about these questions. He was born in India in A.D. 476.

Many historians think that Aryabhata realized that the stars appear to move from east to west because Earth rotates from west to east. He also wrote that the moon and the planets shine because they reflect light from the sun. And he made all these inferences using just his eyes and his mind. The first telescopes wouldn't come along for more than a thousand years!

Lab zone® Do the Inquiry Warm-Up *Earth's Sky.*

Vocabulary
- satellite • planet • meteor
- comet • star • constellation

Skills
- Reading: Identify the Main Idea
- Inquiry: Predict

What Can You See in the Night Sky?

Depending on how dark the sky is where you are, you might see 2,000 or 3,000 stars using just your eyes. 🔑 On a clear night, you may see stars, the moon, planets, meteors, and comets.

Academic Standards for Science

6.2.1 Describe and model how the position, size and relative motions of the earth, moon, and sun cause day and night, solar and lunar eclipses and phases of the moon.

6.NS.2 Plan and carry out investigations.

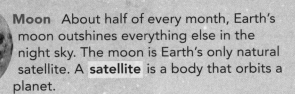

Moon About half of every month, Earth's moon outshines everything else in the night sky. The moon is Earth's only natural satellite. A **satellite** is a body that orbits a planet.

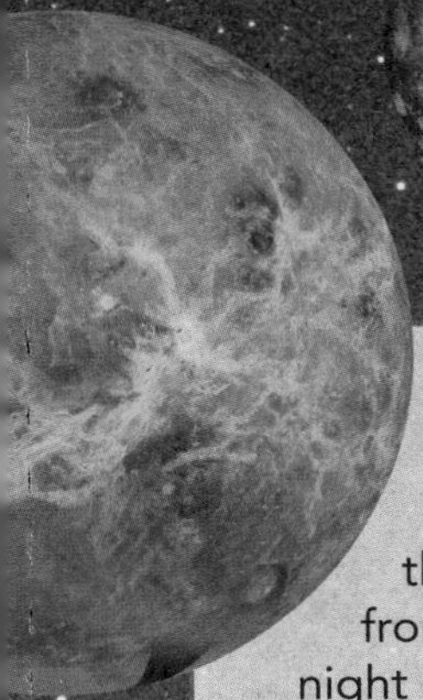

Planets You may see objects that move from night to night against the background stars. These are planets. A **planet** is an object that orbits the sun, is large enough to have become rounded by its own gravity, and has cleared the area of its orbit. There are eight planets in the solar system. Five are visible from Earth without a telescope: Mercury, Venus, Mars, Jupiter, and Saturn.

Meteors and Comets Have you ever seen a "shooting star"? These sudden bright streaks are called **meteors.** A meteor is the streak of light produced when a small object burns up entering Earth's atmosphere. You can see a meteor on almost any night. Comets are rarer. A **comet** is a cold mixture of dust and ice that gives up a long trail of light as it approaches the sun.

Stars Stars appear as tiny points of light. However, scientists infer that a **star** is a giant ball of hot gas, mainly composed of hydrogen and helium. As seen from Earth, the positions of stars relative to each other do not seem to change.

FIGURE 1 ....
These photos show examples of stars, planets, and other objects.

✎ **Observe** What can you observe about the objects shown on this page? Include at least two different objects.

_____

_____

_____

_____

_____

185

Constellations For thousands of years humans have seen patterns in groups of stars and given names to them. 🔑 **A constellation is a pattern or group of stars that people imagined to represent a figure, animal, or object.** Astronomers also use the word *constellation* for an area of the sky and all the objects in that area.

Different cultures have identified different constellations. In Western culture, there are 88 constellations. Most constellation names used today come from the ancient Greeks, who probably took them from the Egyptians and Mesopotamians.

Some constellations' names come from Latin. The constellation Leo, for example, is named from the Latin word meaning "lion." Some constellations are named for people or animals in Greek myths. You may have read some of these myths in school. Do the names *Pegasus* or *Perseus* sound familiar? They are mythological characters and also constellations.

Eastern Horizon

Southern Horizon

FIGURE 2 ···

> INTERACTIVE ART **How to Use a Star Chart**
To use a star chart at night, follow these steps.

1. Choose the chart that fits your location and season. This is a summer chart for the Northern Hemisphere. (There are charts for the other seasons in the Appendix.)

2. Hold the chart upright in front of you. Turn the chart so the label at the bottom matches the direction you face. (*Hint:* If you are looking at the Big Dipper, you are looking north.)

3. Hold the chart at eye level. Compare the figures on the bottom half of the chart to the sky in front of you.

apply it!

❶ **Interpret Diagrams** Find these constellations in **Figure 2**. Then write each constellation's name by its picture.

❷ CHALLENGE Choose another constellation from **Figure 2**. What does it represent? Do research to find out.

_____

_____

6.NS.2

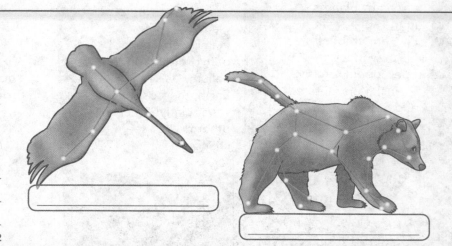

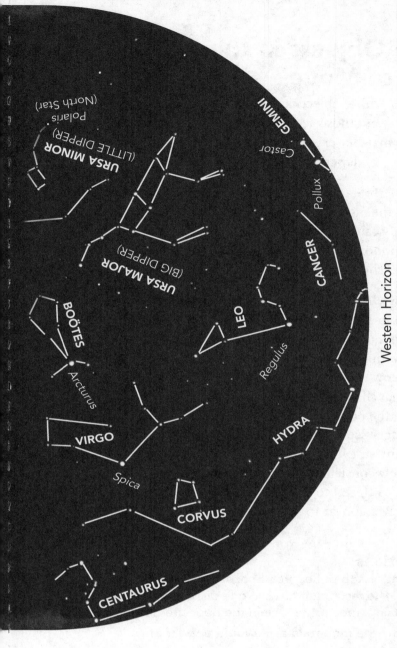

Northern Horizon

Western Horizon

Finding Constellations

A star chart, like the one shown in **Figure 2,** can help you find constellations in the night sky. Read the instructions for how to use the chart. It may seem a little strange at first, but with some practice, these charts are easy to use. Here is one tip to help you get started.

You can probably recognize the Big Dipper. This group of stars is actually not a constellation itself. It is part of the constellation Ursa Major, or the Great Bear. The two stars at the end of the dipper's "bowl" are called the Pointers.

Picture an imaginary line between those two stars. If you continue it away from the "bowl," the first fairly bright star you'll reach is called Polaris (po LA ris). Polaris is commonly called the North Star. It is located close to the sky's North Pole.

In the Appendix, you can find star charts for all four seasons. Take one outside on a clear night and see what you can find!

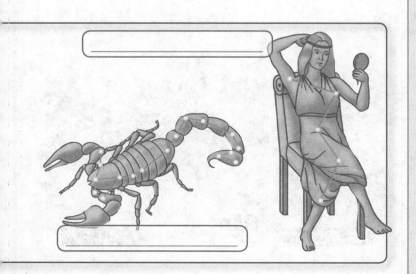

Lab zone® Do the Quick Lab *Observing the Night Sky.*

Assess Your Understanding

got it? ······································

O **I get it!** Now I know that objects visible in the night sky include _____

_____

_____

_____

O **I need extra help with** _____

_____

_____

Go to **MY SCIENCE COACH** *online for help with this subject.*

6.2.1

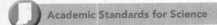

Academic Standards for Science

6.2.1 Describe and model how the position, size and relative motions of the earth, moon, and sun cause day and night, solar and lunar eclipses and phases of the moon.

6.NS.1 Make predictions based on prior knowledge.

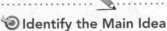

Identify the Main Idea
Underline the main idea in the paragraph called Star Motions.

How Do Objects in the Sky Appear to Move?

Stars, planets, and other objects appear to move over time. They do move in space, but those actual motions and their apparent, or visible, motions may be very different. 🔑 **The apparent motion of objects in the sky depends on the motions of Earth.**

Star Motions Stars generally appear to move from east to west through the night. As Aryabhata thought, this apparent motion is actually caused by Earth turning from west to east. The sun's apparent motion during the day is also caused by Earth's motion. **Figure 3** shows how this kind of apparent motion occurs.

Seasonal Changes Constellations and star patterns remain the same year after year, but which ones you can see varies from season to season. For example, you can find Orion in the eastern sky on winter evenings. But by spring, you'll see Orion in the west, disappearing below the horizon shortly after sunset.

These seasonal changes are caused by Earth's orbit around the sun. Each night, the position of most stars shifts slightly to the west. Soon you no longer see stars once visible in the west, and other stars appear in the east.

There are a few constellations that you can see all year long. These are the ones closest to the North Star. As Earth rotates, these constellations never appear to rise or set.

FIGURE 3 ⋯⋯⋯⋯⋯⋯⋯⋯⋯⋯⋯⋯⋯⋯⋯⋯⋯⋯⋯⋯⋯⋯⋯⋯⋯⋯⋯

Opposite Motions   6.NS.1

The restaurant on top of Seattle's Space Needle rotates much as Earth does. The restaurant turns in one direction, which makes objects outside appear to move in the opposite direction.

△ **Predict Draw the mountain as it would appear at each time shown.**

Motion of restaurant   6:00 P.M.   6:35 P.M.   7:20 P.M.

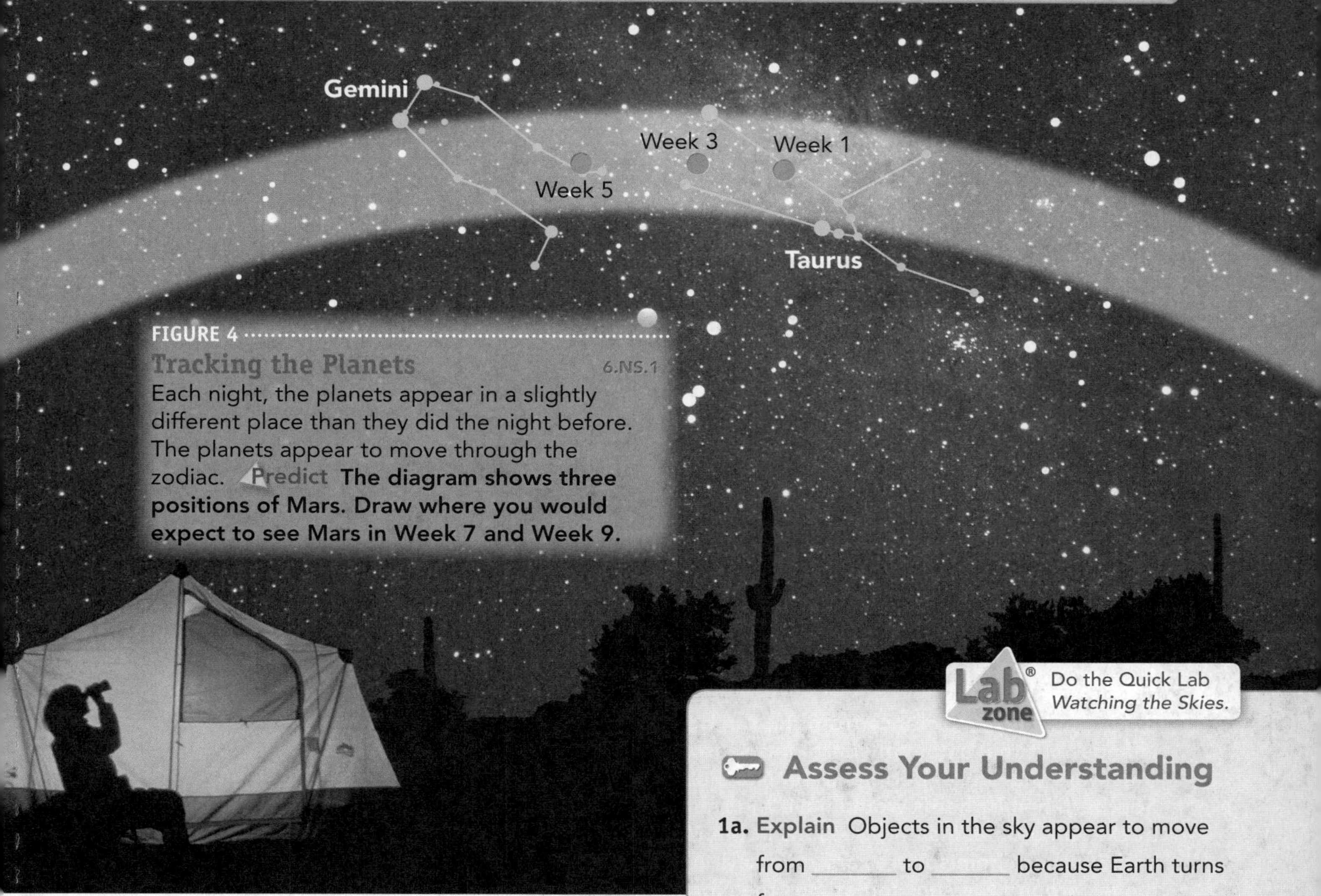

Gemini

Week 3

Week 1

Week 5

Taurus

FIGURE 4 ....

Tracking the Planets   6.NS.1

Each night, the planets appear in a slightly different place than they did the night before. The planets appear to move through the zodiac. *Predict* **The diagram shows three positions of Mars. Draw where you would expect to see Mars in Week 7 and Week 9.**

Do the Quick Lab *Watching the Skies.*

Planets

Planets appear to move against the background of stars, as shown in **Figure 4**. Because the planets all orbit the sun in about the same plane, they appear to move through a narrow band in the sky. This band is called the zodiac. It includes constellations such as Taurus, Leo, and Virgo.

Some planets, when they are visible, can be seen all night long. Mars, Jupiter, and Saturn are all farther from the sun than Earth is. Sometimes, Earth passes between them and the sun. When this occurs, the planets are visible after sunset, once the sun's bright light no longer blocks the view.

You can see Venus and Mercury only in the evening or morning. They are closer to the sun than Earth, and so they always appear close to the sun. Venus is the brightest object in the night sky, other than the moon. Mercury appears low in the sky and is visible for a limited time around sunrise or sunset.

Assess Your Understanding

1a. Explain Objects in the sky appear to move from _____ to _____ because Earth turns from _____ to _____.

6.2.1

b. Make Generalizations What determines whether a planet is visible all night long?

_____

_____

_____

_____

6.2.1

got it? ....

○ **I get it!** Now I know that objects in the sky appear to move _____

_____

○ **I need extra help with** _____

Go to **my science** ⓢ **coach** *online for help with this subject.*
6.2.1

189

Earth in Space

UNLOCK THE BIG ?

🔑 **How Does Earth Move?**
6.2.1, 6.NS.1, 6.DP.10

🔑 **What Causes Seasons?**
6.2.5, 6.NS.8

my planet diary

The Seasons

Misconception: The seasons change because Earth's distance from the sun changes.

Fact: Seasons are the result of Earth's tilted axis.

Evidence: Earth's distance from the sun does change, but that's not why Earth has seasons. If that were the cause, people in the Northern and Southern hemispheres would have the same seasons at the same time. Instead, seasons in the Northern and Southern hemispheres are reversed. As Earth moves around the sun, sometimes the Northern Hemisphere is tilted toward the sun. At other times the Southern Hemisphere is tilted toward the sun.

MISCONCEPTION

Before you read the rest of this lesson, answer the questions below.

1. Why are summers generally warmer than winters?

_____

_____

_____

_____

2. Where on Earth is the tilt of Earth least likely to affect seasons? Why?

_____

_____

_____

_____

> **PLANET DIARY** Go to **Planet Diary** to learn more about Earth's motions.

January 21

Where are you and what are you doing today?

 Lab zone® Do the Inquiry Warm-Up *What Causes Day and Night?*

Vocabulary

- axis • rotation • revolution • orbit
- calendar • solstice • equinox

Skills

↻ Reading: Sequence

△ Inquiry: Infer

How Does Earth Move?

Until a few hundred years ago, most people thought that Earth stood still and the sun, moon, and stars moved around it. But today, scientists know that Earth itself moves and that objects seem to move across the sky because of Earth's motion. ☞ **Earth moves in space in two major ways: rotation and revolution.**

Rotation The imaginary line that passes through Earth's center and the North and South poles is Earth's **axis.** The spinning of Earth on its axis is called **rotation.**

Earth's rotation causes day and night, as you can see in **Figure 1.** As Earth rotates eastward, the sun appears to move west across the sky. As Earth continues to turn to the east, the sun appears to set in the west. Sunlight can't reach the side of Earth facing away from the sun, so it is night there. It takes Earth about 24 hours to rotate once. As you know, each 24-hour cycle of day and night is called a day.

> **Academic Standards for Science**
>
> **6.2.1** Describe and model how the position, size and relative motions of the earth, moon, and sun cause day and night, solar and lunar eclipses and phases of the moon.
>
> **6.NS.1** Make predictions based on research and prior knowledge.
>
> **6.DP.10** Communicate the solution using drawings.

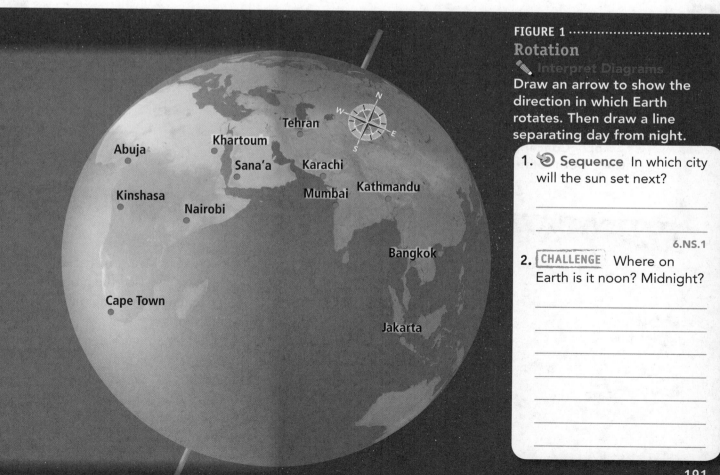

FIGURE 1 ⋯⋯⋯⋯⋯⋯⋯

Rotation

✎ Interpret Diagrams

Draw an arrow to show the direction in which Earth rotates. Then draw a line separating day from night.

1. ↻ **Sequence** In which city will the sun set next?

_____

_____

6.NS.1

2. CHALLENGE Where on Earth is it noon? Midnight?

_____

_____

_____

_____

_____

_____

191

Revolution In addition to rotating, Earth travels around the sun. **Revolution** is the movement of one object around another. One revolution of Earth around the sun is called a year. Earth's path, or **orbit,** is a slightly elongated circle, or ellipse. Earth's orbit brings the planet closest to the sun in January.

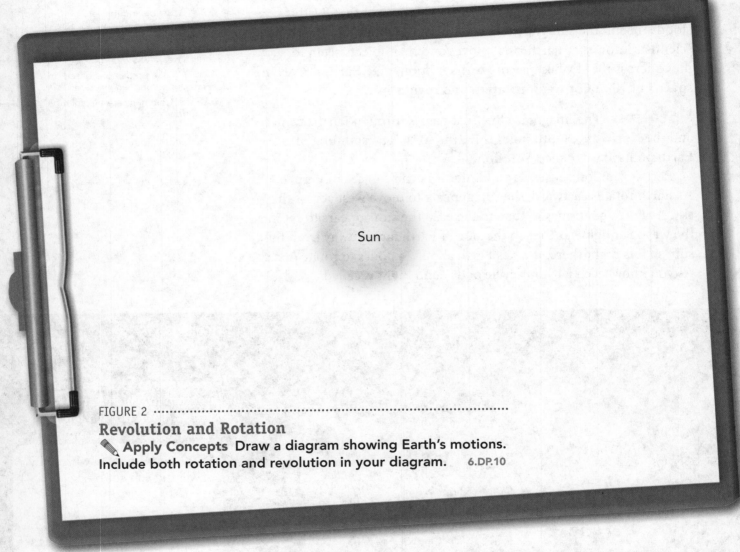

Sun

FIGURE 2 ···
Revolution and Rotation
✎ **Apply Concepts** Draw a diagram showing Earth's motions. Include both rotation and revolution in your diagram. 6.DP.10

✎ **Sequence** Which calendar discussed in this section was developed most recently?

Calendars People of many cultures have divided time based on the motions of Earth and the moon. They have used the motions to establish calendars. A **calendar** is a system of organizing time that defines the beginning, length, and divisions of a year.

The most common calendar today is divided into years, months, and days. One year equals the time it takes Earth to complete one orbit. One day equals the time it takes Earth to turn once on its axis. People also divide the year into months based on the moon's cycle. The time from one full moon to another is about 29 days, though modern months do not match the moon's cycle exactly.

The History of the Calendar

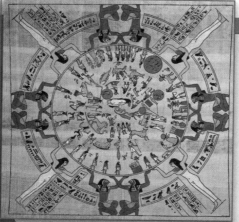

Egyptian

The ancient Egyptians created one of the first calendars. Based on star motions, they calculated that the year was about 365 days long. They divided the year into 12 months of 30 days each, with an extra 5 days at the end.

Roman

The Romans borrowed the Egyptian calendar. But Earth's orbit actually takes about 365¼ days. The Romans adjusted the Egyptian calendar by adding one day every four years. You know this fourth year as "leap year," when February is given 29 days instead of its usual 28. Using leap years helps to ensure that annual events, such as the beginning of summer, occur on the same date each year.

Gregorian

The Roman calendar was off by a little more than 11 minutes a year. Over the centuries, these minutes added up. By the 1500s, the beginning of spring was about ten days too early. To straighten things out, Pope Gregory XIII dropped ten days from the year 1582. He also made some other minor changes to the Roman system to form the calendar that we use today.

Lab zone® Do the Quick Lab *Sun Shadows.*

Assess Your Understanding

1a. Identify What are the two major motions of Earth as it travels through space?

_____

6.2.1

b. Explain Which motion causes day and night?

_____

6.2.1

c. Infer Why do people use Earth's motions to determine units of time?

_____

_____

6.2.1

got it?

○ **I get it!** Now I know that Earth moves by _____

_____

○ **I need extra help with** _____

Go to **MY SCIENCE COACH** online for help with this subject.

6.2.1

193

Academic Standards for Science

6.2.5 Demonstrate that the seasons in both hemispheres are the result of the inclination of the earth on its axis which in turn causes changes in sunlight intensity and length of day.

6.NS.8 Analyze data, and use it to identify patterns and make inferences based on these patterns.

What Causes Seasons?

Many places that are far from Earth's equator and its poles have four distinct seasons: winter, spring, summer, and autumn. But there are differences in temperature from place to place. For instance, it is generally warmer near the equator than near the poles. Why?

How Sunlight Hits Earth **Figure 3** shows how sunlight strikes Earth's surface. Notice that, near the equator, sunlight hits Earth's surface from almost overhead. Near the poles, sunlight arrives at a steep angle. As a result, it is spread out over a greater area. That's why it is warmer near the equator than near the poles.

Earth's Tilted Axis If Earth's axis were straight up and down relative to its orbit, temperatures in an area would remain fairly constant year-round. There would be no seasons. 🔑 **Earth has seasons because its axis is tilted as it revolves around the sun.**

Notice in **Figure 4** that Earth's axis is always tilted at an angle of 23.5° from the vertical. The North Pole always points in the same direction. As Earth revolves around the sun, the north end of its axis is tilted away from the sun for part of the year and toward the sun for part of the year. Summer and winter are caused by Earth's tilt as it revolves around the sun.

FIGURE 3 ·······························
Sunlight on Earth
The diagram shows how Earth's tilted axis affects the strength of sunlight in different places.

⚠️**Infer** Draw a circle around the area where sunlight is most direct. Mark an X on the places that sunlight reaches, but where it is less direct.

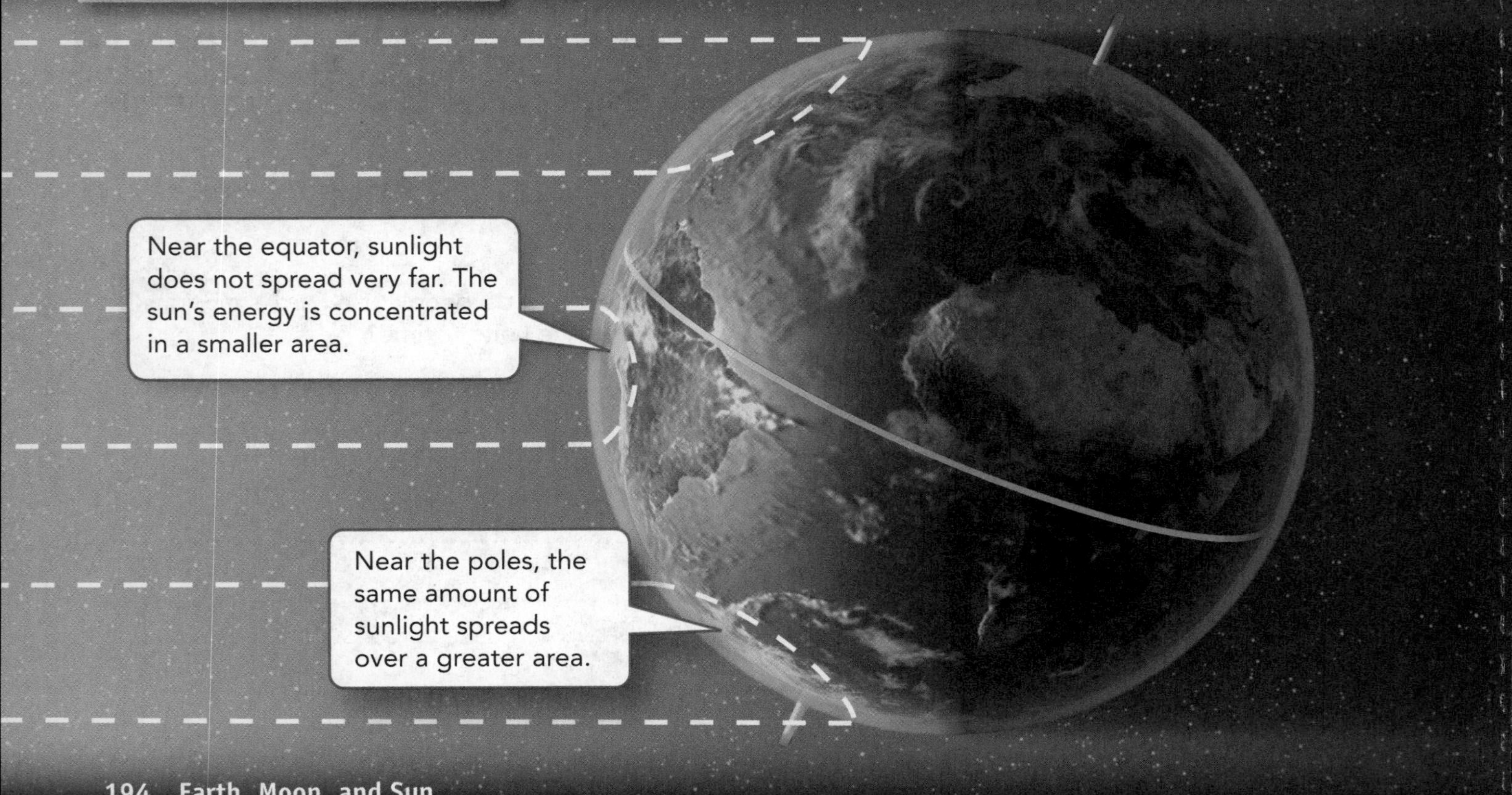

Near the equator, sunlight does not spread very far. The sun's energy is concentrated in a smaller area.

Near the poles, the same amount of sunlight spreads over a greater area.

June In June, the north end of Earth's axis is tilted toward the sun. In the Northern Hemisphere, the noon sun is high in the sky and there are more hours of daylight than darkness. The sun's rays are concentrated. It is summer in the Northern Hemisphere.

At the same time south of the equator, the sun's energy is spread over a larger area. The sun is low in the sky and days are shorter than nights. It is winter in the Southern Hemisphere.

December In December, people in the Southern Hemisphere receive the most direct sunlight, so it is summer. At the same time, the sun's rays in the Northern Hemisphere are more slanted and there are fewer hours of daylight. So it is winter in the Northern Hemisphere.

March

June

December

September

FIGURE 4 ·························
▷ INTERACTIVE ART **Seasons**
The diagram shows how Earth moves during the year. It is not drawn to scale.

✎ **Make Generalizations** Describe the weather and sunlight in the Northern and Southern hemispheres in March and September.

_____
_____
_____
_____
_____
_____
_____
_____

Solstices

The sun appears farthest north of the equator once each year and farthest south once each year. Each of these days is known as a **solstice** (SOHL stis). The day when the sun appears farthest north is the summer solstice in the Northern Hemisphere and the winter solstice in the Southern Hemisphere. This solstice occurs around June 21 each year. It is the longest day of the year in the Northern Hemisphere and the shortest day in the Southern Hemisphere. As you can see in **Figure 5,** the sun rises to the northeast and sets to the northwest.

Similarly, around December 21, the sun appears farthest south. This is the winter solstice in the Northern Hemisphere and the summer solstice in the Southern Hemisphere. The sun rises to the southeast and sets to the southwest.

Equinoxes

Halfway between the solstices, neither hemisphere is tilted toward the sun. The noon sun is directly overhead at the equator, rises due east, and sets due west. Each of these days is known as an **equinox,** which means "equal night." During an equinox, day and night are each about 12 hours long everywhere. The vernal (spring) equinox occurs around March 21 and marks the beginning of spring in the Northern Hemisphere. The fall, or autumnal, equinox occurs around September 22. It marks the beginning of fall in the Northern Hemisphere.

FIGURE 5 ·····································
Solstices and Equinoxes
The diagrams show the apparent path of the sun at the solstices and equinoxes in the Northern Hemisphere. The sun rises and sets farthest north at the June solstice and farthest south at the December solstice.

✎ **Apply Concepts** Draw the sun's path at the equinoxes and the December solstice for the Southern Hemisphere.

6.NS.8

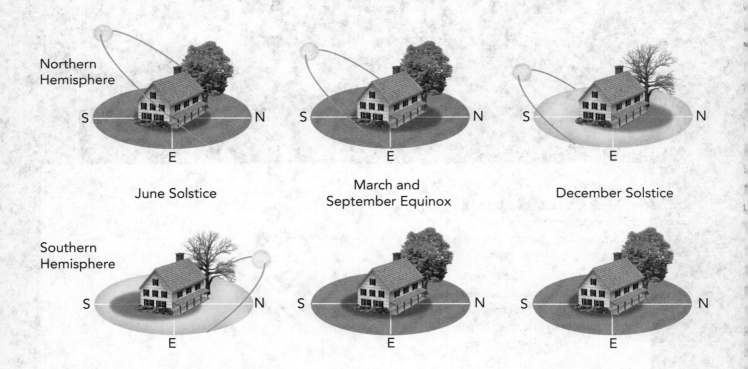

| June Solstice | March and September Equinox | December Solstice |

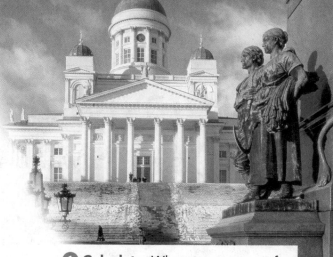

do the math! Sample Problem

Calculating Percents

The table shows the number of hours of sunlight in three cities at different times of year. What percentage of a 24-hour day has sunlight in Guadalajara on January 1?

STEP 1 Divide the number of hours of sunlight by the total number of hours.

$$\frac{\text{Hours of sunlight}}{\text{Total hours}} = \frac{10.90 \text{ hours}}{24 \text{ hours}} = 0.45$$

STEP 2 Multiply by 100 to find the percent.

$$0.45 \times 100 = 45\%$$

In Guadalajara, 45% of a 24-hour day has sunlight on January 1.

1 Calculate What percentage of a day has sunlight in Helsinki on July 1?

2 Calculate What is the difference in the percentage of the day that has sunlight in Helsinki and in Philadelphia on January 1?

3 Infer What percentage of the day would you expect to have sunlight at the equator in January? In June?

City	Approximate Latitude	Hours of Daylight			
		January 1	April 1	July 1	October 1
Helsinki, Finland	60°N	5.98	13.33	18.80	11.45
Philadelphia, United States	40°N	9.38	12.68	14.95	11.77
Guadalajara, Mexico	20°N	10.90	12.37	13.37	11.95

6.NS.8

 Lab zone® Do the Lab Investigation *Reasons for the Seasons.*

🔑 Assess Your Understanding

2a. Define The noon sun is directly overhead at the equator during (a solstice/an equinox).

6.2.5

b. Relate Cause and Effect What causes the seasons? _____

_____

_____

6.2.5

c. Predict How would the seasons be different if Earth were not tilted on its axis? Explain.

_____

_____

_____

_____

_____

6.2.5

got it? ·

○ **I get it!** Now I know that Earth's seasons are caused by _____

_____

○ **I need extra help with** _____

Go to **MY SCIENCE COACH** online for help with this subject.

6.2.5

Gravity and Motion

UNLOCK THE BIG ?

🔑 **What Determines Gravity?**
6.2.2

🔑 **What Keeps Objects in Orbit?**
6.2.2, 6.NS.1, 6.NS.8

MY PLANET DIARY

Gravity Assists

You might think that gravity only brings objects down. But gravity can also speed things up and send them flying! If a space probe comes close to a planet, the planet's gravity changes the probe's path. Engineers plan space missions to take advantage of these "gravity assists." A gravity assist can shorten the probe's interplanetary trip by many years. The diagram shows how the probe *Voyager 2* used gravity assists to visit all four outer planets!

Path of spacecraft

TECHNOLOGY

Use what you know about gravity to answer this question.

How does a planet's gravity change the path of a space probe?

_____

_____

_____

▶ **PLANET DIARY** Go to **Planet Diary** to learn more about gravity.

 Do the Inquiry Warm-Up **What Factors Affect Gravity?**

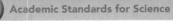

Academic Standards for Science

6.2.2 Recognize that gravity is a force that keeps celestial bodies in regular and predictable motion, holds objects to earth's surface, and is responsible for ocean tides.

What Determines Gravity?

Earth revolves around the sun in a nearly circular orbit. The moon orbits Earth in the same way. But what keeps Earth and the moon in orbit? Why don't they just fly off into space?

The first person to answer these questions was the English scientist Isaac Newton. In the 1600s, Newton realized that there must be a force acting between Earth and the moon that kept the

Vocabulary
- force • gravity • law of universal gravitation
- mass • weight • inertia • Newton's first law of motion

Skills
- ↻ Reading: Ask Questions
- △ Inquiry: Draw Conclusions

Gravity Newton hypothesized that the force that pulls an apple to the ground also pulls the moon toward Earth, keeping it in orbit. This force, called **gravity,** attracts all objects toward each other. Newton's **law of universal gravitation** states that every object in the universe attracts every other object. ⚷ **The strength of the force of gravity between two objects depends on two factors: the masses of the objects and the distance between them.**

Gravity, Mass, and Weight The strength of gravity depends in part on the masses of each of the objects. **Mass** is the amount of matter in an object. Because Earth is so massive, it exerts a much greater force on you than this book does.

The measure of the force of gravity on an object is called **weight.** Mass doesn't change, but an object's weight can change depending on its location. On the moon, you would weigh about one sixth as much as on Earth. This is because the moon has less mass than Earth, so the pull of the moon's gravity on you would also be less.

Gravity and Distance Gravity is also affected by the distance between two objects. The force of gravity decreases rapidly as distance increases. If the distance between two objects doubles, the force of gravity decreases to one fourth of its original value.

did you know?

You could say we owe our understanding of gravity to disease! In 1665, Isaac Newton was a student. Then a disease called plague shut down the university for 18 months. Newton had to go home. While he was there, he thought of the ideas that led to his theory. (But it may not be true that he got the idea when an apple fell from a tree.)

FIGURE 1 ....
> VIRTUAL LAB **Gravity, Mass, and Distance**
✏ **Compare and Contrast** Draw arrows showing the force of gravity in the second and third pictures.

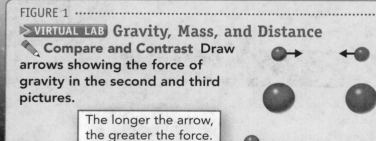

The longer the arrow, the greater the force.

Lab zone Do the Quick Lab *What's Doing the Pulling?*

⚷ Assess Your Understanding

got it? ....

○ **I get it!** Now I know that the force of gravity depends on _____

_____

○ **I need extra help with** _____

Go to **my science** ⓢ **coach** *online for help with this subject.*

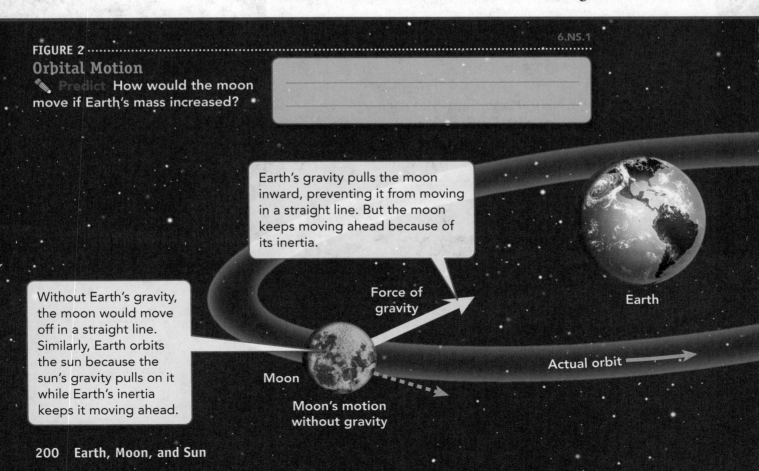

What Keeps Objects in Orbit?

If the sun and Earth are constantly pulling on one another because of gravity, why doesn't Earth fall into the sun? Similarly, why doesn't the moon crash into Earth? The fact that such collisions have not occurred shows that there must be another factor at work. That factor is called inertia.

Inertia The tendency of an object to resist a change in motion is **inertia.** You feel the effects of inertia every day. When you are riding in a car and it stops suddenly, you keep moving forward. If you didn't have a seat belt on, your inertia could cause you to bump into the car's windshield or the seat in front of you. The more mass an object has, the greater its inertia. An object with greater inertia is more difficult to start or stop.

Isaac Newton stated his ideas about inertia as a scientific law. **Newton's first law of motion** says that an object at rest will stay at rest and an object in motion will stay in motion with a constant speed and direction unless acted on by a force.

Orbital Motion Why do Earth and the moon remain in orbit? **Newton concluded that inertia and gravity combine to keep Earth in orbit around the sun and the moon in orbit around Earth.** You can see how this occurs in **Figure 2.**

Academic Standards for Science

6.2.2 Recognize that gravity is a force that keeps celestial bodies in regular and predictable motion, holds objects to earth's surface, and is responsible for ocean tides.

6.NS.1 Make predictions based on research and prior knowledge.

6.NS.8 Analyze data, and use it to identify patterns and make inferences based on these patterns.

Ask Questions Before you read the paragraphs under Inertia, write a question you would like to have answered. Look for the answer as you read.

_____

_____

_____

_____

FIGURE 2
Orbital Motion
Predict **How would the moon move if Earth's mass increased?**

6.NS.1

Earth's gravity pulls the moon inward, preventing it from moving in a straight line. But the moon keeps moving ahead because of its inertia.

Without Earth's gravity, the moon would move off in a straight line. Similarly, Earth orbits the sun because the sun's gravity pulls on it while Earth's inertia keeps it moving ahead.

Force of gravity

Earth

Actual orbit

Moon

Moon's motion without gravity

do the math! Analyzing Data

Gravity Versus Distance

As a rocket leaves a planet's surface, the force of gravity between the rocket and the planet changes. Use the graph to answer the questions below.

❶ **Read Graphs** The variables being graphed

are _____

and _____

❷ **Read Graphs** What is the force of gravity on the rocket at the planet's surface?

_____

❸ **Read Graphs** What is the force of gravity on the rocket at two units (twice the planet's radius from its center)?

_____

❹ **Make Generalizations** In general, how does the force of gravity on the rocket change as its distance from the planet increases?

_____

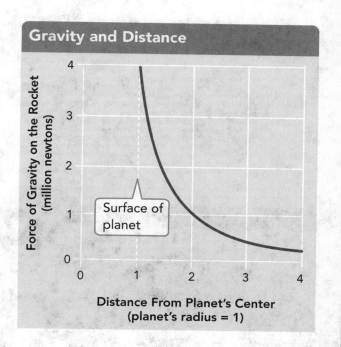

Gravity and Distance

Force of Gravity on the Rocket (million newtons)

Surface of planet

Distance From Planet's Center (planet's radius = 1)

6.NS.8

Lab zone ® Do the Quick Lab *Around and Around We Go.*

🔑 Assess Your Understanding

1a. Identify What two factors keep a planet in orbit around the sun?

_____

6.2.2

b. Draw Conclusions What keeps Earth from falling into the sun?

_____

6.2.2

c. CHALLENGE How would a planet move if the sun suddenly disappeared? Explain.

_____

_____

_____

_____

6.2.2, 6.NS.1

got it? ···

○ **I get it!** Now I know that objects are kept in orbit by _____

_____

○ **I need extra help with** _____

Go to MY SCIENCE ⓢ COACH online for help with this subject.

6.2.2

4 Phases and Eclipses

🔑 **What Causes the Moon's Phases?**
6.2.1, 6.NS.11

🔑 **What Are Eclipses?**
6.2.1, 6.DP.10

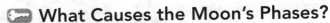

MY PLANET DIARY

BLOG

Posted by: Nicole

Location: Bernhard's Bay, New York

One night, my mom, dad, and I were coming home from eating dinner. When we got out of the car, we saw that the moon was turning red. We looked at the moon for a while. Then our neighbor called and said that it was a lunar eclipse. It was an amazing sight.

Think about your own experiences as you answer the question below.

What is the most interesting or unusual event you have ever seen in the sky?

_____

_____

_____

_____

 Do the Inquiry Warm-Up
How Does the Moon Move?

▶ PLANET DIARY Go to **Planet Diary** to learn more about eclipses.

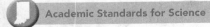

Academic Standards for Science

6.2.1 Describe and model how the position, size and relative motions of the earth, moon, and sun cause day and night, solar and lunar eclipses and phases of the moon.

6.NS.11 Communicate findings using models.

What Causes the Moon's Phases?

Have you ever been kept awake by bright moonlight? The light streaming through your window actually comes from the sun! The moon does not shine with its own light. Instead, it reflects light from the sun. When the moon is full, this light may be bright enough to read by! But at other times, the moon is just a thin crescent in the sky. The different shapes of the moon you see from Earth are called **phases.** Phases are caused by the motions of the moon around Earth.

Vocabulary

- phase
- eclipse
- solar eclipse
- umbra
- penumbra
- lunar eclipse

Skills

⟳ **Reading:** Relate Text and Visuals

△ **Inquiry:** Make Models

Motions of the Moon When you look up at the moon, you may see what looks like a face. What you are really seeing is a pattern of light-colored and dark-colored areas on the moon's surface that just happens to look like a face. Oddly, this pattern never seems to move. The same side of the moon, the "near side," always faces Earth. The "far side" of the moon always faces away from Earth. Why? The answer has to do with the moon's motions.

Like Earth, the moon moves through space in two ways. The moon revolves around Earth and also rotates on its own axis. The moon rotates once on its axis in the same time that it takes to revolve once around Earth. Thus, a "day" on the moon is the same length as a month on Earth. For this reason, the same side of the moon always faces Earth, as you can see in **Figure 1**.

As the moon orbits Earth, the relative positions of the moon, Earth, and sun change. ⟬══ **The changing relative positions of the moon, Earth, and sun cause the phases of the moon.**

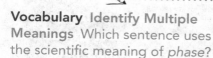

Vocabulary Identify Multiple Meanings Which sentence uses the scientific meaning of *phase*?

○ The doctor told the parent that the child was just going through a phase.

○ The moon goes through a cycle of phases every month.

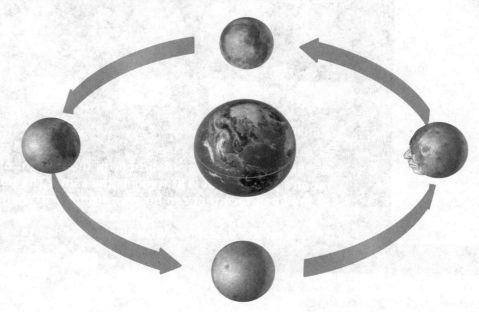

FIGURE 1 ....

The Moon's Motion
The diagram shows the moon's rotation and revolution. ✎ **Infer** Find the face on the **rightmost view of the moon. Draw the face as it would appear on each view.**

CHALLENGE How would the moon appear from Earth if the moon did not rotate?

_____

_____

Phases of the Moon

Half the moon is almost always in sunlight. But since the moon orbits Earth, you see the moon from different angles. The phase of the moon you see depends on how much of the sunlit side of the moon faces Earth.

During the new moon phase, the side of the moon facing Earth is not lit. As the moon revolves around Earth, you see more of the lit side of the moon, until you see all of the lit side. As the month continues, you see less of the lit side. You can see these changes in **Figure 2.** About 29.5 days after the last new moon, a new moon occurs again.

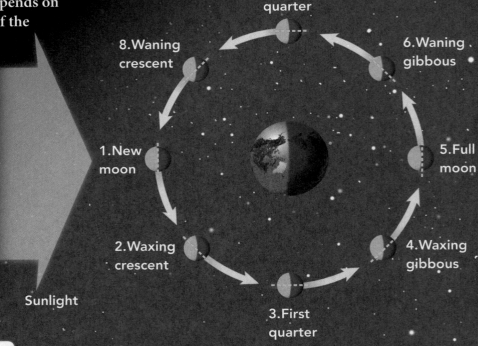

Sunlight

1.New moon
2.Waxing crescent
3.First quarter
4.Waxing gibbous
5.Full moon
6.Waning gibbous
7.Third quarter
8.Waning crescent

FIGURE 2 ······················
Moon Phases
As the moon revolves around Earth, the amount of the moon's surface that is lit remains the same. The part of the lit surface that can be seen from Earth changes.
✎ Interpret Diagrams **Match each photo to its phase shown on the diagram. Write the number of the phase.**

apply it!

⚠ **Make Models** Describe a way to model the moon's phases using items you might have at home.

_____

_____

_____

_____

_____

6.NS.11

Do the Quick Lab
Moon Phases.

🔑 Assess Your Understanding

got it?······················

○ **I get it!** Now I know that moon phases are caused by _____

_____

○ **I need extra help with** _____

Go to **MY SCIENCE ⓢ COACH** *online for help with this subject.*

6.2.1

What Are Eclipses?

The moon's orbit around Earth is slightly tilted with respect to Earth's orbit around the sun. As a result, the moon travels above and below Earth's orbit. But on rare occasions, Earth, the moon, and the sun line up.

When an object in space comes between the sun and a third object, it casts a shadow on that object, causing an **eclipse** (ih KLIPS) to take place. There are two types of eclipses: solar eclipses and lunar eclipses. (The words *solar* and *lunar* come from the Latin words for "sun" and "moon.")

Academic Standards for Science

6.2.1 Describe and model how the position, size and relative motions of the earth, moon, and sun cause day and night, solar and lunar eclipses and phases of the moon.

6.DP.10 Communicate the solution using drawings.

Solar Eclipses During a new moon, the moon lies between Earth and the sun. A **solar eclipse** occurs when the moon passes directly between Earth and the sun, blocking sunlight from Earth. The moon's shadow then hits Earth.

Total Solar Eclipses The very darkest part of the moon's shadow is the **umbra** (UM bruh). You can see how the umbra strikes Earth in Figure 3. Within the umbra, the sun's light is completely blocked. Only people within the umbra experience a total solar eclipse. During a total solar eclipse, the sky grows as dark as night. The air gets cool and the sky becomes an eerie color. You can see the stars and the solar corona, which is the faint outer atmosphere of the sun.

Partial Solar Eclipses The moon casts another part of its shadow that is less dark than the umbra. This larger part of the shadow is called the **penumbra** (peh NUM bruh). In the penumbra, part of the sun is visible from Earth. During a solar eclipse, people in the penumbra see only a partial eclipse.

FIGURE 3 ·······
Solar Eclipse
The diagram shows the moon's penumbra and umbra during an eclipse. It is not drawn to scale.

Relate Text and Visuals
Mark an X to show where a total solar eclipse would be visible. Circle the area in which a partial solar eclipse would be visible.

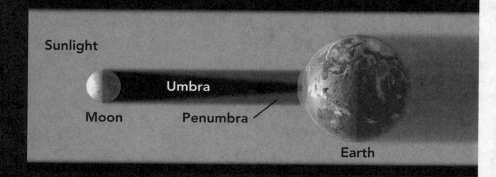

Sunlight · Moon · Umbra · Penumbra · Earth

Lunar Eclipses During most months, the moon moves near Earth's shadow but not quite into it. A **lunar eclipse** occurs at a full moon when Earth is directly between the moon and the sun. You can see a lunar eclipse in Figure 4. 🔑 During a lunar eclipse, Earth blocks sunlight from reaching the moon. Lunar eclipses occur only when there is a full moon because the moon is closest to Earth's shadow at that time.

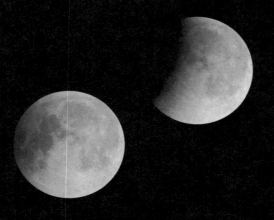

✏️ **Relate Text and Visuals** Mark an X on the photograph above that shows a total eclipse.

Total Lunar Eclipses Like the moon's shadow in a solar eclipse, Earth's shadow has an umbra and a penumbra. When the moon is in Earth's umbra, you see a total lunar eclipse. Unlike a total solar eclipse, a total lunar eclipse can be seen anywhere on Earth that the moon is visible. So you are more likely to see a total lunar eclipse than a total solar eclipse.

Partial Lunar Eclipses For most lunar eclipses, Earth, the moon, and the sun are not quite in line, and only a partial lunar eclipse results. A partial lunar eclipse occurs when the moon passes partly into the umbra of Earth's shadow. The edge of the umbra appears blurry, and you can watch it pass across the moon for two or three hours.

FIGURE 4 ·
Lunar Eclipse
As the moon moves through Earth's shadow, total and partial eclipses occur. This diagram is not to scale.

✏️ **Infer** Draw a circle labeled *T* to show where the moon would be during a total eclipse. Draw two circles labeled *P* to show two places the moon could be during a partial eclipse.

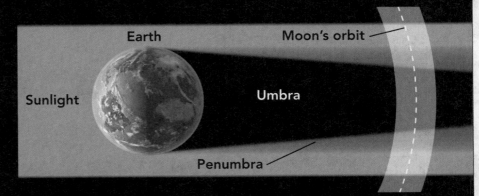

Earth

Moon's orbit

Sunlight

Umbra

Penumbra

Seasons and Shadows

How do Earth, the moon, and the sun interact?

FIGURE 5 ···

▶ **INTERACTIVE ART** Look at the diagram below. (The diagram is not to scale.) Identify what season it is in the Northern Hemisphere, what the phase of the moon is, and what kind of eclipse, if any, could occur.

Season

_____

Moon Phase

_____

Eclipse

_____

Use the above diagram as a model. Draw the arrangement of Earth, the moon, and the sun during a total lunar eclipse in December.

6.DP.10

Do the Quick Lab *Eclipses.*

🔑 Assess Your Understanding

1a. Explain A (solar/lunar) eclipse occurs when the moon passes into Earth's shadow. A (solar/lunar) eclipse occurs when Earth passes into the moon's shadow.

6.2.1

b. **ANSWER THE BIG ?** How do Earth, the moon, and the sun interact? _____

_____

_____

_____

6.2.1

got it? ···

○ **I get it!** Now I know that eclipses occur when _____

_____

○ **I need extra help with** _____

Go to **MY SCIENCE ⓢ COACH** online for help with this subject.

6.2.1

207

LESSON

5 Tides

UNLOCK THE BIG

?

🔑 **What Are Tides?**
6.2.2, 6.NS.8

MY PLANET DIARY

A River in Reverse

If you were visiting New Brunswick in Canada, you might see the Saint John River flowing into the ocean. But six hours later, you might find that the river changed direction while you were gone! How could this happen? The Saint John River really does reverse course twice a day. At low tide, it empties into the Bay of Fundy, shown below. At high tide, the Bay of Fundy's tide pushes into the river, forcing the river to run in the opposite direction. The Bay of Fundy's tides are among the highest in the world.

FUN FACT

Use your experience to answer the questions.

1. Why does the Saint John River change direction?

_____
_____
_____

2. Have you ever seen a natural event that surprised you? Why was it surprising?

_____
_____
_____

▶ PLANET DIARY Go to **Planet Diary** to learn more about tides.

 Do the Inquiry Warm-Up *When Is High Tide?*

High tide

Low tide

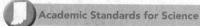

Vocabulary
- tide
- spring tide
- neap tide

Skills
- Reading: Relate Cause and Effect
- Inquiry: Observe

What Are Tides?

The reversing Saint John River is caused by ocean **tides,** the rise and fall of ocean water that occurs every 12.5 hours or so. The water rises for about six hours, then falls for about six hours.

The Tide Cycle   The force of gravity pulls the moon and Earth (including the water on Earth's surface) toward each other. ⊙ **Tides are caused mainly by differences in how much gravity from the moon and the sun pulls on different parts of Earth.**

At any one time on Earth, there are two places with high tides and two places with low tides. As Earth rotates, one high tide occurs on the side of Earth that faces the moon. The second high tide occurs on the opposite side of Earth. **Figure 1** explains why.

> **Academic Standards for Science**
>
> **6.2.2** Recognize that gravity is a force that keeps celestial bodies in regular and predictable motion, holds objects to earth's surface, and is responsible for ocean tides.
>
> **6.NS.8** Analyze data, using appropriate mathematical manipulation as required, and use it to identify patterns and make inferences based on these patterns.

⊙ **Relate Cause and Effect** As you read **Figure 1,** underline the causes of high and low tides.

FIGURE 1 ·······································

> **ART IN MOTION** **Tides**

You can think of Earth as a ball surrounded by a layer of water, as shown here. The layer is really much thinner than this, but is drawn thicker so it is easier to see.

 — North Pole

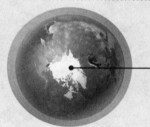

The Near Side   The moon's gravity pulls a little more strongly on the water on the side closest to the moon than on Earth as a whole. This difference causes a bulge of water on the side of Earth closest to the moon. This bulge causes high tide.

The Far Side   The moon's gravity pulls more weakly on the water on the far side of Earth than on Earth as a whole. Since Earth is pulled more strongly, the water is "left behind." Water flows toward the far side, causing high tide. Halfway between the high tides, water flows toward the high tides, causing low tide.

✎ **Interpret Diagrams**
Write an *H* where high tides occur and an *L* where low tides occur.

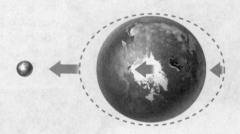

The Sun's Role Even though the sun is about 150 million kilometers from Earth, it is so massive that its gravity affects the tides. The sun pulls the water on Earth's surface toward it. 🔑 Changes in the positions of Earth, the moon, and the sun affect the heights of the tides during a month.

New Moon
The sun, the moon, and Earth are nearly in a line during a new moon. The gravity of the sun and the moon pull in the same direction. Their combined forces produce a tide with the greatest difference between consecutive low and high tides, called a **spring tide.** The term "spring tide" comes from an Old English word, *springen,* meaning "to jump."

First Quarter
During the moon's first-quarter phase, the line between Earth and the sun is at right angles to the line between Earth and the moon. The sun's pull is at right angles to the moon's pull. This arrangement produces a **neap tide,** a tide with the least difference between consecutive low and high tides. Neap tides occur twice a month.

Full Moon
At full moon, the moon and the sun are on opposite sides of Earth. Since there are high tides on both sides of Earth, a spring tide is also produced. It doesn't matter in which order the sun, Earth, and the moon line up.

Third Quarter
✏️ **Infer** Draw the position of the moon and the tide bulges at third quarter. What kind of tide occurs?

_____

The table shows high and low tides at four times in May 2008, in St. John, New Brunswick. St. John is on the Bay of Fundy.

High and Low Tides at St. John, New Brunswick

Date	High Tide (meters)	Low Tide (meters)
May 6–7	8.7	0.0
May 13–14	7.1	1.7
May 21	7.5	1.2
May 26	6.9	2.0

1 Interpret Data Spring tides occurred at two of the times shown. Which two? How do you know?

_____

_____

2 CHALLENGE Would the tide be higher when the moon is on the same side of Earth as New Brunswick or on the opposite side? Why?

_____

_____

_____

_____

_____

6.NS.8

Vocabulary Identify Multiple Meanings Does a spring tide always happen in the season of spring? Explain your answer.

_____

_____

_____

_____

_____

_____

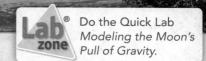
Do the Quick Lab *Modeling the Moon's Pull of Gravity.*

🔑 Assess Your Understanding

1a. Review Most coastal areas have _____ high tides and _____ low tides each day.

6.2.2

b. Relate Cause and Effect What causes tides?

_____

_____

_____

6.2.2

c. Observe Look at the diagrams on the previous page. What is the angle formed by the sun, Earth, and the moon during a neap tide? A spring tide?

_____

_____

_____

6.2.2, 6.NS.8

got it?

○ **I get it!** Now I know that tides are _____

_____

○ **I need extra help with** _____

Go to **MY SCIENCE COACH** online for help with this subject.

6.2.2

Earth's Moon

UNLOCK THE BIG ?

🔑 **What Is the Moon Like?**

6.2.4

my planet Diary

VOICES FROM HISTORY

Galileo Galilei

In 1609, the Italian astronomer Galileo Galilei turned a new tool—the telescope—toward the moon. What he saw amazed him: wide dark areas and strange spots and ridges.

> *I have been led to that opinion ... that I feel sure that the surface of the Moon is not perfectly smooth ...but that, on the contrary, it is ... just like the surface of the Earth itself, which is varied everywhere by high mountains and deep valleys.*

Today, scientists know that Galileo was right. Powerful telescopes have shown the mountains and craters on the moon, and astronauts have walked and driven over the moon's surface.

✏️ **Communicate** Discuss Galileo's observations with a partner. Then answer the questions below.

1. What conclusions did Galileo draw about the moon?

_____

_____

2. How do you think it would feel to make an observation that no one had made before?

_____

_____

_____

▷ **PLANET DIARY** Go to **Planet Diary** to learn more about Earth's moon.

Lab zone® Do the Inquiry Warm-Up *Why Do Craters Look Different From Each Other?*

Vocabulary
- maria • crater
- meteoroid

Skills
⊙ Reading: Compare and Contrast
△ Inquiry: Develop Hypotheses

What Is the Moon Like?

For thousands of years, people could see the moon, but didn't know much about it. Galileo's observations were some of the first to show details on the moon's surface. Scientists have since learned more about the moon's features. ⟁ **The moon is dry and airless and has an irregular surface. Compared to Earth, the moon is small and has large variations in its surface temperature.**

Surface Features As **Figure 1** shows, the moon has many unusual structures, including maria, craters, and highlands.

Maria Dark, flat areas, called **maria** (MAH ree uh), are hardened rock formed from huge lava flows that occurred 3–4 billion years ago. The singular form of *maria* is *mare* (MAH ray).

Craters Large round pits called **craters** can be hundreds of kilometers across. These craters were caused by the impacts of **meteoroids,** chunks of rock or dust from space. Maria have relatively few craters. This means that most of the moon's craters formed from impacts early in its history, before maria formed.

Highlands Some of the light-colored features you can see on the moon's surface are highlands, or mountains. The peaks of the lunar highlands and the rims of the craters cast dark shadows. The highlands cover most of the moon's surface.

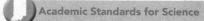

Academic Standards for Science

6.2.4 Compare and contrast the planets of the solar system with one another and with asteroids and comets with regard to their size, composition, distance from sun, surface features and ability to support life.

FIGURE 1 ·······························
Moon Features
This photograph shows the features of the northern part of the side of the moon that you can see from Earth.

✎ **Relate Diagrams and Photos** How is the photograph different from Galileo's drawing on the previous page?

_____

_____

_____

_____

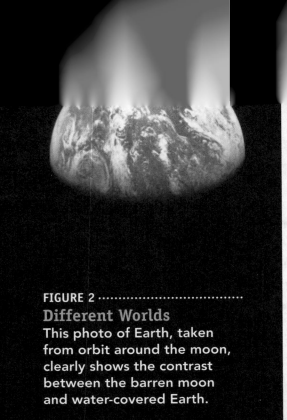

FIGURE 2 ....
Different Worlds
This photo of Earth, taken from orbit around the moon, clearly shows the contrast between the barren moon and water-covered Earth.

Size and Density The moon is 3,476 kilometers across, a little less than the distance across the United States. This is about one fourth of Earth's diameter. However, the moon has only one eightieth as much mass as Earth. Though Earth has a very dense core, its outer layers are less dense. The moon's average density is similar to the density of Earth's outer layers. Its gravity is about one sixth of Earth's.

Temperature At the moon's equator, temperatures range from a torrid 130°C in direct sunlight to a frigid −170°C at night. Temperatures at the poles are even colder. Temperatures vary so much because the moon does not have an atmosphere. The moon's surface gravity is so weak that gases can easily escape into space.

Water For many years, people thought the moon had no water, except for small amounts of ice. In 2009, scientists using data from several space probes determined that a thin layer of water exists in the moon's soil. The total amount of water is very small, but it is found in many places on the moon's surface.

Origins of the Moon Scientists have suggested many possible theories for how the moon formed. The theory that seems to best fit the evidence is called the collision-ring theory. About 4.5 billion years ago, when Earth was very young, the solar system was full of rocky debris. Scientists theorize that a planet-sized object collided with Earth. Material from the object and Earth's outer layers was ejected into orbit around Earth, where it formed a ring. Gravity caused this material to clump together to form the moon.

✎ Compare and Contrast
Complete the table below to compare and contrast Earth and the moon.

		Density	Temperatures	Atmosphere	Water
Earth					
Moon					

apply it!

Within your lifetime, tourists may be able to travel to the moon. If you were taking a trip to the moon, what would you pack? Remember that the moon is dry, has almost no liquid water, and has no atmosphere.

1 **Solve Problems** On the packing list to the right, list five items you would need on the moon.

2 [CHALLENGE] List two items that you could not use on the moon. Why would they not work?

_____

_____

_____

_____

_____

_____

Things to Pack

1. _____
2. _____
3. _____
4. _____
5. _____

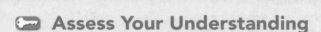 **Lab zone**® Do the Quick Lab *Moonwatching.*

🔑 Assess Your Understanding

1a. List What are the three main surface features on the moon?

_____
_____

6.2.4

b. 🔄 **Compare and Contrast** How does the moon's gravity compare with Earth's?

_____

6.2.4

c. 🔺 **Develop Hypotheses** Write a hypothesis explaining why the moon has very little liquid water.

_____
_____
_____

6.2.4, 6.NS.1

got it? ●●

○ **I get it!** Now I know that the characteristics of Earth's moon are _____
_____

○ **I need extra help with** _____

Go to **MY SCIENCE** 🔵 **COACH** *online for help with this subject.*

6.2.4

215

6 Study Guide

Interactions between Earth, the moon, and the sun cause _____,
_____, _____, and _____.

LESSON 1 The Sky From Earth
6.2.1, 6.NS.1, 6.NS.2

🔑 On a clear night, you may see stars, the moon, planets, meteors, and comets.

🔑 A constellation is a pattern or grouping of stars imagined by people to represent figures.

🔑 The apparent motion of objects in the sky depends on the motions of Earth.

Vocabulary
- satellite • planet • meteor • comet
- star • constellation

LESSON 2 Earth in Space
6.2.1, 6.2.5, 6.NS.1, 6.NS.8, 6.DP.10

🔑 Earth moves in space in two major ways: rotation and revolution.

🔑 Earth has seasons because its axis is tilted as it revolves around the sun.

Vocabulary
- axis • rotation
- revolution
- orbit • calendar
- solstice • equinox

LESSON 3 Gravity and Motion
6.2.2, 6.NS.1, 6.NS.8

🔑 The strength of the force of gravity between two objects depends on two factors: the masses of the objects and the distance between them.

🔑 Newton concluded that inertia and gravity combine to keep Earth in orbit around the sun and the moon in orbit around Earth.

Vocabulary
- force • gravity • law of universal gravitation
- mass • weight • inertia
- Newton's first law of motion

LESSON 4 Phases and Eclipses
6.2.1, 6.NS.11, 6.DP.10

🔑 The changing relative positions of the moon, Earth, and sun cause the phases of the moon.

🔑 A solar eclipse occurs when the moon passes directly between Earth and the sun, blocking sunlight from Earth. During a lunar eclipse, Earth blocks sunlight from reaching the moon.

Vocabulary
- phase • eclipse • solar eclipse • umbra
- penumbra • lunar eclipse

LESSON 5 Tides
6.2.2, 6.NS.8

🔑 Tides are caused by differences in how much gravity from the moon and the sun pulls on different parts of Earth.

🔑 Changes in the positions of Earth, the moon, and the sun affect the heights of the tides during a month.

Vocabulary
- tide • spring tide • neap tide

LESSON 6 Earth's Moon
6.2.4

🔑 The moon is dry and airless and has an irregular surface. Compared to Earth, the moon is small and has large variations in its surface temperature.

Vocabulary
- maria • crater
- meteoroid

Review and Assessment

LESSON 1 The Sky From Earth

1. Which of the following objects is found in Earth's atmosphere?

a. comet **b.** meteor

c. moon **d.** planet

6.2.4

2. Over time, people have given names to groups of stars, called _____

6.2

3. Predict The constellation Orion appears in the eastern sky in December. Where would you expect it to appear in March? Why?

_____
_____
_____

6.2.1, 6.NS.1

4. [Write About It] Suppose you were camping on a summer night. Describe what objects you might see in the sky and how the sky would change throughout the night.

6.2.1, 6.2.4, 6.NS.1

LESSON 2 Earth in Space

5. What is Earth's annual motion around the sun called?

a. month **b.** revolution

c. rotation **d.** seasons

6.2.1

6. The _____ occurs when the sun is farthest north of the equator.

6.2.5

7. Infer Mars's axis is tilted at about the same angle as Earth's axis. Do you think Mars has seasons? Explain your answer.

_____
_____
_____

6.2.1, 6.2.4

8. [Write About It] Write a guide for younger children explaining how Earth's motions are related to the lengths of days and years.

6.2.1, 6.NS.11

LESSON 3 Gravity and Motion

9. The tendency of an object to resist a change in motion is called

a. force. **b.** gravity.

c. inertia. **d.** weight.

6.2.2

10. An object is kept in orbit by _____ and _____

6.2.2

11. Relate Cause and Effect If you move two objects farther apart, how does the force of gravity between the two objects change?

_____

6.2.2

12. Compare and Contrast How are weight and mass different? _____
_____
_____

6.2.2

13. Explain Explain Newton's first law of motion in your own words. _____
_____
_____
_____
_____
_____

6.2.2

Use this illustration to answer Question 14.

450 N

14. math! How much would the person above weigh on the moon? _____

6.2.2, 6.NS.8

217

LESSON 4 Phases and Eclipses

15. The moon's shadow falling on Earth causes a

    a. full moon.   **b.** lunar eclipse.

    c. phase.   **d.** solar eclipse.

                                      6.2.1

16. The darkest part of the moon's shadow is the

_____

                                      6.2.1

17. Relate Cause and Effect Why does the moon

have phases? _____

_____

_____

                                      6.2.1

18. Make Generalizations Which occurs more often, a partial or a total lunar eclipse? Why?

_____

_____

_____

                                      6.2.1

LESSON 5 Tides

19. About how long passes between high tides?

    a. 6 hours   **b.** 12 hours

    c. 24 hours   **d.** 48 hours

                                      6.2.2

20. The least difference between high and low

tides occurs during a _____

                                      6.2.2

Use the diagram to answer Question 21.

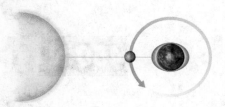

21. Interpret Diagrams Does the diagram show a spring or a neap tide? How do you know?

_____

_____

                                      6.2.2

LESSON 6 Earth's Moon

22. What caused the moon's craters?

    a. maria   **b.** meteoroids

    c. tides   **d.** volcanoes

                                        6.2.4

23. The moon's light-colored highlands are

_____

                                      6.2.4

24. Explain Why do temperatures vary so much

on the moon? _____

_____

_____

                                      6.2.4

25. **Write About It** Suppose you were hired to design a spacesuit for use on the moon. What characteristics of the moon would be important for you to consider? Explain.

                               6.2.4, 6.NS.11

APPLY THE BIG ? How do Earth, the moon, and the sun interact?

26. Can more people see a total solar eclipse or a total lunar eclipse? Explain your answer.

_____

_____

_____

_____

_____

_____

_____

_____

_____

_____

                                      6.2.1

Indiana ISTEP+ Practice

Multiple Choice

Circle the letter of the best answer.

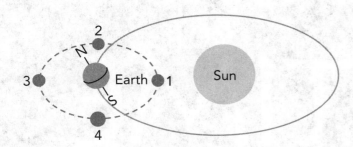

1. Which of the following can occur when the moon is at location 1?

   A. only a lunar eclipse

   B. only a solar eclipse

   C. both a solar and a lunar eclipse

   D. neither a solar nor a lunar eclipse

   6.2.1

2. On what does the force of gravity between two objects depend?

   A. mass and weight

   B. speed and distance

   C. weight and speed

   D. mass and distance

   6.2.2

3. The dark, flat areas on the moon are called

   A. craters.

   B. highlands.

   C. maria.

   D. meteoroids.

   6.2.4

4. Which type of object visible from Earth orbits the sun and has cleared the area of its orbit?

   A. star

   B. planet

   C. moon

   D. meteor

   6.2.4

Constructed Response

Write your answer to Question 5 on the lines below.

5. What happens at a spring tide?

   _____

   _____

   _____

   6.2.2

Extended Response

Use the diagram below to answer the question.

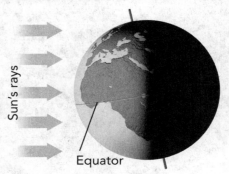

6. In the Northern Hemisphere, is it the summer solstice, winter solstice, or one of the equinoxes? Explain how you know.

   6.2.5

KEEPING TRACK OF TIME

▲ This sun stone is sometimes called the Aztec calendar. It shows the 20 days in the Aztec month. The Aztec calendar was a solar calendar, with a total of 365 days in a year.

What day of the week is your birthday this year? Better check the calendar.

Calendars were invented to keep track of important events, such as planting schedules and festivals.

Early people noticed certain patterns in nature. The seasons change. The sun rises and sets. The moon changes phases. These patterns became the basis for calendars even before people understood that Earth rotates on an axis and revolves around the sun or that the moon revolves around Earth.

Calendars were lunar (based on the moon), solar (based on the sun), or lunisolar (based on a combination). But none was completely accurate—important events shifted around from one year to the next.

The Gregorian calendar, introduced in 1582, is the standard calendar in use today. It is more accurate than most calendars, but even it requires some tinkering. We add an extra day almost every four years, giving us a leap year. Century years (like 2000) are not leap years unless they are divisible by 400.

Research It There are about 40 different kinds of calendars in use today. Pick one and research it. Write an essay describing the calendar and how it is different from the Gregorian calendar. What does the calendar tell you about the society that uses it?

 6.NS.2

AFTER APOLLO: EXPLORING THE MOON

This is no ordinary footprint. It was made by an astronaut on the moon's dusty surface. Because there is no wind to weather it, it could last for a very long time.

No one has set foot on the moon since the two Apollo 17 astronauts did in 1972. But the moon has not been abandoned. Robotic spacecraft and rovers have taken over from humans.

In 2007, China and Japan sent robotic space probes to photograph and map the moon. In late 2008, India launched its moon orbiter and released a briefcase-sized probe onto the moon's surface, where it beamed back images. Next up? The National Aeronautic and Space Administration's Lunar Reconnaissance Orbiter, which will search for good landing sites and resources. Its goal is to help put humans back on the moon in the near future.

Research It Choose one of the international moon missions and prepare a timeline, from initial design to moon orbit.

6.NS.11

◀ The Lunar Reconnaissance Orbiter was designed to orbit approximately 50 kilometers above the moon's surface, collecting detailed information about its environment.

WHAT MIGHT SATURN'S RINGS BE MADE OF?

Why are objects in the solar system different from each other?

This photograph from the *Cassini* space probe shows Saturn and part of its magnificent system of rings. Space probes such as *Cassini* have helped scientists learn more about the objects in the solar system.

Infer What do you think Saturn's rings are made of? How might they have formed?

▷ UNTAMED SCIENCE Watch the **Untamed Science** video to learn more about the solar system.

_____

_____

_____

_____

_____

_____

The Solar System

7 Getting Started

Check Your Understanding

1. Background Read the paragraph below and then answer the question.

> Tyrone is watching a movie. He sees astronauts explore a planet that **revolves** around a star. As the astronauts travel, they notice that the planet **rotates**. Tyrone knows that **gravity** holds the planet in orbit around the star.

- What causes day and night on a planet?

_____

_____

> **Revolution** is the motion of one object around another.
>
> An object **rotates** when it spins around a central axis.
>
> **Gravity** is the force that attracts all objects toward each other.

> **MY READING WEB** If you had trouble completing the question above, visit **My Reading Web** and type in *The Solar System*.

Vocabulary Skill

Greek Word Origins Many science words come to English from Greek. In this chapter, you will learn the term *geocentric*. *Geocentric* comes from the Greek word parts *ge*, meaning "Earth," and *kentron*, meaning "center."

ge
Earth + *kentron*
center = *geocentric*
having Earth at the center

Learn these Greek word parts to help you remember the vocabulary terms.

Greek Word	Meaning	Example
helios	sun	heliocentric, *adj.*
chromas	color	chromosphere, *n.*
sphaira	sphere	photosphere, *n.*

2. Quick Check Predict the meaning of *heliocentric*.

_____

_____

planet

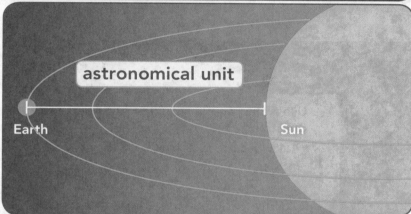

astronomical unit

Earth | Sun

solar system

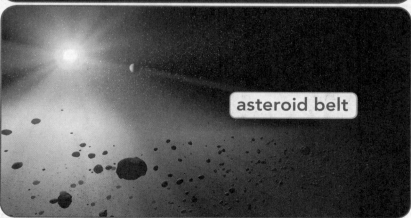

asteroid belt

Chapter Preview

LESSON 1
- geocentric • heliocentric
- ellipse

🔄 **Sequence**
△ **Make Models**

LESSON 2
- solar system • astronomical unit
- planet • dwarf planet
- planetesimal

🔄 **Identify Supporting Evidence**
△ **Calculate**

LESSON 3
- core • nuclear fusion
- radiation zone • convection zone
- photosphere • chromosphere
- corona • solar wind • sunspot
- prominence • solar flare

🔄 **Relate Cause and Effect**
△ **Interpret Data**

LESSON 4
- terrestrial planet
- greenhouse effect

🔄 **Compare and Contrast**
△ **Communicate**

LESSON 5
- gas giant • ring

🔄 **Outline**
△ **Pose Questions**

LESSON 6
- asteroid belt • Kuiper belt
- Oort cloud • comet
- coma • nucleus • asteroid
- meteoroid • meteor • meteorite

🔄 **Summarize**
△ **Classify**

> **VOCAB FLASH CARDS** For extra help
with vocabulary, visit **Vocab Flash
Cards** and type in *The Solar System.*

Models of the Solar System

UNLOCK
THE BIG

?

 What Was the Geocentric Model?
6.2.4

 How Did the Heliocentric Model Develop?
6.2.4, 6.NS.11, 6.DP.10

MY PLANET DiARY

CAREER

Picturing the Solar System

When Walter Myers was seven years old, he found a book with drawings of astronauts walking on the moons of Saturn. Ever since, he's been making space pictures himself. At first, he used pencil. Today, he works on computers. He likes using computers because he can create images that are more like photographs, such as the ones below.

As an artist, Mr. Myers can show scenes that haven't been photographed, such as ideas for future spacecraft and the views from another planet's moons. Mr. Myers especially likes creating views of what human visitors to other planets might see. His work has appeared in books, magazines, Web sites, and even on television!

Use what you have read to answer these questions.

1. What tool does Walter Myers use?

_____

2. Why do people use art or other models to show objects in the solar system?

_____
_____
_____

> PLANET DIARY Go to **Planet Diary** to learn more about models of the solar system.

 Lab zone Do the Inquiry Warm-Up
What Is at the Center?

Vocabulary
- geocentric
- heliocentric
- ellipse

Skills
- Reading: Sequence
- Inquiry: Make Models

What Was the Geocentric Model?

From here on Earth, it seems as if our planet is stationary and that the sun, moon, and stars are moving around Earth. But is the sky really moving above you? Centuries ago, before there were space shuttles or even telescopes, people had no easy way to find out.

Ancient Observations Ancient observers, including the Greeks, Chinese, and Mayans, noticed that the patterns of the stars didn't change over time. Although the stars seemed to move, they stayed in the same position relative to one another. These people also observed planets, which moved among the stars.

Many early observers thought Earth was at the center of the universe. Some Chinese observers thought Earth was under a dome of stars. Many Greek astronomers thought that Earth was inside rotating spheres nested inside each other. These spheres contained the stars and planets. Since *ge* is the Greek word for "Earth," an Earth-centered model is known as a **geocentric** (jee oh SEN trik) model. 🔑 **In a geocentric model, Earth is at the center of the revolving planets and stars.**

Ptolemy's Model About A.D. 140, the Greek astronomer Ptolemy (TAHL uh mee) further developed the geocentric model. Like the earlier Greeks, Ptolemy thought that Earth was at the center of the universe. In Ptolemy's model, however, the planets moved in small circles carried along in bigger circles.

Ptolemy's geocentric model explained the motions observed in the sky fairly accurately. As a result, the geocentric model of the universe was widely accepted for nearly 1,500 years after Ptolemy.

ⓘ **Academic Standards for Science**

6.2.4 Compare and contrast the planets of the solar system with one another and with asteroids and comets with regard to their size, composition, distance from sun, surface features and ability to support life.

apply it!

Critique Scientific Explanations and Models Describe an experience from everyday life that appears to support the geocentric model.

_____

_____

_____

_____

_____

_____

Lab zone Do the Quick Lab *Going Around in Circles.*

🔑 Assess Your Understanding

got it? ....

○ **I get it!** Now I know that the geocentric model is _____

_____

○ **I need extra help with** _____

Go to **my science** 🔍 **coach** *online for help with this subject.*

6.2.4

Academic Standards for Science

6.2.4 Compare and contrast the planets of the solar system with one another and with asteroids and comets with regard to their size, composition, distance from sun, surface features and ability to support life.

6.NS.11 Communicate findings using models.

6.DP.10 Communicate the solution using drawings.

How Did the Heliocentric Model Develop?

Not everybody believed in the geocentric system. An ancient Greek scientist named Aristarchus developed a sun-centered model called a heliocentric (hee lee oh SEN trik) system. *Helios* is Greek for "sun." In a `heliocentric` system, Earth and the other planets revolve around the sun. This model was not well received in ancient times, however, because people could not accept that Earth was not at the center of the universe.

FIGURE 1 ·······

Changing Models

Make Models **Draw each model of the solar system. Include the sun, Earth, the moon, and Jupiter. Include Jupiter's moons in Galileo's model.**

CHALLENGE Why might people not have believed Galileo's discoveries?

_____

_____

6.NS.11, 6.DP.10

A.D.   **1500**   **1550**

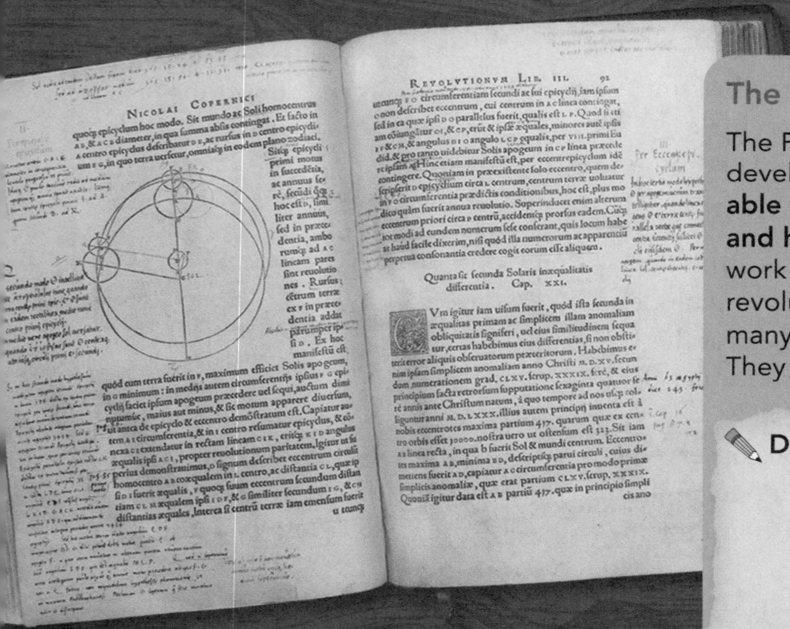

The Copernican Revolution

The Polish astronomer Nicolaus Copernicus further developed the heliocentric model. **Copernicus was able to work out the arrangement of the known planets and how they move around the sun.** He published his work in 1543. Copernicus's theory would eventually revolutionize the science of astronomy. But at first many people were unwilling to accept his theory. They needed more evidence to be convinced.

Draw Copernicus's model.

Sequence **Which astronomer did his work first?**

- Tycho Brahe
- Nicolaus Copernicus
- Galileo Galilei
- Johannes Kepler

Brahe and Kepler

Ptolemy and Copernicus both assumed that planets moved in perfect circles. Their models fit existing observations fairly well. But in the late 1500s, the Dutch astronomer Tycho Brahe (TEE koh BRAH uh) made much more accurate observations. Brahe's assistant, Johannes Kepler, used the observations to figure out the shape of the planets' orbits. When he used circular orbits, his calculations did not fit the observations. **After years of detailed calculations, Kepler found that the orbit of each planet is an ellipse. An ellipse is an oval shape.**

✎ Draw Kepler's model.

Tycho Brahe's Observatory

1600   **1650**

Galileo's Evidence

In the 1500s and early 1600s, most people still believed in the geocentric model. **However, evidence collected by the Italian scientist Galileo Galilei gradually convinced others that the heliocentric model was correct.** In 1610, Galileo used a telescope to discover four moons around Jupiter. These moons proved that not everything in the sky revolves around Earth. Galileo also discovered that Venus goes through a series of phases similar to the moon's. But Venus would not have a full set of phases if both it and the sun circled around Earth. Therefore, Galileo reasoned, the geocentric model must be incorrect.

✎ Draw Galileo's model.

Lab zone® Do the Quick Lab A Loopy Ellipse.

🔑 Assess Your Understanding

1a. Review (Kepler/Copernicus) discovered that planets move in ellipses.

6.2.4

b. Relate Evidence and Explanation What discoveries by Galileo support the heliocentric model?

_____

_____

_____

6.2.4

got it?

○ **I get it!** Now I know that the heliocentric model was developed _____

_____

○ **I need extra help with** _____

Go to **MY SCIENCE ⑤ COACH** *online for help with this subject.*

6.2.4

Introducing the Solar System

UNLOCK
THE BIG
?

🗝 **What Makes Up the Solar System?**
6.2.3, 6.2.4, 6.NS.3, 6.NS.8

🗝 **How Did the Solar System Form?**
6.2.4

my PLANET DiaRY

Extreme Conditions

Imagine a place where the sun shines 11 times brighter than it does on Earth. How could you keep anything cool there? Engineers had to solve just that problem when designing the Mercury *MESSENGER* spacecraft. In 2008, this spacecraft began to visit Mercury, where temperatures can reach up to 370°C. Engineers designed a sunshade to protect *MESSENGER*'s instruments. It's made from ceramic fabric! The fabric, made of elements such as silicon, aluminum, and boron, is resistant to heat. It reflects most of the sun's heat away from the *MESSENGER* spacecraft, keeping all the instruments at a comfortable room temperature (about 20°C).

TECHNOLOGY

Use what you have read to answer the questions below.

1. Why did engineers need to design a sunshade for Mercury *MESSENGER*?

_____

_____

_____

2. What other challenges do you think there would be for engineers designing a spacecraft to travel to Mercury?

_____

_____

_____

> PLANET DIARY Go to **Planet Diary** to learn more about the solar system.

Lab
zone

® Do the Inquiry Warm-Up
How Big Is Earth?

Vocabulary
- solar system
- astronomical unit
- planet
- dwarf planet
- planetesimal

Skills
- Reading: Identify Supporting Evidence
- Inquiry: Calculate

What Makes Up the Solar System?

Mercury is just one of many objects that make up the solar system. **Our solar system consists of the sun, the planets, their moons, and a variety of smaller objects**. The sun is at the center of the solar system, with other objects orbiting around it. The force of gravity holds the solar system together.

Distances in the Solar System Distances within the solar system are so large that they cannot be easily measured in meters or kilometers. Instead, scientists often use a unit called the astronomical unit. One **astronomical unit** (AU) equals the average distance between Earth and the sun, about 150,000,000 kilometers. The solar system extends more than 100,000 AU from the sun.

Academic Standards for Science

6.2.3 Understand that the sun, an average star where nuclear reactions occur, is the central and largest body in the solar system.

6.2.4 Compare and contrast the planets of the solar system with one another and with asteroids and comets with regard to their size, composition, distance from sun, surface features and ability to support life.

6.NS.3 Collect quantitative data and use appropriate units to label numerical data.

6.NS.8 Analyze data, using appropriate mathematical manipulation as required, and use it to identify patterns and make inferences based on these patterns.

do the math!

Converting Units

To convert from astronomical units (AU) to kilometers (km), you can multiply the number of AU by 150,000,000.

1 Calculate Mars is 1.52 AU from the sun. About how many kilometers is Mars from the sun? _____

2 Apply Concepts If you know an object's distance from the sun in kilometers, how can you find its distance in AU? _____

_____

6.NS.3, 6.NS.8

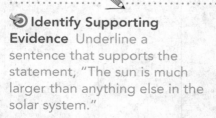

1 AU

Earth   Sun

The Sun At the center of our solar system is the sun. The sun is much larger than anything else in the solar system. About 99.85 percent of the mass of the solar system is contained within the sun. Despite being more than a million times the volume of Earth, our sun is actually a very ordinary mid-sized star. Using telescopes, we see stars that have volumes a thousand times greater than the sun's! This turns out to be a very good thing for us. Large stars burn out and die quickly, but our sun will last for five billion more years.

Identify Supporting Evidence Underline a sentence that supports the statement, "The sun is much larger than anything else in the solar system."

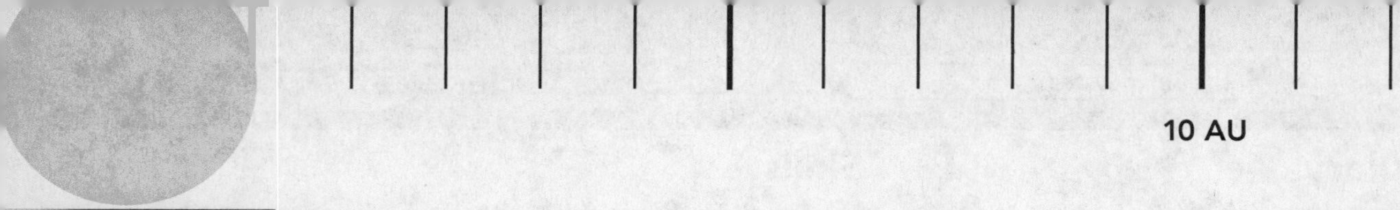

FIGURE 1 ···

> **INTERACTIVE ART** **The Solar System**

The planets' sizes are shown to scale, but their distances from the sun are not.

✎ **Mark the position of each planet on the distance scale above.**

1. **Interpret Data** Where is the largest gap between planets?

_____

6.NS.8

2. **CHALLENGE** Could you show the planets' relative sizes and distances from the sun in the same diagram on one page? Why or why not?

_____

_____

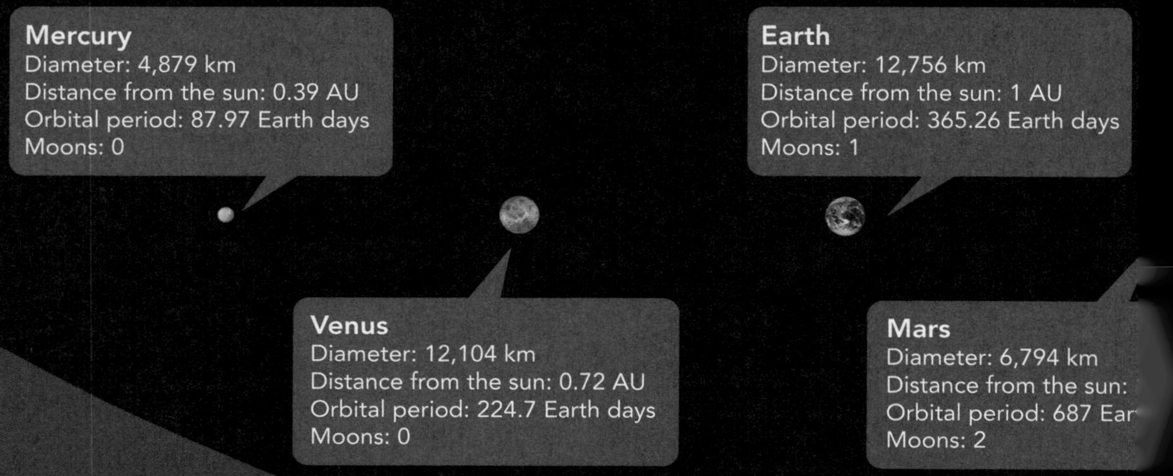

Mercury
Diameter: 4,879 km
Distance from the sun: 0.39 AU
Orbital period: 87.97 Earth days
Moons: 0

Earth
Diameter: 12,756 km
Distance from the sun: 1 AU
Orbital period: 365.26 Earth days
Moons: 1

Venus
Diameter: 12,104 km
Distance from the sun: 0.72 AU
Orbital period: 224.7 Earth days
Moons: 0

Mars
Diameter: 6,794 km
Distance from the sun:
Orbital period: 687 Ear
Moons: 2

Planets

There are many different objects in the solar system. How do you decide what is a planet and what isn't? In 2006, astronomers decided that a **planet** must be round, orbit the sun, and have cleared out the region of the solar system along its orbit. The first four planets are small and are mostly made of rock and metal. The last four planets are very large and are mostly made of gas and liquid. Like Earth, each planet has a "day" and a "year." Its day is the time it takes to rotate on its axis. Its year is the time it takes to orbit the sun. **Figure 1** shows some basic facts about the planets.

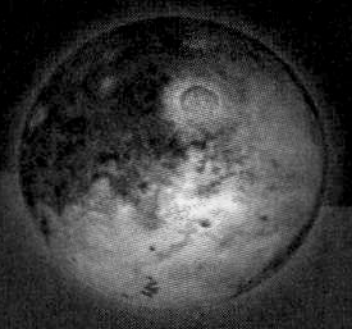

Dwarf Planets

For many years, Pluto was considered the planet in the solar system. But Pluto share area of its orbit with other objects. Pluto is considered a dwarf planet. A **dwarf plane** object that orbits the sun and has enough to be spherical, but has not cleared the ar orbit. There are five known dwarf planets solar system: Pluto, Eris, Ceres, Makemak (MAH keh MAH keh), and Haumea (how MAY u .... observe more distant objects, th

Satellites

Except for Mercury and Venus, every planet in the solar system has at least one natural satellite, or moon. Earth has the fewest moons, with just one. Jupiter and Saturn each have more than 60! Some dwarf planets also have satellites.

Smaller Objects

The solar system also includes many smaller objects that orbit the sun. Some, called asteroids, are small, mostly rocky bodies. Many asteroids are found in an area between the orbits of Mars and Jupiter. Comets are another large group of solar system objects. Comets are loose balls of ice and rock that usually have very long, narrow orbits.

Saturn
Diameter: 120,536 km
Distance from the sun: 9.54 AU
Orbital period: 29.47 Earth years
Moons: 60+

Neptune
Diameter: 49,258 km
Distance from the sun: 30.07 AU
Orbital period: 163.72 Earth years
Moons: 13+

Uranus
Diameter: 51,118 km
Distance from the sun: 19.19 AU
Orbital period: 83.75 Earth years
Moons: 20+

Jupiter
Diameter: 142,984 km
Distance from the sun: 5.20 AU
Orbital period: 11.86 Earth years
Moons: 60+

Lab zone® Do the Lab Investigation *Speeding Around the Sun.*

🔑 Assess Your Understanding

1a. Sequence List the planets in order of increasing distance from the sun.

_____
_____
_____

6.2.4

b. Make Generalizations What is the relationship between a planet's distance from the sun and the length of its year?

_____
_____

6.2.4

got it?

○ **I get it!** Now I know that the solar system includes _____

_____
_____

○ **I need extra help with** _____

_____

Go to **MY SCIENCE** 💬 **COACH** *online for help with this subject.*

6.2.4

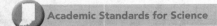

Academic Standards for Science

6.2.4 Compare and contrast the planets of the solar system with one another and with asteroids and comets with regard to their size, composition, distance from sun, surface features and ability to support life.

<figure>
FIGURE 2 ··

> **ART IN MOTION** **Formation of the Solar System**

✎ **Sequence** Write the numbers 1 through 4 in the circles to put the images in order.
</figure>

How Did the Solar System Form?

Where did the objects in the solar system come from? ⚿ **Scientists think the solar system formed about 4.6 billion years ago from a cloud of hydrogen, helium, rock, ice, and other materials pulled together by gravity.**

A Spinning Disk The process began as gravity pulled the cloud's material together. The cloud collapsed and started to rotate, forming a disk. Most of the material was pulled to the center. As this material became tightly packed, it got hotter and the pressure on it increased.

Eventually, the temperature and pressure became so high that hydrogen atoms were pressed together to form helium. This process, called nuclear fusion, releases large amounts of energy. Once nuclear fusion began, the sun gave off light and became a stable star. Sunlight is one form of the energy produced by fusion.

The Planets Form Away from the sun, planets began to form as gravity pulled rock, ice, and gas together. The rock and ice formed small bodies called **planetesimals** (pla nuh TE suh muhlz). Over time, planetesimals collided and stuck together, eventually combining to form all the other objects in the solar system.

Inner Planets Close to the sun, the solar system was very hot. Most water evaporated, preventing ice from forming. The bodies that formed in this region were comparatively low in mass. Their gravity was too weak to hold on to light gases such as hydrogen and helium. This is why the inner planets are small and rocky.

Outer Planets At greater distances from the sun, temperatures were cooler. Ice formed, adding mass to the planets that formed at these distances. As the planets grew, their gravity was strong enough to hold hydrogen and helium, forming the gas giant planets. Beyond the gas giants, temperatures were even lower. Ice and other materials produced comets and dwarf planets.

EXPLORE THE BIG ?

Solve THE SOLAR SYSTEM

Why are objects in the solar system different from each other?

FIGURE 3 ·······················
Use the clues to complete the puzzle.
Then answer the question.

ACROSS

3 The planet farthest from the sun
4 A loose, icy body with a long, narrow orbit
6 A gas giant planet that is smaller than Jupiter but larger than Neptune
7 The smallest planet in the solar system
8 An object that orbits a planet

DOWN

1 The largest planet in the solar system
2 A planet that formed closer to the sun than Earth but not closest to the sun
5 A small rocky body that orbits the sun

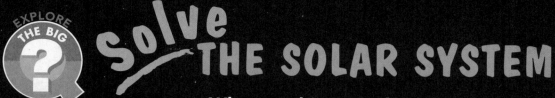

Why are the objects in clues 2 and 6 so different?

_____

_____

_____

Lab zone®   Do the Quick Lab
Clumping Planets.

🔑 Assess Your Understanding

2a. **Explain** What force formed the solar system?

_____

_____
6.2.2

b. ANSWER THE BIG ? Why are objects in the solar system different from each other?

_____

_____

_____

_____
6.2.4

got it?

○ I get it! Now I know that the solar system formed when _____

_____

_____

○ I need extra help with _____

Go to my science 🔵ˢ coach *online for help with this subject.*
6.2.4

Indiana

LESSON

3 The Sun

UNLOCK THE BIG ?

🔑 **What Is the Structure of the Sun?**
6.2.3, 6.NS.8

🔑 **What Features Can You See on the Sun?**
6.2.3

my planeT DiaRY

DISASTER

Left in the Dark

On March 13, 1989, a flood of electric particles from the sun reached Earth, causing a magnetic storm. Bright streamers of color filled the sky as far south as Jamaica. But in Quebec, Canada, the storm brought problems. At 2:45 A.M., the entire electric power system collapsed. People woke up with no heat or light. Traffic snarled as traffic lights and subways stopped working.

How could particles from the sun take out a power system? The magnetic storm caused an electrical surge through the power lines. Electric stations couldn't handle the extra electricity, and they blew out, taking the power system with them.

✏️ **Communicate** Discuss the Quebec blackout with a partner. Then answer the questions below.

1. What caused the Quebec blackout of 1989?

_____

_____

2. How would your life be affected if a magnetic storm shut down electricity in your area?

_____

_____

_____

▶ PLANET DIARY Go to **Planet Diary** to learn more about the sun.

Do the Inquiry Warm-Up *How Can You Safely Observe the Sun?*

Vocabulary

- core • nuclear fusion • radiation zone
- convection zone • photosphere • chromosphere
- corona • solar wind • sunspot • prominence
- solar flare

Skills

↩ Reading: Relate Cause and Effect

△ Inquiry: Interpret Data

What Is the Structure of the Sun?

Unlike Earth, the sun has no solid surface. About three fourths of the sun's mass is hydrogen, and about one fourth is helium. There are tiny amounts of other elements. **The sun has an interior and an atmosphere. The interior includes the core, the radiation zone, and the convection zone. Figure 1** shows the sun's interior.

> **Academic Standards for Science**
>
> **6.2.3** Understand that the sun, an average star where nuclear reactions occur, is the central and largest body in the solar system.
>
> **6.NS.8** Analyze data, and use it to identify patterns and make inferences based on these patterns.

FIGURE 1 ....

Layers of the Sun

The diagram shows the layers of the sun's interior.

✎ **Apply Concepts** Draw arrows to show energy as it passes from the sun's core through the radiation and convection zones. Underline clues in the text that help you determine the path.

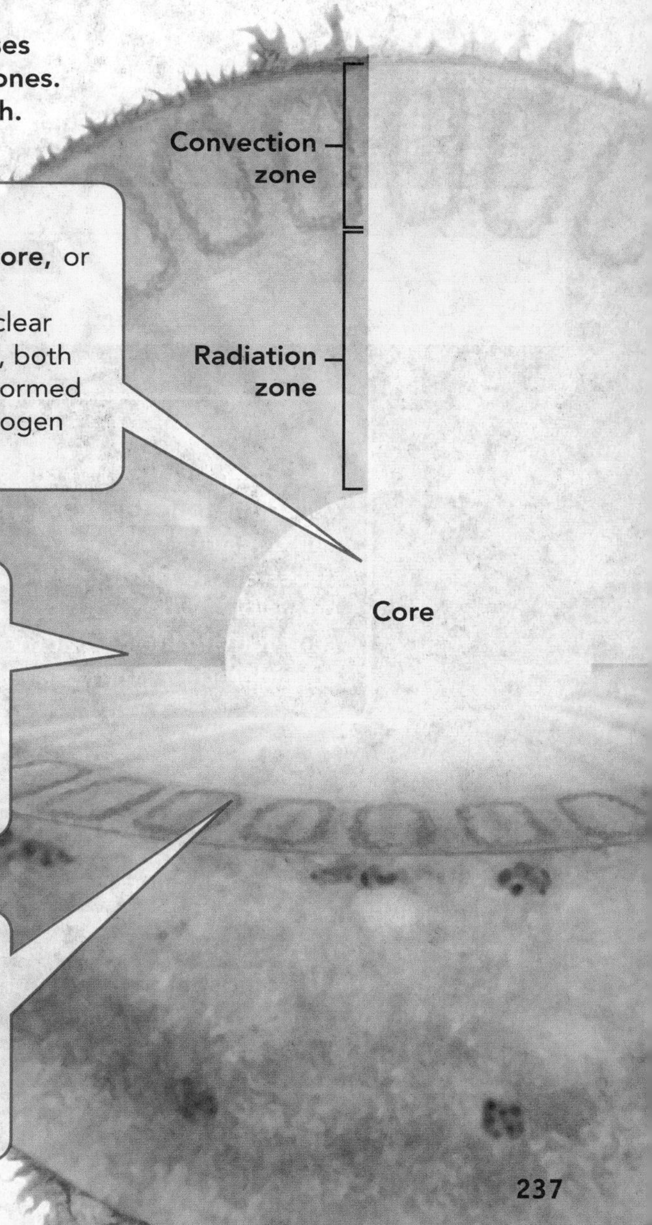

Convection zone

Radiation zone

Core

The Core

The sun produces an enormous amount of energy in its **core,** or central region, through nuclear fusion. In the process of **nuclear fusion,** hydrogen atoms join to form helium. Nuclear fusion requires extremely high temperature and pressure, both of which are found in the core. The total mass of helium formed by nuclear fusion is slightly less than the mass of the hydrogen that goes into it. The remaining mass becomes energy.

The Radiation Zone

The energy produced in the sun's core moves outward through the radiation zone. The **radiation zone** is a region of very tightly packed gas where energy moves mainly in the form of electromagnetic radiation. Because the radiation zone is so dense, energy can take more than 100,000 years to move through it.

The Convection Zone

The **convection zone** is the outermost layer of the sun's interior. Hot gases rise from the bottom of the convection zone and gradually cool as they approach the top. Cooler gases sink, forming loops of gas that move energy toward the sun's surface.

237

eek Word Origins
~~l~~ *photos* means
~~bes~~ *photosphere*

The Sun's Atmosphere

The sun has an atmosphere that stretches far into space, as you can see in **Figure 2**. The layers of the atmosphere become less dense the farther they are from the radiation zone. Like the sun's interior, the atmosphere is primarily composed of hydrogen and helium. 🔑 The sun's atmosphere includes the photosphere, the chromosphere, and the corona. Each layer has unique properties.

ART The Sun's Atmosphere

~~is~~ a combination of two photographs of the ~~sun. One sho~~ws the sun's surface and was taken through a ~~filter~~ that shows the sun's features. The other ~~shows the co~~rona and was taken during an eclipse.

~~Relate T~~ext and Visuals On the photograph, label the ~~photosphere~~ and corona. Shade in the area of the chromosphere.

~~Predict~~ Why can the chromosphere and corona only be seen ~~d~~uring an eclipse?

_____

_____

_____

The Photosphere

The inner layer of the sun's atmosphere is called the **photosphere** (FOH tuh sfeer). The sun does not have a solid surface, but the gases of the photosphere are thick enough to be visible. When you look at an image of the sun, you are looking at the photosphere. It is considered to be the sun's surface layer.

~~chromos~~phere

~~At the beginning a~~nd end of a total eclipse, a reddish ~~glow appears~~ just around the photosphere. This ~~glow comes f~~rom the middle layer of the sun's ~~atmosphere, t~~he **chromosphere** (KROH muh sfeer). ~~The Greek wo~~rd *chroma* means "color," so the ~~chromospher~~e is the "color sphere."

_____

do the math! Analyzing Data

Solar Temperature
Use the table to answer the questions.

Layer	Temperature (°C)
Core	About 15,000,000
Radiation and Convection Zones	About 4,000,000
Photosphere	About 6,000
Inner Chromosphere	About 4,300
Outer Chromosphere	About 8,300
Corona	About 1,000,000

1 Interpret Data Which layer is hottest?

_____

2 Compare and Contrast How does the temperature change in the sun's atmosphere differ from the temperature change in the sun's interior?

_____

_____

6.NS.8

The Corona
During a total solar eclipse, an even fainter layer of the sun becomes visible, as you can see in **Figure 2**. This outer layer, which looks like a white halo around the sun, is called the **corona**, which means "crown" in Latin. The corona extends into space for millions of kilometers. It gradually thins into streams of electrically charged particles called the **solar wind.**

Do the Quick Lab
Layers of the Sun.

🔑 Assess Your Understanding

1a. List List the layers of the sun's interior and atmosphere, starting from the center.

_____

_____

_____

6.2.3

b. **Compare and Contrast** What is one key difference between the radiation and convection zones?

_____

_____

_____

_____

6.2.3

got it? •••••••••••••••••••••••••••••••••

○ **I get it!** Now I know that the sun's

structure includes _____

_____

○ **I need extra help with** _____

_____

Go to **my science** Ⓢ **coach** *online for help with this subject.*   6.2.3

239

Academic Standards for Science

6.2.3 Understand that the sun, an average star where nuclear reactions occur, is the central and largest body in the solar system.

What Features Can You See on the Sun?

For hundreds of years, scientists have used special telescopes to study the sun. They have spotted a variety of features on the sun's surface. ⚿ **Features on or just above the sun's surface include sunspots, prominences, and solar flares.**

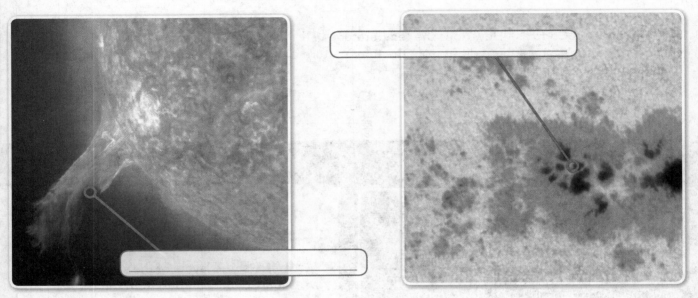

FIGURE 3 ·······

Sunspots and Prominences
Sunspots look dark in regular photographs. Some photos of the sun are taken with special filters that show the sun's structure. Sunspots may appear white in these photos. Sunspots are visible in both of the photos above. ✎ **Classify Label a prominence and a sunspot in the photos.**

Sunspots Photographs show dark areas on the sun's surface. These **sunspots** are areas of gas on the sun's surface that are cooler than the gases around them. Cooler gases don't give off as much light as hotter gases, which is why sunspots look dark. Sunspots look small, but in fact they can be larger than Earth. The number of sunspots varies in a regular cycle, with the most sunspots appearing about once every 11 years.

Prominences Sunspots usually occur in groups. Huge loops of gas called **prominences** often link different parts of sunspot regions. You can compare sunspots and prominences in **Figure 3.**

Solar Flares Sometimes the loops in sunspot regions suddenly connect, releasing large amounts of magnetic energy. The energy heats gas on the sun to millions of degrees Celsius, causing the gas to erupt into space. These eruptions are called **solar flares.**

⟳ **Relate Cause and Effect**
When prominences join, they cause (sunspots/solar flares).

Solar Wind The solar wind is made up of electrical particles from the sun. Solar flares can greatly increase the solar wind, which means that more particles reach Earth's upper atmosphere. Earth's atmosphere and magnetic field normally block these particles. But near the North and South poles, the particles can enter Earth's atmosphere. There, they create powerful electric currents that cause gas molecules in the atmosphere to glow. These particles cause auroras near the poles. They can also cause magnetic storms like the one that caused the blackout in Quebec in 1989. **Figure 4** shows how the solar wind interacts with Earth's magnetic field.

FIGURE 4 ....

Solar Wind

Particles from the solar wind spread through the solar system. When they reach Earth, they interact with Earth's magnetic field. (Note: The diagram is not to scale.)

✎ **Make Generalizations** The corona is the least dense layer of the sun's atmosphere. How do you think the density of the solar wind compares to the density of the corona?

_____

_____

_____

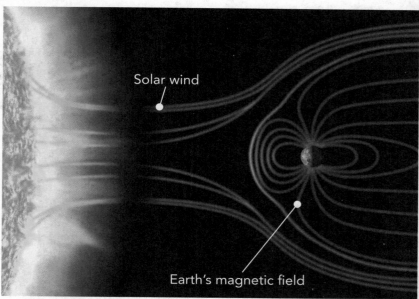

Solar wind

Earth's magnetic field

Lab zone® Do the Quick Lab *Viewing Sunspots.*

🔑 Assess Your Understanding

2a. Define (Prominences/sunspots) are loops of gas that extend from the sun's surface.

6.2.3

b. Explain Why do sunspots look darker than the rest of the sun's photosphere?

_____

_____

_____

6.2.3

c. ↻ **Relate Cause and Effect** How is the solar wind related to magnetic storms on Earth?

_____

_____

_____

_____

_____

6.2.3

got it? ....

○ **I get it!** Now I know that features on the sun include _____

○ **I need extra help with** _____

Go to MY SCIENCE Ⓢ COACH *online for help with this subject.*

6.2.3

4 The Inner Planets

 What Do the Inner Planets Have in Common?
6.2.4, 6.NS.8

What Are the Characteristics of the Inner Planets?
6.2.4, 6.NS.1, 6.NS.11, 6.DP.1, 6.DP.4

MY PLANET DiARY

What's in a Name?

Where in the solar system could you find Lewis and Clark's guide Sacagawea, artist Frida Kahlo, writer Helen Keller, and abolitionist Sojourner Truth all in the same place? On Venus! In fact, almost every feature on Venus is named for a real, fictional, or mythological woman.

In general, the person or people who discover an object or feature in the solar system get to choose its name. But scientists have agreed on some guidelines. Features on Mercury are named for authors, artists, and musicians. Many craters on Mars are named for towns on Earth. And most of the craters on Earth's moon are named for astronomers, physicists, and mathematicians.

FUN FACT

After you read the information to the left, answer the questions below.

1. Who decides what to name a newly discovered feature in the solar system?

_____

_____

2. If you discovered a new planet, how would you decide what to name its features?

_____

_____

_____

▶ **PLANET DIARY** Go to **Planet Diary** to learn more about the inner planets.

Lab**zone** Do the Inquiry Warm-Up *Ring Around the Sun.*

Vocabulary
- terrestrial planet
- greenhouse effect

Skills
- Reading: Compare and Contrast
- Inquiry: Communicate

What Do the Inner Planets Have in Common?

Earth, Mercury, Venus, and Mars are more like each other than they are like the outer planets. ⟳ **The inner planets are small and dense and have rocky surfaces.** The inner planets are often called the **terrestrial planets,** from the Latin word *terra*, which means "Earth." **Figure 1** summarizes data about the inner planets.

The terrestrial planets all have relatively high densities. They are rich in rocky and metallic materials, including iron and silicon. Each has a solid surface. All except Mercury have atmospheres.

 Academic Standards for Science

6.2.4 Compare and contrast the planets of the solar system with one another and with asteroids and comets with regard to their size, composition, distance from sun, surface features and ability to support life.

6.NS.8 Analyze data, using appropriate mathematical manipulation as required, and use it to identify patterns and make inferences based on these patterns.

FIGURE 1 ·······································
⟩ INTERACTIVE ART
The Inner Planets
✎ **Interpret Data** Use the table to answer the questions below.

1. Which planet is largest?

   _____

2. Which planet has the most moons?

   _____

3. Which planet is most similar to Earth in size?

   _____

   6.NS.8

Planet	 Mercury	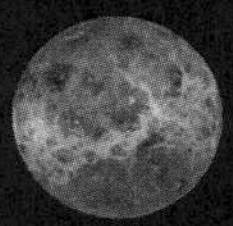 Venus	 Earth	 Mars
Diameter (km)	4,879	12,104	12,756	6,794
Period of rotation (Earth days)	58.9	244	1.0	1.03
Average distance from sun (AU)	0.39	0.72	1.0	1.52
Period of revolution (Earth days)	88	224.7	365.2	687
Number of moons	0	0	1	2

Note: Planets are not shown to scale.

 Lab zone Do the Quick Lab *Characteristics of the Inner Planets.*

⟳ Assess Your Understanding

got it? ······································

○ I get it! Now I know that the inner planets are _____

○ I need extra help with _____

Go to **MY SCIENCE** ⟩ **COACH** *online for help with this subject.*

6.2.4

243

Academic Standards for Science

6.2.4 Compare and contrast the planets of the solar system with one another and with asteroids and comets with regard to their size, composition, distance from sun, surface features and ability to support life.

6.NS.11 Communicate findings using models.

6.DP.1 Identify a need or problem to be solved.

6.DP.4 Select a solution to the need or problem.

Size of Mercury compared to Earth

I'm visiting the planets! As you read this lesson and the next one, keep track of how far I've traveled.

What Are the Characteristics of the Inner Planets?

Though the four inner planets have many features in common, they differ in size and composition as well as distance from the sun.

Mercury Would you like to visit a place where the temperature can range from 430°C to below −170°C? 🔑 **Mercury is the smallest terrestrial planet and the planet closest to the sun.** Mercury is not much larger than Earth's moon. The interior of Mercury is probably made up mainly of the dense metal iron.

Mercury's Surface As you can see in **Figure 2,** Mercury has flat plains and craters on its surface. Most of these craters formed early in the history of the solar system. Since Mercury has no water and not much atmosphere, the craters have not worn away over time.

Mercury's Atmosphere Mercury has virtually no atmosphere. Because Mercury's mass is small, its gravity is weak. Gas particles can easily escape into space. However, astronomers have detected small amounts of sodium and other gases around Mercury.

During the day, the side of Mercury facing the sun can reach temperatures of 430°C. Because there is so little atmosphere, the planet's heat escapes at night. Then the temperature drops below −170°C.

Exploring Mercury Much of what astronomers know about Mercury has come from space probes. *Mariner 10* flew by Mercury three times in 1974 and 1975. *Mercury MESSENGER* has passed Mercury several times, and will begin orbiting Mercury in 2011.

TOTAL AU:

SOL ☉ TOURS

INTERPLANETARY FREQUENT TRAVELER REWARDS PROGRAM

SPF 1000000

FIGURE 2 ···
Mercury
The photo shows Mercury's cratered surface.

✎ **Answer the questions below.**

1. **Solve Problems** List three things a visitor to Mercury would need to bring.

_____

_____

_____

2. CHALLENGE Refer to **Figure 1.** How many Mercury days are there in a Mercury year?

_____

Thick clouds cover the surface.

Blue regions are flat plains covered by lava flows.

Venus from space

Venus's surface

FIGURE 3 ···

Venus

This figure combines images of Venus taken from space with a camera (left) and radar (right). Radar is able to penetrate Venus's thick clouds to reveal the surface. The colors in both images are altered to show more details.

✎ **Infer** Why do scientists need to use radar to study Venus's surface?

_____

_____

Size of Venus compared to Earth

Venus Venus is so similar in size and mass to Earth that it is sometimes called "Earth's twin." Venus's density and internal structure are similar to Earth's. But in other ways Venus and Earth are very different. ⊙━ **Venus has a thick atmosphere, an unusual pattern of rotation, and the hottest surface of any planet.**

Venus's Atmosphere Venus's atmosphere is so thick that it is always cloudy. As you can see in **Figure 3,** astronomers can see only a smooth cloud cover over Venus. The thick clouds are made mostly of droplets of sulfuric acid.

At Venus's surface, you would quickly be crushed by the weight of its atmosphere. The pressure of Venus's atmosphere is 90 times greater than the pressure of Earth's atmosphere. You couldn't breathe on Venus because its atmosphere is mostly carbon dioxide.

Venus's Rotation Venus takes about 7.5 Earth months to revolve around the sun. It takes about 8 months for Venus to rotate once on its axis. Thus, Venus rotates so slowly that its day is longer than its year! Oddly, Venus rotates from east to west, the opposite direction from most other planets and moons. Astronomers hypothesize that this unusual rotation was caused by a very large object that struck Venus billions of years ago. Such a collision could have caused the planet to change its direction of rotation. Another hypothesis is that Venus's thick atmosphere could have somehow altered its rotation.

A Hot Planet Because Venus is closer to the sun than Earth is, it receives more solar energy than Earth does. Much of this radiation is reflected by Venus's atmosphere. However, some radiation reaches the surface and is later given off as heat. The carbon dioxide in Venus's atmosphere traps heat so well that Venus has the hottest surface of any planet. At 460°C, its average surface temperature is hot enough to melt lead. This trapping of heat by the atmosphere is called the **greenhouse effect. Figure 4** shows how the greenhouse effect occurs.

Exploring Venus The first probe to land on Venus's surface and send back data, *Venera 7*, landed in 1970. It survived for only a few minutes because of the high temperature and pressure. Later probes were more durable and sent images and data back to Earth.

The *Magellan* probe reached Venus in 1990, carrying radar instruments. Radar works through clouds, so *Magellan* was able to map nearly the entire surface. The *Magellan* data confirmed that Venus is covered with rock. Venus's surface has more than 10,000 volcanoes. Lava flows from these volcanoes have formed plains.

More recent probes have included *Venus Express,* from the European Space Agency, as well as brief visits by space probes headed for other planets. Images from *Venus Express* have helped scientists understand how Venus's clouds form and change.

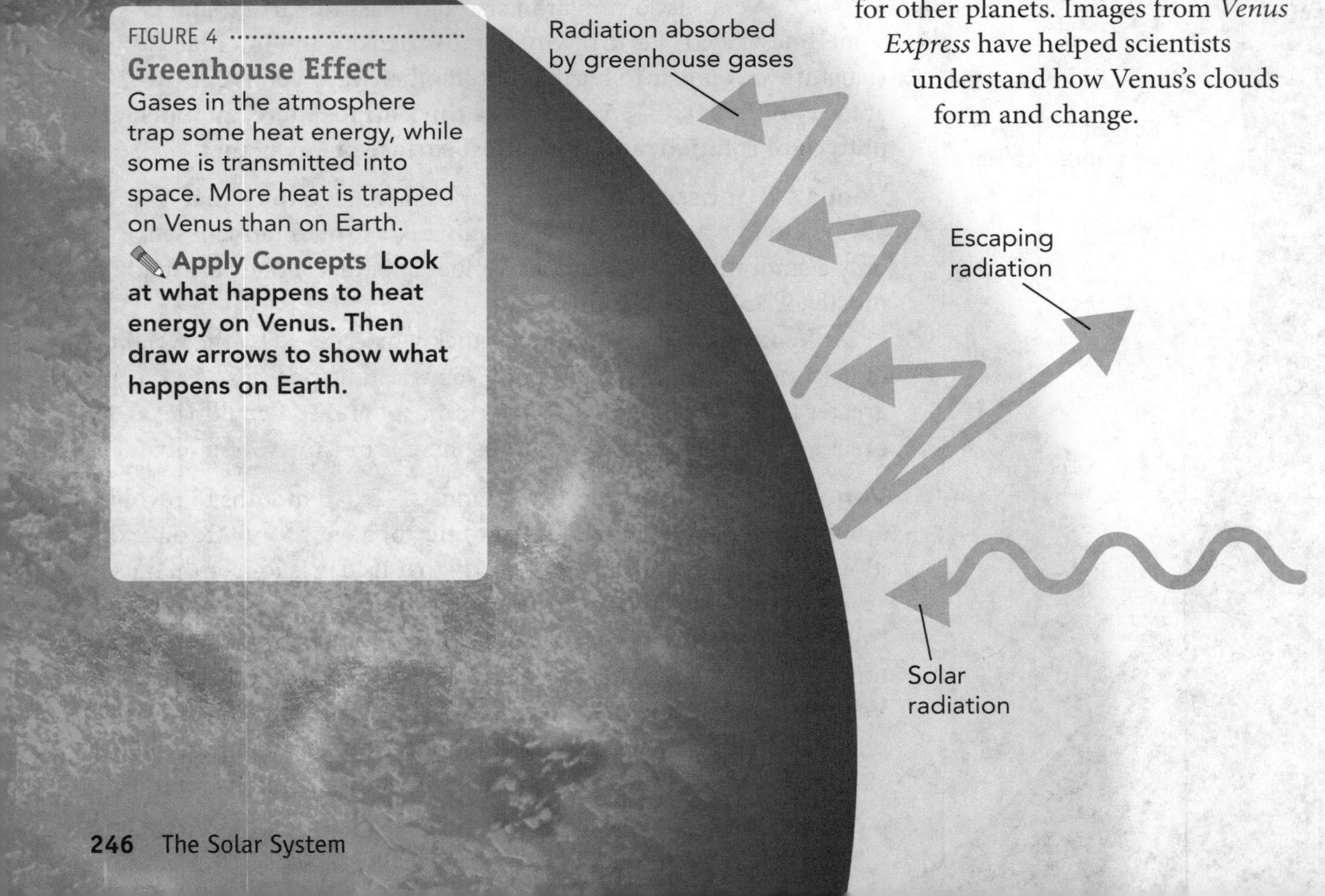

Compare and Contrast
List one feature Venus has in common with Earth and one feature that is different.

In common: _____

_____

Different: _____

_____

_____

FIGURE 4 ·····························

Greenhouse Effect
Gases in the atmosphere trap some heat energy, while some is transmitted into space. More heat is trapped on Venus than on Earth.

✎ **Apply Concepts** Look at what happens to heat energy on Venus. Then draw arrows to show what happens on Earth.

Radiation absorbed by greenhouse gases

Escaping radiation

Solar radiation

Earth There's only one planet in the solar system where you could live easily: Earth. 🔑 **Earth has liquid water and a suitable temperature range and atmosphere for living things to survive.**

The Water Planet Earth is unique in our solar system in having liquid water on its surface. In fact, most of Earth's surface, about 70 percent, is covered with water.

Earth's Temperature Scientists sometimes speak of Earth as having "Goldilocks" conditions—in other words, Earth is "just right" for life as we know it. Earth is not too hot and not too cold. If Earth were a little closer to the sun, it would be so hot that liquid water would evaporate. If it were a little farther away and colder, water would always be solid ice.

Earth's Atmosphere Earth has enough gravity to hold on to most gases. These gases make up Earth's atmosphere. Earth is the only planet with an atmosphere that is rich in oxygen. Oxygen makes up about 20 percent of Earth's atmosphere. Nearly all the rest is nitrogen, with small amounts of other gases such as argon, carbon dioxide, and water vapor.

Like Venus, Earth experiences a greenhouse effect. Earth's atmosphere traps heat, though less heat than Venus's atmosphere does. Without the atmosphere, Earth would be much colder.

FIGURE 5 ·············

Earth's Structure
Earth has three main layers—a crust, a mantle, and a core. The crust includes the solid, rocky surface. Under the crust is the mantle, a layer of hot rock. Earth has a dense core made mainly of iron and nickel.

✏️ **Relate Text and Visuals**
Label the layer of Earth with the highest density.

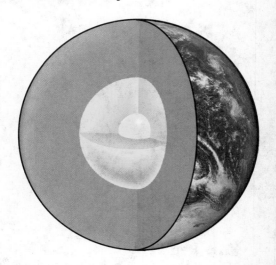

Solar radiation

Size of Mars
compared to Earth

Mars Mars is called the "red planet." **Figure 6** shows why. This reddish color is due to the breakdown of iron-rich rocks, leaving a rusty dust behind. 🔑 **Though Mars is too cold for liquid water, it does have water ice now and had liquid water in the past.**

Mars's Atmosphere The atmosphere of Mars is more than 95 percent carbon dioxide. You could walk around on Mars, but you would have to wear an airtight suit and carry your own oxygen. Mars has few clouds, and they are very thin compared to clouds on Earth. Temperatures on the surface range from −140°C to 20°C.

Water and Ice Images of Mars taken from space show a variety of features that look as if they were made by ancient streams, lakes, or floods. Scientists think that liquid water flowed on Mars's surface in the distant past. Scientists infer that Mars must have been much warmer and had a thicker atmosphere at that time.

Today, Mars's atmosphere is so thin that any liquid water would quickly turn into a gas. So where is Mars's water now? Some is located in the planet's two polar ice caps. Scientists thought the ice caps contained frozen carbon dioxide, but recent data show that the caps are almost entirely made of frozen water. Observations from the space probes *Mars Global Surveyor* and *Mars Reconnaissance Orbiter* have found large ice deposits just under the surface.

FIGURE 6 ···

The Red Planet
Remote-controlled landers such as *Phoenix*, *Spirit*, and *Opportunity* have sent back pictures of the surface of Mars.

✎ **Design a Solution** If you were designing a lander to work on Mars, where on Earth would you test it? Why? 6.NS.1, 6.DP.1, 6.DP.4

Communicate Choose one of the inner planets other than Earth. Describe an alien that could live there. Include at least three features of your alien that make it well suited for the planet you chose. Draw your alien to the right.

_____

_____

_____

_____

_____

6.NS.11

FIGURE 7 ··································

Olympus Mons
This computer-generated image is based on data from the *Mars Global Surveyor* mission.

Volcanoes Some regions of Mars have giant volcanoes. There are signs that lava flowed from the volcanoes in the past, but the volcanoes are rarely active today. Olympus Mons, shown in **Figure 7,** is the largest volcano in the solar system. It is as large as Missouri and is nearly three times as tall as Mount Everest!

Mars's Moons Mars has two very small moons. Phobos, the larger moon, is about 22 kilometers across. Deimos is even smaller, about 13 kilometers across. Like Earth's moon, Phobos and Deimos are covered with craters.

Exploring Mars Many space probes have visited Mars. Recent missions have focused on finding signs of water and possible life on Mars. Rovers called *Spirit* and *Opportunity* found traces of salts and minerals that form in the presence of water. The *Phoenix* mission took samples of soil and found frozen water near the north polar cap. Orbiting spacecraft such as *Mars Express* have detected methane gas in Mars's atmosphere. This gas might be a clue that microscopic life forms exist on Mars, even today!

Lab zone® Do the Quick Lab *Greenhouse Effect.*

Assess Your Understanding

1a. Name Which inner planet has the thickest atmosphere? _____

6.2.4

b. Relate Cause and Effect Why is Venus hotter than Mercury? _____

_____

_____

6.2.4

got it?

○ **I get it!** Now I know that the inner planets differ in _____

_____

○ **I need extra help with** _____

Go to **MY SCIENCE** Ⓢ **COACH** *online for help with this subject.*

6.2.4

The Outer Planets

UNLOCK THE BIG ?

🔑 **What Do the Outer Planets Have in Common?**
6.2.4, 6.NS.8

🔑 **What Are the Characteristics of Each Outer Planet?**
6.2.4, 6.NS.1, 6.NS.8

MY PLANET DIARY

Predicting a Planet

In the 1840s, astronomers were puzzled. Uranus didn't move as expected, based on the theory of gravity. Astronomers John Couch Adams and Urbain Leverrier independently hypothesized that Uranus was being affected by another planet's gravity. They calculated where this planet should be. Another astronomer, Johann Galle, aimed his telescope at the place Leverrier predicted. On September 23, 1846, he discovered the new planet—Neptune.

DISCOVERY

✎ **Communicate** **Work with a partner to answer the question.**

What science skills did the astronomers use when they discovered Neptune?

_____

_____

_____

_____

▷ PLANET DIARY Go to **Planet Diary** to learn more about the outer planets.

 ® Do the Inquiry Warm-Up
How Big Are the Planets?

ⓘ **Academic Standards for Science**

6.2.4 Compare and contrast the planets of the solar system with one another and with asteroids and comets with regard to their size, composition, distance from sun, surface features and ability to support life.

6.NS.8 Analyze data, using appropriate mathematical manipulation as required, and use it to identify patterns and make inferences based on these patterns.

What Do the Outer Planets Have in Common?

If you could visit the outer planets, you wouldn't have a solid place to stand! 🔑 **The four outer planets are much larger and more massive than Earth, and they do not have solid surfaces.** Because these four planets are so large, they are often called **gas giants.** **Figure 1** summarizes some basic facts about the gas giants.

Composition Jupiter and Saturn are composed mainly of hydrogen and helium. Uranus and Neptune contain some of these gases, but also ices of ammonia and methane. Because they are so massive, the gas giants exert a very strong gravitational force. This gravity keeps gases from escaping, forming thick atmospheres.

Vocabulary
- gas giant
- ring

Skills
- Reading: Outline
- Inquiry: Pose Questions

Despite the name "gas giant," much of the material in these planets is actually liquid because the pressure inside the planets is so high. The outer layers are extremely cold because they are far from the sun. Temperatures increase greatly within the planets.

Moons and Rings All the gas giants have many moons, ranging from 13 around Neptune to more than 60 around Jupiter! These moons vary from tiny balls of rock and ice barely a kilometer across to moons larger than Mercury. Some of these moons even have their own atmospheres!

In addition, each of the gas giants is surrounded by a set of rings. A **ring** is a thin disk of small particles of ice and rock. Saturn's rings are the largest and most complex.

As you visit each planet, don't forget to keep track of how many AU you've collected!

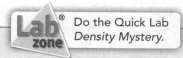
TOTAL AU:
SOL TOURS
INTERPLANETARY FREQUENT TRAVELER REWARDS PROGRAM

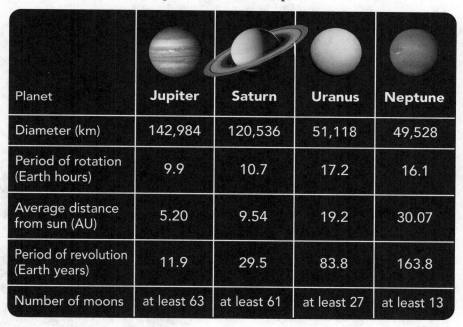

Planet	Jupiter	Saturn	Uranus	Neptune
Diameter (km)	142,984	120,536	51,118	49,528
Period of rotation (Earth hours)	9.9	10.7	17.2	16.1
Average distance from sun (AU)	5.20	9.54	19.2	30.07
Period of revolution (Earth years)	11.9	29.5	83.8	163.8
Number of moons	at least 63	at least 61	at least 27	at least 13

Note: Planets are not shown to scale.

FIGURE 1 ·····································
INTERACTIVE ART
The Outer Planets
The table summarizes data about the outer planets.

✎ **Estimate** Earth's diameter is about 12,750 km. About how many times larger is Jupiter's diameter than Earth's?

_____

6.NS.8

Lab zone Do the Quick Lab
Density Mystery.

⟳ Assess Your Understanding

got it? ··

○ **I get it!** Now I know that the gas giants all _____

_____

○ **I need extra help with** _____

Go to MY SCIENCE COACH *online for help with this subject.*

6.2.4

251

Academic Standards for Science

6.2.4 Compare and contrast the planets of the solar system with one another and with asteroids and comets with regard to their size, composition, distance from sun, surface features and ability to support life.

6.NS.1 Make predictions and develop testable questions based on research and prior knowledge.

6.NS.8 Analyze data.

Size of Jupiter compared to Earth

What Are the Characteristics of Each Outer Planet?

Since telescopes were first invented, scientists have studied the features of the outer planets and their moons. Today, space-based telescopes and space probes including the *Voyager*, *Galileo*, and *Cassini* missions have revealed many details of these planets that are not visible from Earth. Scientists are constantly discovering new information about these planets and their moons.

Jupiter 🔑 **Jupiter is the largest and most massive planet.** Jupiter's enormous mass dwarfs the other planets. In fact, its mass is about $2\frac{1}{2}$ times that of all the other planets combined!

Jupiter's Atmosphere Like all of the gas giants, Jupiter has a thick atmosphere made up mainly of hydrogen and helium. One notable feature of Jupiter's atmosphere is its Great Red Spot, a storm that is larger than Earth! The storm's swirling winds are similar to a hurricane, as you can see in **Figure 2**. Unlike hurricanes on Earth, however, the Great Red Spot shows no signs of going away.

Jupiter's Structure Astronomers think that Jupiter probably has a dense core of rock and iron at its center. A thick mantle of liquid hydrogen and helium surrounds this core. Because of the weight of Jupiter's atmosphere, the pressure at Jupiter's core is estimated to be about 30 million times greater than the pressure at Earth's surface.

✏️ **Outline** As you read, make an outline about Jupiter.

I. Atmosphere

  A. _____

    _____

  B. _____

II. Structure

  A. _____

    _____

  B. _____

    _____

  C. _____

    _____

FIGURE 2 ···

The Great Red Spot
This storm is about 20,000 km long and 12,000 km wide. The largest tropical storm on Earth was 2,200 km across.

✏️ **Calculate** Think of the storm on Earth as a square and the Great Red Spot as a rectangle. About how many Earth storms would fit inside the Great Red Spot?

6.NS.8

Jupiter's Moons The Italian astronomer Galileo Galilei discovered Jupiter's largest moons in 1610. These moons, shown in **Figure 3,** are named Io, Europa, Ganymede, and Callisto. Since Galileo's time, astronomers have discovered dozens of additional moons orbiting Jupiter. Many of these are small moons that have been found in the last few years thanks to improved technology.

FIGURE 3 ·······································

The Moons of Jupiter

Jupiter's four largest moons are larger than Earth's moon. Each has characteristics that set it apart from the others.

✎ **Relate Text and Visuals** Based on the photograph, match each description below to its moon.

❶ Ganymede is Jupiter's largest moon. It is larger than Mercury! Its surface is divided into dark and bright areas.

❷ Callisto is second to Ganymede in size, but has less ice. It has the most craters of any of Jupiter's moons.

❸ Io is not icy, unlike most of Jupiter's moons. It may have as many as 300 active volcanoes. The eruptions from those volcanoes constantly change the moon's surface.

❹ Europa is covered with ice. There may be liquid water below the ice—and if there's water, there might be life!

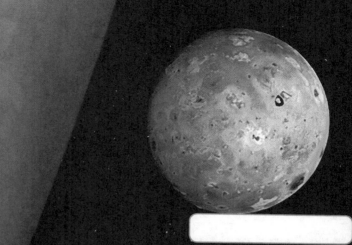

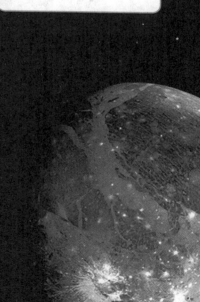

TOTAL AU:

SOL ☾ TOURS

INTERPLANETARY
FREQUENT TRAVELER
REWARDS PROGRAM

Titan This giant moon has a thick atmosphere.

TOTAL AU:

SOL & TOURS

INTERPLANETARY FREQUENT TRAVELER REWARDS PROGRAM

FIGURE 4 ....

The Saturn System

Recent space probes have shown details of Saturn and its moons.

✎ **Answer the questions below.**

1. **Make Judgments** Would it be easier to build a space colony on Saturn or on one of its moons? Why?

_____

_____

2. CHALLENGE Look at the photographs of Mimas and Tethys. What can you infer about the history of these moons?

_____

_____

Mimas A giant impact nearly broke Mimas apart, leaving the enormous crater shown here.

Iapetus This moon has light and dark areas.

✎ **Develop Hypotheses** What might the light areas be?

_____

6.NS.1

Saturn The second-largest planet in the solar system is Saturn. Saturn, like Jupiter, has a thick atmosphere made up mainly of hydrogen and helium. Saturn's atmosphere also contains clouds and storms, but they are less dramatic than those on Jupiter. The *Cassini* space probe found unusual six-sided cloud patterns around Saturn's north pole. Scientists aren't sure what causes these patterns.

Saturn's Rings 🔑 **Saturn has the most spectacular rings of any planet.** These rings are made of chunks of ice and rock, each traveling in its own orbit around Saturn. From Earth, it looks as though Saturn has only a few rings and that they are divided from each other by narrow, dark regions. Space probes have shown that each of these obvious rings is divided into many thinner rings. Saturn's rings are broad and thin, like a compact disc. Some rings are kept in place by gravity from tiny moons that orbit on either side of the ring.

Saturn's Moons Saturn's largest moon, Titan, is larger than the planet Mercury. It is also the only moon in the solar system that has a thick atmosphere. The atmosphere is composed mostly of nitrogen and methane. Some of these gases break down high in the atmosphere, forming a haze that is somewhat like smog on Earth. In 2005, the *Huygens* probe landed on Titan's surface. Photos from *Huygens* show features that may have been formed by flowing liquid. A few scientists think that Titan might support life.

Scientists have learned a great deal about Saturn's moons from the *Cassini* space probe. Giant craters and trenches cut cross Mimas (MY mus) and Tethys (TEE this). Ice and water erupt in geysers from the surface of Enceladus (en SEL uh dus). In 2009, scientists discovered a ring of material that may come from the outermost moon, Phoebe (FEE bee). **Figure 4** shows some of the members of the Saturn system.

Size of Saturn compared to Earth

did you know?

Saturn has the lowest density of any planet. If you could build a bathtub big enough, Saturn would float!

Tethys In this photo, you can just see a group of canyons that circle this moon.

Enceladus This photo shows faint bluish plumes erupting from the surface of Enceladus.

✏️ **Make Generalizations** Eruptions from Enceladus form one of Saturn's rings. What is that ring most likely made of?

Size of Uranus
compared to Earth

Uranus

Uranus Although the gas giant Uranus (YOOR uh nus) is about four times the diameter of Earth, it is still much smaller than Jupiter and Saturn. Uranus is twice as far from the sun as Saturn, so it is much colder. Uranus looks blue-green because of traces of methane in its atmosphere. Like the other gas giants, Uranus is surrounded by a group of thin, flat rings, although they are much darker than Saturn's rings.

Uranus's Moons Photographs from *Voyager 2* show that Uranus's five largest moons have icy, cratered surfaces. The craters show that rocks from space have hit the moons. Uranus's moons also have lava flows on their surfaces, suggesting that material has erupted from inside each moon. *Voyager 2* images revealed 10 moons that had never been seen before. Recently, astronomers discovered several more moons, for a total of at least 27.

A Tilted Planet 🔑 **Uranus's axis of rotation is tilted at an angle of about 90 degrees from the vertical.** Viewed from Earth, Uranus rotates from top to bottom instead of from side to side, as other planets do. You can see the tilt in **Figure 5.** Uranus's rings and moons rotate around this tilted axis. Astronomers think that billions of years ago, an object hit Uranus and knocked it on its side. Images from the *Voyager 2* space probe allowed scientists to determine that Uranus rotates in about 17 hours.

FIGURE 5 ·······························

A Sideways Planet
✏️ **Compare and Contrast** How do day and night at Uranus's equator change as Uranus revolves around the sun?

_____
_____
_____
_____
_____
_____
_____

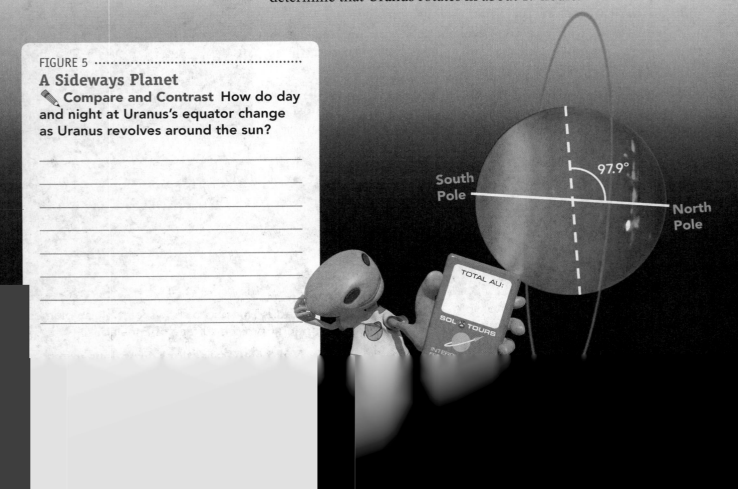

South Pole

North Pole

97.9°

TOTAL AU:

SOL TOURS

Neptune Neptune is similar in size and color to Uranus. **Neptune is a cold, blue planet. Its atmosphere contains visible clouds.** The color comes from methane in the atmosphere. Neptune's interior is hot due to energy left over from its formation. As this energy rises, it produces clouds and storms in the atmosphere.

Size of Neptune compared to Earth

Neptune's Atmosphere In 1989, *Voyager 2* flew by Neptune and photographed a Great Dark Spot about the size of Earth. Like the Great Red Spot on Jupiter, the Great Dark Spot was probably a giant storm. But it didn't last long. Images taken five years later showed that the spot was gone.

Neptune's Moons Astronomers have discovered at least 13 moons orbiting Neptune. The largest moon is Triton, which has a thin atmosphere. *Voyager 2* images show that the area of Triton's south pole is covered by nitrogen ice.

FIGURE 6 ....
Changing Neptune
The photograph above was taken in 1989. The photograph below was taken in 2002.

✏️ **Interpret Photos** How did Neptune change?

_____

_____

_____

_____

apply it!

Congratulations! You've earned enough AU in your travels to qualify for a free mission to one planet or moon of your choice!

❶ **Make Judgments** Which planet or moon do you choose? List three reasons for your choice.

_____

_____

❷ **Pose Questions** What is one question you would want your mission to answer?

_____

6.NS.1

🔑 **Assess Your Understanding**

1. Describe Describe one feature of each outer planet that distinguishes it from the others.

_____

_____

_____

_____

6.2.4

Lab zone Do the Quick Lab *Make a Model of Saturn.*

got it?

○ **I get it!** Now I know that the outer planets differ in _____

_____

○ **I need extra help with** _____

Go to **MY SCIENCE** 🔎 **COACH** online for help with this subject.

6.2.4

LESSON 6

Small Solar System Objects

 How Do Scientists Classify Small Objects in the Solar System?

6.2.4, 6.NS.1

MY PLANET DIARY

Posted by: Haley

Location: Constantia, New York

During the summer my dad and I go outside when it gets dark. We like to go stargazing. I have even seen shooting stars! Shooting stars are very hard to spot. You have to stare at the sky and sometimes you will see one shoot by. They only stick around for one split second, but it is really amazing to see one. This is my favorite thing to do when it gets dark during the summer!

BLOG

✏ **Communicate** Discuss your answers to these questions with a partner.

1. What do you think shooting stars are?

_____

_____

_____

_____

2. What do you like to observe in the night sky?

_____

_____

_____

> PLANET DIARY   Go to **Planet Diary** to learn more about small solar system objects.

 Lab zone Do the Inquiry Warm-Up *Collecting Micrometeorites.*

Vocabulary
- asteroid belt • Kuiper belt • Oort cloud
- comet • coma • nucleus • asteroid
- meteoroid • meteor • meteorite

Skills
↻ Reading: Summarize
△ Inquiry: Classify

How Do Scientists Classify Small Objects in the Solar System?

The solar system contains many small objects that, like the planets, orbit the sun. 🔑 **Scientists classify these objects based on their sizes, shapes, compositions, and orbits. The major categories include dwarf planets, comets, asteroids, and meteoroids.**

Areas of the Solar System Most of the small objects in the solar system are found in three areas: the asteroid belt, the Kuiper belt, and the Oort cloud. The **asteroid belt** is a region of the solar system between Mars and Jupiter. Beyond Neptune's orbit is a region called the **Kuiper belt** (KY per) which extends to about 100 times Earth's distance from the sun. Beyond the Kuiper belt, the **Oort cloud** (ort) stretches out more than 1,000 times the distance between the sun and Neptune. **Figure 1** shows these areas.

Academic Standards for Science

6.2.4 Compare and contrast the planets of the solar system with one another and with asteroids and comets with regard to their size, composition, distance from sun, surface features and ability to support life.

6.NS.1 Make predictions based on research and prior knowledge.

FIGURE 1 ···

Areas of the Solar System
The diagram below shows the relative positions of the asteroid belt, the Kuiper belt, and the Oort cloud.

✏ **Relate Text and Visuals** As you read this lesson, write a C to show where a comet would most likely come from. Write a P to show where you would expect to find a plutoid. Write an A to show where you would expect to find an asteroid.

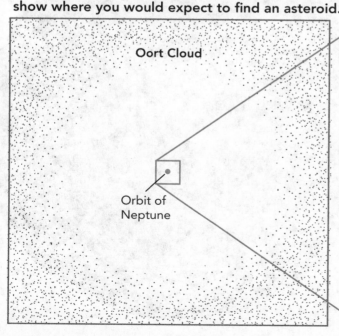

Oort Cloud

Orbit of
Neptune

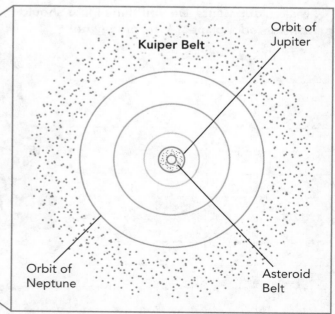

Kuiper Belt

Orbit of
Jupiter

Orbit of
Neptune

Asteroid
Belt

Vocabulary Greek Word
Origins The word *comet* comes
from the Greek word *kometes,*
meaning "long hair." Why do
you think this word is used?

_____

_____

_____

Dwarf Planets

Dwarf Planets "What happened to Pluto?" You may have found yourself asking this question as you have learned about the solar system. For many years, Pluto was considered a planet. But then scientists discovered other objects that were at least Pluto's size. Some were even farther away than Pluto. Scientists began debating how to define a planet.

Defining Dwarf Planets In 2006, astronomers developed a new category of objects, called dwarf planets. These objects orbit the sun and have enough gravity to pull themselves into spheres, but they have other objects in the area of their orbits. As of 2009, scientists had identified five dwarf planets: Pluto, Eris, Makemake, Haumea, and Ceres. Eris is believed to be the largest dwarf planet so far. There are at least a dozen more objects that may turn out to be dwarf planets, once scientists are able to study them.

Like planets, dwarf planets can have moons. Pluto has three moons: Charon, Nix, and Hydra. Haumea has two and Eris has one.

Kuiper Belt Objects All the known dwarf planets except Ceres orbit beyond Neptune. (Ceres orbits in the asteroid belt.) A dwarf planet that orbits beyond Neptune is also called a plutoid. Most plutoids orbit the sun in the Kuiper belt, though Eris may be beyond it. The Kuiper belt also includes many other objects that are too small to be considered dwarf planets.

FIGURE 2
> VIRTUAL LAB **Planet or Not?**
This figure shows one artist's idea of what the surface of Pluto looks like.

Make Judgments Do you think Pluto should be considered a planet? Why or why not?

_____

_____

_____

_____

_____

_____

_____

_____

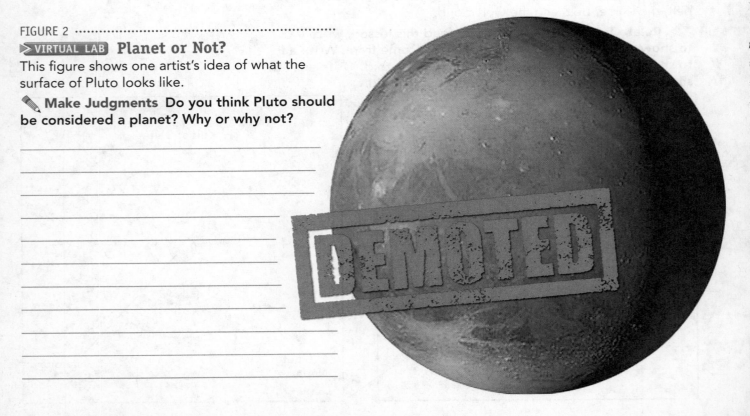

Comets

A comet is one of the most dramatic objects you can see in the night sky. On a dark night, you can see its fuzzy white head and long, streaming tails. **Comets** are loose collections of ice, dust, and small rocky particles whose orbits can be very long, narrow ellipses. Some comets have smaller orbits that bring them near Earth regularly. Most comets originate in the Oort cloud.

A Comet's Head When a comet gets close to the sun, the energy in sunlight turns the ice into gas, releasing gas and dust. Clouds of gas and dust form a fuzzy outer layer called a **coma. Figure 3** shows the coma and the **nucleus,** the solid inner core of a comet. The nucleus is usually only a few kilometers across.

A Comet's Tail As a comet approaches the sun, it heats up and starts to glow. Some of its gas and dust stream outward, forming a tail. Most comets have two tails—a gas tail and a dust tail. The gas tail points away from the sun and the dust tail points along the path the comet has taken. A comet's tail can be more than 100 million kilometers long and from Earth, appears to stretch across most of the sky. The material is stretched out very thinly, however.

> ✎ **Summarize** Write a few sentences to summarize the structure of a comet.
>
> _____
> _____
> _____
> _____
> _____
> _____

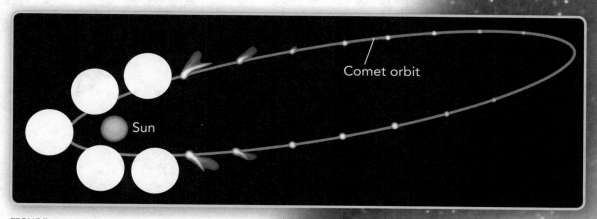

Comet orbit

Sun

FIGURE 3 ···

A Comet's Orbit

Comets, as shown here, have long, narrow orbits. Their tails tend to grow longer as they approach the sun.

✎ **Apply Concepts Complete the diagram above by adding the comet's tails.**

Gas tail

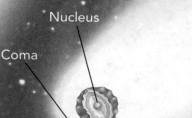

Nucleus

Coma

Dust tail

Asteroids Hundreds of small, irregular, rocky objects orbit the sun. These **asteroids** are rocky objects, most of which are too small and too numerous to be considered planets or dwarf planets. Astronomers have discovered more than 100,000 asteroids, and they are constantly finding more.

Small Bodies Most asteroids are small—less than a kilometer in diameter. Only Ceres, Pallas, Vesta, and Hygiea are more than 300 kilometers across. (Ceres is both a dwarf planet and the largest asteroid.) Most asteroids are not spherical. Scientists hypothesize that asteroids are leftover pieces of the early solar system that never came together to form a planet.

Asteroid Orbits Most asteroids orbit the sun in the asteroid belt. Some, however, have very elliptical orbits that bring them closer to the sun than Earth's orbit. Someday, an asteroid will hit Earth. One or more large asteroids did hit Earth about 65 million years ago, filling the atmosphere with dust and smoke and blocking out sunlight around the world. Scientists hypothesize that many species of organisms, including the dinosaurs, became extinct as a result.

know?

The Holcomb Observatory at Butler University, in Indianapolis, is one of the largest public observatories in the world. It is home to a 38-inch telescope used by astronomers and students. Recently, researchers at the observatory have been measuring the orbits and other characteristics of asteroids.

apply it!

Classify For each description below, classify the object as a dwarf planet, comet, asteroid, or meteoroid.

❶ This object is slightly smaller than Pluto. It orbits the sun beyond Neptune and is spherical. _____

❷ This object is irregularly shaped. It orbits the sun just outside the orbit of Mars. _____

❸ This object is a chunk of rock and metal. It was once part of another object that orbited the sun. _____

❹ This object is composed of ice and rock. It orbits the sun in an elongated orbit, taking many years to complete one orbit.

_____

❺ CHALLENGE Which two types of objects are hardest to tell apart? Why? _____

_____

_____

Meteoroids Chunks of rock or dust smaller than asteroids are called **meteoroids.** Meteoroids are generally less than 10 meters across. Some meteoroids form when asteroids collide. Others form when comets break up, creating dust clouds.

Meteors and Meteorites When a meteoroid enters Earth's atmosphere, friction with the air creates heat and produces a streak of light. This streak is a **meteor.** (People often call meteors shooting stars, but they are not stars.) Most meteors come from tiny bits of rock or dust that burn up completely. But some larger meteoroids do not burn up. Meteoroids that pass through the atmosphere and are found on Earth's surface are called **meteorites.** Meteorite impacts can leave craters, such as the one shown in **Figure 4.**

Meteor Showers Meteor showers occur when Earth passes through an area with many meteoroids. Some of these groups of meteoroids are bits of comets that broke up. These meteor showers occur every year as Earth passes through the same areas. Meteor showers are often named for the constellation from which they appear to come. The Perseids, Geminids, and Orionids are examples of meteor showers.

FIGURE 4 ···

Meteor Crater

Meteor Crater in Arizona formed about 50,000 years ago from the impact of a meteorite 50–100 meters wide. ✎ **Predict** How would a large meteorite impact affect Earth today?

_____

_____

_____

6.NS.1

○ Approximate size of meteorite relative to crater

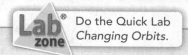
Do the Quick Lab *Changing Orbits.*

🔑 Assess Your Understanding

1a. Review (Comets/Asteroids) are rocky, while (comets/asteroids) are made of ice and dust.

6.2.4

b. Compare and Contrast What is the difference between a dwarf planet and an asteroid?

_____

_____

_____

6.2.4

c. Relate Cause and Effect How and why does a comet change as it approaches the sun?

_____

_____

_____

6.2.4

got it? ···

○ **I get it!** Now I know that small solar system objects include _____

_____

○ I need extra help with _____

Go to **MY SCIENCE** 🔵 **COACH** *online for help with this subject.*

6.2.4

7 Study Guide

Objects in the solar system are different because they formed _____

LESSON 1 Models of the Solar System

6.2.4, 6.NS.11, 6.DP.10

🔑 In a geocentric model, Earth is at the center.

🔑 Copernicus worked out the arrangement of the known planets and how they orbit the sun.

🔑 Kepler found that planets' orbits are ellipses.

🔑 Evidence from Galileo Galilei convinced others that the heliocentric model was correct.

Vocabulary
• geocentric • heliocentric • ellipse

LESSON 2 Introducing the Solar System

6.2.3, 6.2.4, 6.NS.3, 6.NS.8

🔑 Our solar system consists of the sun, the planets, their moons, and smaller objects.

🔑 The solar system formed about 4.6 billion years ago from a cloud of hydrogen, helium, rock, ice, and other materials pulled together by gravity.

Vocabulary
• solar system • astronomical unit • planet
• dwarf planet • planetesimal

LESSON 3 The Sun

6.2.3, 6.NS.8

🔑 The sun's interior consists of the core, the radiation zone, and the convection zone. The sun's atmosphere includes the photosphere, the chromosphere, and the corona.

🔑 Features on or just above the sun's surface include sunspots, prominences, and solar flares.

Vocabulary
• core • nuclear fusion • radiation zone
• convection zone • photosphere
• chromosphere • corona • solar wind
• sunspot • prominence • solar flare

LESSON 4 The Inner Planets

6.2.4, 6.NS.1, 6.NS.11, 6.DP.1, 6.DP.4

🔑 The inner planets are small and dense and have rocky surfaces.

🔑 Mercury is the smallest terrestrial planet and the planet closest to the sun. Venus has a thick atmosphere and the hottest surface of any planet. Earth has a suitable temperature range and atmosphere for living things to survive. Mars has ice and may have had liquid water in the past.

Vocabulary
• terrestrial planet • greenhouse effect

LESSON 5 The Outer Planets

6.2.4, 6.NS.1, 6.NS.8

🔑 The outer planets are much larger than Earth and do not have solid surfaces.

🔑 Jupiter is the largest and most massive planet. Saturn has the most spectacular rings of any planet. Uranus's axis of rotation is tilted at an angle of about 90 degrees from the vertical. Neptune is a cold, blue planet with visible clouds.

Vocabulary
• gas giant • ring

LESSON 6 Small Solar System Objects

6.2.4, 6.NS.1

🔑 Scientists classify small objects based on their sizes, shapes, compositions, and orbits. The major categories include dwarf planets, comets, asteroids, and meteoroids.

Vocabulary
• asteroid belt • Kuiper belt • Oort cloud
• comet • coma • nucleus • asteroid
• meteoroid • meteor • meteorite

Review and Assessment

LESSON 1 Models of the Solar System

1. What object is at the center of a geocentric system?

  a. Earth   **b.** the moon

  c. a star   **d.** the sun

        6.2

2. Kepler discovered that planets move in

_____

        6.2

3. Relate Cause and Effect How did Tycho Brahe's work contribute to the development of the heliocentric model?

_____

_____

_____

        6.2

4. Write About It Suppose you lived at the time of Copernicus. Write a letter to a scientific journal supporting the heliocentric model.

        6.2

LESSON 2 Introducing the Solar System

5. Pluto is an example of a(n)

  a. dwarf planet.   **b.** inner planet.

  c. outer planet.   **d.** planetesimal.

        6.2.4

6. An astronomical unit is equal to _____

_____

        6.2.4

7. Compare and Contrast Compare the conditions that led to the formation of the inner planets with those that led to the formation of the outer planets.

_____

_____

_____

        6.2.4

LESSON 3 The Sun

8. In which part of the sun does nuclear fusion take place?

  a. chromosphere   **b.** convection layer

  c. core   **d.** corona

        6.2.3

9. Relatively cool areas on the sun's surface are called _____

        6.2.3

10. Explain How can the solar wind affect life on Earth? _____

_____

_____

        6.2.3

11. math! The density of the sun's core is about 160 g/cm^3. The density of Earth's core is about 13.0 g/cm^3. About how many times denser is the sun's core than Earth's?

_____

        6.2.3, 6.NS.8

LESSON 4 The Inner Planets

12. What feature is shared by all the inner planets?

  a. thick atmosphere   **b.** rocky surface

  c. ring system   **d.** liquid water

        6.2.4

13. The inner planets are also called _____

_____

        6.2.4

14. Apply Concepts Explain why Venus has the hottest surface of any planet.

_____

_____

_____

_____

        6.2.4

15. Write About It Choose one inner planet. Write a news article describing a visit to that planet's surface. Include descriptive details.

        6.2.4, 6.NS.2

LESSON 5 The Outer Planets

16. Which planet's orbit is farthest from Earth's?

   a. Jupiter   **b.** Neptune

   c. Saturn   **d.** Uranus

                                6.2.4

17. All the gas giants are surrounded by _____

_____

                                6.2.4

Use the illustration to answer Question 18.

18. Interpret Diagrams What planet is shown above? What is unusual about it? What do scientists think caused that unusual feature?

_____

_____

_____

_____

_____

                                6.2.4

19. Predict Do you think astronomers have found all the moons of the outer planets? Explain.

_____

_____

_____

_____

_____

_____

                       6.2.4, 6.NS.1

LESSON 6 Small Solar System Objects

20. Where are most dwarf planets found?

   a. asteroid belt   **b.** Kuiper belt

   c. Oort cloud   **d.** plutoid belt

                                6.2.4

21. A _____ is a meteoroid that reaches Earth's surface.

                                6.2.4

22. Compare and Contrast Compare and contrast asteroids, comets, and meteoroids.

_____

_____

_____

_____

_____

23. Write About It Suppose you could witness a large meteorite or asteroid striking Earth. Write a news report explaining the event.

                                6.2.4

APPLY
THE BIG
? **Why are objects in the solar system different from each other?**

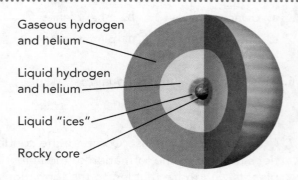

Gaseous hydrogen and helium

Liquid hydrogen and helium

Liquid "ices"

Rocky core

24. What type of planet is shown? Under what conditions would it most likely have formed?

_____

_____

_____

_____

                                6.2.4

Indiana ISTEP+ Practice

Multiple Choice

Circle the letter of the best answer.

1. The table below shows data for five planets.

Planet	Period of Rotation (Earth days)	Period of Revolution (Earth years)	Average Distance from the Sun (million km)
Mars	1.03	1.9	228
Jupiter	0.41	12	779
Saturn	0.45	29	1,434
Uranus	0.72	84	2,873
Neptune	0.67	164	4,495

According to the table, which planet has a "day" that is most similar in length to a day on Earth?

A. Mars
B. Jupiter
C. Neptune
D. Uranus

6.2.4, 6.NS.8

2. What characteristic do all of the outer planets share?

A. They have rocky surfaces.
B. They are larger than the sun.
C. They have many moons.
D. They have thin atmospheres.

6.2.4

3. Which layer of the sun has the highest density?

A. core
B. corona
C. photosphere
D. radiation zone

6.2.3

4. From what region do *most* comets come?

A. asteroid belt
B. inner solar system
C. Kuiper belt
D. Oort cloud

6.2.4

Constructed Response

Write your answer to Question 5 on the lines below.

5. Mercury has a daytime temperature of about 430°C and a nighttime temperature below −170°C. What is the *best* explanation for this?

_____

_____

_____

6.2.4

Extended Response

Use the diagram below to answer Question 6.

6. What model of the solar system is shown above? Give at least two pieces of evidence that support the model.

6.2.4

Mars Rovers

Was there ever water on Mars? The planet is too far away for humans to explore directly. So the National Aeronautics and Space Administration (NASA) dropped robot rovers onto Mars' surface to do the exploring for us. The rovers landed in January 2004, and their mission was to last three months. Their assignment was to collect images that would help determine if water ever existed on the planet. Chemical and physical data from the rovers suggest that there once was water on Mars. There is evidence of erosion as well as of chemicals that would exist in an acidic lake or hot springs. The rovers have continued to send data back to NASA for more than five years!

Design It Find out more about the Mars rover missions and identify problems NASA had with the rovers. Brainstorm potential design solutions and select your best idea. Document the design of your rover. Then select the most appropriate materials to create a prototype for your design. Test and evaluate your design on a sandy surface with some rocks. Record appropriate data, such as how far your rover travels before it gets stuck. Graph your data and then use the information to redesign your rover. See Appendix A on page 350 for more information about the design process.

6.NS.1–6.NS.11, 6.DP.1–6.DP.11

Maria Mitchell

In the mid-1800s, the idea of a woman astronomer seemed far-fetched. But then Maria Mitchell changed everything. In 1847, Mitchell was the first American woman astronomer to use a telescope to find a comet. Later, she taught astronomy at Vassar College, and inspired other young women to follow in her footsteps. She was a true astronomical pioneer.

Write About It Research more about Maria Mitchell's career. Write a biographical essay about her life and work.

 6.NS.2

Maria Mitchell (left) and Mary Whitney in the observatory at Vassar. Mary Whitney studied with Maria Mitchell, and later taught with her. ▶

GOODBYE, PLUTO!

What is a planet? That question was hotly debated by astronomers in 2006. Everyone agreed that a planet must be round and orbit the sun. But some said that a planet must also be dominant in its area of space. And then, the astronomers voted. The result: Pluto was demoted to a dwarf planet.

Research It Find out more about the Pluto decision. Participate in a debate and vote on the definition of *planet*. Write a newspaper article about the result of your debate. Be sure to include information from both sides of the argument.

 6.2.4, 6.NS.2

Why Do Clownfish Play With Poison?

How do living things affect one another?

Clownfish live among the poisonous and stinging tentacles of sea anemones to avoid being eaten by larger fish. Amazingly, the clownfish do not get stung! This is because a fluid called mucus protects the skin of the fish. **Develop Hypotheses How might a sea anemone benefit from having clownfish around?**

_____

_____

_____

_____

_____

_____

_____

> **UNTAMED SCIENCE** Watch the **Untamed Science** video to learn more about interactions between organisms.

Populations and Communities

CHAPTER 8

Academic Standards for Science

6.3, 6.3.1, 6.3.2, 6.3.3, 6.NS.1–6.NS.11, 6.DP.1–6.DP.11

8 Getting Started

Check Your Understanding

1. **Background** Read the paragraph below and then answer the question.

Raquel planted a garden in a sunny area near her home. First, she loosened the **soil**, so the plant roots could easily grow. If days passed with no **precipitation**, she watered the plants. That was all she had to do—the rest of what the plants needed came from the **atmosphere!**

Soil is made up of rock fragments, water, air, and decaying plant and animal matter.

Rain, hail, sleet, and snow are all types of **precipitation.**

Earth's **atmosphere** contains oxygen, carbon dioxide, nitrogen, and other gases.

• How do soil, precipitation, and the atmosphere help a plant grow?

_____

_____

_____

> **MY READING WEB** If you had trouble completing the question above, visit **My Reading Web** and type in *Populations and Communities.*

Vocabulary Skill

Latin Word Origins Some key terms in this chapter contain word parts with Latin origins. The table below lists two of the Latin words that key terms come from.

Latin Word	Meaning of Latin Word	Example
aptare	to fit	adaptation, *n.* a characteristic that allows an organism to live successfully in its environment
migrare	to move	immigration, *n.* movement into a population

2. **Quick Check** The terms *immigration* and *emigration* both come from the Latin word *migrare*. Circle the meaning of *migrare* in the table above.

organism

immigration

adaptation

predation

Chapter Preview

LESSON 1
- organism • habitat
- biotic factor • abiotic factor
- species • population
- community • ecosystem
- ecology

↻ **Compare and Contrast**
△ **Draw Conclusions**

LESSON 2
- birth rate • death rate
- immigration • emigration
- population density
- limiting factor
- carrying capacity

↻ **Relate Cause and Effect**
△ **Infer**

LESSON 3
- natural selection • adaptation
- niche • competition • predation
- predator • prey • symbiosis
- mutualism • commensalism
- parasitism • parasite • host

↻ **Relate Text and Visuals**
△ **Classify**

LESSON 4
- succession • primary succession
- pioneer species
- secondary succession

↻ **Compare and Contrast**
△ **Observe**

▸ **VOCAB FLASH CARDS** For extra help with vocabulary, visit **Vocab Flash Cards** and type in *Populations and Communities.*

273

LESSON 1

Living Things and the Environment

What Does an Organism Get From Its Environment?
6.3

What Are the Two Parts of an Organism's Habitat?
6.3.3, 6.NS.8

How Is an Ecosystem Organized?
6.3, 6.NS.11

MY PLANET DIARY

DISCOVERY

Love Song

The gray, golden brown, and Goodman's mouse lemurs are some of the world's smallest primates. These three lemurs look similar. Looking so similar makes it difficult for the lemurs to find members of their own kind or species during mating season. However, it seems that the lemurs can identify their own species by song. Scientists recorded the mating calls of the three species of lemurs. They discovered that the lemurs reacted more to the calls from their own species. This allows the lemurs to pick the right mate, even at night.

Communicate Answer these questions. Discuss your answers with a partner.

1. If you were looking for your sneakers among several pairs that looked just like yours, what characteristics would make it easier for you to find them?

_____

_____

2. What do you think would happen if a lemur mated with a different kind of lemur?

_____

_____

> PLANET DIARY Go to **Planet Diary** to learn more about habitats.

Golden brown mouse lemur

Goodman's mouse lemur

Gray mouse lemur

Lab zone® Do the Inquiry Warm-Up *What's in the Scene?*

Vocabulary

- organism • habitat • biotic factor • abiotic factor
- species • population • community • ecosystem
- ecology

Skills

- Reading: Compare and Contrast
- Inquiry: Draw Conclusions

What Does an Organism Get From Its Environment?

If you were to visit Alaska, you might see a bald eagle fly by. A bald eagle is one type of **organism,** or living thing. Different types of organisms live in different types of surroundings, or environments. **An organism gets food, water, shelter, and other things it needs to live, grow, and reproduce from its environment.** An environment that provides the things a specific organism needs to live, grow, and reproduce is called its **habitat.**

In a forest habitat, mushrooms grow in the damp soil and woodpeckers build nests in tree trunks. Organisms live in different habitats because they have different requirements for survival and reproduction. Some organisms live on a prairie, with its flat terrain, tall grasses, and low rainfall amounts. A prairie dog, like the one shown in **Figure 1,** obtains the food and shelter it needs from a prairie habitat. It could not survive on this rocky ocean shore. Likewise, the prairie would not meet the needs of a sea star.

> **Academic Standards for Science**
>
> **6.3 Core Standard** Understand that the major source of energy for ecosystems is light produced by major nuclear reactions in the sun.

FIGURE 1 ···
What's Wrong With This Picture?
Most people would never expect to see a prairie dog at the beach.
✎ **List** Give three reasons why this prairie dog would not survive in this habitat.

_____

_____

_____

_____

Do the Quick Lab
Organisms and Their Habitats.

Assess Your Understanding

got it? ···

○ **I get it!** Now I know that an organism's environment provides _____

_____

○ **I need extra help with** _____

Go to **my science COACH** *online for help with this subject.*

6.3

Academic Standards for Science

6.3.3 Describe how certain biotic and abiotic factors, such as quantity of light and water, range of temperatures, and soil composition can limit the number of organisms that an ecosystem can support.

6.NS.8 Analyze data, and use it to identify patterns and make inferences based on these patterns.

⟳ **Compare and Contrast** In the paragraphs at the right, circle how biotic and abiotic factors are similar and underline how they are different.

What Are the Two Parts of an Organism's Habitat?

To meet its needs, a prairie dog must interact with more than just the other prairie dogs around it. ☞ **An organism interacts with both the living and nonliving parts of its habitat.**

Biotic Factors
What living things can you see in the prairie dog's habitat shown in **Figure 2**? The parts of a habitat that are living, or once living, and interact with an organism are called **biotic factors** (by AHT ik). The plants that provide seeds and berries are biotic factors. The ferrets and eagles that hunt the prairie dog are also biotic factors. Worms and bacteria are biotic factors that live in the soil underneath the prairie grass. Prairie dog scat, owl pellets, and decomposing plant matter are also biotic factors.

Abiotic Factors
Not all of the factors that organisms interact with are living. **Abiotic factors** (ay by AHT ik) are the nonliving parts of an organism's habitat. These factors, as shown in **Figure 2**, include sunlight, soil, temperature, oxygen, and water.

FIGURE 2 ···
Factors in a Prairie Habitat
A prairie dog interacts with many biotic and abiotic factors in the prairie habitat.

✎ **Relate Text and Visuals** Add another biotic factor to the picture. For each abiotic factor, draw a line from the text box to an example in the picture.

Sunlight Because sunlight is needed for plants to make their own food, it is an important abiotic factor for most living things.

Soil Soil consists of varying amounts of rock fragments, nutrients, air, water, and the decaying remains of living things. The soil in an area influences the kinds of plants and animals that can live and grow there.

Temperature The temperatures that are typical in an area determine the types of organisms that can live there.

Oxygen Most living things require oxygen to carry out their life processes. Organisms on land obtain oxygen from air. Aquatic organisms obtain oxygen that is dissolved in the water around them.

Water All living things require water to carry out their life processes. Plants and algae need water along with sunlight and carbon dioxide to make their own food. Other living things depend on plants and algae for food.

apply it!

Salt is an abiotic factor found in some environments. To see how the amount of salt affects the hatching of brine shrimp eggs, varying amounts of salt were added to four different 500-mL beakers.

1 Observe In which beaker(s) did the eggs, shown as purple circles, hatch? _____

2 Infer The manipulated variable was

_____

3 Infer The responding variable was _____

_____

4 CHALLENGE Beaker _____ was the control.

5 Draw Conclusions What can you conclude about the amount of salt in the shrimps' natural habitat?

_____
_____
_____

6.NS.8

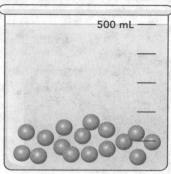

Beaker A
500 mL spring water

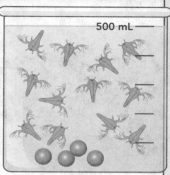

Beaker B
500 mL spring water
+ 2.5 g salt

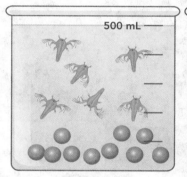

Beaker C
500 mL spring water
+ 7.5 g salt

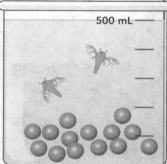

Beaker D
500 mL spring water
+ 15 g salt

 Do the Lab Investigation *World in a Bottle.*

🔑 Assess Your Understanding

1a. Interpret Diagrams List two biotic and two abiotic factors in **Figure 2.**

_____
_____
_____
_____

6.3.3

b. Draw Conclusions Name two abiotic factors in your habitat and explain how your life would be different without them.

_____
_____
_____
_____

6.3.3

got it? ....

O **I get it!** Now I know that the two parts of an organism's habitat are _____

_____

O **I need extra help with** _____

Go to my science COACH online for help with this subject.

6.3.3

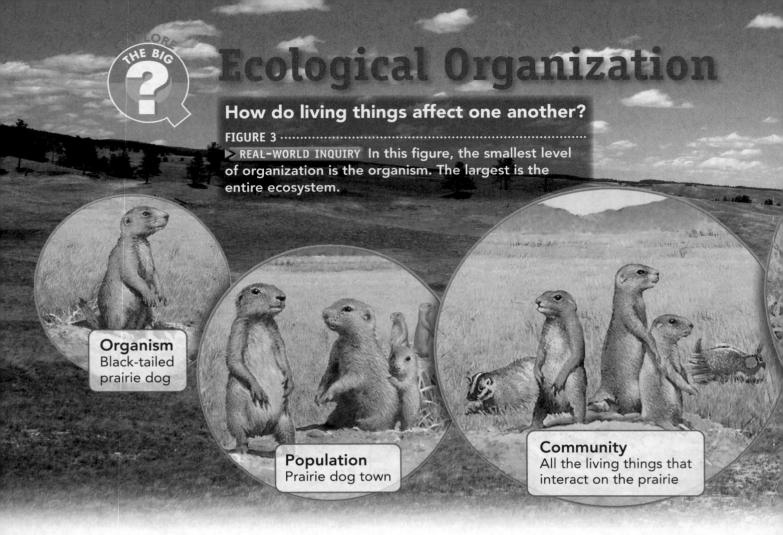

Ecological Organization

How do living things affect one another?

FIGURE 3 ....

▷ REAL-WORLD INQUIRY In this figure, the smallest level of organization is the organism. The largest is the entire ecosystem.

Organism
Black-tailed prairie dog

Population
Prairie dog town

Community
All the living things that interact on the prairie

Academic Standards for Science

6.3 Core Standard Describe that all organisms, including humans, are part of complex systems found in all biomes (freshwater, marine, forest, desert, grassland, tundra).

6.NS.11 Communicate findings using models through oral and written reports.

How Is an Ecosystem Organized?

Most organisms do not live all alone in their habitat. Instead, organisms live together in populations and communities that interact with abiotic factors in their ecosystems.

Organisms Black-tailed prairie dogs that live in prairie dog towns on the Nebraska plains are all members of one species. A **species** (SPEE sheez) is a group of organisms that can mate with each other and produce offspring that can also mate and reproduce.

Populations All the members of one species living in a particular area are referred to as a **population.** The prairie dogs in the Nebraska town are one example of a population.

Communities A particular area contains more than one species of organism. The prairie, for instance, includes prairie dogs, hawks, snakes, and grasses. All the different populations that live together in an area make up a **community**.

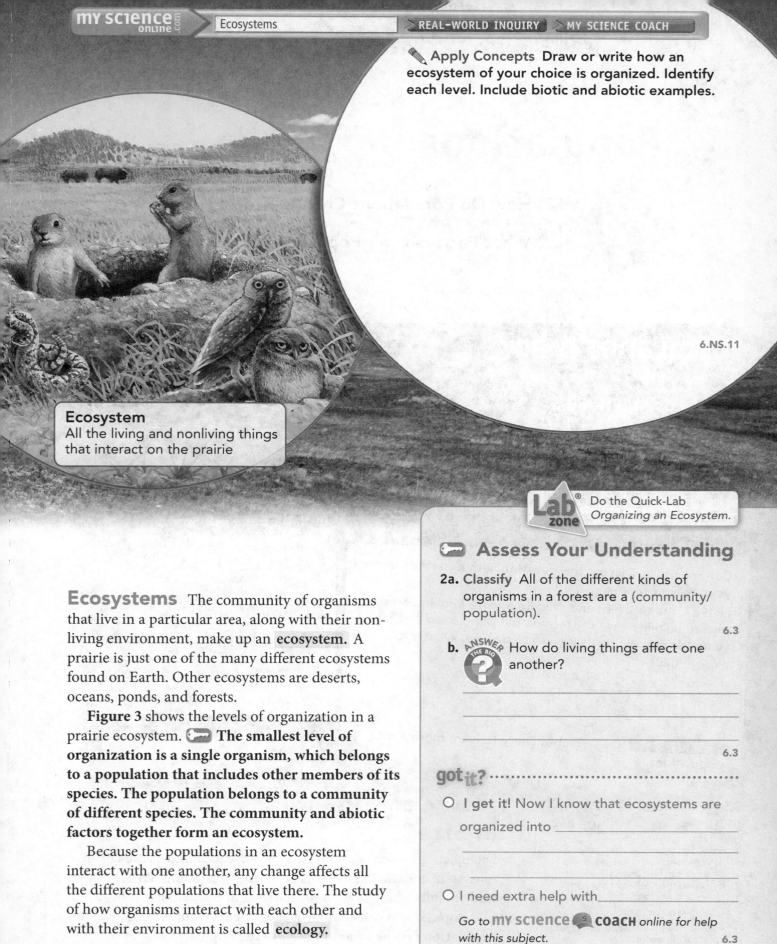

✎ **Apply Concepts** Draw or write how an ecosystem of your choice is organized. Identify each level. Include biotic and abiotic examples.

6.NS.11

Ecosystem
All the living and nonliving things that interact on the prairie

Ecosystems The community of organisms that live in a particular area, along with their non-living environment, make up an **ecosystem**. A prairie is just one of the many different ecosystems found on Earth. Other ecosystems are deserts, oceans, ponds, and forests.

Figure 3 shows the levels of organization in a prairie ecosystem. 🔑 **The smallest level of organization is a single organism, which belongs to a population that includes other members of its species. The population belongs to a community of different species. The community and abiotic factors together form an ecosystem.**

Because the populations in an ecosystem interact with one another, any change affects all the different populations that live there. The study of how organisms interact with each other and with their environment is called **ecology**.

Lab zone® Do the Quick-Lab *Organizing an Ecosystem.*

🔑 **Assess Your Understanding**

2a. Classify All of the different kinds of organisms in a forest are a (community/population).

6.3

b. ANSWER THE BIG ? How do living things affect one another?

_____

_____

_____

6.3

got it? ....

○ I get it! Now I know that ecosystems are organized into _____

_____

_____

○ I need extra help with_____

Go to my science ⑤ coach *online for help with this subject.*

6.3

279

Populations

UNLOCK THE BIG ?

🔑 **How Do Populations Change in Size?**
6.3.2, 6.NS.8, 6.DP.9

🔑 **What Factors Limit Population Growth?**
6.3.3, 6.DP.1

MY PLANET DIARY
for Indiana

Losing Friends

Indiana bats eat pests that bother both people and crops. These bats hibernate in large groups during the winter in a few caves in the Midwest. Just one person disturbing a nest can lead to the deaths of hundreds to thousands of bats. Due to increased awareness and conservation efforts, bat populations have begun to recover.

Communicate Discuss the question with a partner. Write your answer below.

In 1983, the U.S. Fish and Wildlife Service implemented a plan to help increase the Indiana bat population, but for years the population continued to decline. What might explain this?

_____

_____

▷ PLANET DIARY Go to **Planet Diary** to learn more about populations.

SCIENCE STATS

Indiana Bat Population

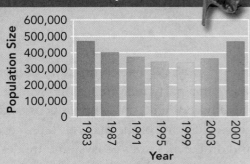

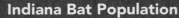

SOURCE: USFWS Indiana Bat Hibernacula Database

Lab zone® Do the Inquiry Warm-Up *Populations.*

How Do Populations Change in Size?

Ecologists are scientists who study biotic and abiotic factors of an ecosystem and the interactions between them. Some ecologists study populations and monitor the sizes of populations over time. 🔑 **Populations can change in size when new members join the population or when members leave the population.**

Academic Standards for Science

6.3.2 Describe how changes caused by organisms in the habitat where they live can be beneficial or detrimental to themselves or the native plants and animals.

6.NS.8 Analyze data.

6.DP.9 Present evidence using mathematical representations.

Vocabulary
- birth rate • death rate • immigration
- emigration • population density
- limiting factor • carrying capacity

Skills
↻ Reading: Relate Cause and Effect
△ Inquiry: Infer

Births and Deaths The most common way in which new individuals join a population is by being born into it. If more individuals are born into a population than die in any period of time, a population can grow. So when the **birth rate,** the number of births per 1,000 individuals for a given time period, is greater than its **death rate,** the number of deaths per 1,000 individuals for a given time period, the population may increase. The main way that individuals leave a population is by dying. If the birth rate is the same as the death rate, then the population may stay the same. In situations where the death rate is higher than the birth rate, then the population may decrease.

do the math!

Depending on the size and age of the female, an American Alligator can lay between 10 and 50 eggs per year.

① **Graph** Using the data table and colored pencils, create a double bar graph showing alligator births and deaths for four years.

② Label the x-axis and y-axis.

③ Write a title for the graph.

④ Fill in the graph using the colors shown.

⑤ **Develop Hypotheses** What factors might explain the number of births and deaths in Year 3?

_____

_____

_____

_____

_____

_____

6.NS.8, 6.DP.9

Data Table

Year	Births	Deaths
1	32	8
2	28	13
3	47	21
4	33	16

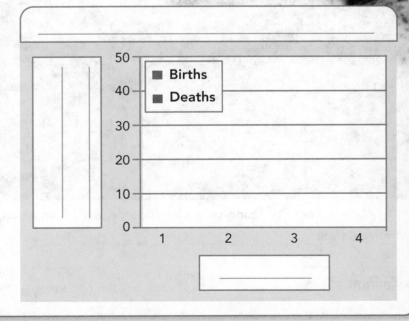

The Population Statement

When the birth rate in a population is greater than the death rate, the population will generally increase. This can be written as a mathematical statement using the "is greater than" sign:

If birth rate > death rate, population size increases.

However, if the death rate in a population is greater than the birth rate, the population size will generally decrease. This can also be written as a mathematical statement:

If death rate > birth rate, population size decreases.

Immigration and Emigration

The size of a population also can change when individuals move into or out of the population. **Immigration** (im ih GRAY shun) means moving into a population. **Emigration** (em ih GRAY shun) means leaving a population. For instance, if food is scarce, some members of an antelope herd may wander off in search of better grassland. If they become permanently separated from the original herd, they will no longer be part of that population.

Vocabulary Latin Word Origins
Both the terms *immigration* ("moving into a population") and *emigration* ("moving out of a population") come from the Latin word *migrare* ("to move"). What do you think the prefixes *im–* and *e–* mean?

_____

_____

_____

_____

FIGURE 1 ······························

Immigration

In 1898, white-tailed deer were almost extinct in Iowa due to over-hunting. The deer population was reestablished as animals from Minnesota, Wisconsin, and Missouri immigrated into Iowa.

Apply Concepts Using your classroom, describe an example of each of the following.

Immigration: _____

_____

Emigration: _____

_____

Graphing Changes in Population

Changes in a population's size can be displayed on a line graph. Figure 2 shows a graph of the changes in a rabbit population. The vertical axis identifies the number of rabbits in the population, while the horizontal axis shows time. The graph represents the size of the rabbit population over a ten-year period.

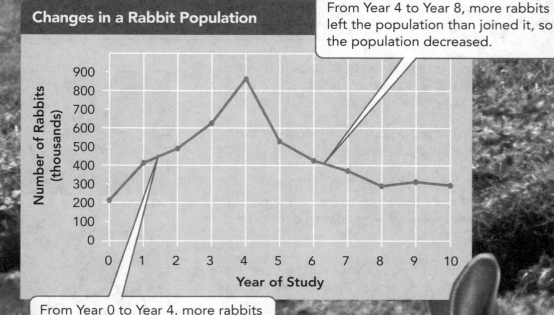

Changes in a Rabbit Population

From Year 4 to Year 8, more rabbits left the population than joined it, so the population decreased.

From Year 0 to Year 4, more rabbits joined the population than left it, so the population increased.

FIGURE 2 ·······························

▶ INTERACTIVE ART **Changes in a Rabbit Population**

✎ This graph shows how the size of a rabbit population changed over ten years.

1. **Interpret Data** In Year _____, the rabbit population reached its highest point.

2. **Read Graphs** What was the size of the rabbit population in that year? _____

3. CHALLENGE How do you think the rabbit population affected the fox population over the same ten-year period? Explain your reasoning.

_____

_____

_____

_____

_____

_____

6.NS.8

Population Density Sometimes an ecologist needs to know more than just the total size of a population. In many situations, it is helpful to know the **population density**—the number of individuals in an area of a specific size. Population density can be written as an equation:

$$\text{Population density} = \frac{\text{Number of individuals}}{\text{Unit area}}$$

For example, suppose you counted 20 butterflies in a garden measuring 10 square meters. The population density would be 20 butterflies per 10 square meters, or 2 butterflies per square meter.

apply it!

In the pond on the top, there are 10 flamingos in 8 square meters. The population density is 1.25 flamingos per square meter.

1 **Calculate** What is the population density of the flamingos in the pond on the bottom?

_____

2 **Infer** If 14 more flamingos landed in the pond on the bottom, what would the population density be then?

_____

3 CHALLENGE What do you think would happen if the population density of flamingos in the pond on the bottom became too great?

_____

_____

_____

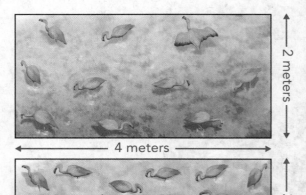

2 meters

4 meters

2 meters

6.NS.8

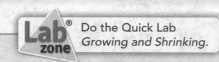
Do the Quick Lab
Growing and Shrinking.

🔑 Assess Your Understanding

1a. Review Two ways to join a population are

_____ and _____.

Two ways to leave a population are _____

and _____.

6.3.2

b. Calculate Suppose a population of 8 wolves has produced 20 young in a year. If 7 wolves have died, how many wolves are in the population now? (Assume no wolves have moved into or out of the population for other reasons.)

_____

6.3.2

got it? ....

○ **I get it!** Now I know that population size changes due to _____

_____

○ **I need extra help with** _____

Go to MY SCIENCE ⬤ COACH online for help with this subject.

6.3.2

What Factors Limit Population Growth?

When the living conditions in an area are good, a population will generally grow. But eventually some environmental factor will cause the population to stop growing. A **limiting factor** is an environmental factor that causes a population to stop growing or decrease in size. **Some limiting factors for populations are weather conditions, space, food, and water.**

Climate Changes in climate conditions, such as temperature and the amount of rainfall, can limit population growth. A cold spring season can kill the young of many species of organisms, including birds and mammals. Unusual events like floods, hurricanes, and the tornado shown in **Figure 3,** can also have long-lasting effects on population size.

FIGURE 3 ·······························

Weather as a Limiting Factor

A tornado or flood can destroy nests and burrows.

✎ Identify **Name two types of natural disasters that you think can also limit population growth.**

_____

_____

Tornado funnel
touching ground

Academic Standards for Science

6.3.3 Describe how certain biotic and abiotic factors, such as quantity of light and water, range of temperatures, and soil composition, can limit the number of organisms that an ecosystem can support.

6.DP.1 Identify a need or problem to be solved.

·············· ✏ ··············

⟳ **Relate Cause and Effect** As you read about the four factors that can limit populations, fill in the graphic organizer below.

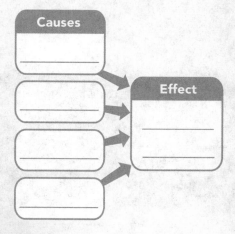

Causes

Effect

Some plants, like the black walnut tree, release chemicals into the environment that discourage other plants from growing too close. This process is called allelopathy (uh luh LOP uh thee).

Space Space is another limiting factor for populations. Gannets are seabirds that are usually seen flying over the ocean. They come to land only to nest on rocky shores. But the nesting shores get very crowded. If a pair does not find room to nest, they will not be able to add any offspring to the gannet population. So nesting space on the shore is a limiting factor for gannets. If there were more nesting space, more gannets would be able to nest. The population could increase.

Figure 4 shows how space is also a limiting factor for plants. The amount of space in which a plant grows determines whether the plant can obtain the sunlight, water, and soil nutrients it needs. For example, many pine seedlings sprout each year in forests. But as the seedlings grow, the roots of those that are too close together run out of space. Branches from other trees may block the sunlight the seedlings need. Some of the seedlings then die, limiting the size of the pine population.

Food and Water Organisms require food and water to survive. When food and water are in limited supply, they can be limiting factors. Suppose a giraffe must eat 10 kilograms of leaves each day to survive. The trees in an area can provide 100 kilograms of leaves a day while remaining healthy. Five giraffes could live easily in this area, because they would need just 50 kilograms of food a day. But 15 giraffes could not all survive—there would not be enough food. No matter how much shelter, water, and other resources there were, the population would not grow much larger than 10 giraffes. The largest population that an area can support is called its **carrying capacity**. The carrying capacity of this giraffe habitat would be 10 giraffes. The size of a population can vary, but usually stays near its carrying capacity because of the limiting factors in its habitat.

FIGURE 4 ⋯⋯⋯⋯⋯⋯⋯⋯⋯⋯⋯⋯⋯⋯⋯⋯⋯⋯⋯

Space as a Limiting Factor
If no more tulip plants can grow in this field, the field has reached its carrying capacity for tulips.
✎ List **Name three things a plant needs to survive.**

_____

Giant pandas live in the mountains of south central China. Most (99 percent) of the pandas' diet is made up of the bamboo plant. Bamboo is not nutrient rich. Pandas spend 55 percent of their day eating between 9 and 38 kilograms of bamboo. Getting enough bamboo to eat can be a challenge. Farming and the timber industry have destroyed the pandas' habitat and bamboo forests. In addition, when a bamboo plant flowers, the plant dies and does not regrow for several years. It is difficult for scientists to know exactly how many giant pandas exist in the wild. The best estimate is that there are about 1,600 of them. Due to the small population size, this species is classified as endangered.

✏️ **Communicate** Write a letter to the editor that describes how food and space may be limiting factors for the giant panda species. Add a headline to your letter.

_____

_____

_____

_____

_____

_____

_____

_____

6.DP.1

Lab zone® Do the Quick Lab *Elbow Room.*

🔑 Assess Your Understanding

2a. Summarize When the climate changes or there is not enough _____ or _____ or _____, a population can (begin/stop) growing in size.

6.3.3

b. Relate Cause and Effect Choose a limiting factor and describe the factor's effect on population growth.

_____

_____

_____

6.3.3

got it? ....

○ I get it! Now I know that populations can be limited when _____

_____

○ I need extra help with _____

Go to **MY SCIENCE** 🖥️ **COACH** *online for help with this subject.*

6.3.3

Interactions Among Living Things

UNLOCK THE BIG ?

🔑 **How Do Adaptations Help an Organism Survive?**
6.3.2

🔑 **What Are Competition and Predation?**
6.3.1, 6.NS.1, 6.NS.8, 6.NS.11, 6.DP.10

🔑 **What Are the Three Types of Symbiosis?**
6.3.1

MY PLANET DIARY

Predator Power

What predator can close its jaws the fastest? You might think it is a lion or a shark, but you would be wrong. It is the trap-jaw ant that has the fastest strike in the animal kingdom. The trap-jaw ant closes its mouth around its prey in 0.13 milliseconds at speeds of 35 to 64 meters per second! The force created when its jaw snaps shut also helps the ant escape danger by either jumping up to 8.3 centimeters high or 39.6 centimeters sideways.

A trap-jaw ant stalks its prey.

FUN FACT

Communicate Answer the questions below. Discuss your answers with a partner.

1. How does the trap-jaw ant's adaptation help it avoid becoming the prey of another organism?

_____

_____

_____

2. What are some adaptations that other predators have to capture prey?

_____

_____

> PLANET DIARY Go to **Planet Diary** to learn more about predators.

 Do the Inquiry Warm-Up
Can You Hide a Butterfly?

Academic Standards for Science

6.3.2 Describe how changes caused by organisms in the habitat where they live can be beneficial or detrimental to themselves or the native plants and animals.

How Do Adaptations Help an Organism Survive?

As day breaks, a sound comes from a nest tucked in the branch of a saguaro cactus. Two young red-tailed hawks are preparing to fly. Farther down the stem, a tiny elf owl peeks out of its nest in a small hole. A rattlesnake slithers around the base of the saguaro, looking for breakfast. Spying a shrew, the snake strikes it with needle-like fangs. The shrew dies instantly.

Vocabulary

- natural selection • adaptation • niche • competition
- predation • predator • prey • symbiosis • mutualism
- commensalism • parasitism • parasite • host

Skills

↻ Reading: Relate Text and Visuals

△ Inquiry: Classify

Figure 1 shows some organisms that live in, on, and around the saguaro cactus. Each organism has unique characteristics. These characteristics affect the individual's ability to survive and reproduce in its environment.

Natural Selection

A characteristic that makes an individual better suited to a specific environment may eventually become common in that species through a process called **natural selection**. Natural selection works like this: Individuals whose unique characteristics are well-suited for an environment tend to survive and produce more offspring. Offspring that inherit these characteristics also live to reproduce. In this way, natural selection results in **adaptations**, the behaviors and physical characteristics that allow organisms to live successfully in their environments. For example, the arctic hare has fur that turns from gray to white in the winter which helps camouflage the hare against the snow.

Individuals with characteristics poorly suited to a particular environment are less likely to survive and reproduce. Over time, poorly suited characteristics may disappear from the species. If a species cannot adapt to changes in its environment, the entire species can disappear from Earth and become extinct.

FIGURE 1 ·······································

Saguaro Community

✎ Describe **Circle two examples of how organisms interact in this scene. Describe each one.**

_____

_____

_____

_____

Purple martin

Red-tailed hawk

Flycatcher

Woodpecker

Elf owl

Saguaro cactus

Wasps

Rattlesnake

Gila monster

Scorpion

Roadrunner

Niche The organisms in the saguaro community have adaptations that result in specific roles. The role of an organism in its habitat is called its **niche.** A niche includes what type of food the organism eats, how it obtains this food, and what other organisms eat it. A niche also includes when and how the organism reproduces and the physical conditions it requires to survive. Some organisms, like the birds in **Figure 2,** share the same habitat but have very specific niches that allow them to live together. 🗝 **Every organism has a variety of adaptations that are suited to its specific living conditions and help it survive.**

apply it!

Organisms occupy many niches in an environment like the one in this picture.

1 Identify List two abiotic factors in the picture.

_____

2 Interpret Diagrams Describe the niche of the squirrel in the picture.

_____

_____

3 Make Generalizations What adaptations might the squirrel have that make it able to live in this environment?

_____

_____

Lab ® Do the Quick Lab
zone *Adaptations for Survival.*

🗝 Assess Your Understanding

1a. Define Adaptations are the _____ and _____ characteristics that allow organisms to live successfully in their environments.

6.3.2

b. Explain How are a snake's sharp fangs an adaptation that help it survive in the saguaro community?

_____

_____

6.3.2

got it? ....

○ **I get it!** Now I know that adaptations are_____

_____

○ **I need extra help with** _____

Go to **MY SCIENCE** ⓢ **COACH** *online for help with this subject.*

6.3.2

What Are Competition and Predation?

During a typical day in the saguaro community, a range of inter-actions takes place among organisms. ☞ **Two major types of interactions among organisms are competition and predation.**

Competition   Different species can share the same habitat and food requirements. For example, the flycatcher and the elf owl both live on the saguaro and eat insects. However, these two species do not occupy exactly the same niche. The flycatcher is active during the day, while the owl is active mostly at night. If two species occupy the same niche, one of the species might eventually die off. The reason for this is **competition.** The struggle between organisms to survive as they attempt to use the same limited resources is called competition. For example, weeds in a garden compete with vegetable crops for soil nutrients, water, and sunlight.

In any ecosystem, there are limited amounts of food, water, and shelter. Organisms that share the same habitat often have adaptations that enable them to reduce competition. For example, the three species of warblers in **Figure 2** specialize in feeding only in a certain part of the spruce tree.

Academic Standards for Science

6.3.1 Describe relationships (predator/prey, consumer/producer or parasite/host) between organisms and determine whether these relationships are competitive or mutually beneficial.

6.NS.1 Make predictions based on research and prior knowledge.

6.NS.8 Analyze data, using appropri-ate mathematical manipulation as required, and use it to identify pat-terns and make inferences based on these patterns.

6.NS.11 Communicate findings using models.

6.DP.10 Communicate the solution using drawings.

Cape May Warbler
This species feeds at the tips of branches near the top of the tree.

Bay-Breasted Warbler
This species feeds in the middle part of the tree.

Yellow-Rumped Warbler
This species feeds in the lower part of the tree and at the bases of the middle branches.

FIGURE 2 ···

Niche and Competition

✏ Each of these warbler species occupies a very specific location in its habitat. By feeding on insects in different areas of the tree, the birds avoid compet-ing for food and are able to live together.

1. Predict What could happen if these warbler species fed in the same location on the tree?   **6.NS.1**

_____

_____

_____

_____

2. List For what resources do the tree and the grass compete?

_____

_____

_____

_____

291

FIGURE 3 ·····················

Predation

This tiger shark and this albatross are involved in a predator-prey interaction.

✎ **Interpret Photos**
Label the predator and the prey in the photo.

Predation In **Figure 3,** a tiger shark bursts through the water to seize an albatross in its powerful jaws. An interaction in which one organism kills another for food or nutrients is called **predation.** The organism that does the killing is the **predator.** The organism that is killed is the **prey.** Even though they do not kill their prey, organisms like cows and giraffes are also considered predators because they eat plants.

Predation can have a major effect on a prey population size. Recall that when the death rate exceeds the birth rate in a population, the population size can decrease. So, if there are too many predators in an area, the result is often a decrease in the size of the prey population. But a decrease in the number of prey results in less food for their predators. Without adequate food, the predator population can decline. Generally, populations of predators and their prey rise and fall in related cycles.

FIGURE 4 ·····················

Predator Adaptations

A jellyfish's tentacles contain a poisonous substance that paralyzes tiny water animals. The sundew is a plant that is covered with sticky bulbs on stalks. When a fly lands on a bulb, it remains snared in the sticky goo while the plant digests it.

✎ **Make Models** Imagine an ideal predator to prey upon a porcupine. Draw or describe your predator below and label its adaptations.   6.NS.11, 6.DP.10

Predator Adaptations Predators, such as those in **Figure 4**, have adaptations that help them catch and kill their prey. A cheetah can run very fast for a short time, enabling it to catch its prey. Some predators, such as owls and bats, have adaptations that enable them to hunt at night when their prey, small mammals and insects, are active.

Prey Adaptations How do organisms avoid being killed by effective predators? The smelly spray of a skunk and the sharp quills of a porcupine help keep predators at a distance. As you can see in **Figure 5**, organisms have many kinds of adaptations that help them avoid becoming prey.

Warning Coloring Like many brightly colored animals, this frog is poisonous. Its bright blue and yellow colors warn predators not to eat it.

False Coloring Predators may be confused by a false eyespot and attack the wrong end of the fish. This allows the fish to swim safely away in the opposite direction.

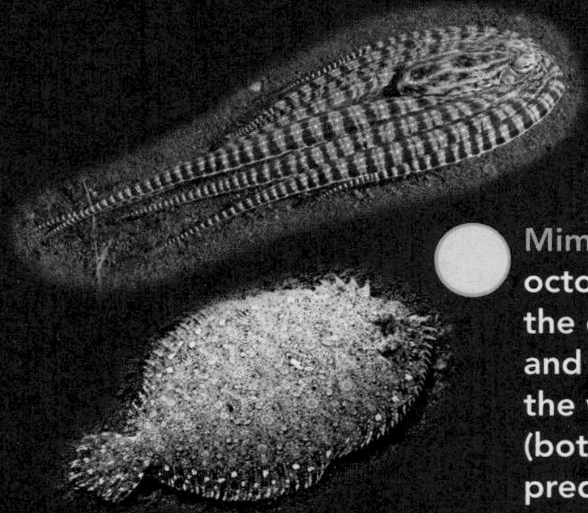

Mimicry The mimic octopus (top) imitates the coloring, shape, and swimming style of the venomous sole fish (bottom) to discourage predators.

Protective Covering Have you ever seen a pinecone with a face? This is a pangolin, a small African mammal. When threatened, the pangolin protects itself by rolling up into a scaly ball.

Camouflage Is it a leaf? Actually, it's a walking leaf insect. But if you were a predator, you might be fooled into looking elsewhere for a meal.

FIGURE 5 ·······

> INTERACTIVE ART **Defense Strategies**

Organisms display a wide range of adaptations that help them avoid becoming prey. ✎ **Communicate** In a group, rate each prey adaptation from 1 (best) to 5 (worst) in the circles. Explain your best choice.

_____

_____

_____

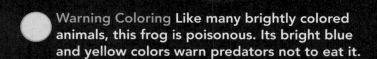

do the math!

Predator-Prey Interactions

On Isle Royale, an island in Lake Superior, the populations of wolves (the predator) and moose (the prey) rise and fall in cycles. Use the graph to answer the questions.

❶ Read Graphs What variable is plotted on the horizontal axis? What two variables are plotted on the vertical axis?

_____

_____

❷ Interpret Data How did the moose population change between 2002 and 2007? What happened to the wolf population from 2003 through 2006?

_____

_____

_____

❸ Draw Conclusions How might the change in moose population have led to the change in the wolf population?

_____

_____

_____

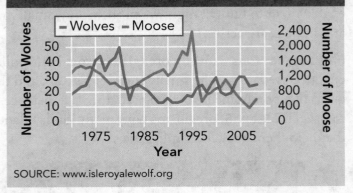

Wolf and Moose Populations on Isle Royale

— Wolves — Moose

Number of Wolves

Number of Moose

Year

SOURCE: www.isleroyalewolf.org

❹ Explain What adaptations does a wolf have that make it a successful predator?

_____

_____

❺ Predict How might disease in the wolf population one year affect the moose population the next year?

_____

_____

_____

6.NS.1, 6.NS.8

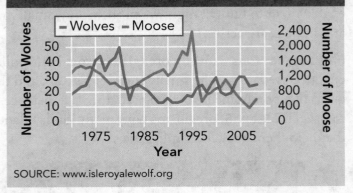 Do the Quick Lab
Competition and Predation.

🔑 Assess Your Understanding

2a. Review Two main ways in which organisms

interact are _____

and _____ .

6.3.1

b. Describe Give an example of competition. Explain your answer.

_____

_____

6.3.1

c. Apply Concepts Owls often prey on mice. What adaptations do you think the mice have that help them avoid becoming prey?

_____

_____

_____

6.3.1

got it? ....

○ **I get it!** Now I know that competition and predation _____

_____

○ **I need extra help with** _____

Go to **MY SCIENCE COACH** *online for help with this subject.*

6.3.1

What Are the Three Types of Symbiosis?

In addition to competition and predation, symbiosis is a third type of interaction among organisms. **Symbiosis** (sim bee OH sis) is any relationship in which two species live closely together and at least one of the species benefits. 🔑 **The three main types of symbiotic relationships are mutualism, commensalism, and parasitism.**

Mutualism In some relationships, two species may depend on one another. This is true for some species of acacia trees and stinging ants in South America. The stinging ants nest only in the acacia tree, whose thorns discourage the ants' predators. The tree also provides the ants' only food. The ants, in turn, attack other animals that approach the tree and clear competing plants away from the base of the tree. This relationship is an example of **mutualism** (MYOO choo uh liz um). A relationship in which both species benefit is called mutualism. Other examples of mutualism can be seen in **Figure 6.**

Academic Standards for Science

6.3.1 Describe specific relationships (predator/prey, consumer/producer or parasite/host) between organisms and determine whether these relationships are competitive or mutually beneficial.

FIGURE 6

Mutualism

✏️ An oxpecker rides and snacks aboard an impala. The oxpecker eat ticks living on the impala's ears. This interaction is an example of mutualism because both organisms benefit.

1. Infer How does the oxpecker benefit?

_____

2. Infer How does the impala benefit?

_____

3. CHALLENGE Explain how the relationship between the hummingbird and the flower is an example of mutualism.

_____
_____
_____

Commensalism

Have you ever seen a bird build a nest in a tree? The bird gets a place to live while the tree is unharmed. This relationship is an example of commensalism. **Commensalism** (kuh MEN suh liz um) is a relationship in which one species benefits and the other species is neither helped nor harmed. In nature, commensalism is not very common because two species are usually either helped or harmed a little by any interaction.

Parasitism

Many family pets get treated with medication to prevent tick and flea bites. Without treatment, pets can suffer from severe health problems as a result of these bites. A relationship that involves one organism living with, on, or inside another organism and harming it is called **parasitism** (PA ruh sit iz um). The organism that benefits is called a **parasite.** The organism it lives on or in is called a **host.** The parasite is usually smaller than the host. In a parasitic relationship, the parasite benefits while the host is harmed. Unlike a predator, a parasite does not usually kill the organism it feeds on. If the host dies, the parasite could lose its source of food or shelter.

Some parasites, like fleas and ticks, have adaptations that enable them to attach to their host and feed on its blood. Other examples of parasitism are shown in **Figure 7**.

◉ Relate Text and Visuals List the names of the parasites and the hosts in **Figure 7**.

Parasites	Hosts

A parasitic cowbird laid its eggs in a yellow warbler's nest. The cowbird chick is outcompeting the warbler chicks for space and food.

Fish lice feed on the blood and other internal fluids of fish.

Dwarf mistletoe is a small parasitic flowering plant that grows into the bark of trees to obtain water and nutrients.

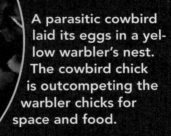

FIGURE 7 ....
Parasitism
There are many examples of parasitic relationships. Besides fleas, ticks, and tapeworms, some plants and birds are parasites. ✎ **Explain Why doesn't a parasite usually kill its host?**

_____

_____

_____

apply it!

Classify Each photograph on the right represents a different type of symbiosis. Classify each interaction as mutualism, commensalism, or parasitism. Explain your answers.

Interaction 1: A remora fish attaches itself to the underside of a shark without harming the shark, and eats leftover bits of food from the shark's meals.

Interaction 2: A vampire bat drinks the blood of horses.

Interaction 3: A bee pollinates a flower.

1 Interaction 1

_____

_____

2 Interaction 2

_____

_____

3 Interaction 3

_____

_____

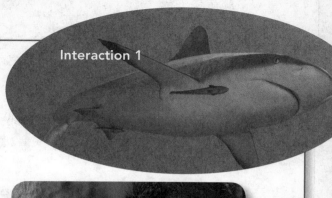
Interaction 1

Interaction 2

Interaction 3

Lab zone® Do the Quick Lab Type of Symbiosis.

Assess Your Understanding

3a. Identify The three types of symbiosis are

_____, _____,

and _____.

6.3.1

b. Classify Microscopic mites live at the base of human eyelashes, where they feed on tiny bits of dead skin. What type of symbiosis could this be? Explain your answer.

_____

_____

_____

6.3.1

c. Compare and Contrast Name each type of symbiosis and explain how the two species are affected.

_____

_____

_____

_____

_____

_____

6.3.1

got it?

○ **I get it!** Now I know that the three types of symbiosis differ in _____

_____

○ **I need extra help with** _____

Go to MY SCIENCE ⬤ COACH online for help with this subject.

6.3.1

Indiana

LESSON

4 Changes in Communities

🔑 How Do Primary and Secondary Succession Differ?

UNLOCK THE BIG ❓

6.3.2

MY PLANET DiARY

Fighting Fire With Fire

Wildfires are often reported in the national news. The images associated with these reports show how damaging these fires can be to property and to some ecosystems. What you may not know is that fire can actually help fight wildfires! Controlled burns, or prescribed burns, are fires that are purposely and carefully set by professional foresters. Prescribed burns are used to remove materials such as dead, dry branches and leaves that can fuel wildfires. A wildfire that occurs in an area that has previously been burned would cause less damage and be easier for firefighters to control.

This forester is carefully igniting a controlled burn.

MISCONCEPTION

Communicate **Discuss these questions with a classmate. Write your answers below.**

1. Why should only professional foresters set prescribed fires?

_____

_____

_____

2. What do you think could be some other benefits to using prescribed burns in an ecosystem?

_____

_____

_____

▶ PLANET DIARY Go to **Planet Diary** to learn more about succession.

 Do the Inquiry Warm-Up *How Communities Change.*

Academic Standards for Science

6.3.2 Describe how changes caused by organisms in the habitat where they live can be beneficial or detrimental to themselves or the native plants and animals.

How Do Primary and Secondary Succession Differ?

Fires, floods, volcanoes, hurricanes, and other natural disasters can change communities very quickly. But even without disasters, communities change. The series of predictable changes that occur in a community over time is called **succession**.

Vocabulary
- succession
- primary succession
- pioneer species
- secondary succession

Skills
- Reading: Compare and Contrast
- Inquiry: Observe

Primary Succession When a new island is formed by the eruption of an undersea volcano or an area of rock is uncovered by a melting sheet of ice, no living things are present. Over time, living things will inhabit these areas. **Primary succession** is the series of changes that occur in an area where no soil or organisms exist.

Figure 1 shows how an area might change following a volcanic eruption. Just like the pioneers that first settled new frontiers, the first species to populate an area are called **pioneer species.** They are often carried to the area by wind or water. Typical pioneer species are mosses and lichens. Lichens are fungi and algae growing in a symbiotic relationship. As pioneer species grow, they help break up the rocks. When the organisms die, they provide nutrients that enrich the thin layer of soil that is forming on the rocks.

As plant seeds land in the new soil, they begin to grow. The specific plants that grow depend on the climate of the area. For example, in a cool, northern area, early seedlings might include alder and cottonwood trees. Eventually, succession may lead to a community of organisms that does not change unless the ecosystem is disturbed. Reaching this mature community can take centuries.

FIGURE 1 ....

> ART IN MOTION **Primary Succession**
Primary succession occurs in an area where no soil and no organisms exist.

✏ **Sequence** In the circles, number the stage of primary succession to show the correct order of events.

Soil Creation
As pioneer species grow and die, soil forms. Some plants grow in this new soil.

Pioneer Species
The first species to grow are pioneer species such as mosses and lichens.

Volcanic Eruption
Shortly after a volcanic eruption, there is no soil, only ash and rock.

Fertile Soil and Maturing Plants
As more plants die, they decompose and make the soil more fertile. New plants grow and existing plants mature in the fertile soil.

FIGURE 2 ···

> ART IN MOTION **Secondary Succession**

Secondary succession occurs following a disturbance to an ecosystem, such as clearing a forest for farmland.

✎ **Describe** Write a brief title that describes what happens at each of the four stages of secondary succession.

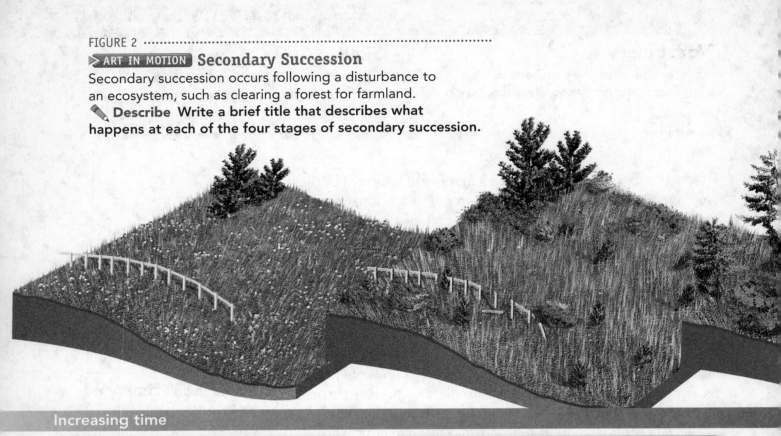

Increasing time

Title: _____

Grasses and wildflowers have taken over this abandoned field.

Title: _____

After a few years, pine seedlings and other trees replace some of the grasses and wildflowers.

---

apply it!

⟳ **Compare and Contrast** Based on your reading, complete the table below.

Factors in Succession	Primary Succession	Secondary Succession
Possible Cause	Volcanic eruption	_____
Type of Area	_____	_____
Existing Ecosystem?	_____	_____

Secondary Succession In October 2007, huge wildfires raged across Southern California. The changes following the California fires are an example of secondary succession. **Secondary succession** is the series of changes that occur in an area where the ecosystem has been disturbed, but where soil and organisms still exist. Natural disturbances that have this effect include fires, hurricanes, and tornadoes. Human activities, such as farming, logging, or mining, may also disturb an ecosystem and cause secondary succession to begin.

🔑 Unlike primary succession, secondary succession occurs in a place where an ecosystem currently exists. Secondary succession usually occurs more rapidly than primary succession because soil already exists and seeds from some plants remain in the soil. You can follow the process of succession in an abandoned field in **Figure 2.** After a century, a hardwood forest is developing. This forest community may remain for a long time.

Title: _____

As tree growth continues, the trees begin to crowd out the grasses and wildflowers.

Title: _____

Eventually, a forest of mostly oak, hickory, and some pine dominates the landscape.

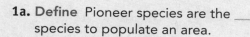
Assess Your Understanding

Lab zone ® Do the Quick Lab
Primary or Secondary.

1a. Define Pioneer species are the _____ species to populate an area.

6.3.2

b. Observe Is grass poking through a sidewalk crack primary or secondary succession? Why?

_____

_____

_____

6.3.2

c. CHALLENGE Why are the changes during succession predictable?

_____

_____

_____

6.3.2

got it? ·

○ **I get it!** Now I know that primary and secondary succession differ in _____

_____

○ **I need extra help with** _____

_Go to_ **MY SCIENCE** 🔊 **COACH** _online for help with this subject._

6.3.2

REVIEW THE BIG ?

Living things interact in many ways, including competition and _____, as well as through symbiotic relationships such as mutualism, commensalism, and _____.

LESSON 1 Living Things and the Environment

6.3, 6.3.3, 6.NS.8, 6.NS.11

🔑 An organism gets the things it needs to live, grow, and reproduce from its environment.

🔑 Biotic and abiotic factors make up a habitat.

🔑 The levels of organization in an ecosystem are organism, population, and community.

Vocabulary
• organism • habitat • biotic factor
• abiotic factor • species • population
• community • ecosystem • ecology

LESSON 2 Populations

6.3.2, 6.3.3, 6.NS.8, 6.DP.1, 6.DP.9

🔑 Populations can change in size when new members join the population or when members leave the population.

🔑 Some limiting factors for populations are weather conditions, space, food, and water.

Vocabulary
• birth rate • death rate • immigration
• emigration • population density
• limiting factor • carrying capacity

LESSON 3 Interactions Among Living Things

6.3.1, 6.3.2, 6.NS.1, 6.NS.8, 6.NS.11, 6.DP.10

🔑 Every organism has a variety of adaptations that are suited to its specific living conditions to help it survive.

🔑 Two major types of interactions among organisms are competition and predation.

🔑 The three main types of symbiotic relationships are mutualism, commensalism, and parasitism.

Vocabulary
• natural selection • adaptation • niche • competition
• predation • predator • prey • symbiosis • mutualism
• commensalism • parasitism • parasite • host

LESSON 4 Changes in Communities

6.3.2

🔑 Unlike primary succession, secondary succession occurs in a place where an ecosystem currently exists.

Vocabulary
• succession
• primary succession
• pioneer species
• secondary succession

Review and Assessment

LESSON 1 Living Things and the Environment

1. A prairie dog, a hawk, and a snake are all members of the same

a. niche.

b. community.

c. species.

d. population.

6.3

2. Grass is an example of a(n) _____ in a habitat.

6.3.3

3. Sequence Put these levels in order from the smallest to the largest: population, organism, ecosystem, community.

_____

_____

6.3

4. Apply Concepts Name two biotic and two abiotic factors you might find in a forest ecosystem.

_____

_____

6.3.3

5. Draw Conclusions In 1815, Mount Tambora, a volcano in Indonesia, erupted. So much volcanic ash and dust filled the atmosphere that 1816 is referred to as the "Year Without a Summer." How might a volcanic eruption affect the abiotic factors in an organism's habitat?

_____

_____

_____

_____

_____

6.3.3

6. Write About It Write at least one paragraph describing your habitat. Describe how you get the food, water, and shelter you need from your habitat. How does this habitat meet your needs in ways that another would not?

6.3

LESSON 2 Populations

7. All of the following are limiting factors for populations except

a. space.

b. food.

c. time.

d. weather.

6.3.3

8. _____ occurs when individuals leave a population.

6.3.3

Use the data table to answer the questions below. Ecologists monitoring a deer population collect data during a 30-year study.

Year	0	5	10	15	20	25	30
Population (thousands)	15	30	65	100	40	25	10

9. Graph Use the data to make a line graph.

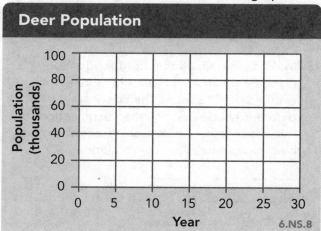

Deer Population

10. Interpret Data In which year was the deer population the highest? The lowest?

_____

6.3.3, 6.NS.8

11. Develop Hypotheses In Year 16 of the study, this region experienced a severe winter. How might this have affected the deer population?

_____

_____

_____

_____

6.3.3, 6.NS.8

303

Interactions Among Living Things

12. In which type of interaction do both species benefit?

a. predation   b. mutualism

c. commensalism   d. parasitism

6.3.1

13. A parasite lives on or inside its _____.

6.3.1

14. Relate Cause and Effect Name two prey adaptations. How does each adaptation protect the organism?

_____

_____

_____

_____

_____

6.3.1

15. Make Generalizations Competition for resources in an area is usually more intense within a single species than between two different species. Suggest an explanation for this observation. (*Hint:* Consider how niches help organisms avoid competition.)

_____

_____

_____

_____

_____

6.3.1

16. Write About It Some scientists think that the relationship between clownfish and sea anemones is an example of commensalism. Other scientists think that the relationship is mutualism. If this relationship is actually mutualism, how might both the clownfish and sea anemone benefit?

6.3.1, 6.NS.11

Changes in Communities

17. The series of predictable changes that occur in a community over time is called

a. natural selection   b. ecology

c. commensalism   d. succession

6.3.2

18. _____ are the first species to populate an area.

6.3.2

19. Classify Lichens and mosses have just begun to grow on the rocky area shown below. What type of succession is occurring? Explain.

_____

_____

6.3.2

APPLY THE BIG ❓ How do living things affect one another?

20. Humans interact with their environment on a daily basis. These interactions can have both positive and negative effects. Using at least four vocabulary terms from this chapter, describe a human interaction and the effect it has on the environment.

_____

_____

_____

_____

_____

_____

_____

_____

_____

_____

6.3.2

Indiana ISTEP+ Practice

Multiple Choice

Circle the letter of the best answer.

1. Symbiotic relationships include mutualism, commensalism, and parasitism. Which of the images below shows mutualism?

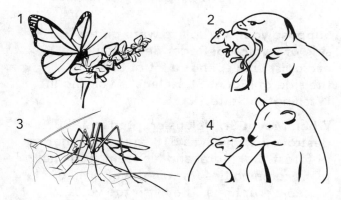

1
2
3
4

A. Image 1
B. Image 2
C. Image 3
D. Image 4

6.3.1

2. In general, which of the following is a true statement about population size?

    A. If birth rate < death rate, population size increases.

    B. If death rate < birth rate, population size decreases.

    C. If birth rate > death rate, population size increases.

    D. If death rate > birth rate, population size increases.

6.3.2

3. Ecosystems have different levels of organization. A group of similar organisms makes up a

_____, which, along with other types of organisms, makes up a(n) _____.

    A. species, population
    B. habitat, ecosystem
    C. population, community
    D. population, habitat

6.3

4. Which of the following is a typical pioneer species?

    A. grass
    B. lichen
    C. pine trees
    D. soil

6.3.1

Constructed Response

Write your answer to Question 5 on the lines below.

5. Three different bird species all live in the same trees in an area, but competition between the birds rarely occurs. What is a likely explanation for this lack of competition?

_____

_____

_____

6.3.1

Extended Response

Use the diagram below and your knowledge of science to help you answer Question 6. Write your answer on a separate piece of paper.

6. An organism interacts with both the biotic and abiotic factors in its habitat. List three biotic factors and three abiotic factors shown in the drawing above.

6.3.3

305

SUCCESSION ECOLOGIST

These lupine plants are growing out of the volcanic ash on Mount St. Helens, 20 years after its last eruption.

Suppose your workplace were on the side of a volcano! Roger del Moral is an ecologist who spends a lot of time on the side of Mount St. Helens, a volcano in Washington State.

When Mount St. Helens erupted in 1980, it destroyed as much as 518 square kilometers of forest. Del Moral and his team study how plant communities form in the aftermath of volcanic eruptions. They visit the volcano regularly to identify plants and estimate the remaining populations of plants to describe how the plant communities are recovering. This work enables researchers to develop more effective ways to help areas recover from human-caused environmental changes.

Del Moral loves his work and says, "My work on Mount St. Helens allows me to follow my passion, train students, and contribute to a better understanding of how the world works."

If you are interested in ecology, try volunteering or interning at a local park or field museum. National parks also have Junior Naturalist programs designed to give you experience in the field.

Compare It Find a park in your neighborhood or town and describe the kinds of plants you find. Make a table in which you list each kind of plant, describe it, describe where it grew, and draw conclusions about the reasons why it might have grown there.

 6.3.2, 6.3.3, 6.NS.11

BINOCULAR BOOT CAMP

▼ Populations of common and rare birds can be estimated based on input from students like you!

Scientists need all the help they can get estimating large populations! Binocular Boot Camp, a program for kids in Sonoma Valley, California, trains kids to identify the songs, calls, and flight patterns of birds. Participants form teams and identify and count as many birds as they can in one afternoon. The information they gather gets entered into a huge database of bird observations.

You don't have to go to Binocular Boot Camp to help, though. For four days in February, schools, clubs, and individuals in the United States and Canada take part in the Great Backyard Bird Count (GBBC). All you need to do is count birds for 15 minutes, then fill out a form to help scientists learn how climate change, habitat change, and other factors affect bird populations.

Research It Find out more about the GBBC. Design a poster or use presentation software to create a presentation to convince your school to participate.

6.NS.11

Bird Radio

How accurate are estimates of bird populations? Scientists at North Carolina State University wondered whether background noise affects scientists' ability to count bird populations. They used Bird Radio to find out.

Bird Radio plays bird songs to simulate a wild bird population. Researchers adjusted background noise and the number of different bird songs. They learned that this affected people's ability to estimate the number of "birds" singing on Bird Radio. Even slight increases in background noise reduced the accuracy of population counts by up to 40 percent!

Design It Research problems facing bird populations. Design a solution by building a birdhouse or a bird feeder. Brainstorm potential designs and document your ideas. Select a design and choose materials to create a prototype. Then test and evaluate your solution by recording the number and types of birds that you observe. Present your observations using graphs or data tables. Finally, redesign your solution based on how well you think it addresses the problem. See Appendix A on page 350 for more information about the design process.

 6.NS.1–6.NS.11, 6.DP.1–6.DP.11

WHERE DOES FOOD COME FROM?

How do energy and matter move through ecosystems?

Flying around hunting for food, this barn owl spots a mouse for dinner. But what did the mouse eat? Perhaps it nibbled on seeds or a caterpillar. Then you might ask, where did the seeds and caterpillar get their food?

△ Develop Hypotheses **Where do living things get their food?**

_____

_____

_____

_____

_____

_____

> UNTAMED SCIENCE Watch the **Untamed Science** video to learn more about ecosystems and biomes.

Ecosystems and Biomes

Indiana
CHAPTER
9

Academic Standards for Science

6.3, 6.3.1, 6.3.2, 6.3.3, 6.3.4, 6.3.5, 6.3.6, 6.3.7,
6.NS.1–6.NS.3, 6.NS.8, 6.NS.11, 6.DP.1–6.DP.8, 6.DP.10

9 Getting Started

Check Your Understanding

1. **Background** Read the paragraph below and then answer the question.

> One morning, Han walks to the park and sits by the pond. He has just studied **ecosystems** in class, and now, looking at the pond, he realizes he sees things in a new way. He notices a turtle sunning itself on a rock, and knows that the sun and rock are **abiotic factors**, while the turtle, and other living things, are **biotic factors.**

> The community of organisms that live in a particular area, along with their nonliving environment, make up an **ecosystem.**
>
> **Abiotic factors** are the nonliving parts of an organism's habitat.
>
> **Biotic factors** are the living parts of an organism's habitat.

• Name one more biotic factor and one more abiotic factor that Han might see at the pond.

_____

_____

> **MY READING WEB** If you had trouble answering the question above, visit **My Reading Web** and type in *Ecosystems and Biomes.*

Vocabulary Skill

Prefixes Some words can be divided into parts. A root is the part of the word that carries the basic meaning. A prefix is a word part that is placed in front of the root to change the word's meaning. The prefixes below will help you understand some vocabulary in this chapter.

Prefix	Meaning	Example
bio-	life	biogeography, *n.* the study of where organisms live
inter-	between	intertidal, *adj.* ocean zone between the highest high-tide line and the lowest low-tide line

2. **Quick Check** Circle the prefix in each boldface word below.
   • There was an **intermission** between the acts of the play.
   • The **biosphere** is the area where life exists.

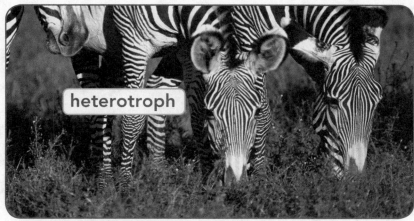

heterotroph

consumer

precipitation

desert

Chapter Preview

LESSON 1
- photosynthesis • autotroph
- heterotroph • chlorophyll

↻ **Sequence**

△ **Classify**

LESSON 2
- producer • consumer
- herbivore • carnivore • omnivore
- scavenger • decomposer
- food chain • food web
- energy pyramid

↻ **Relate Text and Visuals**

△ **Classify**

LESSON 3
- evaporation • condensation
- precipitation • nitrogen fixation

↻ **Sequence**

△ **Infer**

LESSON 4
- biome • climate • desert
- rain forest • emergent layer
- canopy • understory • grassland
- savanna • deciduous tree
- boreal forest • coniferous tree
- tundra • permafrost

↻ **Compare and Contrast**

△ **Draw Conclusions**

> **VOCAB FLASH CARDS** For extra help with vocabulary, visit **Vocab Flash Cards** and type in *Ecosystems and Biomes.*

311

Photosynthesis

🔑 **How Do Living Things Get Energy From the Sun?**
6.3, 6.3.4, 6.3.5

🔑 **What Happens During Photosynthesis?**
6.3.4, 6.3.6

MY PLANET DIARY

MISCONCEPTION

When Is Food Not Food?

Misconception: Some people think that the plant food they give to house and garden plants is food for the plants. It isn't.

Plants make their own food—in the form of sugars—using water, carbon dioxide, and sunlight. So what is the "food" that people add to plants? It's fertilizer. Fertilizer is a mixture of minerals, such as potassium, calcium, and phosphorus. It helps plants grow but doesn't supply them with energy as food does. Farmers add fertilizer to soil to grow better quality crops. People do the same to grow bigger and healthier plants at home.

Communicate Write your answers to the questions below. Then discuss Question 2 with a partner.

1. What is "plant food"?

_____

_____

2. What do you think would happen if you put a small seedling in complete darkness for a month but kept all other environmental conditions the same?

_____

▶ PLANET DIARY Go to **Planet Diary** to learn more about photosynthesis.

Lab ® Do the Inquiry Warm-Up
zone *Where Does the Energy Come From?*

Vocabulary
- photosynthesis
- autotroph
- heterotroph
- chlorophyll

Skills
↻ Reading: Sequence
△ Inquiry: Classify

How Do Living Things Get Energy From the Sun?

On a plain in Africa, a herd of zebras peacefully eats grass. But watch out! A group of lions is about to attack the herd. The lions will kill one of the zebras and eat it.

Both the zebras and the lion you see in **Figure 1** use the food they eat to obtain energy. Every living thing needs energy. All cells need energy to carry out their functions, such as making proteins and transporting substances into and out of the cell. Like the raw materials used within a cell, energy used by living things comes from their environment. Zebra meat supplies the lion's cells with energy. Similarly, grass provides the zebra's cells with energy. But where does the energy in the grass come from? Plants and certain other organisms, such as algae and some bacteria, obtain their energy in a different way. These organisms use the energy in sunlight to make their own food.

Academic Standards for Science

6.3 Core Standard Understand that the major source of energy for eco-systems is light produced by major nuclear reactions in the sun.

6.3.4 Recognize that plants use energy from the sun to make sugar (glucose) by the process of photosynthesis.

6.3.5 Describe how all animals meet their energy needs by consuming other organisms, breaking down their structures, and using the materials to grow and function.

FIGURE 1 ·······

An Energy Chain
All living things need energy.

✎ **Interpret Photos** In the boxes, write the direct source of energy for each organism. Which organism shown does not depend on another organism for food?

apply it!

A spider catches and eats a caterpillar that depends on plant leaves for food.

1 🔄 **Sequence** Draw a diagram of your own that tracks how the sun's energy gets to the spider.

2 ⚠ **Classify** In your diagram, label each organism as a heterotroph or an autotroph.

The Sun as an Energy Source

The process by which a cell captures energy in sunlight and uses it to make food is called **photosynthesis** (foh toh SIN thuh sis). The term *photosynthesis* comes from the Greek words *photos*, which means "light," and *syntithenai*, which means "putting together."

🔑 **Nearly all living things obtain energy either directly or indirectly from the energy of sunlight that is captured during photosynthesis.** Grass obtains energy directly from sunlight because grass makes its own food during photosynthesis. When the zebra eats grass, it gets energy from the sun that has been stored in the grass. Similarly, the lion obtains energy stored in the zebra. The zebra and lion both obtain the sun's energy indirectly from the energy that the grass obtained through photosynthesis.

Producers and Consumers

Plants make their own food through the process of photosynthesis. An organism that makes its own food is called a producer, or an **autotroph** (AWT oh trohf). An organism that cannot make its own food, including animals such as the zebra and the lion, is called a consumer, or a **heterotroph** (HET ur oh trohf). Many heterotrophs obtain food by eating other organisms. Some heterotrophs, such as fungi, absorb their food from other organisms.

Lab zone® Do the Quick Lab *Energy From the Sun.*

🔑 Assess Your Understanding

1a. Identify An organism that makes its own food is a(n) (autotroph/heterotroph).   6.3.4, 6.3.6

b. Explain Why do living things need energy?

_____

6.3.6

c. Apply Concepts Give an example of how energy from the sun gets into your cells.

_____

_____

_____

6.3.6

got it?..

○ **I get it!** Now I know that living things get energy directly from the sun by _____

or indirectly by _____

○ **I need extra help with** _____

Go to **MY SCIENCE** 💬 **COACH** *online for help with this subject.*   6.3, 6.3.4, 6.3.6

What Happens During Photosynthesis?

You've just read that plants make their own food. So how do they do that? **During photosynthesis, plants and some other organisms absorb energy from the sun and use the energy to convert carbon dioxide and water into sugars and oxygen.** You can think of photosynthesis as taking place in two stages. First, plants capture the sun's energy. Second, plants produce sugars.

Stage 1: Capturing the Sun's Energy In the first stage of photosynthesis, energy from sunlight is captured. In plants, this process occurs mostly in the leaves. Recall that chloroplasts are green organelles inside plant cells. The green color comes from pigments, colored chemical compounds that absorb light. The main pigment for photosynthesis in chloroplasts is **chlorophyll**.

Chlorophyll functions something like the solar cells in a solar-powered calculator. Solar cells capture the energy in light and convert it to a form that powers the calculator. Similarly, chlorophyll captures light energy and converts it to a form that is used in the second stage of photosynthesis.

During Stage 1, water in the chloroplasts is split into hydrogen and oxygen, as shown in **Figure 2**. The oxygen is given off as a waste product. The hydrogen is used in Stage 2.

Academic Standards for Science

6.3.4 Recognize that plants use energy from the sun to make sugar (glucose) by the process of photosynthesis.

6.3.6 Recognize that food provides the energy for the work that cells do and is a source of the molecular building blocks that can be incorporated into a cell's structure or stored for later use.

Vocabulary Greek Word Origins The Greek word part *chloros-* means "pale green." Circle two words in the text that begin with this word part. Which word means "a green compound that absorbs light"?

○ Chloroplast
○ Chlorophyll

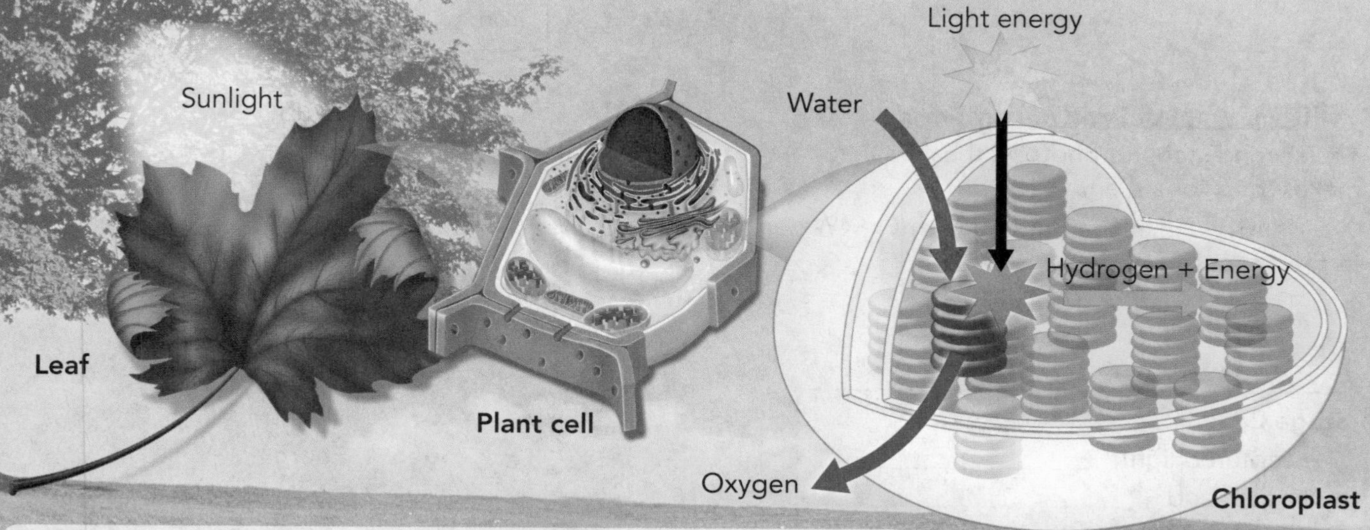

Sunlight
Leaf
Plant cell
Light energy
Water
Hydrogen + Energy
Oxygen
Chloroplast

FIGURE 2
First Stage of Photosynthesis
You might say the first stage of photosynthesis powers the "energy engine" of the living world.

Make Generalizations What do you think this sentence means?

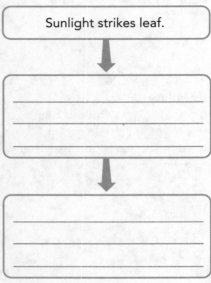

Sequence Complete the flowchart to show the process of photosynthesis.

Photosynthesis

Sunlight strikes leaf.

↓

_____
_____
_____

↓

_____
_____
_____

Stage 2: Using Energy to Make Food

In the second stage of photosynthesis, cells produce sugars. As shown in **Figure 3,** cells use hydrogen (H) that came from the splitting of water in Stage 1. Cells also use carbon dioxide (CO_2) from the air. Carbon dioxide enters the plant through small openings on the undersides of the leaves and moves into the chloroplasts.

Powered by the energy captured in Stage 1, hydrogen and carbon dioxide undergo a series of reactions that result in sugars. One important sugar produced is glucose. It has the chemical formula $C_6H_{12}O_6$. You may know that sugars are a type of carbohydrate. Cells can use the energy in glucose to carry out vital cell functions.

The other product of photosynthesis is oxygen gas (O_2). Recall that oxygen forms during the first stage when water molecules are split apart. Oxygen gas exits a leaf through the openings on its underside. Almost all the oxygen in Earth's atmosphere is produced by living things through the process of photosynthesis.

FIGURE 3 ·····································

> INTERACTIVE ART) Producing Food
The second stage of photosynthesis makes food for a plant.

✎ **Identify** Fill in the missing terms in the spaces provided.

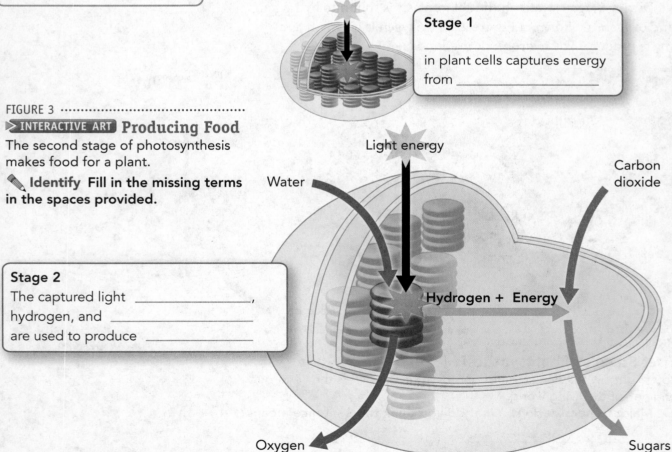

Stage 1
_____
in plant cells captures energy
from _____

Light energy

Water

Carbon dioxide

Hydrogen + Energy

Stage 2
The captured light _____,
hydrogen, and _____
are used to produce _____

Oxygen

Sugars

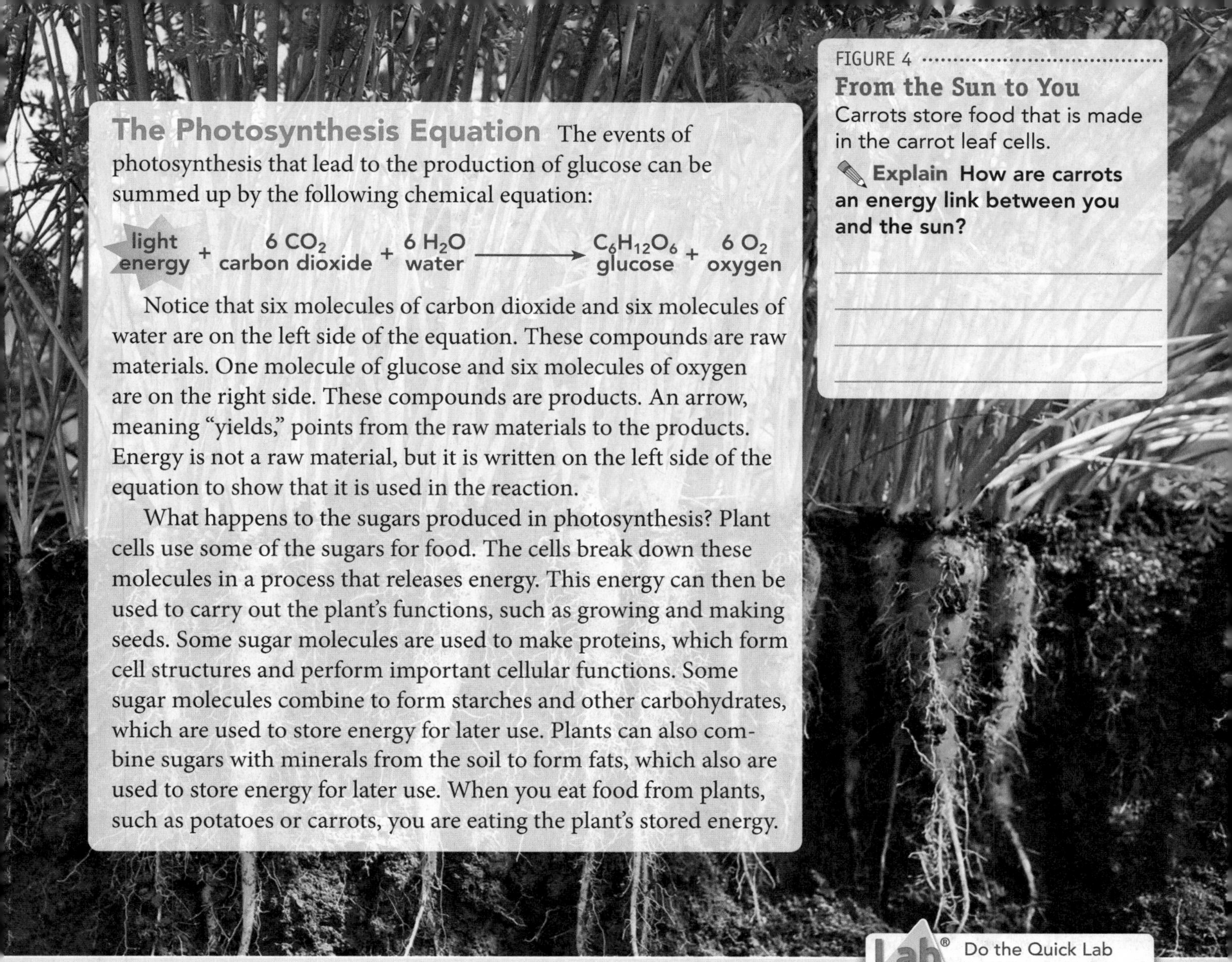

The Photosynthesis Equation

The events of photosynthesis that lead to the production of glucose can be summed up by the following chemical equation:

$$\text{light energy} + \underset{\text{carbon dioxide}}{6\ CO_2} + \underset{\text{water}}{6\ H_2O} \longrightarrow \underset{\text{glucose}}{C_6H_{12}O_6} + \underset{\text{oxygen}}{6\ O_2}$$

Notice that six molecules of carbon dioxide and six molecules of water are on the left side of the equation. These compounds are raw materials. One molecule of glucose and six molecules of oxygen are on the right side. These compounds are products. An arrow, meaning "yields," points from the raw materials to the products. Energy is not a raw material, but it is written on the left side of the equation to show that it is used in the reaction.

What happens to the sugars produced in photosynthesis? Plant cells use some of the sugars for food. The cells break down these molecules in a process that releases energy. This energy can then be used to carry out the plant's functions, such as growing and making seeds. Some sugar molecules are used to make proteins, which form cell structures and perform important cellular functions. Some sugar molecules combine to form starches and other carbohydrates, which are used to store energy for later use. Plants can also combine sugars with minerals from the soil to form fats, which also are used to store energy for later use. When you eat food from plants, such as potatoes or carrots, you are eating the plant's stored energy.

FIGURE 4 ·····················
From the Sun to You
Carrots store food that is made in the carrot leaf cells.

✎ **Explain** How are carrots an energy link between you and the sun?

_____
_____
_____
_____

Lab® Do the Quick Lab
zone *Looking at Pigments.*

⚷ Assess Your Understanding

2a. Name Circle two products of photosynthesis.
glucose/carbon dioxide/oxygen/chlorophyll

6.3.4

b. Interpret Diagrams Refer to **Figure 3** on the facing page. Where does the hydrogen that is used in Stage 2 of photosynthesis come from?

_____
_____

6.3.4

c. CHALLENGE Would you expect a plant to produce more oxygen on a sunny day or a cloudy day? Explain your answer.

_____
_____
_____
_____

6.3.4

got it? ··

O **I get it!** Now I know that during photosynthesis _____
_____

O I need extra help with _____

Go to MY SCIENCE ⓢ COACH *online for help with this subject.*

6.3.4, 6.3.6

Energy Flow in Ecosystems

UNLOCK THE BIG ?

🔑 **What Are the Energy Roles in an Ecosystem?**
6.3.1, 6.3.5, 6.NS.8

🔑 **How Does Energy Move Through an Ecosystem?**
6.3.1, 6.3.5, 6.NS.8, 6.DP.10

MY PLANeT DiaRY

I'll Have the Fish

Scientists have noticed something fishy going on with the wolves in British Columbia, Canada. During autumn, the wolves ignore their typical food of deer and moose and feast on salmon instead. Salmon are very nutritious and lack the big horns and hoofs that can injure or kill wolves. Plus, there are plenty of fish in a small area, making them easier to find and catch.

Many animals, including the wolves, depend upon the salmon's annual mating trip upstream. Losing this important food source to overfishing would hurt the populations of bears, wolves, birds, and many other animals.

DISCOVERY

Communicate Discuss these questions with a classmate. Write your answers below.

1. What are two reasons the wolves may eat fish in autumn instead of deer or moose?

_____

_____

2. What effect could overfishing salmon have on an ecosystem?

_____

_____

_____

_____

_____

> PLANET DIARY Go to **Planet Diary** to learn more about food webs.

 Lab zone® Do the Inquiry Warm-Up *Where Did Your Dinner Come From?*

Vocabulary

- producer • consumer • herbivore • carnivore
- omnivore • scavenger • decomposer • food chain
- food web • energy pyramid

Skills

↻ Reading: Relate Text and Visuals
△ Inquiry: Classify

What Are the Energy Roles in an Ecosystem?

Do you play an instrument in your school band? If so, you know that each instrument has a role in a piece of music. Similar to instruments in a band, each organism has a role in the movement of energy through its ecosystem.

An organism's energy role is determined by how it obtains food and how it interacts with other organisms. **Each of the organisms in an ecosystem fills the energy role of producer, consumer, or decomposer.**

Producers Energy enters most ecosystems as sunlight. Some organisms, like the plants and algae shown in **Figure 1,** and some types of bacteria, capture the energy of sunlight and store it as food energy. These organisms use the sun's energy to turn water and carbon dioxide into food molecules in a process called photosynthesis.

An organism that can make its own food is a **producer.** Producers are the source of all the food in an ecosystem. In a few ecosystems, producers obtain energy from a source other than sunlight. One such ecosystem is found in rocks deep beneath the ground. Certain bacteria in this ecosystem produce their own food using the energy in hydrogen sulfide, a gas that is present in their environment.

Academic Standards for Science

6.3.1 Describe specific relationships between organisms.

6.3.5 Describe how all animals meet their energy needs by consuming other organisms, breaking down their structures, and using the materials to grow and function.

6.NS.8 Analyze data, and use it to identify patterns and make inferences based on these patterns.

FIGURE 1 ·····················

Producers

Producers are organisms that can make their own food.

✎ **Identify** Complete the shopping list below to identify the producers that are part of your diet.

- ◯ wheat
- ◯ corn
- ◯ banana
- ◯
- ◯
- ◯
- ◯
- ◯
- ◯

Tape grass and water milfoil

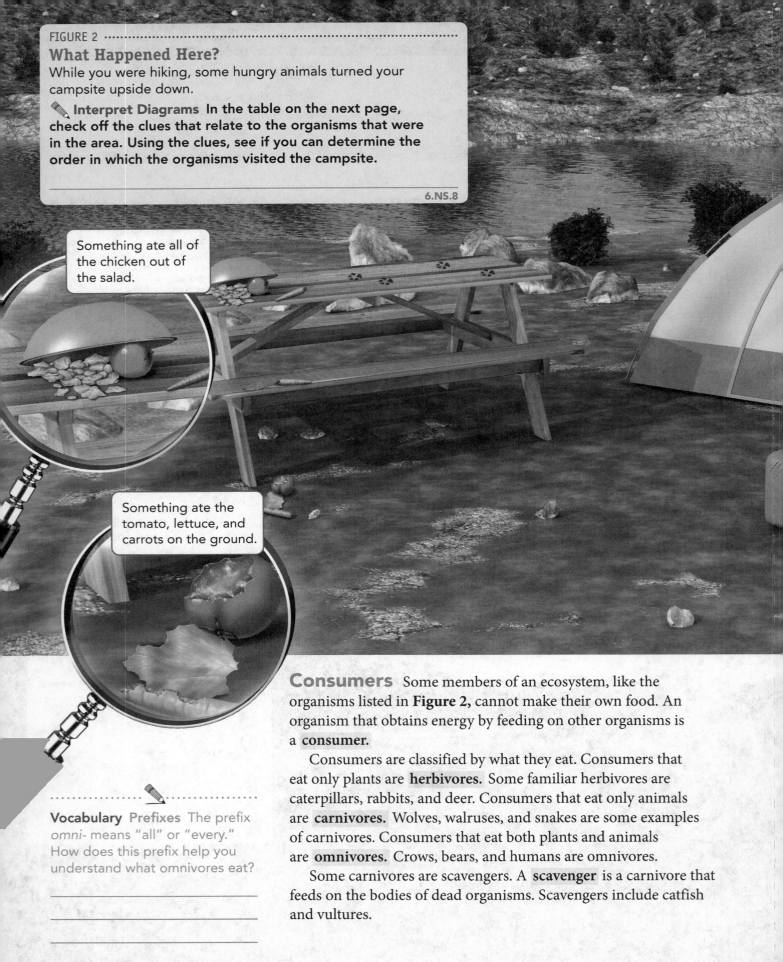

FIGURE 2 ....

What Happened Here?
While you were hiking, some hungry animals turned your campsite upside down.

✏️ **Interpret Diagrams** In the table on the next page, check off the clues that relate to the organisms that were in the area. Using the clues, see if you can determine the order in which the organisms visited the campsite.

6.NS.8

Something ate all of the chicken out of the salad.

Something ate the tomato, lettuce, and carrots on the ground.

Vocabulary Prefixes The prefix *omni-* means "all" or "every." How does this prefix help you understand what omnivores eat?

_____

_____

Consumers Some members of an ecosystem, like the organisms listed in **Figure 2,** cannot make their own food. An organism that obtains energy by feeding on other organisms is a **consumer.**

Consumers are classified by what they eat. Consumers that eat only plants are **herbivores.** Some familiar herbivores are caterpillars, rabbits, and deer. Consumers that eat only animals are **carnivores.** Wolves, walruses, and snakes are some examples of carnivores. Consumers that eat both plants and animals are **omnivores.** Crows, bears, and humans are omnivores.

Some carnivores are scavengers. A **scavenger** is a carnivore that feeds on the bodies of dead organisms. Scavengers include catfish and vultures.

Clues	Bear	Mold	Rabbit	Wolf
Can easily reach the table top				
Grows on food and breaks it down				
Small enough to enter and exit tent				
Gets energy from meat				
Strong enough to open cooler				
Not a picky eater				
Gets energy from plants				

Something ate the apples and beef jerky from inside the tent.

Something ate strawberries, even some of the moldy ones.

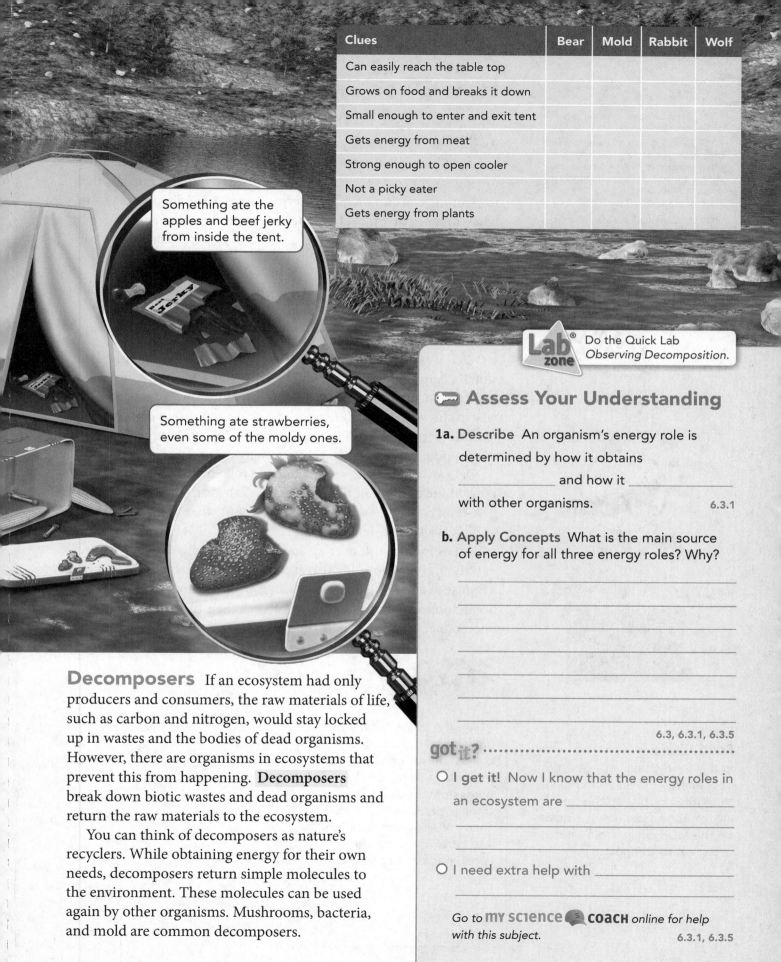

Decomposers If an ecosystem had only producers and consumers, the raw materials of life, such as carbon and nitrogen, would stay locked up in wastes and the bodies of dead organisms. However, there are organisms in ecosystems that prevent this from happening. **Decomposers** break down biotic wastes and dead organisms and return the raw materials to the ecosystem.

You can think of decomposers as nature's recyclers. While obtaining energy for their own needs, decomposers return simple molecules to the environment. These molecules can be used again by other organisms. Mushrooms, bacteria, and mold are common decomposers.

Lab zone® Do the Quick Lab *Observing Decomposition.*

🔑 Assess Your Understanding

1a. Describe An organism's energy role is determined by how it obtains

_____ and how it _____

with other organisms.   6.3.1

b. Apply Concepts What is the main source of energy for all three energy roles? Why?

_____

_____

_____

_____

_____

_____

_____

                                        6.3, 6.3.1, 6.3.5

got it? ··

○ **I get it!** Now I know that the energy roles in

an ecosystem are _____

_____

_____

○ **I need extra help with** _____

_____

Go to **my science coach** *online for help with this subject.*   6.3.1, 6.3.5

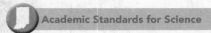
Academic Standards for Science

6.3.1 Describe specific relationships between organisms.

6.3.5 Describe how all animals meet their energy needs by consuming other organisms, breaking down their structures, and using the materials to grow and function.

6.NS.8 Analyze data.

6.DP.10 Communicate the solution using drawings.

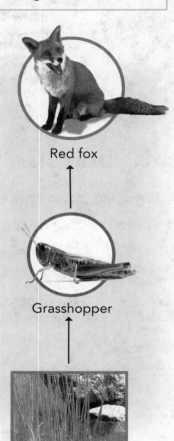

Red fox

Grasshopper

Plants

FIGURE 3 ·····················
Food Chain
In this food chain, you can see how energy moves from plants, to a grasshopper, to the fox. The arrows show how energy moves up the food chain, from one organism to the next.

How Does Energy Move Through an Ecosystem?

As you have read, energy enters most ecosystems as sunlight and is converted into food by producers. This energy is transferred to the organisms that eat the producers, and then to other organisms that feed on the consumers. 🗝 **Energy moves through an ecosystem when one organism eats another.** This movement of energy can be shown as food chains, food webs, and energy pyramids.

Food Chains One way to show how energy moves in an ecosystem is with a food chain. A **food chain** is a series of events in which one organism eats another and obtains energy. You can follow one example of a food chain in **Figure 3.**

Food Webs A food chain shows only one possible path along which energy can move through an ecosystem. Most producers and consumers are part of many food chains. A more realistic way to show the flow of energy through an ecosystem is with a food web. As shown in **Figure 4,** a **food web** consists of many overlapping food chains in an ecosystem.

Organisms may play more than one role in an ecosystem. Look at the crayfish in **Figure 4.** A crayfish is an omnivore that is a first-level consumer when it eats plants. But when a crayfish eats a snail, it is a second-level consumer.

Just as food chains overlap and connect, food webs interconnect as well. A gull might eat a fish at the ocean, but it might also eat a mouse at a landfill. The gull, then, is part of two food webs—an ocean food web and a land food web. All the world's food webs interconnect in what can be thought of as a global food web.

apply it!

△Classify Using what you have learned about food chains, draw or describe a food chain from your local ecosystem. Show at least three organisms in your food chain. Name each organism and label it as a producer, consumer, or decomposer.

6.DP.10

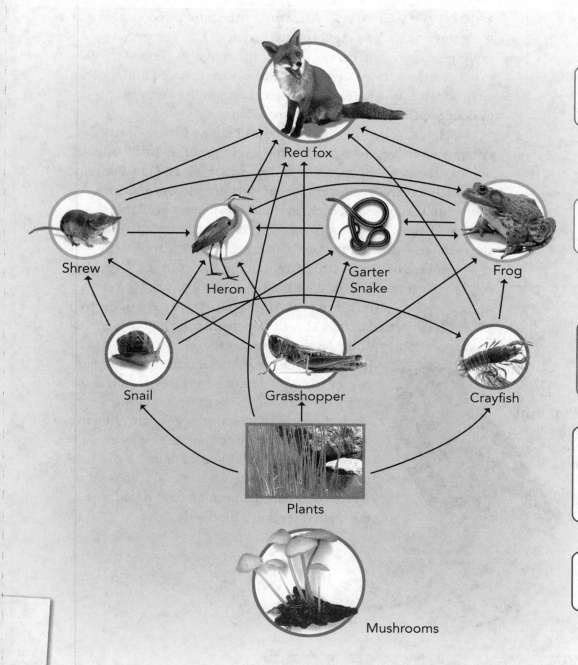

Third-level consumers eat the second-level consumers.

Second-level consumers eat the first-level consumers.

First-level consumers are organisms that feed directly on the producers.

Producers form the base of the food web. The first organism in a food chain is always a producer.

Decomposers consume the wastes and remains of other organisms.

Red fox

Shrew

Heron

Garter Snake

Frog

Snail

Grasshopper

Crayfish

Plants

Mushrooms

FIGURE 4 ···

> INTERACTIVE ART **Food Web**

A food web consists of many interconnected food chains.

✎ **Complete the tasks.**

1. **Interpret Diagrams** Pick two organisms from the food web. Draw arrows connecting them to the decomposers.

2. 🔄 **Relate Text and Visuals** How can the fox be both a second-level and third-level consumer?

_____

_____

_____

_____

_____

_____

323

Look at the energy pyramid.
Why is a pyramid the best shape
to show how energy moves
through an ecosystem?

_____

_____

_____

_____

_____

_____

_____

FIGURE 5 ....

▶ VIRTUAL LAB Energy Pyramid

This energy pyramid diagram
shows the energy available at
each level of a food web
and how it is calculated.
Energy is measured in
kilocalories, or kcal.

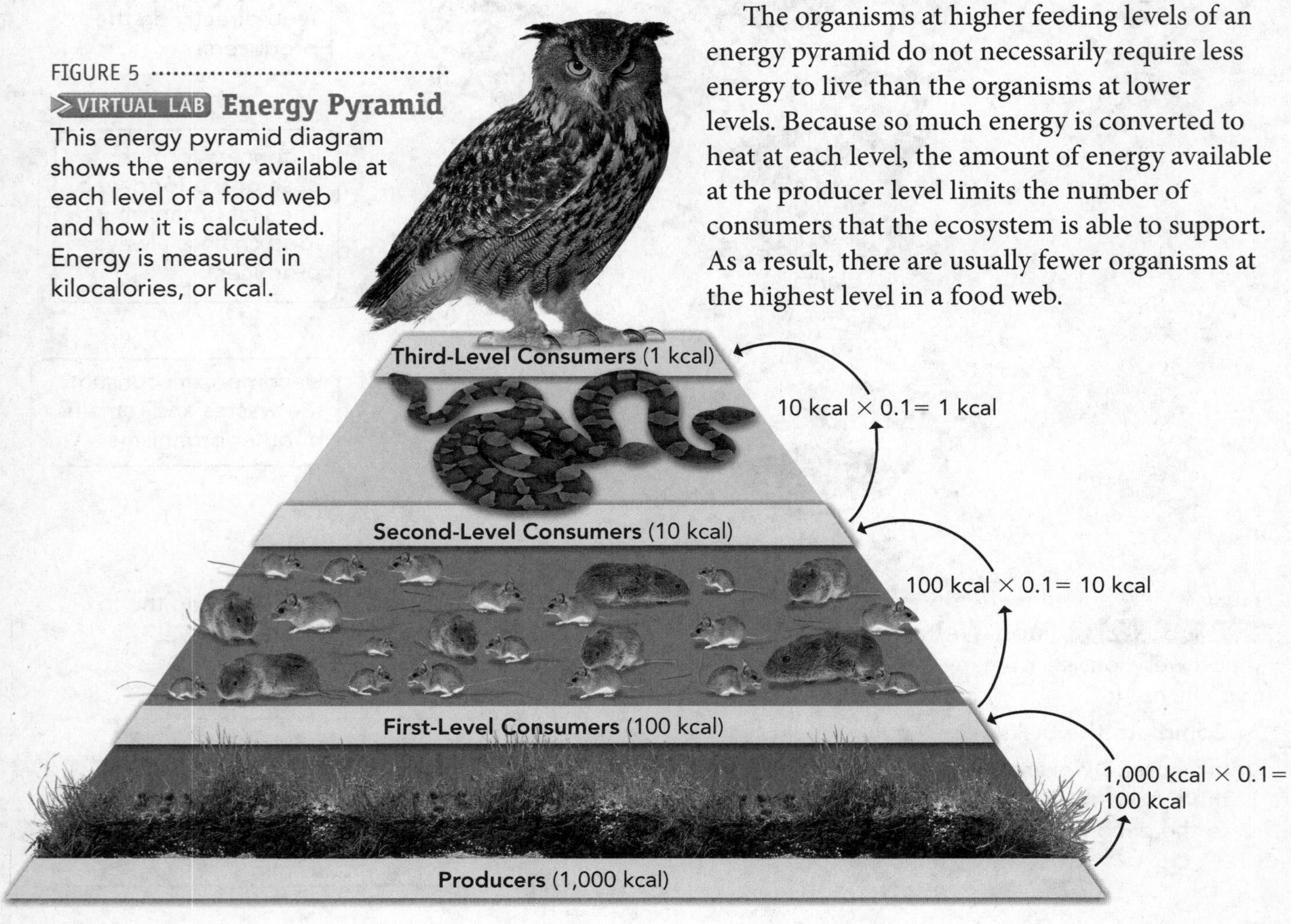

Energy Pyramids When an organism in an ecosystem eats,
it obtains energy. The organism uses some of this energy to move,
grow, reproduce, and carry out other life activities. These activities
produce heat, a form of energy, which is then released into the
environment. When heat is released, the amount of energy that is
available to the next consumer is reduced.

A diagram called an **energy pyramid** shows the amount of
energy that moves from one feeding level to another in a food web.
You can see an energy pyramid in **Figure 5.** 🔑 **The most energy
is available at the producer level of the pyramid. As energy
moves up the pyramid, each level has less energy available than
the level below.** An energy pyramid gets its name from the shape of
the diagram—wider at the base and narrower at the top.

In general, only about 10 percent of the energy at one level of a
food web is transferred to the next higher level. Most of the energy
at each level is converted to heat. Since about 90 percent of the food
energy is converted to heat at each step, there is not enough energy
to support many feeding levels in an ecosystem.

The organisms at higher feeding levels of an
energy pyramid do not necessarily require less
energy to live than the organisms at lower
levels. Because so much energy is converted to
heat at each level, the amount of energy available
at the producer level limits the number of
consumers that the ecosystem is able to support.
As a result, there are usually fewer organisms at
the highest level in a food web.

Third-Level Consumers (1 kcal)

10 kcal × 0.1 = 1 kcal

Second-Level Consumers (10 kcal)

100 kcal × 0.1 = 10 kcal

First-Level Consumers (100 kcal)

1,000 kcal × 0.1 = 100 kcal

Producers (1,000 kcal)

do the math!

Energy Pyramids

Suppose that the producers at the base of an energy pyramid contain 330,000 kilocalories.
Calculate Using **Figure 5** as a guide, label how much energy would be available at each level of the pyramid based on the questions below.

1 If mice ate all of the plants, how much energy would be available to them as first-level consumers?

2 If all of the mice were eaten by snakes, how much energy would the snakes receive?

3 If all of the snakes were eaten by the owl, how much energy would the owl receive?

4 CHALLENGE About how much energy would the owl use for its life processes or lose as heat? _____

5 CHALLENGE How much energy would be stored in the owl's body? _____

6.NS.8

(Pyramid diagram)
- Third-Level Consumers
- Second-Level Consumers
- First-Level Consumers
- 330,000 kcal
- Producers

Do the Lab Investigation
Ecosystem Food Chains.

Assess Your Understanding

2a. Define A food (web/chain) is a series of events in which one organism eats another and obtains energy. A food (web/chain) consists of many overlapping food (webs/chains).   6.3.1

b. Compare and Contrast Why is a food web a more realistic way of portraying an ecosystem than a food chain?

_____
_____
_____
6.3.1

c. Relate Cause and Effect Why are there usually fewer organisms at the top of an energy pyramid?

_____
_____
_____
_____
_____
_____
6.3.1, 6.3.5

got it? ....

○ **I get it!** Now I know that energy moves through an ecosystem when_____
_____

○ **I need extra help with** _____

Go to MY SCIENCE COACH *online for help with this subject.*   6.3.1, 6.3.5

Cycles of Matter

UNLOCK
THE BIG
?

🔑 **What Processes Are Involved in the Water Cycle?**
6.3, 6.3.3

🔑 **How Are the Carbon and Oxygen Cycles Related?**
6.3.2, 6.3.3

🔑 **How Does Nitrogen Cycle Through Ecosystems?**
6.3.2, 6.3.3

MY PLANET DIARY

DISASTER

Canaries and Coal

Have you ever stopped to listen to a bird sing? If you were a coal miner in the early 1900s, your life may have depended on it! Sometimes miners stumbled upon pockets of carbon monoxide, a toxic, odorless gas that makes it difficult for the body to get enough oxygen. Without fresh air circulating in the mineshafts, the miners would fall asleep and eventually die. To prevent this disaster from happening, canaries were used to monitor the air quality. A singing canary indicated that all was well. If the canary stopped singing and died, the miners knew that they needed to quickly leave the mine.

Answer the question below.

Do you think it was ethical, or fair, to use canaries this way? Explain.

_____

_____

_____

_____

▷ **PLANET DIARY** Go to **Planet Diary** to learn more about cycles of matter.

 Do the Inquiry Warm-Up *Are You Part of a Cycle?*

What Processes Are Involved in the Water Cycle?

Academic Standards for Science

6.3 Core Standard Understand that the major source of energy for ecosystems is light produced by major nuclear reactions in the sun.

6.3.3 Describe how certain biotic and abiotic factors can limit the number of organisms that an ecosystem can support.

Recycling is important for ecosystems because matter is limited. To understand how matter cycles through an ecosystem, you need to know a few terms that describe the structure of matter. Matter is made up of tiny particles called atoms. Two or more atoms that are joined and act as a unit make up a molecule. For example, a water molecule consists of two hydrogen atoms and one oxygen atom.

Water is essential for life. The water cycle is the continuous process by which water moves from Earth's surface to the atmosphere and back. 🔑 **The processes of evaporation, condensation, and precipitation make up the water cycle.**

Vocabulary
- evaporation
- condensation
- precipitation
- nitrogen fixation

Skills
- ⟳ Reading: Sequence
- △ Inquiry: Infer

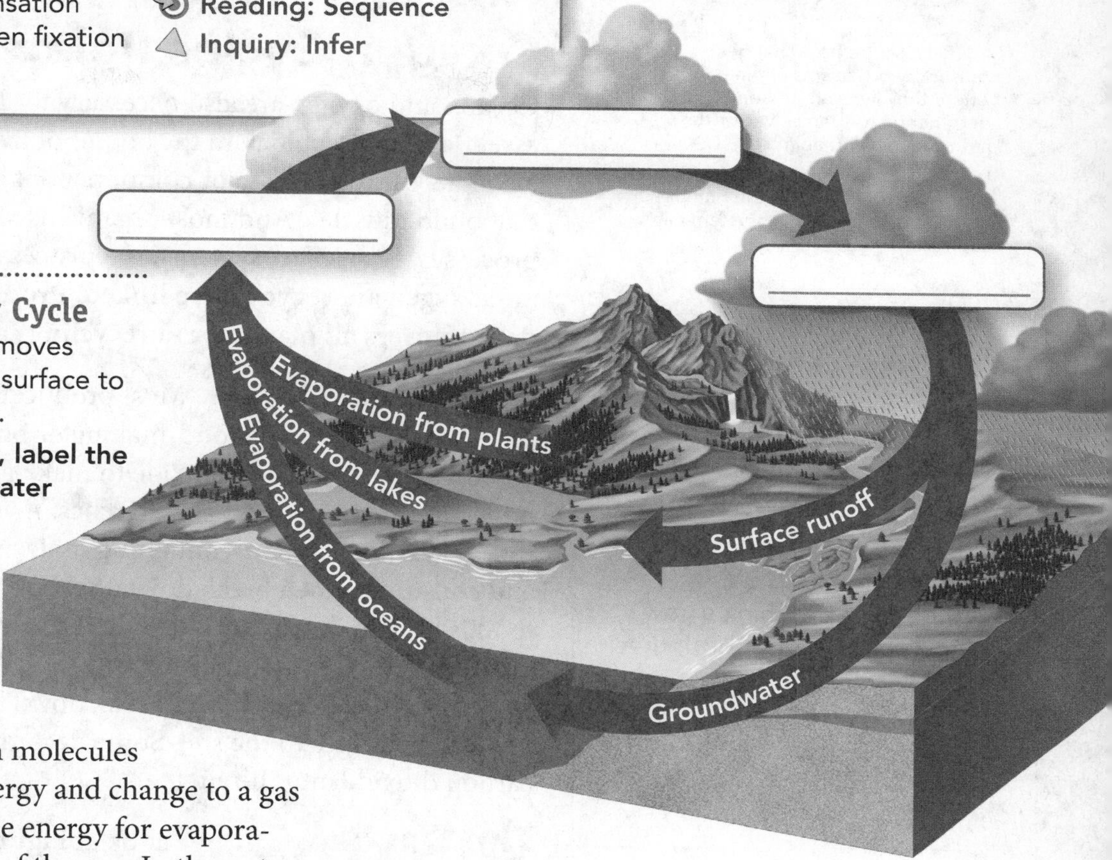

FIGURE 1 ....

> **INTERACTIVE ART** **Water Cycle**

In the water cycle, water moves continuously from Earth's surface to the atmosphere and back.

✎ **Identify** As you read, label the three processes of the water cycle in the diagram.

Evaporation from plants

Evaporation from lakes

Evaporation from oceans

Surface runoff

Groundwater

Evaporation

How does water from the ground get into the air? The process by which molecules of liquid water absorb energy and change to a gas is called **evaporation.** The energy for evaporation comes from the heat of the sun. In the water cycle, liquid water evaporates from oceans, lakes, and other sources and forms water vapor, a gas, in the atmosphere. Smaller amounts of water also evaporate from living things. Plants release water vapor from their leaves. You release liquid water in your wastes and water vapor when you exhale.

Condensation
As water vapor rises higher in the atmosphere, it cools down. The cooled vapor then turns back into tiny drops of liquid water. The process by which a gas changes to a liquid is called **condensation.** The water droplets collect around dust particles and form clouds.

Precipitation
As more water vapor condenses, the drops of water in the clouds grow larger. Eventually the heavy drops fall to Earth as **precipitation**—rain, snow, sleet, or hail. Precipitation may fall into oceans, lakes, or rivers. The precipitation that falls on land may soak into the soil and become groundwater, or run off the land, flowing back into a river or ocean.

Lab zone® Do the Quick Lab *Following Water.*

🔑 Assess Your Understanding

got it? ....

○ **I get it!** Now I know that the processes of the water cycle are _____

_____

_____

○ **I need extra help with** _____

_____

_____

Go to **MY SCIENCE** S **COACH** online for help with this subject.   6.3, 6.3.3

Academic Standards for Science

6.3.2 Describe how changes caused by organisms in the habitat where they live can be beneficial or detrimental to themselves or the native plants and animals.

6.3.3 Describe how certain biotic and abiotic factors can limit the number of organisms that an ecosystem can support.

How Are the Carbon and Oxygen Cycles Related?

Carbon and oxygen are also necessary for life. Carbon is an essential building block in the bodies of living things. For example, carbon is a major component of bones and the proteins that build muscles. And most organisms use oxygen for their life processes. 🔑 **In ecosystems, the processes by which carbon and oxygen are recycled are linked. Producers, consumers, and decomposers all play roles in recycling carbon and oxygen.**

The Carbon Cycle Most producers take in carbon dioxide gas from the air during food-making or photosynthesis. They use carbon from the carbon dioxide to make food—carbon-containing molecules such as sugars and starches. As consumers eat producers, they take in the carbon-containing molecules. Both producers and consumers then break down the food to obtain energy. As the food is broken down, producers and consumers release carbon dioxide and water into the environment. When producers and consumers die, decomposers break down their remains and return carbon molecules to the soil. Some decomposers also release carbon dioxide into the air.

The Oxygen Cycle Look at **Figure 2.** Like carbon, oxygen cycles through ecosystems. Producers release oxygen as a result of photosynthesis. Most organisms take in oxygen from the air or water and use it to carry out their life processes.

Human Impact Human activities also affect the levels of carbon and oxygen in the atmosphere. When humans burn oil and other plant-based fuels, carbon dioxide is released into the atmosphere. Carbon dioxide levels can also rise when humans clear forests for lumber, fuel, and farmland. Increasing levels of carbon dioxide are a major factor in global warming. As you know, producers take in carbon dioxide during photosynthesis. When trees are removed from the ecosystem, there are fewer producers to absorb carbon dioxide. There is an even greater effect if trees are burned down to clear a forest. When trees are burned down, additional carbon dioxide is released during the burning process.

apply it!

Producers, consumers, and decomposers all play a role in recycling carbon and oxygen.

Infer On the lines below, describe how you think a cow eating grass is part of both the carbon and oxygen cycles.

_____

_____

_____

_____

_____

_____

_____

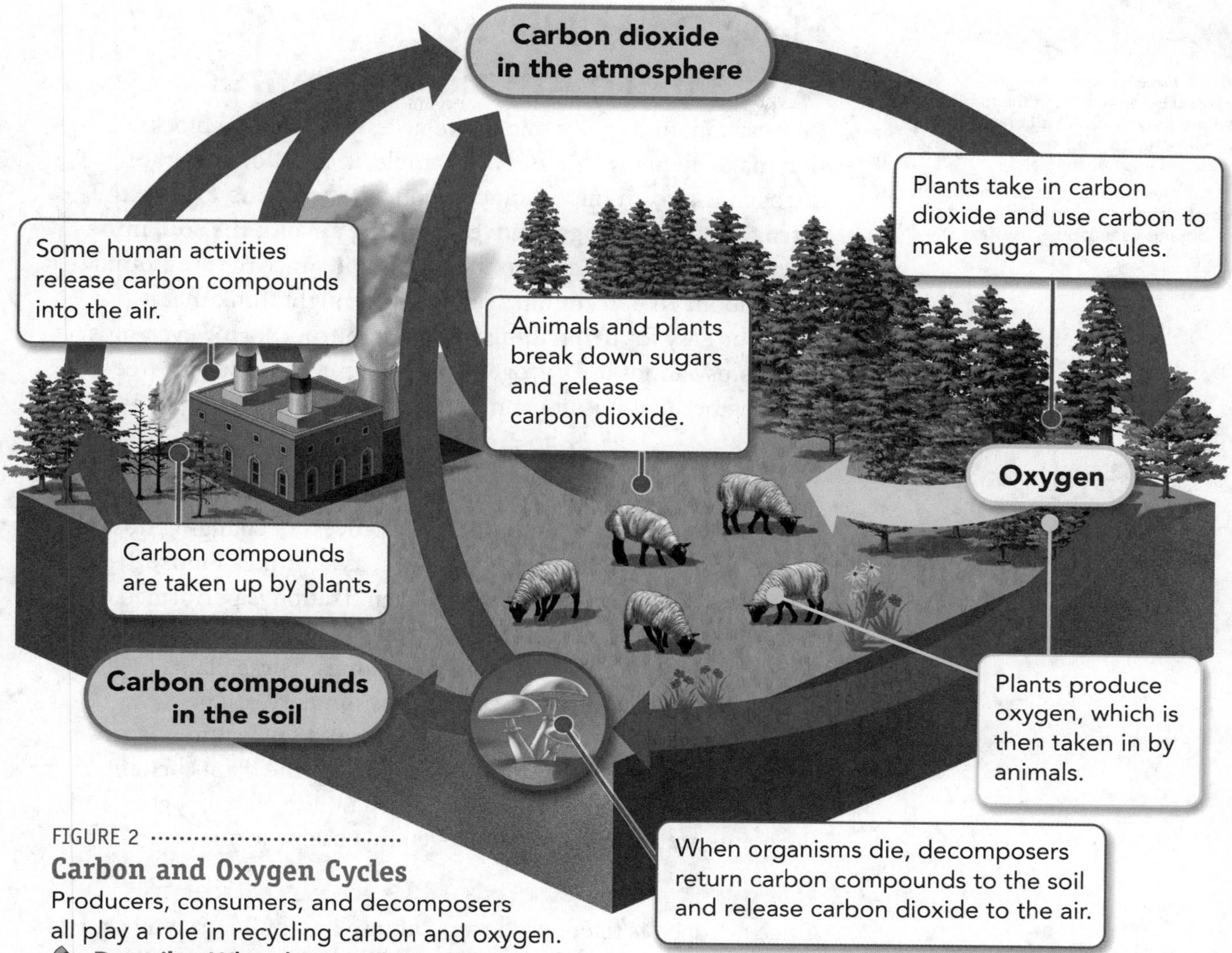

Carbon dioxide in the atmosphere

Some human activities release carbon compounds into the air.

Plants take in carbon dioxide and use carbon to make sugar molecules.

Animals and plants break down sugars and release carbon dioxide.

Carbon compounds are taken up by plants.

Oxygen

Carbon compounds in the soil

Plants produce oxygen, which is then taken in by animals.

When organisms die, decomposers return carbon compounds to the soil and release carbon dioxide to the air.

FIGURE 2 ·······························

Carbon and Oxygen Cycles
Producers, consumers, and decomposers all play a role in recycling carbon and oxygen.
✏ **Describe** When humans burn fuel or cut down trees, they (increase/decrease) levels of carbon dioxide in the atmosphere.

Lab zone Do the Quick Lab
Carbon and Oxygen Blues.

🔑 **Assess Your Understanding**

1a. Identify Carbon and oxygen are both

_____ in an ecosystem.

6.3.2, 6.3.3

b. Develop Hypotheses How might the death of all the producers in a community affect the carbon and oxygen cycles?

_____

_____

_____

_____

6.3.2, 6.3.3, 6.NS.1

got it?

○ **I get it!** Now I know that the carbon and

oxygen cycles are related by _____

_____

_____

_____

○ **I need extra help with** _____

Go to **MY SCIENCE** ⬢ **COACH** *online for help with this subject.*

6.3.2, 6.3.3

Academic Standards for Science

6.3.2 Describe how changes caused by organisms in the habitat where they live can be beneficial or detrimental to themselves or the native plants and animals.

6.3.3 Describe how certain biotic and abiotic factors can limit the number of organisms that an ecosystem can support.

How Does Nitrogen Cycle Through Ecosystems?

Like carbon, nitrogen is one of the necessary building blocks that make up living things. For example, in addition to carbon, nitrogen is also an important component of proteins. 🔑 **In the nitrogen cycle, nitrogen moves from the air into the soil, into living things, and back into the air or soil.** Since the air around you is about 78 percent nitrogen gas, you might think that it would be easy for living things to obtain nitrogen. However, most organisms cannot use nitrogen gas. Nitrogen gas is called "free" nitrogen because it is not combined with other kinds of atoms.

Nitrogen Fixation Most organisms can use nitrogen only after it has been "fixed," or combined with other elements to form nitrogen-containing compounds. The process of changing free nitrogen into a usable form of nitrogen, as shown in **Figure 4,** is called **nitrogen fixation.** Most nitrogen fixation is performed by certain kinds of bacteria. These bacteria live in bumps called nodules (NAHJ oolz) on the roots of legumes. These plants include clover, beans, peas, alfalfa, peanuts, and some trees.

The relationship between the bacteria and the legumes is an example of mutualism. Both the bacteria and the plants benefit from this relationship: The bacteria feed on the plants' sugars, and the plants are supplied with nitrogen in a usable form.

Return of Nitrogen to the Environment

Once nitrogen is fixed, producers can use it to build proteins and other complex compounds. Nitrogen can cycle from the soil to producers and then to consumers many times. At some point, however, bacteria break down the nitrogen compounds completely. These bacteria then release free nitrogen back into the air, causing the cycle to continue.

FIGURE 3 ···

Growth in Nitrogen-Poor Soil

Pitcher plants can grow in nitrogen-poor soil because they obtain nitrogen by trapping insects in their tube-shaped leaves. The plants then digest the insects and use their nitrogen compounds.

✏ **Circle the correct word in each sentence.**

1. **Identify** If nitrogen in the soil isn't (fixed/free), then most organisms cannot use it.

2. CHALLENGE The relationship between the pitcher plant and the insects is an example of (competition/predation/symbiosis).

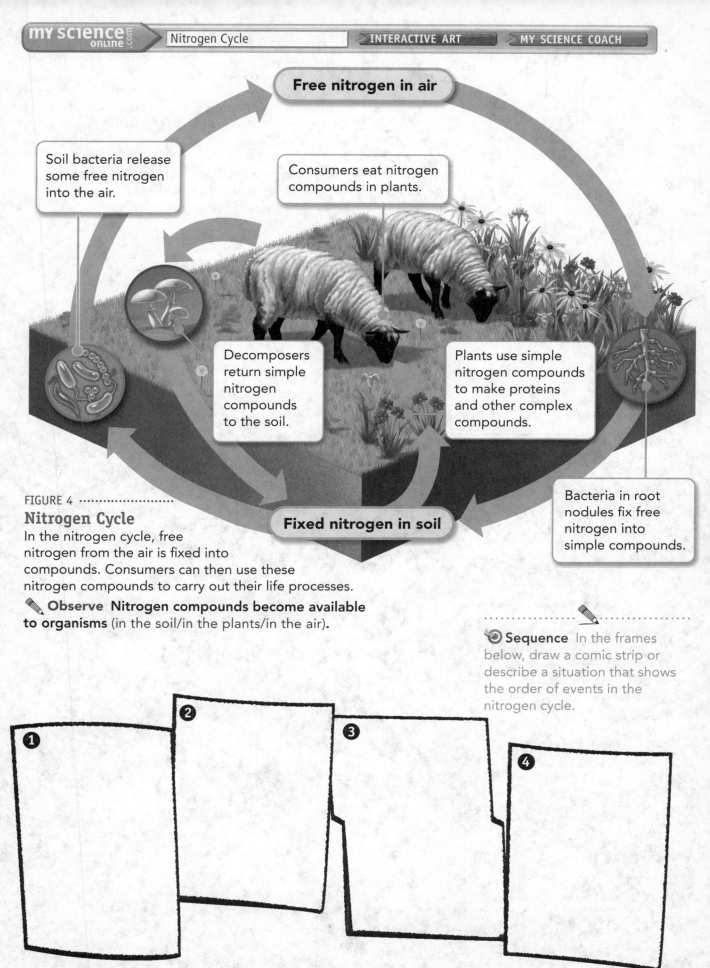

Free nitrogen in air

Soil bacteria release some free nitrogen into the air.

Consumers eat nitrogen compounds in plants.

Decomposers return simple nitrogen compounds to the soil.

Plants use simple nitrogen compounds to make proteins and other complex compounds.

Bacteria in root nodules fix free nitrogen into simple compounds.

Fixed nitrogen in soil

FIGURE 4 ·······················

Nitrogen Cycle

In the nitrogen cycle, free nitrogen from the air is fixed into compounds. Consumers can then use these nitrogen compounds to carry out their life processes.

✎ **Observe Nitrogen compounds become available to organisms** (in the soil/in the plants/in the air).

✎ **Sequence** In the frames below, draw a comic strip or describe a situation that shows the order of events in the nitrogen cycle.

❶

❷

❸

❹

331

Cycles of Matter

EXPLORE THE BIG ?

How do energy and matter move through ecosystems?

FIGURE 5 ....

> **INTERACTIVE ART** Energy and matter are constantly being cycled through an ecosystem. These cycles can occur at the same time.

✎ **Interpret Diagrams** Using colored pencils, draw arrows to represent the following in the figure below: water cycle (blue), carbon cycle (purple), oxygen cycle (yellow), nitrogen cycle (orange), food chain (green). Label each cycle.

 Do the Quick Lab *Playing Nitrogen Cycle Roles.*

🔑 Assess Your Understanding

2a. Describe (Fixed/Free) nitrogen is not combined with other kinds of atoms.

6.3.2, 6.3.3

b. Predict What might happen in a community if farmers did not plant legume crops?

_____

_____

_____

_____

_____

_____

_____

_____

6.3.2, 6.3.3, 6.NS.1

c. ANSWER THE BIG ❓ How do energy and matter move through ecosystems?

_____

_____

_____

_____

_____

_____

_____

_____

6.3.3, 6.3.5

got it? ....

○ I get it! Now I know that the nitrogen cycle

_____

_____

_____

○ I need extra help with _____

_____

Go to **MY SCIENCE** 🅂 **COACH** *online for help with this subject.*   6.3.2, 6.3.3

333

Indiana

LESSON

4 Biomes

UNLOCK THE BIG ?

🔑 **What Are the Six Major Biomes?**
6.3, 6.NS.8

Special formations on the roots of the Bald Cypress help it survive in areas with lots of water.

my PLANET DIARY _for_ Indiana

Trees With Knees?

When you think of all the sites to see in your home state of Indiana, you may not think of swamps. But located along the Hoosier state's southwestern corner, where the Wabash and Ohio rivers meet, is Twin Swamps Natural Preserve. There you can find not one, but two swamps!

The Twin Swamps Natural Preserve was created in 1987 to help protect Indiana's bald cypress trees. These trees have special adaptations on their roots—called knees—that help them live in wet lowland areas, such as swamps and river bottoms. Logging and the building of dams on local rivers and streams have destroyed much of the trees' habitat. This has left them in danger of disappearing forever.

FIELD TRIP

Communicate Discuss the question with a partner. Write your answer below.

Why might the building of dams on rivers and streams negatively affect the bald cypress?

_____

_____

_____

▶ PLANET DIARY Go to **Planet Diary** to learn more about biomes.

Lab zone® Do the Inquiry Warm-Up _How Much Rain Is That?_

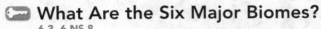

Academic Standards for Science

6.3 Core Standard Describe that all organisms, including humans, are part of complex systems found in all biomes.

6.NS.8 Analyze data.

What Are the Six Major Biomes?

Imagine that you are taking part in an around-the-world scientific expedition. On this expedition you will collect data on the typical climate and organisms of each of Earth's biomes. A **biome** is a group of ecosystems with similar climates and organisms.

🔑 **The six major biomes are desert, rain forest, grassland, deciduous forest, boreal forest, and tundra.** It is mostly the **climate**—the average annual temperature and amount of precipitation—in an area that determines its biome. Climate limits the species of plants that can grow in an area. In turn, the species of plants determine the kinds of animals that live there.

Vocabulary

- biome • climate • desert • rain forest
- emergent layer • canopy • understory • grassland
- savanna • deciduous tree • boreal forest
- coniferous tree • tundra • permafrost

Skills

- Reading: Compare and Contrast
- Inquiry: Draw Conclusions

Desert Biomes The first stop on your expedition is a desert. You step off the bus into the searing heat. A **desert** is an area that receives less than 25 centimeters of rain per year. Some of the driest deserts may not receive any precipitation in a year! Deserts often undergo large shifts in temperature during the course of a day. A scorching hot desert like the Namib Desert in Africa cools rapidly each night when the sun goes down. Other deserts, such as the Gobi in central Asia, have a yearly average temperature that is below freezing.

Organisms that live in the desert, like the fennec in **Figure 1**, must be adapted to little or no rain and to extreme temperatures. For example, the stem of a saguaro cactus has folds that are similar to the pleats in an accordion. The stem expands to store water when it is raining. Gila monsters can spend weeks at a time in their cool underground burrows. Many other desert animals are most active at night when the temperatures are cooler.

FIGURE 1 ....
Desert
Organisms must be adapted to live in the desert.

✎ **Complete these tasks.**

1. [CHALLENGE] How do you think the fennec's ears and fur are adaptations to the desert's extreme temperatures?

_____
_____
_____

2. **List** Write five things you'll need to be well adapted to desert conditions. Pack carefully!

Supply List

○ wide-brimmed hat
○ _____
○ _____
○ _____
○ _____
○ _____

Equator

Desert Biomes
☐ Desert

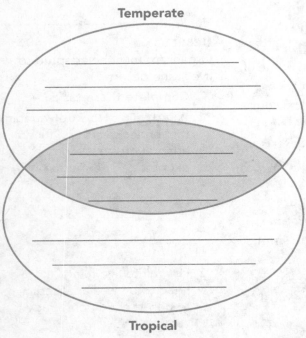

✎ **Compare and Contrast** As you read about temperate and tropical rain forests, fill in the Venn diagram.

Temperate

_____

_____

_____

_____

_____

_____

_____

_____

_____

Tropical

FIGURE 2

Temperate Rain Forests

The sugar pine is the tallest kind of pine tree, reaching heights of 53 to 61 meters. It also produces the largest pine cones. A sugar pine cone can reach a length of 30 to 56 centimeters. The sugar pine cone shown here is actual size!

✎ **Identify** What conditions do you think allow a tree to grow so tall?

_____

_____

_____

_____

Rain-Forest Biomes

The second stop on your expedition is a rain forest. **Rain forests** are forests in which large amounts of rain fall year-round. This biome is living up to its name—it's pouring! After a short shower, the sun reappears. However, very little sunlight reaches the ground.

Plants are everywhere in the rain forest. Some plants, like the vines hanging from tree limbs, even grow on other plants! And animals are flying, creeping, and slithering all around you.

Temperate Rain Forests You may think that a rain forest is a warm, humid "jungle" in the tropics. But there is another type of rain forest. The Pacific Northwest of the United States receives more than 300 centimeters of rain a year. Huge trees grow there, including redwoods, cedars, and firs. Many ecologists refer to this ecosystem as a temperate rain forest. The term *temperate* means "having moderate temperatures."

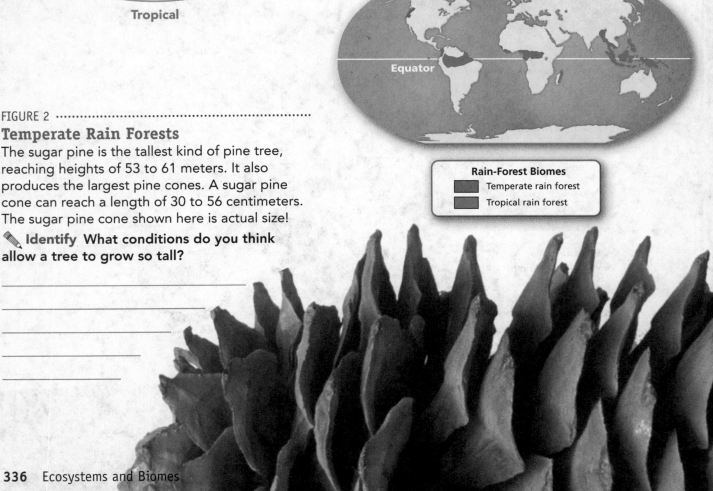

Equator

Rain-Forest Biomes
- Temperate rain forest
- Tropical rain forest

Tropical Rain Forests As you can see on the map, tropical rain forests are found in regions close to the equator. The climate is warm and humid all year long, and there is a lot of rain. Because of these climate conditions, an amazing variety of plants grow in tropical rain forests.

Trees in the rain forest form several distinct layers. The tallest layer of the rain forest which receives the most sunlight and can reach up to 70 meters, is the **emergent layer.** Underneath, trees up to 50 meters tall form a leafy roof called the **canopy.** Below the canopy, a layer of shorter trees and vines, around 15 meters high, form an **understory.** Understory plants grow well in the shade formed by the canopy. The forest floor is nearly dark, so only a few plants live there. Look at the tree layers in **Figure 3.**

The abundant plant life in tropical rain forests provides habitats for many species of animals. Ecologists estimate that millions of species of insects live in tropical rain forests. These insects serve as a source of food for many reptiles, birds, and mammals. Many of these animals, in turn, are food sources for other animals. Although tropical rain forests cover only a small part of the planet, they probably contain more species of plants and animals than all the other biomes combined.

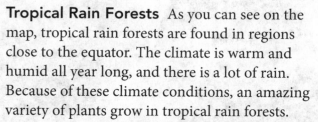

FIGURE 3 ···

Tropical Rain Forests
On the edge of this tropical rain forest, an amazing variety of organisms can be found in the different layers.

✎ **Relate Text and Visuals** Based on your reading, label the four distinct layers of the tropical rain forest in the boxes above.

Rhea, South America **A**

Cassowary, Australia **B**

Ostrich, Africa **C**

FIGURE 4 ··························

Grasslands

The rhea, cassowary, and ostrich are grassland birds that live on different continents.

✎ **Interpret Maps** On the world map, identify the continents in which these three birds are located. List three characteristics that these grassland birds all share.

_____

_____

_____

_____

_____

8.NS.8

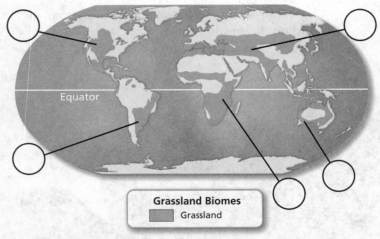

Equator

Grassland Biomes
⬛ Grassland

Grassland Biomes The third stop on the expedition is a grassy plain called a prairie. Temperatures are more comfortable here than they were in the desert. The breeze carries the scent of soil warmed by the sun. This rich soil supports grasses as tall as you. Startled by your approach, sparrows dart into hiding places among the waving grass stems.

Although the prairie receives more rain than a desert, you may notice only a few scattered areas of trees and shrubs. Ecologists classify prairies, which are generally found in the middle latitudes, as grasslands. A **grassland** is an area that is populated mostly by grasses and other nonwoody plants. Most grasslands receive 25 to 75 centimeters of rain each year. Fires and droughts are common in this biome. Grasslands that are located closer to the equator than prairies are known as savannas. A **savanna** receives as much as 120 centimeters of rain each year. Scattered shrubs and small trees grow on savannas, along with grass.

Grasslands are home to many of the largest animals on Earth— herbivores such as elephants, bison, antelopes, zebras, giraffes, kangaroos, and rhinoceroses. Grazing by these large herbivores maintains the grasslands. Their grazing keeps young trees and bushes from sprouting and competing with the grass for water and sunlight. You can see some grassland birds in **Figure 4.**

Deciduous Forest Biomes Your trip to the fourth biome takes you to another forest. It is now late summer. Cool mornings here give way to warm days. Several members of the expedition are busy recording the numerous plant species. Others are looking through binoculars, trying to identify the songbirds.

You are now visiting a deciduous forest biome. Many of the trees in this forest are **deciduous trees** (dee SIJ oo us), trees that shed their leaves and grow new ones each year. Oaks and maples are examples of deciduous trees. Deciduous forests receive enough rain to support the growth of trees and other plants, at least 50 centimeters of rain per year. Temperatures can vary greatly during the year. The growing season usually lasts five to six months.

The variety of plants in a deciduous forest creates many different habitats. Many species of birds live in different parts of the forest, eating the insects and fruits in their specific areas. Mammals such as chipmunks and skunks live in deciduous forests. In a North American deciduous forest you might also see wood thrushes and white-tailed deer.

If you were to return to this biome in the winter, you would not see much wildlife. Many of the bird species migrate, or fly great distances, to warmer areas. Some of the mammals hibernate, or enter a state of greatly reduced body activity similar to sleep. Look at **Figure 5.** During the winter months, animals that hibernate get energy from fat stored in their bodies.

did you
know? ....

Some of Indiana's oldest deciduous trees, which are predominately found in the southern third of the state, are over 250 years old. A number of the state's oldest oak trees were producing acorns since before the time of the American Revolution!

FIGURE 5 ·······························

Deciduous Forest
Most of the trees in a deciduous forest have leaves that change color and drop to the forest floor each autumn. In the leaves, this dormouse hibernates through the winter.

✏ **Infer Is hibernation an adaptation to life in a deciduous forest? Explain your answer.**

_____

_____

_____

_____

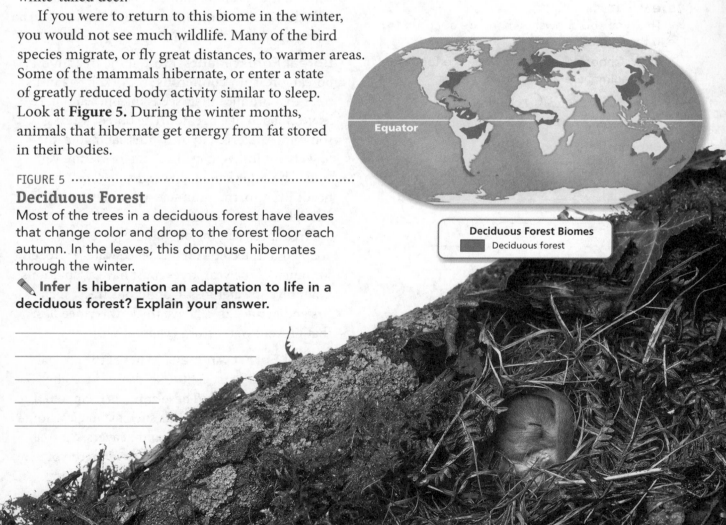

Equator

Deciduous Forest Biomes
■ Deciduous forest

FIGURE 6 ·······································

Boreal Forest

🖎 This lynx and snowshoe hare are adapted to life in the boreal forest.

1. **Infer** Choose the best answer. The feet of each animal are an adaptation to its

   ⭘ food.   ⭘ climate.
   ⭘ predators.   ⭘ all of the above

2. **Explain** Defend your answer.

   _____

   _____

   _____

   _____

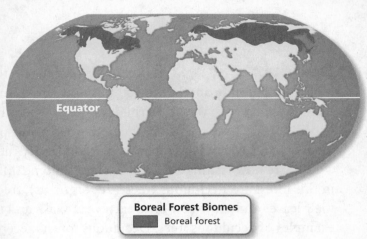

Boreal Forest Biomes
Boreal forest

Boreal Forest Biomes Now the expedition heads north to a colder biome, the boreal forest. The term *boreal* means "northern," and **boreal forests** are dense forests found in upper regions of the Northern Hemisphere. The expedition leaders claim they can identify a boreal forest by its smell. When you arrive, you catch a whiff of the spruce and fir trees that blanket the hillsides. Feeling the chilly early fall air, you pull a jacket and hat out of your bag.

Boreal Forest Plants Most of the trees in the boreal forest are **coniferous trees** (koh NIF ur us), trees that produce their seeds in cones and have leaves shaped like needles. The boreal forest is sometimes referred to by its Russian name, the *taiga* (TY guh). Winters in these forests are very cold. The snow can reach heights well over your head! Even so, the summers are rainy and warm enough to melt all the snow.

Tree species in the boreal forest are well adapted to the cold climate. Since water is frozen for much of the year, trees must have adaptations that prevent water loss. Coniferous trees, such as firs and hemlocks, all have thick, waxy needles that prevent water from evaporating.

Boreal Forest Animals Many of the animals of the boreal forest eat the seeds produced by the coniferous trees. These animals include red squirrels, insects, and birds such as finches. Some herbivores, such as moose and beavers, eat tree bark and new shoots. The variety of herbivores in the boreal forest supports many predators, including lynx, otters, and great horned owls. **Figure 6** shows an herbivore and its predator.

Tundra Biomes As you arrive at your last stop, the driving wind gives you an immediate feel for this biome. The **tundra** is extremely cold and dry. Expecting deep snow, many are surprised to learn that the tundra may receive no more precipitation than a desert.

Most of the soil in the tundra is frozen all year. This frozen soil is called **permafrost.** During the short summer, the top layer of soil thaws, but the underlying soil remains frozen. Because rainwater cannot soak into the permafrost, shallow ponds and marshy areas appear in the summer.

Tundra Plants Mosses, grasses, and dwarf forms of a few trees can be found in the tundra. Most of the plant growth takes place during the long days of the short summer season. North of the Arctic Circle, the sun does not set during midsummer.

Tundra Animals In summer, the insects are abundant. Insect-eating birds take advantage of the plentiful food by eating as much as they can. But when winter approaches, these birds migrate south. Mammals of the tundra include caribou, foxes, and wolves. The mammals that remain on the tundra during the winter grow thick fur coats. What can these animals find to eat on the tundra in winter? The caribou scrape snow away to find lichens. Wolves follow the caribou and look for weak members of the herd to prey upon.

FIGURE 7 ···
Tundra
Although the ground is frozen for most of the year, mosses, grasses, and dwarf willow trees grow here.

✎ **Communicate** Discuss with a partner why there are no tall trees on the tundra. Describe two factors that you think may influence tree growth.

_____
_____
_____
_____
_____
_____
_____
_____

Equator

Tundra Biomes

Tundra

Mountains and Ice
■ Mountains
☐ Ice

Mountains and Ice

Some land areas are not classified as biomes. Recall that biomes are defined by abiotic factors such as climate and soil, and by biotic factors such as plant and animal life. Because the organisms that live in these areas vary, mountain ranges and land covered with thick ice sheets are not considered biomes.

The climate of a mountain changes from its base to its summit. If you were to hike all the way up a tall mountain, you would pass through a series of biomes. At the base, you might find grasslands. As you climbed, you might pass through deciduous forest and then boreal forest. As you neared the top, your surroundings would resemble the cold, dry tundra.

Other places are covered year-round with thick ice sheets. Most of Greenland and Antarctica fall into this category. Organisms that are adapted to life on ice include leopard seals and polar bears.

FIGURE 8 ···································
▶ INTERACTIVE ART **Mountains**
Mountains are not part of any major biome.

do the math!

Biome Climates

An ecologist collected climate data from two locations. The graph shows the monthly average temperatures in the two locations. The total yearly precipitation in Location A is 250 centimeters. In Location B, the total yearly precipitation is 14 centimeters.

❶ **Read Graphs** Provide a title for the graph. What variable is plotted on the horizontal axis? On the vertical axis?

_____

❷ **Interpret Data** Study the graph. How would you describe the temperature over the course of a year in Location A? In Location B?

_____
_____

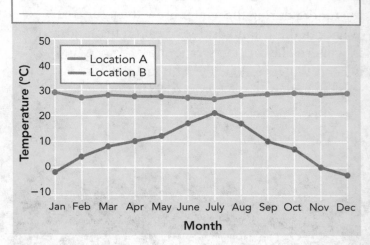

❸ **Draw Conclusions** Given the precipitation and temperature data for these locations, in which biome would you expect each to be located?

_____
_____
_____

6.NS.8

apply it!

Key of Earth Biomes
- ☐ Desert
- ☐ Temperate rain forest
- ☐ Tropical rain forest
- ☐ Grassland
- ☐ Deciduous rain forest
- ☐ Boreal forest
- ☐ Tundra

1 Interpret Maps Using the colors shown in the biome maps throughout this lesson, color in the key above. Use the key to color in the areas on the map of North America.

2 Draw Conclusions Where are most of the boreal forests located? Why are there no boreal forests in the Southern Hemisphere?

_____
_____
_____
_____
_____

3 Describe Mark the area in which you live with an X on the map. What is the climate like where you live? How do you think your climate affects which organisms live there?

_____
_____
_____
_____
_____
_____

6.NS.8

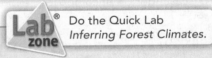
Do the Quick Lab
Inferring Forest Climates.

🔑 Assess Your Understanding

1a. Review _____ and _____ are the two main factors that determine an area's biome.

6.3

b. Infer What biome might you be in if you were standing on a bitterly cold, dry plain with only a few, short trees scattered around?

_____

6.3

got it? ....

○ **I get it!** Now I know that the six major biomes are _____

_____

○ **I need extra help with** _____

Go to **MY SCIENCE** 💬 **COACH** *online for help with this subject.*

6.3

Study Guide

Producers, _____, and _____ help to cycle energy through ecosystems.

LESSON 1 **Photosynthesis**

6.3, 6.3.4, 6.3.5, 6.3.6

🔑 Nearly all living things obtain energy either directly or indirectly from the energy of sunlight that is captured during photosynthesis.

🔑 During photosynthesis, plants and some other organisms absorb energy from the sun and use the energy to convert carbon dioxide and water into sugars and oxygen.

Vocabulary
- photosynthesis   • autotroph
- heterotroph   • chlorophyll

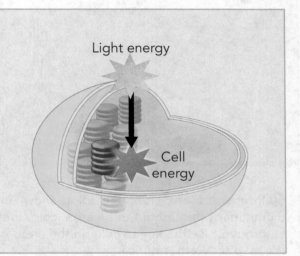

Light energy

Cell energy

LESSON 2 **Energy Flow in Ecosystems**

6.3.1, 6.3.5, 6.NS.8, 6.DP.10

🔑 Each of the organisms in an ecosystem fills the energy role of producer, consumer, or decomposer.

🔑 Energy moves through an ecosystem when one organism eats another.

🔑 The most energy is available at the producer level of the pyramid. As energy moves up the pyramid, each level has less energy available than the level below.

Vocabulary
- producer   • consumer   • herbivore   • carnivore   • omnivore
- scavenger   • decomposer   • food chain   • food web   • energy pyramid

---

LESSON 3 **Cycles of Matter**

6.3, 6.3.2, 6.3.3

🔑 The processes of evaporation, condensation, and precipitation make up the water cycle.

🔑 The processes by which carbon and oxygen are recycled are linked. Producers, consumers, and decomposers play roles in recycling both.

🔑 Nitrogen moves from the air into the soil, into living things, and back into the air or soil.

Vocabulary
- evaporation   • condensation
- precipitation   • nitrogen fixation

LESSON 4 **Biomes**

6.3, 6.NS.8

🔑 The six major biomes are desert, rain forest, grassland, deciduous forest, boreal forest, and tundra.

Vocabulary
- biome   • climate   • desert   • rain forest
- emergent layer   • canopy   • understory
- grassland   • savanna   • deciduous tree
- boreal forest   • coniferous tree   • tundra
- permafrost

Review and Assessment

LESSON 1 **Photosynthesis**

1. Which of the following organisms are autotrophs?

a. fungi   **b.** rabbits

c. humans   **d.** oak trees

6.3.4

2. Plants are green because of

_____, the main

photosynthetic pigment in chloroplasts.

6.3.4

3. Interpret Diagrams Fill in the missing labels in the diagram below.

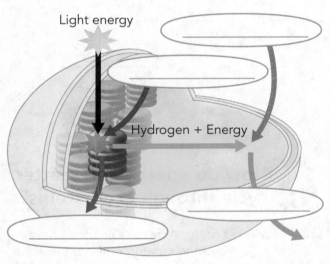

Light energy

Hydrogen + Energy

6.3.4, 6.3.6

4. Predict Suppose a volcano threw so much ash into the air that it blocked much of the sunlight. How might this event affect the ability of animals to obtain energy to live?

_____

_____

_____

6.3.3, 6.3.5, 6.NS.1

5. **Write About It** How do you get energy? Describe the path of energy from the sun to you, using at least two vocabulary terms you learned in this lesson.

6.3, 6.3.1, 6.3.5, 6.NS.11

LESSON 2 **Energy Flow in Ecosystems**

6. A diagram that shows how much energy is available at each feeding level in an ecosystem is a(n)

a. food web.   **b.** food chain.

c. water cycle.   **d.** energy pyramid.

6.3.1

7. A(n) _____ is a consumer that eats only plants.

6.3.1, 6.3.5

8. Interpret Diagrams Which organisms in the illustration are producers? Consumers?

_____

_____

_____

_____

_____

_____

_____

6.3.5

9. Compare and Contrast How are food chains and food webs different?

_____

_____

_____

_____

6.3.1

10. **Write About It** Think about your own food web. Name the producers and consumers that make up your diet.

_____

_____

_____

_____

_____

6.3.1, 6.3.5

345

LESSON 3 Cycles of Matter

11. When drops of water in a cloud become heavy enough, they fall to Earth as

   a. permafrost.   **b.** evaporation.

   c. precipitation.   **d.** condensation.

   6.3.3

12. Evaporation, condensation, and precipitation are the three main processes in the

_____

   6.3.3

13. Infer Which process is responsible for the droplets visible on the glass below? Explain.

14. Classify Which group of organisms is the source of oxygen in the oxygen cycle? Explain.

   6.3.3, 6.3.4

15. Make Generalizations Describe the roles of producers and consumers in the carbon cycle.

   6.3.3

16. Draw Conclusions What would happen if all the nitrogen-fixing bacteria disappeared?

   6.3.2, 6.3.3

LESSON 4 Biomes

17. Little precipitation and extreme temperatures are main characteristics of which biome?

   a. desert   **b.** grassland

   c. boreal forest   **d.** deciduous forest

   6.3

18. A _____ is a group of ecosystems with similar climates and organisms.

   6.3

19. Compare and Contrast How are the tundra and desert similar? How are they different?

   6.3

APPLY THE BIG ? How do energy and matter cycle through ecosystems?

20. Many acres of the Amazon rain forest have been destroyed to create farmland. Describe how the amount of energy in the food web for this area might be affected. How might the carbon and oxygen cycle also be affected?

   6.3.2, 6.3.3, 6.3.4, 6.3.5, 6.NS.1

Indiana ISTEP+ Practice

Multiple Choice

Circle the letter of the best answer.

1. At which level of this energy pyramid is the *least* energy available?

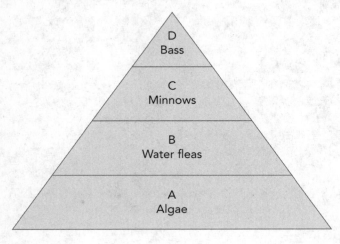

A. Level A   B. Level B
C. Level C   D. Level D

6.3.1

2. What is the source of energy used in photosynthesis?

A. glucose   B. sunlight
C. chlorophyll   D. DNA

6.3.4

3. Which pair of terms could apply to the same organism?

A. carnivore and producer
B. consumer and carnivore
C. scavenger and herbivore
D. producer and omnivore

6.3.1, 6.3.6

4. Many Canadian forests contain coniferous trees, such as fir and spruce. The winter is long and cold. Which term describes this biome?

A. tundra   B. grassland
C. boreal forest   D. deciduous forest

6.3

Constructed Response

Write your answer to Question 5 on the lines below.

5. What is the difference between an autotroph and a heterotroph?

_____

_____

_____

6.3

Extended Response

Use the diagram below and your knowledge of science to help you answer Question 6. Write your answer on a separate piece of paper.

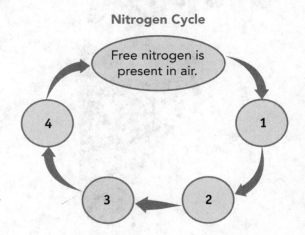

6. Describe each numbered part of the cycle shown in the diagram above.

6.3.3

Clothing That FIGHTS BACK

Humans live in every biome on Earth, even some harsh environments that our bodies are not adapted for—deserts, rain forests, and tundra. In less extreme climates, we also face risks from our surroundings. But we have learned to protect ourselves by building shelters and wearing clothing.

UV (ultraviolet) radiation from the sun can damage your skin and cause cancer. A plain T-shirt offers some protection, but not as much as you might think—it may still allow between 7 and 20 percent of the sun's UV radiation through. Now, you can choose clothing made with chemicals that absorb UV radiation. These clothes offer better protection against the sun because they have a higher UPF (ultraviolet protection factor). They are also lightweight, so they're not as sticky in warm weather.

Design It Scientists also have created bug-repellent clothing, waterproof-breathable clothing, and insulated clothing. Research the climate in a biome of your choosing. Identify aspects of the climate that create problems for surviving in that biome. Design an item of clothing that might help protect humans in that climate. First, brainstorm potential solutions and select your best idea. Document your design with labeled drawings and then select materials for your design. Explain how you would go about testing and evaluating your design. See Appendix A on page 350 for more information about the design process.

6.NS.1, 6.NS.2, 6.NS.8, 6.DP.1–6.DP.8

Museum of Science.

Trees: Environmental Factories

Some of the most important members of your community don't volunteer. They consume huge amounts of water and they make a mess. Despite these drawbacks, these long-standing community members do their share. Who are these individuals? They're trees!

Keeping it clean: Trees remove pollutants from the air. Some researchers have calculated the value of the environmental cleaning services that trees provide. One study valued the air-cleaning service that trees in the Chicago area provide at more than $9 million every year.

Keeping it cool: Trees provide shade and lower air temperature by the process of transpiration. Pollutants, like ozone and smog, form more easily when air temperatures are high, so by keeping the air cool, trees also keep it clean.

Acting locally and globally: Trees help fight global environmental problems such as climate change. Trees remove carbon dioxide from the air and store the carbon as they grow. Experts estimate that urban trees in the United States remove more than 700 million tons of carbon from the air every year.

Helping the local economy: Trees are also good for business. One study found that shoppers spend more money in urban areas where trees are planted than they do in similar areas that don't have trees!

Research It Examine a topographical map of the area where you live. Compare it to an aerial photograph from a library or local archive. Identify areas with a lot of trees, and areas that you think could benefit from more trees. Create a proposal to plant trees in one of the areas you identified. What kinds of trees will you plant? What do those trees need in order to grow well?

 6.NS.1–6.NS.3, 6.NS.11, 6.DP.1–6.DP.5

Schools, clubs, and civic groups all over the United States volunteer to plant trees in their communities. ▶

APPENDIX A

The Design Process

Engineers are people who use scientific and technological knowledge to solve practical problems. To design new products, engineers usually follow the process described here, even though they may not follow these steps in the same order each time.

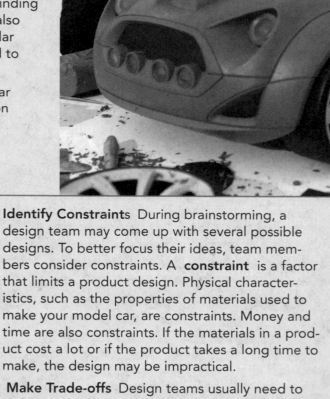

Lab zone®
Do the Indiana Design Project
Rubber Band Rovers

Identify a Need

Before engineers begin designing a new product, they must first identify the need they are trying to meet or the problem they want to solve. For example, suppose you are a member of a design team in a company that makes model cars. Your team has identified a need: a model car that is inexpensive and easy to assemble.

Research the Problem

Engineers often begin by gathering information that will help them with their new design. This research may include finding articles in books, magazines, or on the Internet. It may also involve talking to other engineers who have solved similar problems. Engineers often perform experiments related to the product they want to design.

For your model car, you could look at cars that are similar to the one you want to design. You might do research on the Internet. You could also test some materials to see whether they will work well in a model car.

Design a Solution

Brainstorm Ideas When engineers design new products, they usually work in teams. Design teams often hold brainstorming meetings in which any team member can contribute ideas. **Brainstorming** is a creative process in which one team member's suggestions often spark ideas in other group members. Brainstorming can lead to new approaches to solving a design problem.

Document the Process As the design team works, its members document, or keep a record of, the process. Having access to documentation enables others to repeat, or replicate, the process in the future. Design teams document their research sources, ideas, lists of materials, and so on because any part of the process may be a helpful resource later.

Identify Constraints During brainstorming, a design team may come up with several possible designs. To better focus their ideas, team members consider constraints. A **constraint** is a factor that limits a product design. Physical characteristics, such as the properties of materials used to make your model car, are constraints. Money and time are also constraints. If the materials in a product cost a lot or if the product takes a long time to make, the design may be impractical.

Make Trade-offs Design teams usually need to make trade-offs. In a **trade-off**, engineers give up one benefit of a proposed design in order to obtain another. In designing your model car, you might have to make trade-offs. For example, you might decide to give up the benefit of sturdiness in order to obtain the benefit of lower cost.

Select a Solution After considering the constraints and trade-offs of the possible designs, engineers then select one idea to develop further. That idea represents the solution that the team thinks best meets the need or solves the problem that was identified at the beginning of the process. The decision includes selecting the materials that will be used in the first attempt to build a product.

Create, Test, and Evaluate a Prototype

Once the team has chosen a design plan, the engineers build a prototype. A **prototype** is a working model used to test a design. Engineers evaluate the prototype to see whether it meets the goal. They must determine whether it works well, is easy to operate, is safe to use, and holds up to repeated use.

Part of the evaluation includes collecting data in the form of measurements. For example, think of your model car. Once you decide how to build your prototype, what would you want to know about it? You might want to measure how much baggage it could carry or how its shape affects its speed.

Troubleshoot and Redesign

Few prototypes work perfectly, which is why they need to be tested. Once a design team has tested a prototype, the members analyze the results and identify any problems. The team then tries to **troubleshoot,** or fix the design problems. Troubleshooting allows the team to redesign the prototype to improve on how well the solution meets the need.

Communicate the Solution

A team needs to communicate the final design to the people who will manufacture and use the product. To do this, teams may use sketches, detailed drawings, computer simulations, and word descriptions. The team may also present the evidence that was collected when the prototype was tested. This evidence may include mathematical representations, such as graphs and data tables, that support the choice for the final design.

Academic Standards for Science

The Design Process

6.DP.1 Identify a need or problem to be solved.

6.DP.2 Brainstorm potential solutions.

6.DP.3 Document the design throughout the entire design process so that it can be replicated in a portfolio/notebook with drawings including labels.

6.DP.4 Select a solution to the need or problem.

6.DP.5 Select the most appropriate materials to develop a solution that will meet the need.

6.DP.6 Create the solution through a prototype.

6.DP.7 Test and evaluate how well the solution meets the goal.

6.DP.8 Evaluate and test the design using measurement.

6.DP.9 Present evidence using mathematical representations (graphs, data tables).

6.DP.10 Communicate the solution including evidence using mathematical representations (graphs, data tables), drawings or prototypes.

6.DP.11 Redesign to improve the solution based on how well the solution meets the need.

Science, Engineering and Technology

6.4 Apply a form of energy to design and construct a simple mechanical device.

6.4.1 Understand how to apply potential or kinetic energy to power a simple device.

6.4.2 Construct a simple device that uses potential or kinetic energy to perform work.

6.4.3 Describe the transfer of energy amongst energy interactions.

Safety Symbols

These symbols warn of possible dangers in the laboratory and remind you to work carefully.

 Safety Goggles Wear safety goggles to protect your eyes in any activity involving chemicals, flames or heating, or glassware.

 Lab Apron Wear a laboratory apron to protect your skin and clothing from damage.

 Breakage Handle breakable materials, such as glassware, with care. Do not touch broken glassware.

 Heat-Resistant Gloves Use an oven mitt or other hand protection when handling hot materials such as hot plates or hot glassware.

 Plastic Gloves Wear disposable plastic gloves when working with harmful chemicals and organisms. Keep your hands away from your face, and dispose of the gloves according to your teacher's instructions.

 Heating Use a clamp or tongs to pick up hot glassware. Do not touch hot objects with your bare hands.

 Flames Before you work with flames, tie back loose hair and clothing. Follow instructions from your teacher about lighting and extinguishing flames.

 No Flames When using flammable materials, make sure there are no flames, sparks, or other exposed heat sources present.

 Corrosive Chemical Avoid getting acid or other corrosive chemicals on your skin or clothing or in your eyes. Do not inhale the vapors. Wash your hands after the activity.

 Poison Do not let any poisonous chemical come into contact with your skin, and do not inhale its vapors. Wash your hands when you are finished with the activity.

 Fumes Work in a well-ventilated area when harmful vapors may be involved. Avoid inhaling vapors directly. Only test an odor when directed to do so by your teacher, and use a wafting motion to direct the vapor toward your nose.

 Sharp Object Scissors, scalpels, knives, needles, pins, and tacks can cut your skin. Always direct a sharp edge or point away from yourself and others.

 Animal Safety Treat live or preserved animals or animal parts with care to avoid harming the animals or yourself. Wash your hands when you are finished with the activity.

 Plant Safety Handle plants only as directed by your teacher. If you are allergic to certain plants, tell your teacher; do not do an activity involving those plants. Avoid touching harmful plants such as poison ivy. Wash your hands when you are finished with the activity.

 Electric Shock To avoid electric shock, never use electrical equipment around water, or when the equipment is wet or your hands are wet. Be sure cords are untangled and cannot trip anyone. Unplug equipment not in use.

 Physical Safety When an experiment involves physical activity, avoid injuring yourself or others. Alert your teacher if there is any reason you should not participate.

 Disposal Dispose of chemicals and other laboratory materials safely. Follow the instructions from your teacher.

 Hand Washing Wash your hands thoroughly when finished with an activity. Use soap and warm water. Rinse well.

 General Safety Awareness When this symbol appears, follow the instructions provided. When you are asked to develop your own procedure in a lab, have your teacher approve your plan before you go further.

Using a Laboratory Balance

The laboratory balance is an important tool in scientific investigations. You can use a balance to determine the masses of materials that you study or experiment with in the laboratory.

Different kinds of balances are used in the laboratory. One kind of balance is the triple-beam balance. The balance that you may use in your science class is probably similar to the balance illustrated in this Appendix. **To use the balance properly, you should learn the name, location, and function of each part of the balance you are using. What kind of balance do you have in your science class?**

The Triple-Beam Balance

The triple-beam balance is a single-pan balance with three beams calibrated in grams. The back, or 100-gram, beam is divided into ten units of 10 grams each. The middle, or 500-gram, beam is divided into five units of 100 grams each. The front, or 10-gram, beam is divided into ten units of 1 gram each. Each of the units on the front beam is further divided into units of 0.1 gram. What is the largest mass you could find with a triple-beam balance?

The following procedure can be used to find the mass of an object with a triple-beam balance:

1. Place the object on the pan.
2. Move the rider on the middle beam notch by notch until the horizontal pointer on the right drops below zero. Move the rider back one notch.
3. Move the rider on the back beam notch by notch until the pointer again drops below zero. Move the rider back one notch.
4. Slowly slide the rider along the front beam until the pointer stops at the zero point.
5. The mass of the object is equal to the sum of the readings on the three beams.

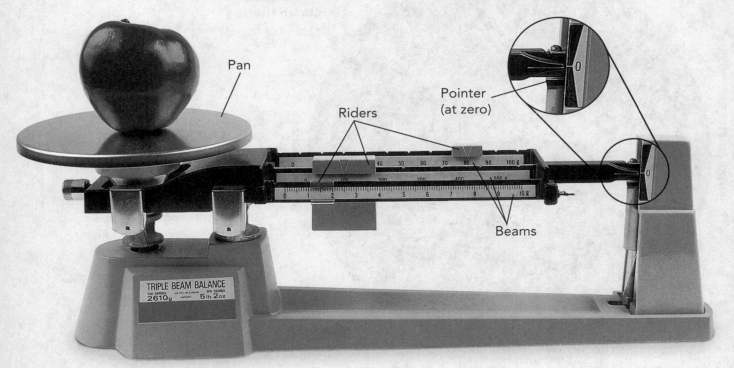

Pan

Riders

Pointer
(at zero)

Beams

TRIPLE BEAM BALANCE
700 SERIES   U.S. PAT. NO. 5,110,116   800 SERIES
2610g   CAPACITY   5 lb 2 oz

Star Charts

Use these star charts to locate bright stars and major constellations in the night sky at different times of year. Choose the appropriate star chart for the current season.

Autumn Sky This chart works best at the following dates and times: September 1 at 10:00 P.M., October 1 at 8:00 P.M., or November 1 at 6:00 P.M. Look for the constellations Ursa Minor (the Little Dipper) and Cassiopeia in the northern sky, and for the star Deneb, which is nearly overhead in autumn.

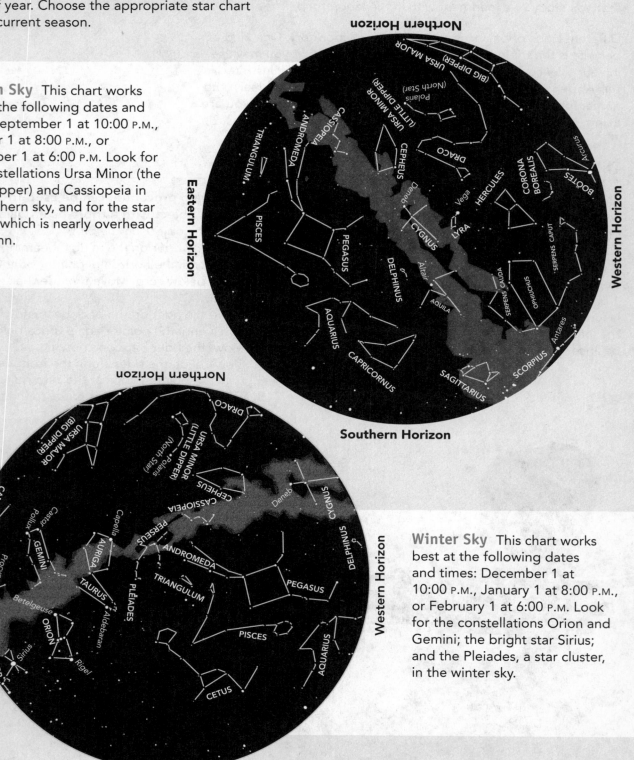

Winter Sky This chart works best at the following dates and times: December 1 at 10:00 P.M., January 1 at 8:00 P.M., or February 1 at 6:00 P.M. Look for the constellations Orion and Gemini; the bright star Sirius; and the Pleiades, a star cluster, in the winter sky.

How to Use the Star Charts

Using a flashlight and a compass, hold the appropriate chart and turn it so that the direction you are facing is at the bottom of the chart. These star charts work best at 34° north latitude, but can be used at other central latitudes.

Spring Sky This chart works best at the following dates and times: March 1 at 10:00 P.M., March 15 at 9:00 P.M., or April 1 at 8:00 P.M. Look for the constellations Ursa Major (which contains the Big Dipper), Boötes, and Leo in the spring sky. The bright stars Arcturus and Spica can be seen in the east.

Northern Horizon

Eastern Horizon

Western Horizon

Southern Horizon

DRACO · URSA MINOR (LITTLE DIPPER) · Polaris (North Star) · CEPHEUS · CASSIOPEIA · ANDROMEDA · TRIANGULUM · PERSEUS · Capella · ARIES · BOÖTES · URSA MAJOR (BIG DIPPER) · Arcturus · AURIGA · TAURUS · Pleiades · Castor · Pollux · GEMINI · Aldebaran · ERIDANUS · CANCER · LEO · Regulus · Procyon · Betelgeuse · ORION · VIRGO · CANIS MINOR · Sirius · Rigel · Spica · CANIS MAJOR · LEPUS · CORVUS · HYDRA · COLUMBA · VELA

Northern Horizon

Eastern Horizon

Western Horizon

Southern Horizon

CASSIOPEIA · CEPHEUS · Deneb · CYGNUS · DRACO · URSA MINOR (LITTLE DIPPER) · Polaris (North Star) · GEMINI · DELPHINUS · LYRA · Vega · HERCULES · CORONA BOREALIS · URSA MAJOR (BIG DIPPER) · Castor · Pollux · CANCER · Altair · AQUILA · SERPENS CAUDA · SERPENS CAPUT · OPHIUCHUS · BOÖTES · Arcturus · LEO · Regulus · SAGITTARIUS · VIRGO · HYDRA · Spica · SCORPIUS · Antares · LIBRA · CORVUS · CENTAURUS

Summer Sky This chart works best at the following dates and times: May 15 at 11:00 P.M., June 1 at 10:00 P.M., or June 15 at 9:00 P.M. Look for the bright star Arcturus in the constellation Boötes overhead in early summer. Toward the east, look for the bright stars Vega, Altair, and Deneb, which form a triangle.

355

GLOSSARY

A

abiotic factor A nonliving part of an organism's habitat. (276)
factor abiótico La parte sin vida del hábitat de un organismo.

accuracy How close a measurement is to the true or accepted value. (50)
exactitud Cuán cerca está una medida del valor verdadero o aceptado.

adaptation An inherited behavior or physical characteristic that helps an organism survive and reproduce in its environment. (289)
adaptación Comportamiento o característica física hereditaria que le permite a un organismo sobrevivir y reproducirse en su ambiente.

amorphous solids A solid made up of particles that are not arranged in a regular pattern. (126)
sólido amorfo Sólido constituido por partículas que no están dispuestas en un patrón regular.

anomalous data Data that do not fit with the rest of a data set. (54)
datos anómalos Información que no encaja con los otros datos de un conjunto de datos.

asteroid One of the rocky objects revolving around the sun that are too small and numerous to be considered planets. (262)
asteroide Uno de los cuerpos rocosos que se mueven alrededor del Sol y que son demasiado pequeños y numerosos como para ser considerados planetas.

asteroid belt The region of the solar system between the orbits of Mars and Jupiter, where many asteroids are found. (259)
cinturón de asteroides Región del sistema solar entre las órbitas de Marte y Júpiter, donde se encuentran muchos asteroides.

astronomical unit A unit of distance equal to the average distance between Earth and the sun, about 150 million kilometers. (231)
unidad astronómica Unidad de medida equivalente a la distancia media entre la Tierra y el Sol, aproximadamente 150 millones de kilómetros.

atom The basic particle from which all elements are made; the smallest particle of an element that has the properties of that element. (94)
átomo Partícula básica de la que todos los elementos están formados; partícula más pequeña de un elemento, que tiene las propiedades de ese elemento.

autotroph An organism that is able to capture energy from sunlight or chemicals and use it to produce its own food. (314)
autótrofo Organismo capaz de capturar y usar la energía solar o de sustancias químicas para producir su propio alimento.

axis An imaginary line that passes through a planet's center and its north and south poles, about which the planet rotates. (191)
eje Línea imaginaria alrededor de la cual gira un planeta, y que atraviesa su centro y sus dos polos, norte y sur.

B

biome A group of ecosystems with similar climates and organisms. (334)
bioma Grupo de ecosistemas con organismos y climas parecidos.

biotic factors A living or once living part of an organism's habitat. (276)
factor biótico Parte viva, o que alguna vez tuvo vida, del hábitat de un organismo.

birth rate The number of births per 1,000 individuals for a certain time period. (281)
tasa de natalidad Número de nacimientos por 1.000 individuos durante un período de tiempo determinado.

boiling Vaporization that occurs at and below the surface of a liquid. (135)
ebullición Evaporación que ocurre en y bajo la superficie de un líquido.

boiling point The temperature at which a liquid boils. (135)
punto de ebullición Temperatura a la cual hierve un líquido.

boreal forests Dense forest of evergreens located in the upper regions of the Northern Hemisphere. (340)
bosque boreal Bosque denso donde abundan las plantas coníferas y que se encuentra en las regiones más al norte del Hemisferio Norte.

Boyle's law A principle that describes the relationship between the pressure and volume of a gas at constant temperature. (144)
ley de Boyle Principio que describe la relación entre la presión y el volumen de un gas a una temperatura constante.

brainstorming A process in which group members freely suggest any creative solutions that come to mind. (350)
lluvia de ideas Proceso mediante el cual los miembros de un grupo sugieren libremente cualquier solución creativa que se les ocurre.

C

calendar A system of organizing time that defines the beginning, length, and divisions of a year. (192)
calendario Sistema de organización del tiempo que define el principio, la duración y las divisiones de un año.

canopy A leafy roof formed by tall trees in a rain forest. (337)
dosel Techo de hojas que forman los árboles en la selva tropical.

carnivore A consumer that obtains energy by eating only animals. (320)
carnívoro Consumidor que adquiere su energía al alimentarse de animales solamente.

carrying capacity The largest population that a particular environment can support. (286)
capacidad de carga Población mayor que un ambiente en particular puede mantener.

Charles's law A principle that describes the relationship between the temperature and volume of a gas at constant pressure. (142)
ley de Charles Principio que describe la relación entre la temperatura y el volumen de un gas a una presión constante.

chemical bond The force of attraction that holds two atoms together. (94)
cambio químico Cambio en el cual una o más sustancias se combinan o se descomponen para formar sustancias nuevas.

chemical change A change in which one or more substances combine or break apart to form new substances. (107)
cambio químico Cambio en el cual una o más sustancias se combinan o se descomponen para formar sustancias nuevas.

chemical energy A form of potential energy that is stored in chemical bonds between atoms. (111)
energía química Forma de energía potencial almacenada en los enlaces químicos de los átomos.

chemical formula Symbols that show the elements in a compound and the ratio of atoms. (95)
fórmula química Símbolos que muestran los elementos de un compuesto y la cantidad de átomos.

chemical property A characteristic of a substance that describes its ability to change into different substances. (90)
propiedad química Característica de una sustancia que describe su capacidad de convertirse en sustancias diferentes.

chemistry The study of the properties of matter and how matter changes. (89)
química Estudio de las propiedades de la materia y de sus cambios.

chlorophyll A green photosynthetic pigment found in the chloroplasts of plants, algae, and some bacteria. (315)
clorofila Pigmento verde fotosintético de los cloroplastos de las plantas, algas y algunas bacterias.

chromosphere The middle layer of the sun's atmosphere. (238)
cromósfera Capa central de la atmósfera solar.

classifying The process of grouping together items that are alike in some way. (7)
clasificación Proceso de agrupar cosas según sus semejanzas.

climate The average annual conditions of temperature, precipitation, winds, and clouds in an area. (334)
clima Condiciones promedio anuales de temperatura, precipitación, viento y nubosidad de un área.

coma The fuzzy outer layer of a comet. (261)
coma Capa exterior y difusa de un cometa.

comet A loose collection of ice and dust that orbits the sun, typically in a long, narrow orbit. (185)
cometa Cuerpo poco denso de hielo y polvo que orbita alrededor del Sol. Generalmente su órbita es larga y estrecha.

commensalism A type of symbiosis between two species in which one species benefits and the other species is neither helped nor harmed. (296)
comensalismo Tipo de relación simbiótica entre dos especies en la cual una especie se beneficia y la otra especie ni se beneficia ni sufre daño.

community All the different populations that live together in a particular area. (278)
comunidad Todas las poblaciones distintas que habitan en un área específica.

competition The struggle between organisms to survive as they attempt to use the same limited resources in the same place at the same time. (291)
competencia Lucha por la supervivencia entre organismos que se alimentan de los mismos recursos limitados en el mismo lugar y al mismo tiempo.

compound A substance made of two or more elements chemically combined in a specific ratio, or proportion. (95)
compuesto Sustancia formada por dos o más elementos combinados químicamente en una razón o proporción específica.

GLOSSARY

condensation The change in state from a gas to a liquid. (136)
condensación Cambio del estado gaseoso al estado líquido.

coniferous trees A tree that produces its seeds in cones and that has needle-shaped leaves coated in a waxy substance to reduce water loss. (340)
árbol conífero Árbol que produce sus semillas en piñones y que tiene hojas en forma de aguja y cubiertas por una sustancia cerosa que reduce la pérdida de agua.

constellation A pattern or grouping of stars that people imagine to represent a figure or object. (186)
constelación Patrón de estrellas que se dice se asemeja a una figura u objeto.

constraint Any factor that limits a design. (350)
restricción Cualquier factor que limita un diseño.

consumer An organism that obtains energy by feeding on other organisms. (320)
consumidor Organismo que obtiene energía al alimentarse de otros organismos.

controlled experiment An experiment in which only one variable is manipulated at a time. (22)
experimento controlado Experimento en el cual sólo se manipula una variable a la vez.

convection zone The outermost layer of the sun's interior. (237)
zona de convección Capa más superficial del interior del Sol.

core The central region of the sun, where nuclear fusion takes place. (237)
núcleo Región central del Sol, donde ocurre la fusión nuclear.

corona The outer layer of the sun's atmosphere. (239)
corona Capa externa de la atmósfera solar.

crater A large round pit caused by the impact of a meteoroid. (213)
cráter Gran hoyo redondo que se forma por el impacto de un meteorito.

crystalline solid A solid that is made up of crystals in which particles are arranged in a regular, repeating pattern. (126)
sólido cristalino Sólido constituido por cristales en los que las partículas están colocadas en un patrón regular repetitivo.

cultural bias An outlook influenced by the beliefs, social forms, and traits of a group. (12)
prejuicio cultural Opinión influenciada por las creencias, costumbres sociales y características de un grupo.

D

data Facts, figures, and other evidence gathered through observations. (23)
dato Hechos, cifras u otra evidencia reunida por medio de observaciones.

death rate The number of deaths per 1,000 individuals for a certain time period. (281)
tasa de mortalidad Número de muertes per 1.000 individuos durante un período de tiempo determinado.

deciduous tree A tree that sheds its leaves during a particular season and grows new ones each year. (339)
árbol caducifolio Árbol que pierde las hojas durante una estación específica y al que le salen hojas nuevas cada año.

decomposer An organism that gets energy by breaking down biotic wastes and dead organisms, and returns raw materials to the soil and water. (321)
descomponedor Organismo que obtiene energía al descomponer desechos bióticos y organismos muertos, y que devuelve materia prima al suelo y al agua.

deductive reasoning A way to explain things by starting with a general idea and then applying the idea to a specific observation. (15)
razonamiento deductivo Manera de explicar las cosas en la que se aplica una idea general a una observación específica.

density The measurement of how much mass of a substance is contained in a given volume. (44)
densidad Medida de la masa de una sustancia que tiene un volumen dado.

dependent variable The factor that changes as a result of changes to the independent variable in an experiment; also called responding variable. (21)
variable dependiente factor que cambia a causa de los cambios de la variable independiente de un experimento; también se denomina variable de respuesta.

desert A dry region that on average receives less than 25 centimeters of precipitation per year. (335)
desierto Región seca en la que se registra un promedio menor de 25 centímetros de precipitación anual.

directly proportional A term used to describe the relationship between two variables whose graph is a straight line passing through the point (0, 0). (143)
directamente proporcional Término empleado para describir la relación entre dos variables cuya gráfica forma una línea recta que pasa por el punto (0, 0).

dwarf planet An object that orbits the sun and is spherical, but has not cleared the area of its orbit. (232)

planeta enano Un cuerpo esférico que orbita alrededor del Sol, pero que no ha despejado las proximidades de su órbita.

E

eclipse The partial or total blocking of one object in space by another. (205)

eclipse Bloqueo parcial o total de un cuerpo en el espacio por otro.

ecology The study of how organisms interact with each other and their environment. (279)

ecología Estudio de la forma en que los organismos interactúan entre sí y con su medio ambiente.

ecosystem The community of organisms that live in a particular area, along with their nonliving environment. (279)

ecosistema Comunidad de organismos que viven en un área específica, y el medio ambiente que los rodea.

elastic potential energy The energy of stretched or compressed objects. (161)

energía elástica potencial Energía de los cuerpos estirados o comprimidos.

electrical energy The energy of electric charges. (166)

energía eléctrica Energía de las cargas eléctricas.

electromagnetic energy The energy of light and other forms of radiation, which travels through space as waves. (167)

energía electromagnética Energía de la luz y otras formas de radiación, que viaja a través del espacio en forma de ondas.

element A pure substance that cannot be broken down into other substances by chemical or physical means. (93)

elemento Sustancia que no se puede descomponer en otras sustancias por medios químicos o físicos.

ellipse An oval shape, which may be elongated or nearly circular; the shape of the planets' orbits. (229)

elipse Forma ovalada que puede ser alargada o casi circular; la forma de la órbita de los planetas.

emergent layer The tallest layer of the rain forest that receives the most sunlight. (337)

capa emergente Capa superior de la selva tropical, que recibe la mayor cantidad de luz solar.

emigration Movement of individuals out of a population's area. (282)

emigración Traslado de individuos fuera del área de una población.

endothermic change A change in which energy is absorbed. (111)

cambio endotérmico Cambio en el que se absorbe energía.

energy The ability to do work or cause change. (156)

energía Capacidad para realizar un trabajo o producir cambios.

energy pyramid diagram that shows the amount of energy that moves from one feeding level to another in a food web. (324)

pirámide de energía Diagrama que muestra la cantidad de energía que fluye de un nivel de alimentación a otro en una red alimentaria.

energy transformation A change from one form of energy to another; also called an energy conversion. (168)

transformación de la energía Cambio de una forma de energía a otra; también se le llama conversión de energía.

equinox Either of the two days of the year on which neither hemisphere is tilted toward or away from the sun. (196)

equinoccio Cualquiera de los de dos días del año en el que ningún hemisferio se retrae o inclina hacia el Sol.

estimate An approximation of a number based on reasonable assumptions. (49)

estimación Aproximación de un número basada en conjeturas razonables.

ethics The study of principles about what is right and wrong, fair and unfair. (13)

ética Estudio de los principios de qué es lo bueno y lo malo, lo justo y lo injusto.

evaluating Comparing observations and data to reach a conclusion about them. (8)

evaluar Comparar observaciones y datos para llegar a una conclusión.

evaporation The process by which molecules at the surface of a liquid absorb enough energy to change to a gas. (135)

evaporación Proceso mediante el cual las moléculas en la superficie de un líquido absorben suficiente energía para pasar al estado gaseoso.

exothermic change A change in which energy is released. (111)
reacción exotérmica Reacción que libera energía generalmente en forma de calor.

experimental bias A mistake in the design of an experiment that makes a particular result more likely. (12)
prejuicio experimental Error en el diseño de un experimento que aumenta la probabilidad de un resultado.

F

feedback Output that changes a system or allows the system to adjust itself. (64)
retroalimentación Salida que cambia un sistema o permite que éste se ajuste.

field Any area outside of the laboratory. (76)
campo Cualquier área fuera del laboratorio.

fluid Any substance that can flow. (127)
fluido Cualquier sustancia que puede fluir.

food chain A series of events in an ecosystem in which organisms transfer energy by eating and by being eaten. (322)
cadena alimentaria Serie de sucesos en un ecosistema por medio de los cuales los organismos transmiten energía al comer o al ser comidos por otros.

food web The pattern of overlapping feeding relationships or food chains among the various organisms in an ecosystem. (322)
red alimentaria Patrón de las relaciones de alimentación intercruzadas o de cadenas alimentarias entre los diferentes organismos de un ecosistema.

force A push or pull exerted on an object. (198)
fuerza Empuje o atracción que se ejerce sobre un cuerpo.

freezing The change in state from a liquid to a solid. (134)
congelación Cambio del estado líquido al sólido.

G

gas A state of matter with no definite shape or volume. (129)
gas Estado de la materia sin forma ni volumen definidos.

gas giant The name often given to the outer planets: Jupiter, Saturn, Uranus, and Neptune. (250)
gigantes gaseosos Nombre que normalmente se da a los cuatro planetas exteriores: Júpiter, Saturno, Urano y Neptuno.

geocentric Term describing a model of the universe in which Earth is at the center of the revolving planets and stars. (227)
geocéntrico Término que describe un modelo del universo en el cual la Tierra se encuentra al centro de los planetas y estrellas que circulan a su alrededor.

graph A picture of information from a data table; shows the relationship between variables. (56)
gráfica Representación visual de la información de una tabla de datos; muestra la relación entre las variables.

grassland An area populated mostly by grasses and other nonwoody plants that gets 25 to 75 centimeters of rain each year. (338)
pradera Área poblada principalmente por hierbas y otras plantas no leñosas, y donde caen entre 25 y 75 centímetros de lluvia cada año.

gravitational potential energy Potential energy that depends on the height of an object. (160)
energía gravitatoria potencial Energía potencial que depende de la altura de un cuerpo.

gravity The attractive force between objects; the force that moves objects downhill. (199)
gravedad Fuerza que atrae a los cuerpos entre sí; fuerza que mueve un cuerpo cuesta abajo.

greenhouse effect The trapping of heat near a planet's surface by certain gases in the planet's atmosphere. (246)
efecto invernadero Retención de calor cerca de la superficie de un planeta debido a la presencia de ciertos gases en la atmósfera.

H

habitat An environment that provides the things a specific organism needs to live, grow, and reproduce. (275)
hábitat Medio que provee lo que un organismo específico necesita para vivir, crecer y reproducirse.

heliocentric Term describing a model of the solar system in which Earth and the other planets revolve around the sun. (228)
heliocéntrico Término que describe un modelo del universo en el cual la Tierra y los otros planetas giran alrededor del Sol.

herbivores A consumer that obtains energy by eating only plants. (320)
herbívoro Consumidor que come sólo plantas para obtener energía.

heterotroph An organism that cannot make its own food and gets food by consuming other living things. (314)
heterótrofo Organismo que no puede producir sus propios alimentos y que se alimenta al consumir otros seres vivos.

host An organism that a parasite lives with, in, or on, and which provides a source of energy or a suitable environment for the parasite to live. (296)
huésped Organismo dentro del o sobre el cual vive un parásito y que provee una fuente de energía o un medio ambiente apropiado para la existencia del parásito.

hypothesis A possible explanation for a set of observations or answer to a scientific question; must be testable. (20)
hipótesis Explicación posible de un conjunto de observaciones o respuesta a una pregunta científica; se debe poder poner a prueba.

I

immigration Movement of individuals into a population's area. (282)
inmigración Movimiento de individuos al área de una población.

independent variable The one factor that a scientist changes during an experiment; also called manipulated variable. (21)
variable independiente el único factor que un científico altera durante un experimento; también se denomina variable manipulada.

inductive reasoning Using specific observations to make generalizations. (15)
razonamiento inductivo Usar observaciones específicas para hacer generalizaciones.

inertia The tendency of an object to resist a change in motion. (200)
inercia Tendencia de un cuerpo de resistirse a cambios de movimiento.

inferring The process of making an inference, an interpretation based on observations and prior knowledge. (6)
inferir Proceso de hacer una inferencia; interpretación basada en observaciones y conocimientos previos.

input Material, energy, or information that goes into a system. (64)
entrada Material, energía o informacion que se agrega a un sistema.

International System of Units A system of units used by scientists to measure the properties of matter. (39)
Sistema Internacional de Unidades (SI) Sistema de unidades que los científicos usan para medir las propiedades de la materia.

inversely proportional A term used to describe the relationship between two variables whose product is constant. (145)
inversamente proporcional Término usado para describir la relación entre dos variables cuyo producto es constante.

K

kinetic energy Energy that an object has due to its motion. (158)
energía cinética Energía que tiene un cuerpo debido a su movimiento.

Kuiper belt A region where many small objects orbit the sun and that stretches from beyond the orbit of Neptune to about 100 times Earth's distance from the sun. (259)
cinturón de Kuiper Región en la cual muchos cuerpos pequeños giran alrededor del Sol y que se extiende desde más allá de la órbita de Neptuno hasta aproximadamente cien veces la distancia entre la Tierra y el Sol.

L

law of conservation of energy The rule that energy cannot be created or destroyed. (172)
ley de conservación de la energía Regla que dice que la energía no se puede crear ni destruir.

law of conservation of mass The principle that the total amount of matter is neither created nor destroyed during any chemical or physical change. (109)
ley de conservación de la masa Principio que establece que la cantidad total de materia no se crea ni se destruye durante cambios químicos o físicos.

law of universal gravitation The scientific law that states that every object in the universe attracts every other object. (199)
ley de gravitación universal Ley científica que establece que todos los cuerpos del universo se atraen entre sí.

limiting factor An environmental factor that causes a population to decrease in size. (285)
factor limitante Factor ambiental que causa la disminución del tamaño de una población.

linear graph A line graph in which the data points yield a straight line. (60)
gráfica lineal Gráfica en la cual los puntos de los datos forman una línea recta.

liquid A state of matter that has no definite shape but has a definite volume. (127)
líquido Estado de la materia que no tiene forma definida pero sí volumen definido.

lunar eclipse The blocking of sunlight to the moon that occurs when Earth is directly between the sun and the moon. (206)
eclipse lunar Bloqueo de la luz solar que ilumina la Luna que ocurre cuando la Tierra se interpone entre el Sol y la Luna.

M

---

making models The process of creating representations of complex objects or processes. (8)
hacer modelos Proceso de crear representaciones de objetos o procesos complejos.

maria Dark, flat areas on the moon's surface formed from huge ancient lava flows. (213)
maria Áreas oscuras y llanas de la superficie lunar formadas por enormes flujos de lava antiguos.

mass A measure of how much matter is in an object. (41)
masa Medida de cuánta materia hay en un cuerpo.

matter Anything that has mass and takes up space. (89)
materia Cualquier cosa que tiene masa y ocupa un espacio.

mean The numerical average of a set of data. (53)
media Promedio numérico de un conjunto de datos.

mechanical energy Kinetic or potential energy associated with the motion or position of an object. (162)
energía mecánica Energía cinética o potencial asociada con el movimiento o la posición de un cuerpo.

median The middle number in a set of data. (53)
mediana Número del medio de un conjunto de datos.

melting The change in state from a solid to a liquid. (133)
fusión Cambio del estado sólido a líquido.

melting point The temperature at which a substance changes from a solid to a liquid; the same as the freezing point, or temperature at which a liquid changes to a solid. (133)
punto de fusión Temperatura a la que una sustancia cambia de estado sólido a líquido; es lo mismo que el punto de congelación (la temperatura a la que un líquido se vuelve sólido).

meteor A streak of light in the sky produced by the burning of a meteoroid in Earth's atmosphere. (185)
meteoro Rayo de luz en el cielo producido por el incendio de un meteoroide en la atmósfera terrestre.

meteorite A meteoroid that passes through the atmosphere and hits Earth's surface. (263)
meteorito Meteoroide que pasa por la atmósfera y toca la superficie terrestre.

meteoroids A chunk of rock or dust in space, generally smaller than an asteroid. (213)
meteoroide Un trozo de roca o polvo, generalmente más pequeño que un asteroide, que existe en el espacio.

metric system A system of measurement based on the number 10. (39)
sistema métrico Sistema de medidas basado en el número 10.

mixture Two or more substances that are together in the same place but their atoms are not chemically bonded. (96)
mezcla Dos o más sustancias que están en el mismo lugar pero cuyos átomos no están químicamente enlazados.

mode The number that appears most often in a list of numbers. (53)
moda Número que aparece con más frecuencia en una lista de números.

model A representation of a complex object or process, used to help people understand a concept that they cannot observe directly. (63)
modelo Representación de un objeto o proceso complejo que se usa para explicar un concepto que no se puede observar directamente.

molecule A neutral group of two or more atoms held together by covalent bonds. (94)
molécula Grupo neutral de dos o más átomos unidos por medio de enlaces covalentes.

mutualism A type of symbiosis in which both species benefit from living together. (295)
mutualismo Tipo de relación simbiótica entre dos especies en la cual ambas especies se benefician de su convivencia.

N

natural selection The process by which organisms that are best adapted to their environment are most likely to survive and reproduce. (289)
selección natural Proceso por el cual los organismos que se adaptan mejor a su ambiente tienen mayor probabilidad de sobrevivir y reproducirse.

neap tide The tide with the least difference between consecutive low and high tides. (210)
marea muerta Marea con la mínima diferencia entre las mareas altas y bajas consecutivas.

Newton's first law of motion The scientific law that states that an object at rest will stay at rest and an object in motion will stay in motion with a constant speed and direction unless acted on by a force. (200)
Primera ley de movimiento de Newton Ley científica que establece que un cuerpo en reposo se mantendrá en reposo y un cuerpo en movimiento se mantendrá en movimiento con una velocidad y dirección constantes a menos que se ejerza una fuerza sobre él.

niche How an organism makes its living and interacts with the biotic and abiotic factors in its habitat. (290)
nicho Forma en que un organismo vive e interactúa con los factores bióticos y abióticos de su hábitat.

nitrogen fixation The process of changing free nitrogen gas into nitrogen compounds that plants can absorb and use. (330)
fijación del nitrógeno Proceso que consiste en transformar el gas de nitrógeno libre en compuestos de nitrógeno que las plantas pueden absorber y usar.

nonlinear graph A line graph in which the data points do not fall along a straight line. (60)
gráfica no lineal Gráfica lineal en la que los puntos de datos no forman una línea recta.

nuclear energy The potential energy stored in the nucleus of an atom. (165)
energía nuclear Energía potencial almacenada en el núcleo de un átomo.

nuclear fusion The process in which two atomic nuclei combine to form a larger nucleus, forming a heavier element and releasing huge amounts of energy; the process by which energy is produced in stars. (237)
fusión nuclear Unión de dos núcleos atómicos que produce un elemento con una mayor masa atómica y que libera una gran cantidad de energía; el proceso mediante el cual las estrellas producen energía.

nucleus 1. In cells, a large oval organelle that contains the cell's genetic material in the form of DNA and controls many of the cell's activities. **2.** The central core of an atom which contains protons and neutrons. **3.** The solid core of a comet. (261)
núcleo 1. En las células, orgánulo grande y ovalado que contiene el material genético de la célula en forma de ADN y que controla muchas de las funciones celulares. **2.** Parte central del átomo que contiene los protones y los neutrones. **4.** Centro sólido de un cometa.

O

objective 1. A lens that gathers light from an object and forms a real image. **2.** Describes the act of decision-making or drawing conclusions based on available evidence. (14)
objetivo 1. Lente que reúne la luz de un objeto y forma una imagen real. **2.** Describe el acto de tomar una decisión o llegar a una conclusión basándose en la evidencia disponible.

observing The process of using one or more of your senses to gather information. (5)
observar Proceso de usar uno o más de tus sentidos para reunir información.

omnivore A consumer that obtains energy by eating both plants and animals. (320)
omnívoro Consumidor que come plantas y animales para obtener energía.

Oort cloud A spherical region of comets that surrounds the solar system. (259)
nube de Oort Región esférica de cometas que rodea al sistema solar.

orbit The path of an object as it revolves around another object in space. (192)
órbita Trayectoria de un cuerpo a medida que gira alrededor de otro en el espacio.

organism A living thing. (275)
organismo Un ser vivo.

output Material, energy, result, or product that comes out of a system. (64)
salida Material, energía, resultado o producto que un sistema produce.

GLOSSARY

P

parasite An organism that benefits by living with, on, or in a host in a parasitism interaction. (296)
parásito Organismo que se beneficia al vivir dentro de o sobre un huésped en una relación parasítica.

parasitism A type of symbiosis in which one organism lives with, on, or in a host and harms it. (296)
parasitismo Tipo de relación simbiótica en la cual un organismo vive con o en un huésped y le hace daño.

penumbra The part of a shadow surrounding the darkest part. (205)
penumbra Parte de la sombra que rodea su parte más oscura.

percent error A calculation used to determine how accurate, or close to the true value, an experimental value really is. (52)
error porcentual Cálculo usado para determinar cuán exacto, o cercano al valor verdadero, es realmente un valor experimental.

permafrost Permanently frozen soil found in the tundra biome climate region. (341)
permagélido Suelo que está permanentemente congelado y que se encuentra en el bioma climático de la tundra.

personal bias An outlook influenced by a person's likes and dislikes. (12)
prejuicio personal Perspectiva influenciada por las preferencias de un individuo.

phase One of the different apparent shapes of the moon as seen from Earth. (202)
fase Una de las distintas formas aparentes de la Luna vistas desde la Tierra.

photosphere The inner layer of the sun's atmosphere that gives off its visible light; the sun's surface. (238)
fotósfera Capa más interna de la atmósfera solar que provoca la luz que vemos; superficie del Sol.

photosynthesis The process by which plants and other autotrophs capture and use light energy to make food from carbon dioxide and water. (314)
fotosíntesis Proceso por el cual las plantas y otros autótrofos absorben la energía de la luz para producir alimentos a partir del dióxido de carbono y el agua.

physical change A change that alters the form or appearance of a material but does not make the material into another substance. (105)
cambio físico Cambio que altera la forma o apariencia de un material, pero que no convierte el material en otra sustancia.

physical property A characteristic of a pure substance that can be observed without changing it into another substance. (90)
propiedad física Característica de una sustancia pura que se puede observar sin convertirla en otra sustancia.

pioneer species The first species to populate an area during succession. (299)
especies pioneras La primera especie que puebla un área durante la sucesión.

planet An object that orbits a star, is large enough to have become rounded by its own gravity, and has cleared the area of its orbit. (185)
planeta Cuerpo que orbita alrededor de una estrella, que tiene suficiente masa como para permitir que su propia gravedad le dé una forma casi redonda, y que además ha despejado las proximidades de su órbita.

planetesimals One of the small asteroid-like bodies that formed the building blocks of the planets. (234)
planetesimal Uno de los cuerpos pequeños parecidos a asteroides que dieron origen a los planetas.

population All the members of one species living in the same area. (278)
población Todos los miembros de una especie que viven en el mismo lugar.

population density The number of individuals in an area of a specific size. (284)
densidad de población Número de individuos en un área de un tamaño específico.

potential energy The energy an object has because of its position; also the internal stored energy of an object, such as energy stored in chemical bonds. (160)
energía potencial Energía que tiene un cuerpo por su posición; también es la energía interna almacenada de un cuerpo, como la energía almacenada en los enlaces químicos.

power The rate at which one form of energy is transformed into another. (157)
potencia Rapidez de la conversión de una forma de energía en otra.

precipitation Any form of water that falls from clouds and reaches Earth's surface as rain, snow, sleet, or hail. (327)
precipitación Cualquier forma del agua que cae de las nubes y llega a la superficie de la tierra como lluvia, nieve, aguanieve o granizo.

precision How close a group of measurements are to each other. (50)
precisión Cuán cerca se encuentran un grupo de medidas.

predation An interaction in which one organism kills another for food or nutrients. (292)
depredación Interacción en la cual un organismo mata a otro para alimentarse u obtener nutrientes de él.

predator The organism that does the killing in a predation interaction. (292)
depredador Organismo que mata durante la depredación.

predicting The process of forecasting what will happen in the future based on past experience or evidence. (7)
predecir Proceso de pronosticar lo que va a suceder en el futuro, basándose en evidencia o experiencias previas.

pressure The force pushing on a surface divided by the area of that surface. (130)
presión 1. Fuerza que actúa contra una superficie, dividida entre el área de esa superficie. **2.** Fuerza que actúa sobre las rocas y que cambia su forma o volumen.

prey An organism that is killed and eaten by another organism in a predation interaction. (292)
presa Organismo que es consumido por otro organismo en el proceso de depredación.

primary succession The series of changes that occur in an area where no soil or organisms exist. (299)
sucesión primaria Serie de cambios que ocurren en un área donde no existe suelo ni organismos.

process A sequence of actions in a system. (64)
proceso Secuencia de acciones en un sistema.

producer An organism that can make its own food. (319)
productor Organismo que puede generar su propio alimento.

prominence A huge, reddish loop of gas that protrudes from the sun's surface, linking parts of sunspot regions. (240)
prominencia Enorme burbuja de gas rojiza que sobresale de la superfice solar, y conecta partes de las manchas solares.

prototype A working model used to test a design. (350)
prototipo Modelo funcional usado para probar un diseño.

----------------- **Q** -----------------

qualitative observation An observation that deals with characteristics that cannot be expressed in numbers. (5)
observación cualitativa Observación que se centra en las características que no se pueden expresar con números.

quantitative observation An observation that deals with a number or amount. (5)
observación cuantitativa Observación que se centra en un número o cantidad.

----------------- **R** -----------------

radiation zone A region of very tightly packed gas in the sun's interior where energy is transferred mainly in the form of electromagnetic radiation. (237)
zona radioactiva Región al interior del Sol de gases densamente acumulados y donde se transmite energía principalmente en la forma de radiación electromagnética.

rain forests A forest that receives at least 2 meters of rain per year, mostly occurring in the tropical wet climate zone. (336)
selva tropical Bosque donde caen al menos 2 metros de lluvia al año, principalmente en la zona climática tropical húmeda.

range The difference between the greatest value and the least value in a set of data. (53)
rango Diferencia entre el mayor y el menor valor de un conjunto de datos.

revolution The movement of an object around another object. (192)
revolución Movimiento de un cuerpo alrededor de otro.

ring A thin disk of small ice and rock particles surrounding a planet. (251)
anill Disco fino de pequeñas partículas de hielo y roca que rodea un planeta.

rotation The spinning motion of a planet on its axis. (191)
rotación Movimiento giratorio de un planeta sobre su eje.

GLOSSARY

——————————— S ———————————

safety symbols A sign used to alert you to possible sources of accidents in an investigation. (73)
símbolos de seguridad Señal de alerta sobre elementos que pueden causar accidentes durante una investigación.

satellite **1.** An object that orbits a planet. **2.** Any object that orbits around another object in space. (185)
satélite **1.** Cuerpo que orbita alrededor de un planeta. **2.** Cualquier cuerpo que orbita alrededor de otro cuerpo en el espacio.

savanna A grassland located close to the equator that may include shrubs and small trees and receives as much as 120 centimeters of rain per year. (338)
sabana Pradera que puede tener arbustos y árboles pequeños, ubicada cerca del ecuador y donde pueden caer hasta 120 centímetros de lluvia al año.

scavenger A carnivore that feeds on the bodies of dead or decaying organisms. (320)
carroñero Carnívoro que se alimenta de los restos de organismos muertos o en descomposición.

science A way of learning about the natural world through observations and logical reasoning; leads to a body of knowledge. (5)
ciencia Estudio del mundo natural a través de observaciones y del razonamiento lógico; conduce a un conjunto de conocimientos.

scientific inquiry The ongoing process of discovery in science; the diverse ways in which scientists study the natural world and propose explanations based on evidence they gather. (19)
indagación científica Proceso continuo de descubrimiento en la ciencia; diversidad de métodos con los que los científicos estudian el mundo natural y proponen explicaciones del mismo basadas en la evidencia que reúnen.

scientific investigation The process by which a scientist asks a question about the natural world, collects and analyzes data to help answer that question, and communicates the results to the scientific community. (9)
investigación científica Proceso por el que un científico hace preguntas acerca del mundo natural, recopila y analiza datos para responder esas preguntas y comunica los resultados a la comunidad científica.

scientific law A statement that describes what scientists expect to happen every time under a particular set of conditions. (26)
ley científica Enunciado que describe lo que los científicos esperan que suceda cada vez que se da una serie de condiciones determinadas.

scientific theory A well-tested explanation for a wide range of observations or experimental results. (26)
teoría científica Explicación comprobada de una gran variedad de observaciones o resultados de experimentos.

secondary succession The series of changes that occur in an area where the ecosystem has been disturbed, but where soil and organisms still exist. (300)
sucesión secundaria Serie de cambios que ocurren en un área después de la perturbación de un ecosistema, pero donde todavía hay suelo y organismos.

significant figures All the digits in a measurement that have been measured exactly, plus one digit whose value has been estimated. (50)
cifras significativas En una medida, todos los dígitos que se han medido con exactitud, más un dígito cuyo valor se ha estimado.

skepticism An attitude of doubt. (11)
escepticismo Actitud de duda.

solar eclipse The blocking of sunlight to Earth that occurs when the moon is directly between the sun and Earth. (205)
eclipse solar Bloqueo de la luz solar que ilumina la Tierra que ocurre cuando la Luna se interpone entre el Sol y la Tierra.

solar flares An eruption of gas from the sun's surface that occurs when the loops in sunspot regions suddenly connect. (240)
destello solar Erupción de los gases de la superficie solar que ocurre cuando las burbujas de las manchas solares se conectan repentinamente.

solar system The system consisting of the sun and the planets and other objects that revolve around it. (231)
sistema solar Sistema formado por el Sol, los planetas y otros cuerpos que giran alrededor de él.

solar wind A stream of electrically charged particles that emanate from the sun's corona. (239)
viento solar Flujo de partículas cargadas que emanan de la corona del Sol.

solid A state of matter that has a definite shape and a definite volume. (125)
sólido Estado en el que la materia tiene forma y volumen definidos.

solstice Either of the two days of the year on which the sun reaches its greatest distance north or south of the equator. (196)
solsticio Uno de los dos días del año en el que el Sol alcanza la mayor distancia al norte o al sur del ecuador.

sound energy Energy in the form of a disturbance that travels as a wave through a medium, such as air. (165)
energía acústica Energía que consiste en una alteración que una onda transporta a través de un medio, como el aire.

species A group of similar organisms that can mate with each other and produce offspring that can also mate and reproduce. (278)
especie Grupo de organismos semejantes que pueden cruzarse y producir descendencia fértil.

spring tide The tide with the greatest difference between consecutive low and high tides. (210)
marea viva Marea con la mayor diferencia entre las mareas altas y bajas consecutivas.

star A ball of hot gas, primarily hydrogen and helium, that undergoes nuclear fusion. (185)
estrella Bola de gases calientes, principalmente hidrógeno y helio, en cuyo interior se produce una fusión nuclear.

subjective Describes the influence of personal feelings on a decision or conclusion. (14)
subjetivo Describe la influencia de sentimientos personales sobre una decisión o conclusión.

sublimation The change in state from a solid directly to a gas without passing through the liquid state. (137)
sublimación Cambio del estado sólido directamente a gas, sin pasar por el estado líquido.

substance A single kind of matter that is pure and has a specific set of properties. (89)
sustancia ipo único de materia que es pura y tiene propiedades específicas.

succession The series of predictable changes that occur in a community over time. (298)
sucesión Serie de cambios predecibles que ocurren en una comunidad a través del tiempo.

sunspot 1. A dark area of gas on the sun's surface that is cooler than surrounding gases. 2. A relatively dark, cool region on the surface of the sun. (240)
mancha solar 1. Área gaseosa oscura de la superficie solar, que es más fría que los gases que la rodean. 2. Región relativamente fría y oscura de la superficie solar.

surface tension The result of an inward pull among the molecules of a liquid that brings the molecules on the surface closer together; causes the surface to act as if it has a thin skin. (128)
tensión superficial Resultado de la atracción hacia el centro entre las moléculas de un líquido, que hace que las moléculas de la superficie se acerquen mucho, y que la superficie actúe como si tuviera una piel delgada.

symbiosis Any relationship in which two species live closely together and that benefits at least one of the species. (295)
simbiosis Cualquier relación en la cual dos especies viven muy cerca y al menos una de ellas se beneficia.

system 1. A group of parts that work together as a whole. 2. A group of related parts that work together to perform a function or produce a result. (64)
sistema 1. Partes de un grupo que trabajan en conjunto. 2. Grupo de partes relacionadas que trabajan conjuntamente para realizar una función o producir un resultado.

—————————— **T** ——————————

temperature How hot or cold something is; a measure of the average energy of motion of the particles of a substance; the measure of the average kinetic energy of the particles of a substance. (110)
temperatura Cuán caliente o frío es algo; medida de la energía de movimiento promedio de las partículas de una sustancia; medida de la energía cinética promedio de las partículas de una sustancia.

terrestrial planets The name often given to the four inner planets: Mercury, Venus, Earth, and Mars. (243)
planetas telúricos Nombre dado normalmente a los cuatro planetas interiores: Mercurio, Venus, Tierra y Marte.

thermal energy The total kinetic and potential energy of all the particles of an object. (110)
energía térmica Energía cinética y potencial total de las partículas de un cuerpo.

tide The periodic rise and fall of the level of water in the ocean. (209)
marea La subida y bajada periódica del nivel de agua del océano.

trade-off An exchange in which one benefit is given up in order to obtain another. (350)
sacrificar una cosa por otra Intercambio en el que se renuncia a un beneficio para obtener otro.

troubleshooting The process of analyzing a design problem and finding a way to fix it. (350)
solución de problemas Proceso por el cual se analiza un problema de diseño y se halla una forma de solucionarlo.

tundra An extremely cold, dry biome climate region characterized by short, cool summers and bitterly cold winters. (341)
tundra Bioma de la región climática extremadamente fría y seca, que se caracteriza por veranos cortos y frescos e inviernos sumamente fríos.

GLOSSARY

——————— U ———————

umbra The darkest part of a shadow. (205)
umbr La parte más oscura de una sombra.

understory A layer of shorter trees and vines that grows in the shade of a forest canopy. (337)
sotobosque Capa de árboles de poca altura y plantas trepadoras que crecen bajo la sombra del dosel de un bosque.

——————— V ———————

vaporization The change of state from a liquid to a gas. (135)
vaporización Cambio del estado de líquido a gas.

variable A factor that can change in an experiment. (21)
variable Factor que puede cambiar en un experimento.

viscosity A liquid's resistance to flowing. (128)
viscosidad Resistencia a fluir que presenta un líquido.

volume The amount of space that matter occupies. (42)
volumen Cantidad de espacio que ocupa la materia.

——————— W ———————

weight A measure of the force of gravity acting on an object. (41)
peso Medida de la fuerza de gravedad que actúa sobre un objeto.

work Force exerted on an object that causes it to move. (156)
trabajo Fuerza que se ejerce sobre un cuerpo para moverlo.

INDEX

Page numbers for key terms are printed in **boldface** type.

INDEX

INDEX

Page numbers for key terms are printed in **boldface** type.

INDEX

Page numbers for key terms are printed in **boldface** type.

ACKNOWLEDGMENTS

Staff Credits

The people who made up the *Interactive Science* team—representing composition services, core design digital and multimedia production services, digital product development, editorial, editorial services, manufacturing, and production—are listed below:

Jan Van Aarsen, Samah Abadir, Ernie Albanese, Chris Anton, Zareh Artinian, Bridget Binstock, Suzanne Biron, Niki Birbilis, MJ Black, Nancy Bolsover, Stacy Boyd, Jim Brady, Katherine Bryant, Michael Burstein, Pradeep Byram, Jessica Chase, Jonathan Cheney, Arthur Ciccone, Allison Cook-Bellistri, Rebecca Cottingham, AnnMarie Coyne, Bob Craton, Chris Deliee, Paul Delsignore, Michael Di Maria, Diane Dougherty, Kristen Ellis, Kelly Engel, Theresa Eugenio, Amanda Ferguson, Jorgensen Fernandez, Kathryn Fobert, Alicia Franke, Louise Gachet, Julia Gecha, Mark Geyer, Steve Gobbell, Paula Gogan-Porter, Jeffrey Gong, Sandra Graff, Robert M. Graham, Adam Groffman, Lynette Haggard, Christian Henry, Karen Holtzman, Susan Hutchinson, Sharon Inglis, Marian Jones, Sumy Joy, Sheila Kanitsch, Courtenay Kelley, Chris Kennedy, Toby Klang, Greg Lam, Russ Lappa, Margaret LaRaia, Ben Leveillee, Thea Limpus, Charles Luey, Dotti Marshall, Kathy Martin, Robyn Matzke, John McClure, Mary Beth McDaniel, Krista McDonald, Tim McDonald, Rich McMahon, Cara McNally, Bernadette McQuilkin, Melinda Medina, Angelina Mendez, Maria Milczarek, Claudi Mimo, Mike Napieralski, Deborah Nicholls, Dave Nichols, William Oppenheimer, Jodi O'Rourke, Ameer Padshah, Lorie Park, Celio Pedrosa, Jonathan Penyack, Linda Zust Reddy, Jennifer Reichlin, Stephen Rider, Charlene Rimsa, Walter Rodriguez, Stephanie Rogers, Marcy Rose, Rashid Ross, Anne Rowsey, Logan Schmidt, Amanda Seldera, Laurel Smith, Nancy Smith, Ted Smykal, Emily Soltanoff, Cindy Strowman, Dee Sunday, Barry Tomack, Elizabeth Tustian, Patricia Valencia, Ana Sofia Villaveces, Stephanie Wallace, Amanda Watters, Christine Whitney, Brad Wiatr, Heidi Wilson, Heather Wright, Rachel Youdelman.

Photography

All otherwise unacknowledged photos are copyright © 2011 Pearson Education.

Cover, Front and Back
Cardinal, Arnold Images/Photolibrary New York; **leaves,** Pixtal Images/Photolibrary New York.

Front Matter
Page vi monument, Carroteater/Shutterstock; **vii barn,** Visions LLC/Photolibrary New York; **vi–vii fields,** Alexey Stiop/Alamy; **vii flag,** Stacey Lynn Payne; **vii cardinal,** Tom Vezo/Peter Arnold Images/Photolibrary New York; **viii,** Masa Ushioda/Photolibrary New York; **ix,** George Ostertag/Photolibrary New York; **x,** Nordic Photos/Photolibrary New York; **xi,** Michael C. York/AP Images; **xii,** Max Rossi/Reuters; **xiii,** Tom Fox/Dallas Morning News/Corbis; **xiv,** ESA/J. Clarke (Boston University)/Z. Levay (STScl)/NASA; **xv,** Gary Bell/Zefa/Corbis; **xvi,** Marko König/Corbis; **xvii laptop,** iStockphoto; **xvii TV,** iStockphoto; **xxiv laptop,** iStockphoto; **xxi br,** JupiterImages/Getty Images; **xxiv laptop,** iStockphoto; **xxvi ml,** Arctic-Images/Corbis; **xxvi br,** John Cancalosi/Nature Picture Library; **xxvii l,** Digital Art/Corbis; **xxvii r,** NASA Langley Research Center (NASA-LaRC); **xxviii ml,** Max Rossi/Reuters; **xxviii mr,** NASA Solarsystem Collection; **xxix,** Robert Postma/Design Pics/Corbis.

Chapter 1
Pages xxx–1 spread, Masa Ushioda/Photolibrary New York; **10 inset,** photo courtesy of the Elwood Haynes Museum; **3,** Poznyakov/Shutterstock; **3,** Holmes Garden Photos/Alamy; **4,** Bates Littlehales/National Geographic Stock; **5,** Poznyakov/Shutterstock; **6,** Jeff Rotman/Alamy; **7 tr,** Courtesy of the US Fish and Wildlife Services; **9 l,** Bioluminescence Team 2009, NOAA-OER/NOAA; **9 r,** Bill Bachman/Photo Researchers, Inc.; **10 m,** Fabrice Bettex/Alamy; **11 b,** Gregory Kendall/Shutterstock; **11 t,** Bill Frische/Shutterstock; **16 bkgrnd,** Dreams3D/Shutterstock; **17 bkgrnd,** Science Source/Photo Researchers, Inc.; **18,** Frank Greenaway/Dorling Kindersley; **19,** Christa DeRidder/Shutterstock; **20,** Regien Paassen/Shutterstock; **21 bkgrnd,** Roman marble bust in high relief (ca. 2 CE). Museo Nazionale Romano (Palazzo Altemps), Rome/Photo by Vanni/Art Resource, New York; **22 tl,** Rolf Nussabaumer/Nature Picture Library; **24,** Al Mueller/Shutterstock; **25,** Juice Images/Corbis; **26,** Holmes Garden Photos/Alamy; **27,** Photolibrary New York; **28 m,** Photo Network/Alamy; **28 t,** Jeff Rotman/Alamy; **29 m,** Gregory Kendall/Shutterstock.

Chapter 1 Feature
Page 32 bkgrnd, Suzanne Tucker/Shutterstock; **32 inset,** Aaron Peterson/Alamy; **33,** Mark Thomas/Photo Researchers, Inc.

Chapter 2
Pages 34–35, George Ostertag/Photolibrary New York; **37 m,** John Cancalosi/Nature Picture Library; **37 b,** Issei Kato/Reuters; **37 t,** Thomas Aichinger/VW Pics/Zuma Press; **37 inset,** Martyn F. Chillmaid/Photo Researchers, Inc.; **38,** Robert Galbraith/Reuters; **40,** Joseph T.Collins/Photo Researchers, Inc.; **42 bkgrnd,** Arthur Cupak Mauritius/Photolibrary New York; **42 inset,** Creativ Studio; Heinemann/Westend61/Photolibrary New York; **43 inset,** Ian O'Leary/Mode Images/Photolibrary New York; **44–45 spread,** Thomas Aichinger/VW Pics/Zuma Press; **46,** Joe Gough/Shutterstock; **47 b,** Willie J. Allen Jr./St. Petersburg Times/Zuma Press; **47 t,** Laszlo Dobos/Shutterstock; **48,** Jim Stem/St. Petersburg Times/Zuma Press; **48,** Pertusinas/Shutterstock; **48 bkgrnd,** Karin Hildebrand Lau/Shutterstock; **49,** John Cancalosi/Nature Picture Library; **50–51 bkgrnd,** John Casey/Fotolia; **51 inset,** Martyn F. Chillmaid/Photo Researchers, Inc.; **52,** Steven Coling/Shutterstock; **53,** Elyse Butler/Aurora/Getty Images; **54,** Heiko Kiera/Shutterstock; **55 t,** Steve Byland/Shutterstock; **55 b,** J. Pat Carter/AP Images; **56 bkgrnd,** Barrie Watts/Dorling Kindersley; **57,** NASA/Goddard Space Flight Center Scientific Visualization Studio, and Virginia Butcher (SSAI); **57 bkgrnd,** Stephen St. John/National Geographic Image Collection; **58 l,** Imagebroker/Alamy; **59 r,** Geoff Brightling/Dorling Kindersley; **59 l,** Ryan M. Bolton/Shutterstock; **60 inset,** Central Science Laboratory/Photo Researchers, Inc.; **60–61 bkgrnd,** Luchschen/Shutterstock; **61 tr,** Daboost/Shutterstock; **62,** Dmitry Naumov/Shutterstock; **63,** Issei Kato/Reuters; **65,** Ahmad Masood/Reuters; **67,** Science Source/Photo Researchers, Inc.; **68 l,** Goddard Space Flight Center

ACKNOWLEDGMENTS

Scientific Visualization Studio/Additional support provided by Sarah Dewitt (NASA/GSFC) and Fred Kemman (HTSI)/NASA; **68 bkgrnd,** Bill Brooks/Alamy; **70–71 spread,** NASA; **72 b,** Joseph T. Collins/Photo Researchers, Inc.; **72 t,** Science Source/Photo Researchers; **74,** Richard Haynes; **76,** Science Source/Photo Researchers; **78 inset,** Central Science Laboratory/Photo Researchers, Inc.

Chapter 2 Feature
Page 82 bkgrnd, Rick Fischer/Masterfile; **82 inset,** Car Culture/Corbis; **83,** Andy Crawford/Dorling Kindersley.

Chapter 3
Pages 84–85 spread, Nordic Photos/Photolibrary New York; **87 t,** Nigel Hicks/Dorling Kindersley; **87 b,** John Shaw/Science Source; **88 t,** *The Head of Medusa* (ca 1590), Michelangelo Merisi da Caravaggio. Oil on canvas glued to wood. Diameter: 21 5/8 in (55 cm). Pre-restoration. Uffizi Gallery, Florence, Italy/Photograph copyright © Nicolo Orsi Battaglini/Art Resource NY; **88 b,** *The Head of Medusa* (ca 1590), Michelangelo Merisi da Caravaggio. Oil on canvas glued to wood. Diameter: 21 5/8 in (55 cm). Restored 2005. Uffizi Gallery, Florence, Italy/Photograph copyright © Scala/Ministero per i Beni e le Attività culturali/Art Resource NY; **88–89 spread,** Katy Williamson/Dorling Kindersley; **90 spread,** ArabianEye/Getty Images; **90 bl,** Wave RF/Photolibrary New York; **90 br,** iStockphoto; **91 b,** Andy Crawford/Dorling Kindersley; **91 t,** Nicole Hill/Rubberball/Photolibrary New York; **92,** Courtesy of Prof Mark Welland and Dr Ghim Wei Ho, Nanoscience Centre, University of Cambridge, UK; **92–93 spread,** Ashok Rodrigues/iStockphoto; **93 tr,** iStockphoto; **93 bl,** iStockphoto; **93 bl,** Dorling Kindersley; **93 t,** PhotoObjects/JupiterUnlimited; **94 bkgrnd,** Max Blain/Shutterstock; **95 tr,** Steve Gorton/Dorling Kindersley; **95 bl,** Mark A. Schneider/Photo Researchers, Inc.; **95 tl,** Albert J. Copley/age Fotostock/Photolibrary New York; **97 ml,** Charles D. Winters/Photo Researchers, Inc.; **98 bkgrnd,** Patrick Robert/Corbis; **98 inset,** Juergen Hasenkopf/Alamy; **100–101 spread,** Mark Lennihan/AP Images; **102–103 spread,** The Granger Collection, New York; **103 b,** Dorling Kindersley; **103 m,** Charles D. Winters/Photo Researchers, Inc.; **103 t,** Steve Gorton/Dorling Kindersley; **104 b,** iStockphoto; **105,** Carolyn Kaster/AP Images; **106,** iStockphoto; **107 r,** Courtesy of North Carolina State Bureau of Investigation, Raleigh NC; **107 b,** iStockphoto; **108 t,** Erasmus Weathervane (2008), Rodney Graham. Copper and steel. Whitechapel Gallery, London. Reproduced by permission of artist. Photo: Anthony Upton/AP Images; **110 inset,** Jonathan Hayward/AP Images; **110 spread,** Umit Bektas/Reuters; **111 r,** John Shaw/Science Source; **112 ml,** Matthew J. Sroka/Reading Eagle/AP Images; **112 mr,** iStockphoto; **112–113 b,** Amr Nabil/AP Images; **112–113 t,** Jakub Semeniuk/iStockphoto; **113 m1,** iStockphoto; **114 t,** Nigel Hicks/Dorling Kindersley; **114 b,** Umit Bektas/Reuters.

Chapter 3 Feature
Page 118, *The Alchemist* (ca. 1640), Hendrick Heerschon. Oil on canvas. The Fisher Collection, Pittsburgh/Alamy; **119 bkgrnd,** Lawrence Berkeley National Laboratory/Science Photo Library/Photo Researchers, Inc.; **119 inset,** American Institute of Physics/Photo Researchers, Inc.

Chapter 4
Pages 120–121 spread, Michael C. York/AP Images; **123 m1,** BC Photography/Alamy; **123 inset,** Ryan Pyle/Corbis; **123 m2,** SuperStock; **123 b,** Charles D. Winters/Photo Researchers, Inc.; **124–125 bkgrnd,** James M. Bell/Photo Researchers, Inc.; **126 l,** Sue Atkinson/Fresh Food Images/Photolibrary New York; **126 r,** Mark A. Schneider/Photo Researchers, Inc.; **128,** BC Photography/Alamy; **129,** Charles D. Winters/Photo Researchers, Inc.; **131,** Frits Meyst/Adventure4ever; **132,** Simon Butcher/Imagestate/Photolibrary New York; **133 m2,** SuperStock; **134,** Winfield Parks/National Geographic Society; **136 b,** Bob Lyndall; **137 inset,** Charles D. Winters/Photo Researchers, Inc.; **137 bkgrnd,** Neal Preston/Corbis; **137 tr,** Frank Greenaway/Dorling Kindersley; **138 tl,** Michael S. Quinton/National Geographic Stock; **138 br,** Andreas Kuehn/Getty Images; **139 b,** epa European Pressphoto Agency creative account/Alamy; **139 t,** Photolibrary New York; **140,** Kat Fahrer/Middletown Journal/AP Images; **146 t,** Mark A. Schneider/Photo Researchers, Inc.; **146 m,** epa European Pressphoto Agency creative account/Alamy.

Chapter 4 Feature
Page 150, Sami Sarkis/Getty Images; **151 ml,** Ted Kinsman/Photo Researchers, Inc.; **151 t,** Stephen Lockett/Alamy.

Chapter 5
Pages 152–153 spread, Max Rossi/Reuters; **155 m2,** Lance Aram Rothstein/St Petersburg Times/Zuma Press; **155 b,** Gilbert Iundt/TempSport/Corbis; **156 bkgrnd,** Josiah Davidson/Getty Images; **157,** DesignPics Inc./Index Stock Imagery/Photolibrary New York; **159 bkgrnd,** Zia Soleil/Iconica/Getty Images; **163 bkgrnd,** Heinz Kluetmeier/Sports Illustrated/Getty Images; **164 bkgrnd,** Lance Aram Rothstein/St Petersburg Times/Zuma Press; **165 bkgrnd,** Nick Suydam/Alamy; **165 bkgrnd,** Roland Weihrauch/AFP/Getty Images; **168 bkgrnd,** Michael Goulding/Orange County Register/Zuma Press; **170 l,** Fundamental Photographs, NYC; **171 bkgrnd,** Gilbert Iundt/TempSport/Corbis; **174 tl,** Creatas/JupiterUnlimited; **174 t,** Russell Burden/Photolibrary New York; **174 m,** Roland Weihrauch/AFP/Getty Images; **176 mr,** Copyright © 2009 Globus Brothers.

Chapter 5 Feature
Page 178 bkgrnd, Dave Reede/AGE Fotostock; **178 inset,** L.G. Patterson/AP Images; **179 bkgrnd,** Imagebroker/Alamy; **179 inset,** Earl Roberge/Photo Researchers, Inc.

Chapter 6
Pages 180–181 spread, Tom Fox/Dallas Morning News/Corbis; **183 m2,** John W. Bova/Photo Researchers, Inc.; **183 m2,** John W. Bova/Photo Researchers, Inc.; **183 m2,** John W. Bova/Photo Researchers, Inc.; **183 b,** Space Frontiers/Getty; **184,** The Inter-University Centre for Astronomy and Astrophysics, Pune India; **184–185 bl,** NASA; **185 bkgrnd,** UVimages/Amana Images/Corbis; **185 m,** NASA; **185 r,** T. Rector (University of Alaska Anchorage), Z. Levay and L. Frattare (Space Telescope Science Institute) and National Optical Astronomy Observatory/Association of Universities for Research in Astronomy/National Science Foundation/Solar System Exploration/NASA; **188 bkgrnd,** Ted Spiegel/Corbis; **189 bkgrnd,** Frank Zullo/Photo Researchers, Inc.;

190 t, Robert Harding Picture Library Ltd/Alamy; 190 b, John White Photos/Alamy; 193 t, Ragab Papyrus Institute Cairo/ Gianni Dagli Orti/The Art Archive/The Picture Desk; 193 ml, Dea/A. Dagli Orti/Getty Images; 193 br, Science Museum Pictorial/SSPL; 197, Gavin Hellier/Photolibrary New York; 198–199 spread, Paul & Lindamarie Ambrose/Getty Images; 202 tr, Jeff Vanuga/Corbis; 202 bkgrnd, UV Images/Amana Images/Corbis; 205 tr, Space Frontiers/Getty; 206 bkgrnd, Tom Fox/Dallas Morning News/Corbis; 208 l, Michael P. Gadomski/Science Source; 208 r, Michael P. Gadomski/Science Source; 211 bkgrnd, David Chapman/Photolibrary New York; 212 inset, Omikron/Photo Researchers, Inc.; 212–213 spread, JPL/USGS/NASA; 214 t, NASA Langley Research Center (NASA-LaRC); 214 b, JPL/USGS/NASA; 214–215 spread, Apollo 11 Image Library/NASA; 216 br, Omikron/Photo Researchers, Inc.

Chapter 6 Feature
Page 220 ml, Andy Crawford/University Museum of Archaeology and Anthropology, Cambridge/Dorling Kindersley; 220 tl, iStockphoto; 220 bl, iStockphoto; 221 both, NASA.

Chapter 7
Pages 222–223 spread, ESA/J. Clarke (Boston University)/ Z. Levay (STScI)/NASA; 225 b, JPL/Caltech/T. Pyle (SSC)/ NASA; 225 t, NASA Lunar and Planetary Laboratory; 226 inset, Walter Myers; 226–227 spread, Walter Myers; 228 tr, Detlev van Ravenswaay/Photo Researchers, Inc.; 228 bl, Crawford Library/Royal Observatory, Edinburgh/ Photo Researchers, Inc.; 229 r, Pictorial Press Ltd/Alamy; 229 l, SPL/Photo Researchers, Inc.; 230–231 spread, Johns Hopkins University Applied Physics Laboratory/NASA; 232 inset, Friedrich Saurer/Alamy; 232–233 spread, NASA Lunar and Planetary Laboratory; 235 bkgrnd, NASA Lunar and Planetary Laboratory; 238–239 spread, Space Frontiers/ Hulton Archive/Getty Images; 238–239 inset, NASA Solar and Heliospheric Observatory Collection; 240 r, SOHO/ ESA/NASA; 240 l, SOHO-EIT Consortium/ESA/NASA; 242 l, Magellan Project/JPL/NASA; 242 ml, Bettmann/Corbis; 242 mr, Bettmann/Corbis; 242–243 r, Library of Congress Department of Prints and Photographs [LC-USZ62-119343]; 243 l, Messenger Teams/Johns Hopkins University Applied Physics Laboratory/NASA; 243 ml, Magellan Project/JPL/ NASA; 243 mr, Apollo 17 Crew/NASA; 243 r, NASA; 244 bl, Messenger Teams/Johns Hopkins University Applied Physics Laboratory/NASA; 244 tr, Messenger Teams/Johns Hopkins University Applied Physics Laboratory/NASA; 244 tl, Apollo 17 Crew/NASA; 245 br, NASA; 245 bl, Apollo 17 Crew/NASA; 245 tr, JPL/USGS/NASA; 245 t1, NASA; 248 spread, Mars Exploration Rover Mission/JPL/NASA; 248 m, JPL/CalTech/ NASA; 248 tr, NASA; 249 inset, Goddard Space Flight Center Scientific Visualization Studio, and Virginia Butcher (SSAI)/NASA; 250, Judy Dole/The Image Bank/Getty Images; 251 l, JPL/NIX/NASA; 251 ml, JPL/NASA; 251 mr, ESA/L. Sromovsky (University of Wisconsin, Madison)/ H. Hammel (Space Science Institute)/K. Rages (SETI)/NASA; 251 r, NASA; 252 tl, JPL/NIX/NASA; 252 tr, Apollo 17 Crew/NASA; 252 br, JPL/NASA; 253 bkgrnd, NASA; 254 bl, JPL/Space Science Institute/NASA; 254 ml, JPL/NASA; 254–255 spread, JPL/ NASA; 255 br, JPL/Space Science Institute/NASA; 255 bl,

Science Source/Photo Researchers Inc.; 255 t1, Apollo 17 Crew/NASA; 255 t2, JPL/NASA; 256 b, Lawrence Sromovsky, University of Wisconsin-Madison/ W. M. Keck Observatory; 256 tr, Apollo 17 Crew/NASA; 256 tl, ESA/L. Sromovsky (University of Wisconsin, Madison)/H. Hammel (Space Science Institute)/K. Rages (SETI)/NASA; 257 mr, L. Sromovsky/P. Fry (University of Wisconsin-Madison)/NASA; 257 tl, Apollo 17 Crew/NASA; 257 tl, NASA; 261 bkgrnd, Jerry Lodriguss/ Photo Researchers, Inc.; 262 inset, JPL/NASA; 262 bkgrnd, JPL/Caltech/T. Pyle (SSC)/NASA; 263, Dr. Marli Miller/Getty Images; 264 t, SOHO-EIT Consortium/ESA/NASA; 264 br, Jerry Lodriguss/Photo Researchers, Inc.; 264 bl, JPL/NIX/ NASA.

Chapter 7 Feature
Page 268 bkgrnd, JPL/Cornell University/NASA; 269 tr, Courtesy of the Nantucket Maria Mitchell Association; 269 br, Courtesy of the Nantucket Maria Mitchell Association.

Chapter 8
Pages 270–271 spread, Gary Bell/Zefa/Corbis; 273 m, age Fotostock/SuperStock; 273 b, Imagebroker/Alamy; 274 br, Wildlife/A.Visage/Peter Arnold; 274 tr, Frans Lanting/Corbis; 274 bl, Jörn Köhler; 275 r, Tom Brakefield/Getty; 275, Bruno Morandi/Robert Harding World; 278–279 Jason O. Watson/ Alamy; 280–281, Chris Johns/National Geographic Stock; 282 b, Photodisc/Getty Images; 283, spread Kim Taylor/Nature Picture Library; 285, Weatherstock/Peter Arnold; 286 t, Tim Mannakee/Grand Tour/Corbis; 286–287 bkgrnd, Matt Brown/ Corbis; 287 tr, Taylor S. Kennedy/National Geographic Society; 288 ml, Alex Wild; 291 m, Jim Zipp/Photo Researchers, Inc.; 291 t, Glenn Bartley/Corbis; 291 b, Jim Zipp/Photo Researchers Inc.; 292 t, Bill Curtsinger/National Geographic Stock; 292 bl, Klaas Lingbeek- van Kranen/Getty; 292 br, Imagebroker/Alamy; 292 mr, Sándor F. Szabó/iStockphoto; 293 rm, age Fotostock/SuperStock; 293 tr, Michael D. Kern/ Nature Picture Library; 293 tl, Jeff Hunter/Getty Images; 293 br, Nature's Images/Photo Researchers, Inc.; 293 ml, Ethan Daniels/Alamy; 293 bl, Fabrice Bettex/Alamy; 295 ml, Villiers Steyn/Shutterstock; 295 mr, Steve Byland/Fotolia; 296 ml, Jeff Foott/Getty Images; 296 rt, WaterFrame/Alamy; 296 rb, USGA; 297 t, Steve Jones/Corbis; 297 b, Dietmar Nill/ Nature Picture Library; 297 m, Bruce Dale/Getty; 298 spread, Ilene MacDonald/Alamy; 302 m, WaterFrame/Alamy.

Chapter 8 Feature
Page 306, Courtesy of Roger del Moral; 307 t, Dave & Les Jacobs/Blend Images/Getty Images; 307 b, Chris Gomersall/ Alamy.

Chapter 9
Page 308–309 spread, Marko König/Corbis; 311 t, age Fotostock/SuperStock; 311 m, Dorling Kindersley; 311 b, Karen Huntt/Getty Images; 312, David Cook/BlueShiftStudios/ Alamy; 313 bl, Adrian Bailey/Aurora Photos; 313 br, age Fotostock/SuperStock; 313 bkgrnd, Robbert Koene/Getty Images; 317, Yuji Sakai/Getty Images; 318, Ian McAllister/ Photolibrary New York; 319 inset, Edward Kinsman/Photo Researchers, Inc.; 319 bkgrnd, Jerome Wexler/Photo Researchers, Inc.; 322 m, Jerry Young/Dorling Kindersley; 322 t, Dorling Kindersley; 322 b, Peter Blottman/iStockphoto;

ACKNOWLEDGMENTS

323 ml, Nicholas Homrich/iStockphoto; **323 t2,** Judy Foldetta/ iStockphoto; **323 t4,** Geoff Brightling/Dorling Kindersley; **323 t1,** Rollin Verlinde/Dorling Kindersley; **323 t3,** Jerry Young/ Dorling Kindersley; **323 b,** Neil Fletcher/Dorling Kindersley; **323 mr,** Frank Greenaway/Dorling Kindersley/Courtesy of the Natural History Museum, London; **323 t,** Dorling Kindersley; **323 m,** Jerry Young/Dorling Kindersley; **323 bm,** Peter Blottman/iStockphoto; **324 t,** Eric Isselée/iStockphoto; **324 m1,** Dave King/Dorling Kindersley; **324 m2,** Frank Greenaway/ Dorling Kindersley; **324 b,** Kim Taylor and Jane Burton/Dorling Kindersley; **324 m2,** Frank Greenaway/Dorling Kindersley; **324 m2,** Frank Greenaway/Dorling Kindersley; **324 m2,** Frank Greenaway/Dorling Kindersley; **326,** Juniors Bildarchiv/Alamy; **335 bkgrnd,** Karen Huntt/Getty Images; **328,** Emma Firth/ Dorling Kindersley; **330,** Dr. Paul A. Zahl/Photo Researchers, Inc.; **335 inset,** Floridapfe from S.Korea Kim in cherl/Getty; **336–337 spread,** Peter Chadwick/Dorling Kindersley; **337 m,** Theo Allofs/Corbis; **338 tm,** Arco Images GmbH/Alamy; **338 tl,** Juan Carlos Munoz/Peter Arnold Inc.; **338 tr,** Peter Lillie/ Photolibrary New York; **339 b,** Tim Shepard, Oxford Scientific Films/Dorling Kindersley; **340 tl,** Randy Green/Getty Images; **340 bl,** Tom Brakefield/Corbis; **341 b,** Foto Zihlmann/Fotolia; **342 bkgrnd,** blickwinkel/Alamy; **344 tr,** Peter Blottman/ iStockphoto.

Chapter 9 Feature
Page 348 bkgrnd, Westend 61 GmbH/Alamy; **349 bkgrnd,** Brent Waltermire/Alamy; **349 inset,** JupiterImages/Creatas/ Alamy.

Appendix
Pages 350–351 foreground, Eckehard Schulz/AP Images; **bkgrnd,** Car Culture/Corbis.

this is your book

you can write in it

take note

this space is yours—great for drawing diagrams and making notes

this is your book

you can write in it

take note

this space is yours—great for drawing diagrams and making notes

this is your book

you can write in it